TEST DEVELOPMENT AND VALIDATION

Gary Skaggs

Virginia Tech

Los Angeles | London | New Delhi
Singapore | Washington DC | Melbourne

FOR INFORMATION:

SAGE Publications, Inc.
2455 Teller Road
Thousand Oaks, California 91320
E-mail: order@sagepub.com

SAGE Publications Ltd.
1 Oliver's Yard
55 City Road
London, EC1Y 1SP
United Kingdom

SAGE Publications India Pvt. Ltd.
B 1/I 1 Mohan Cooperative Industrial Area
Mathura Road, New Delhi 110 044
India

SAGE Publications Asia-Pacific Pte. Ltd.
18 Cross Street #10-10/11/12
China Square Central
Singapore 048423

Copyright © 2023 by SAGE Publications, Inc.

All rights reserved. Except as permitted by U.S. copyright law, no part of this work may be reproduced or distributed in any form or by any means, or stored in a database or retrieval system, without permission in writing from the publisher.

All third-party trademarks referenced or depicted herein are included solely for the purpose of illustration and are the property of their respective owners. Reference to these trademarks in no way indicates any relationship with, or endorsement by, the trademark owner.

Printed in the United States of America

Library of Congress Cataloging-in-Publication Data

Names: Skaggs, Gary, author.

Title: Test development and validation / Dr. Gary Skaggs, Virginia Tech.

Identifiers: LCCN 2021051045 | ISBN 9781544377148 (paperback) | ISBN 9781544377179 (adobe pdf) | ISBN 9781544377155 (epub) | ISBN 9781544377162 (epub)

Subjects: LCSH: Social sciences—Methodology. | Social sciences—Research. | Scaling (Social sciences) | Psychometrics.

Classification: LCC H62 .S487 2022 | DDC 300.72–dc23/eng/20211208 LC record available at https://lccn.loc.gov/2021051045

This book is printed on acid-free paper.

Acquisitions Editor: Leah Fargotstein
Product Associate: Kenzie Offley
Production Editor: Vijayakumar
Copy Editor: Christobel Colleen Hopman
Typesetter: TNQ Technologies
Proofreader: Benny Willy Stephen
Indexer: TNQ Technologies
Cover Designer: Lysa Becker
Marketing Manager: Victoria Velasquez

22 23 24 25 10 9 8 7 6 5 4 3 2 1

BRIEF CONTENTS

DETAILED CONTENTS

PART 2 • TEST DEVELOPMENT

PART 3 • VALIDATION

PREFACE

This book is intended for any individual, project team, or organization that wishes to develop and use a test that measures an unobserved human variable, called a construct in this book. In addition to serving as a textbook, this book can serve as a resource for researchers and professionals who wish to develop a test for research and/or applied uses. No particular prior coursework or training is assumed, although it helps if the reader has encountered at least an introduction to descriptive statistics.

For ten years, I have taught a course titled *Instrument Development and Validation* at Virginia Tech. Students enroll in this course because, for their research or as part of a larger team project, they need to create a test to measure an educational or psychological variable for which a test does not currently exist. In addition to teaching this course, I have served as a consultant to researchers and professionals in testing organizations for planning and carrying out test development projects. In both teaching and consulting, I have found that, while it is easy to find how-to guides that outline the steps for test development, it is difficult to find references that give the development process a sound footing on how to interpret test scores, how to support those interpretations, and how to determine the precision of the scores. Ideas about validity and validation, measurement error, and measurement models are often difficult for folks to access because the primary references tend to be highly technical and difficult for professionals without a psychometric background to access. Furthermore, I have found that many professionals may have had a course in test development and/or validity in their past, but the field has progressed since then. As a result, I will provide an historical context to large-scale testing, validity, test theory, and measurement to show how the guiding principles for test development have evolved over time and will continue to do so.

The book is organized in three parts. Part 1, called The Big Picture, is a series of chapters designed to give the reader a conceptual basis for test development. Chapter 1 introduces the concept of measurement, briefly tracing its history in scientific research. Then, an historical context is provided for the ideas of standardization, measuring constructs, and testing methodology. The chapter concludes with an overview of key descriptive statistics and terms. Chapter 2 presents the concept of validity and how it has evolved over time. Two current validity frameworks, Messick's (also embodied in the 2014 *Standards*) and Kane's, are discussed. Every aspect of the test development process is connected to these validity frameworks and how it supports test score validity. Chapter 3 discusses methods for scoring items and tests and how to transform raw scores into scale scores for a more informative score interpretation. This chapter distinguishes norm-referenced and criterion-referenced score interpretations. It concludes with a brief introduction to equating and linking alternate forms of tests. Chapter 4 introduces Classical Test Theory of how it estimates measurement error and what assumptions about measurement error are needed to obtain those estimates.

Part 2, Test Development, is concerned with the process of developing a test, from initial conception to finished product. Chapter 5 presents several frameworks that guide the test development process, including the 2014 *Standards*, Mark Wilson's (2005) construct map, and evidence-centered design. Chapter 6 discusses preparing test specifications, beginning with a construct map and concluding with a test blueprint. Chapter 7 provides guidance on writing and scoring test items, with a particular focus on the most popular formats: multiple-choice, constructed-response, and Likert items. Chapter 8 delves into the mechanics of pilot testing and item analyses in order to evaluate item quality.

Part 3, Validation, links the conceptual basis in Part 1 with the development process in Part 2. In Chapter 9, Rasch Measurement Theory is introduced as a way to scale and score tests for both items scored dichotomously (e.g., correct or incorrect) and polytomously (e.g., Strongly Agree, Agree, Disagree, Strongly Disagree). Chapter 10 discusses fairness in testing and focuses on analyzing item response data to identify items that are potentially biased against population subgroups. Chapter 11 provides guidance on analyzing the underlying structure, or dimensionality, of a test in order to support the types of scores that are reported, such as a single overall score, several distinct scores, or an overall score with subscales. Chapter 12 introduces standard setting methods for the purpose of informing test takers of their performance in relation to a performance standard, such as "pass" or "certified." The last chapter,

Chapter 13, links back to Chapter 2, and presents ways of reporting validity evidence and planning for future efforts at collecting further evidence.

Each of the chapters ends with a set of Exercises and Activities. For some of the chapters, a test development project is proposed. This project forms the primary course requirement in my class and could be used as such by an instructor. The intent of this project is to guide the reader in developing a test from start to finish but also to situate the development process into the larger context of validation. Some of the exercises and activities pose conceptual questions. Brief answers for these can be found on the accompanying website. These can be used for class or small group discussions or could be made into class assignments. Finally, for the more technical chapters, exercises and activities are actual data analysis problems, the answers to which can be found on the website. These provide practice in carrying out a variety of analyses.

A word about software is in order. Unfortunately, there is no single application that conducts all the analyses discussed in the book. Some commercial programs, such as SPSS, SAS, and MPlus, perform some of them. In consideration of the readers' personal resources, I have chosen to illustrate all analyses with software that is free and open-source. jMetrik (www.itemanalysis.com) is an application with an intuitive graphical user interface. jMetrik can be used to create a number of test scores, to score individual items, to conduct classical and Rasch item analyses, and to analyze item response data for potential bias. Additionally, several R packages are used: psych, mirt, and lavaan. These packages are used to conduct classical item analyses, dimensionality analyses, and analyses for potential item bias. R (www.r-project.org) entails a learning curve for new users. There are a number of resources for learning the basics of R. However, I have tried to minimize the necessity of writing code by providing the R code for the analyses used in several chapters. I recommend running the R packages within R Studio (www.rstudio.com). The website that accompanies this book provides sample datasets. The R code for the analyses used in several chapters is provided in Appendix B.

None of the chapters can cover everything there is to know about a particular topic. For readers interested in more in-depth coverage, there is a section called For Further Reading at the end of each chapter. This section contains seminal works on the topic and are often more technical than this book's presentation.

TEACHING RESOURCES

This text includes an array of Instructor teaching materials designed to save you time and to help you keep students engaged. To learn more, visit **sagepub.com** or **edge.sagepub.com/skaggs1e**.

ACKNOWLEDGMENTS

The genesis of this book comes from a doctoral course, titled *Instrument Development and Validation*, that was first developed by my former colleague Ed Wolfe. When Ed left the university, I took custody of the course. Its content and requirements have evolved over time. Comments and suggestions (and some criticisms) made by students and colleagues influenced my thinking in creating this book. In addition, I gained valuable insight into the large-scale testing industry from my professional colleagues and friends, including Joan Auchter, Mary Lyn Bourque, Carol Ezzelle, Steve Ferrara, Bob Lissitz, Steve Sireci, and Joe Willhoft. I'm grateful as well to Virginia Tech for providing a variety of support services that gave me the space and guidance to the write this book. I also want to thank my School of Education colleagues at Virginia Tech, including Serge Hein, Brett Jones, Yasuo Miyazaki, and Jay Wilkins, for their valuable insights into the ideas presented in the book. Finally, I want to thank my wife Margie for her support and encouragement and for putting up with me working the long hours it took to put this book together. SAGE and the author are grateful for feedback from the following reviewers in the development of this text:

Peggy Perkins Auman, Florida A&M University

Tonia Bock, University of St. Thomas

Robert F. Dedrick, University of South Florida

Daniel Eyers, Cardiff University

Magda Hercheui, UCL School of Management

Joseph C. Kush, Duquesne University

Angela M. Lee, University of Nevada, Reno

Vanessa L. Malcarne, San Diego State University

Alecia M. Santuzzi, Northern Illinois University

Julia Englund Strait, University of Houston–Clear Lake

Feng Su, Liverpool Hope University

Carla J. Thompson, University of West Florida

Chia-Lin Tsai, University of Northern Colorado

Guang Zeng, Texas A&M University–Corpus Christi

Jingshun Zhang, Florida Gulf Coast University

Yuchun Zhou, Ohio State University

ABOUT THE AUTHOR

Dr. Gary Skaggs is a Professor in the Educational Research and Evaluation Program at Virginia Tech. He teaches courses in test development and test theory as well as introductory and intermediate statistics. He is the author or coauthor of 81 publications, including articles in peer-reviewed journals, papers in conference proceedings, book chapters, invited lectures, and professional conference papers/presentations. His research interests include test equating, differential item functioning, standard setting, and cognitive diagnostic models. Dr. Skaggs has served as a test and psychometric consultant to numerous professional organizations including the GED Testing Service, Maryland State Board of Education, National Board of Professional Teaching Standards, Carilion Clinic Department of Psychiatry, and the National Association of Secondary School Principals.

THE BIG PICTURE

MEASUREMENT IN THE SOCIAL SCIENCES

Whatever exists at all exists in some amount.

–Edward L. Thorndike

Suppose that you and your organization, or you and your project team, or just you are interested in the idea of "perception of rejuvenation" and are interested in exploring the relationship between that idea and a variety of health outcomes. Or, perhaps your organization wishes to offer a credential, a license, or certification, for a particular set of skills designed to foster rejuvenation in the workplace. For both scenarios, however, there may be no way to measure perception of rejuvenation because a *test* for it does not exist. And so, you are looking to develop one yourself.

One purpose of this book is to lead you through the process of creating a high-quality test to measure ideas like this one. Furthermore, it is not sufficient to merely develop the test. It must be done in such a way as to convince individuals and organizations who may wish to use it that it is actually achieving its intended purpose. Collecting evidence to support the interpretation and uses of the test is a process called validation and is the second primary purpose of this book.

1.1 WHAT DO WE CALL THEM?

We have a nomenclature issue to deal with before we get started. What do we call an instrument that measures mental variables? Mental variables, which we also call constructs or latent variables, are variables that we cannot directly observe. Most textbooks and sponsoring organizations call the instruments measuring these variables as mental measurement instruments. But what do you think of when you hear the terms test or examination? Many people think of a series of questions on which the respondent tries to do his or her best. There is often an accompanying feeling of stress or pressure. There's even a large body of research on *test anxiety*. But not all mental measurement instruments are like this. Other instruments are called inventories, indices, scales, profiles, or simply measures. These instruments usually attempt to describe typical behaviors, attitudes, or emotions. Here are the names of some widely used instruments:

Graduate Record *Exam*

National *Assessment* of Educational Progress

Minnesota Multiphasic Personality *Inventory* (MMPI)

GED *Tests*

The School Counselor Self-Efficacy *Scale*

The Parenting Stress *Index*

The School as a Caring Community *Profile*

Adolescent Diagnostic *Interview*

Myers–Briggs Type *Indicator*

Measures of Musical Abilities

Rating Scale of Communication in Cognitive Decline

All of these have several things in common. They require the respondent to answer questions, complete tasks, or make a performance. The responses or behaviors are scored to provide an interpretation. Every year, I teach a course called Instrument Development and Validation, and to be sure, I would prefer here to use the term instrument. However, to eliminate confusion over naming and to be consistent with most of the professional literature, I'm going to refer to all of these instruments as *tests*. For example, the *Standards for Educational and Psychological Testing* (APA, AERA, & NCME, 2014) is a primary source of guidance, sponsored by three prominent professional organizations, for test development and validation. The *Standards* refer to tests but apply more broadly to instruments measuring constructs. Additionally, people who take tests are commonly called examinees. But since not everyone is actually taking an exam, I will refer to them generically as respondents, that is, people who respond to the questions on a test.

You may have noticed that the above list of instruments does not include *surveys* and *questionnaires*. Questionnaires are data collection instruments designed to collect a wide variety of variables, some of which could be constructs. They are used in survey programs to collect data from a target population. But questionnaires also are likely to include many other variables, such as demographic, physical measurements, personal history, and test scores. They may also include tests. For example, the National Education Longitudinal Survey (NELS), sponsored by the National Center of Education Statistics, contained questionnaires that asked high school students questions about constructs such as self-concept and locus of control. These sets of questions could be considered to be tests embedded within the questionnaires. To be clear, this book is *not* intended to guide the development and validation of questionnaires and surveys. This book considers a set of questions that together are designed to provide a score that measures a construct or mental variable.

1.2 WHAT IS MEASUREMENT?

In thinking about measuring constructs, it's critical to discuss first what we mean by measurement. According to *Merriam-Webster's Collegiate Dictionary* (11th Edition, 2014), measurement is "1: the act or process of measuring, or 2: a figure, extent, or amount obtained by measuring" (p. 769). Okay, so what is measuring? One of several definitions of this term is "to allot or apportion in measured amounts (measuring out three cups)" (p. 769). The definitions of measurement in dictionaries tend to have this circular form. However, the operative word here is *amount*. That is, measuring a variable, say someone's height, is tantamount to determining how many height units someone has. The units can be inches, feet, centimeters, meters, or miles. Measuring height is an exercise in counting height units. This is the original, classical conception of measurement which dates back to Euclid's *Elements*, Book V (Heath, 1908). Consider the Thorndike quote at the beginning of this chapter. It is well known among measurement professionals, but the sentence that follows is less well known:

> *Whatever exists at all exists in some amount. To know it thoroughly involves knowing its quantity.*
>
> (Thorndike, 1918, pp. 16–17)

Unfortunately, this view of measurement does not work well with tests measuring constructs. Implicit in the classical concept of measurement is the idea that counting units results in ratio interpretations. For example, if Person A has 20 units of height and Person B has 10 units of height, not only is there a difference of 10 units but also Person A is *twice* as tall as Person B. This interpretation is clearly difficult, if not impossible, for tests measuring constructs. First, there is no clear unit of measurement. Scores on tests or parts of tests are not equal interval in nature. Consider, for example, one mathematics item "1 + 1 =" and another item "Find the square root of 23." They may both be scored one point for a correct answer, but the difference in mathematics skills between scores of 0 and 1 is not equal to the difference between scores of 1 and 2. Second, a ratio interpretation requires a true zero point. A score of 20 for Person A does not mean twice the amount of the construct as a score of 10 for Person B because a score of 0 does not mean zero amount of the construct. If we adhered to the classical concept of measurement, then it would be nearly impossible to conduct any quantitative-based research in education or the social sciences.

To get around this problem, the psychologist S. S. Stevens expanded the classical concept of measurement to include other interpretations of measuring constructs in addition to ratio scales. His definition of measurement was:

> *Measurement is the assignment of numerals to objects or events according to rule.*
>
> (Stevens, 1946)

For example, in a competition that measures diving skill, a diver performs a certain kind of dive and receives a score of 9.1. There were rules for obtaining that score. For example, if there is a lot of splash entering the pool, 0.2 of a point is deducted. This measurement of diving skill obviously does not fit the classical concept of measurement. There is no absolute 0 point, and it is not even clear that scores are on an equal interval scale. Nevertheless, because there were rules for scoring the dive, rules that were applied equally to all divers, Stevens claims that measurement has taken place. He developed four levels of measurement that are widely taught today in introductory quantitative research methods courses:

- *Nominal/categorical*: Numbers of this type are merely labels for categories, e.g., 1 = female, 2 = male. Many variables, such as marital status, political party affiliation, and geographic region are nominal/categorical in nature. Test scores can also be nominal in nature, e.g., pass or fail.

- *Ordinal*: The numbers indicate relative position or ranking but do not claim to be equal interval, e.g., 1 = first, 2 = second, 3 = third. An example of an ordinal level test score is the percentile rank, or the percentage of respondents with that score or lower.

- *Interval*: The numbers represent equal intervals, e.g., the difference between 5 and 10 is the same as the difference between 10 and 15, but there is no true zero. An example of an interval level variable is the centigrade temperature scale.

- *Ratio*: This level of measurement embodies the original classical concept, where the numbers indicate equal intervals, and there is a true zero. Examples of ratio level variables are length, height, velocity, and reaction time.

So, what is the highest measurement level for scores from tests measuring constructs? This is a point of some debate among psychometricians, but there is a general consensus that test scores fall somewhere between ordinal and interval data. Much depends on how the test is scored. If item scores are simply summed, the resulting scores, called raw or observed scores, are most likely ordinal. As discussed in Chapters 3 and 9, some transformations of raw scores claim to result in an interval scale. However, test scores are clearly not ratio level data, so you can never make an interpretation such as, Person A's self-concept is twice as positive as Person B's even if Person A's score is twice that of Person B's score.

The process of moving psychology from the classical view of measurement to Stevens' concept of levels of measurement being widely adopted actually took place over several decades in the early twentieth century. For the reader interested in this history, I recommend Joel Michell's (1999) account in *Measurement in Psychology: A Critical History of a Methodological Concept.*

1.3 SOME KEY TERMS

I have no wish to bore you with an extensive list of definitions. However, a few terms have different meanings for measurement specialists than they do for the general public or scholars in other disciplines. As a result, it's important to make this distinction so that you know what is meant when I use these terms in this book.

Psychometrics/Psychometricians. Psychometrics is the academic discipline associated with mental measurement. It includes scaling and scoring tests, validation, and test theories. It may also be referred to as quantitative psychology. Psychometricians are professionals who work and conduct research in this discipline. In other words, these are the testing experts. On the other hand, in the field of school psychology, psychometricians are professionals who administer tests. That is different from the use in this book.

Test. A test (or exam or scale or one of the other labels mentioned above) is a device for obtaining a measurement. More specifically, it is a "standard procedure for obtaining a sample of behavior from a specified domain" (Crocker & Algina, 1986, p. 4). The operative words in this definition are *standard* and *sample*. Although we are dealing here with test development, this definition also applies to everyday use. For instance, a thermometer is an instrument for measuring one's body temperature. The measurement is done the same way every time, or by following a set of procedures. Furthermore, each measurement is a sample, e.g., temperature taken in the morning, from a large number of possible occurrences.

Assessment. According to the National Council on Measurement's (NCME) glossary (http://www.ncme.org/resources/glossary), assessment means:

> *Any systematic method of obtaining information from tests and other sources, used to draw inferences about characteristics of people, objects, or programs; a process designed to systematically measure or evaluate the characteristics or performance of individuals, programs, or other entities, for purposes of drawing inferences; sometimes used synonymously with test.*

This rather wordy definition conflates an assessment with a test. In fact, many psychometricians think of assessment as testing. State educational achievement testing programs are often called state assessments, while at the national level, the federal government sponsors the National Assessment of Educational Progress (NAEP). On the other hand, outside of a measurement context (Merriam-Webster, 2014), to assess has a broader meaning: "to determine the importance, value, or size of…." (p.74). This definition of assessment does not need to have anything to do with mental measurement.

Evaluation. Related to assessment (Merriam-Webster, 2014), to evaluate is defined as: "to determine the value of" (p.432). For example, an assessment such as NAEP may discover that 30 percent of third graders are proficient in reading, but reporting that this percentage is below national goals is an evaluation of that assessment.

For other terms related to testing, test development, and validation that are not explicitly defined in this book, I refer the reader to the glossary on the NCME website.

1.4 MEASURING CONSTRUCTS

At the beginning of this chapter, I mentioned that this book is intended to guide the development of tests to measure mental variables most commonly called constructs or latent variables. Much of psychological or educational test development is geared toward measuring how much of some hypothetical variable respondents have. We construct these variables to explain human behavior on the basis of a theory of that construct, but we are never sure if these constructs really exist. These variables are sometimes called traits, but there is a difference in meaning. Traits are thought of as relatively stable characteristics, for example, the Big Five personality traits. So, traits are a type of construct, but the term construct is broader in meaning. For the remainder of this book, for simplicity, I will use the term construct.

1.5 HISTORICAL CONTEXT

Current practice in test development and validation has evolved over the course of time, over 4,000 years as it turns out. It's useful to examine briefly this history in order to see the basic underlying principles on which development procedures rest and why they are important. In particular, there are five major lines of development that converge in terms of methodology even though the purposes of these types of tests vary widely: personnel selection, credentialing, measuring intelligence, educational achievement, and personality.

1.5.1 Personnel Selection Testing in China, the United Kingdom, and United States

The first tests, as we know them today, were used to select individuals for employment. And the first of these dates back over 4,000 years to China. Nation states at that time were led by ruling families, or dynasties. China was no different in that regard. However, unlike other nations, China prioritized hiring the most qualified individuals for government positions. Beginning in 2200 BCE, China administered "examinations" every three years to government officials for determining their fitness for remaining on the job. In 1115 BCE, the Chan dynasty began formal testing to select individuals for high government positions. These positions were highly prized, and millions of Chinese sat for these exams from which a chosen few were hired. The exams were performance-based and covered music, writing, arithmetic, horseman-ship, and prominent ceremonial rites.

In developing these tests, the Chinese government developed methodology that is still used today. First, standardized procedures were implemented so that everyone was measured the same way. For example, scorers did not know who the candidates were. Two examiners scored each response, with a third brought in to mediate differences between the scorers. Additionally, candidates were tested under environmental conditions that were as similar as possible. Finally, the exams themselves were small samples of behavior under controlled conditions that could fairly well predict how individuals would perform in broader conditions.

The Han dynasty (202 BCE–220 AD) undertook major revisions of the civil service examinations. The program became a set of separate exams for law, revenue, military, agriculture, geography, and moral standards. After the invention of paper in 105 AD, these became the first written exams. From this point forward, the Chinese civil service examinations evolved in content and purpose. One key purpose was the promotion of meritocracy, or the hiring of the best qualified candidates as a path to upward mobility. This idea later became a primary driver for the widespread use of college admissions tests. For the reader interested in the Chinese civil service examination system and its intended and unintended consequences, I recommend Benjamin A. Elman's (2013) *Civil Examinations and Meritocracy in Late Imperial China*.

The Chinese examinations became a model for other nations. In the mid-1800s, British visitors to China were so impressed with the examination system that they modeled a testing system after it for selecting candidates for the civil service in India and later in Great Britain. In the late 1800s, legislators in the United States modeled the American civil service examination program after the British system.

1.5.2 Credentialing

Many professions today have a credentialing process in place, for certification or licensure. This process usually involves candidates needing to pass an examination or a series of exams. In particular, licensure procedures for the medical and legal pro-fessions have been in existence for several thousand years. In fact, the early Chinese civil service examinations included credentialing for those two professions. In the early part of this millennium, legal regulations of law and medicine became established in Europe. By the 14th century, credentialing took two primary forms. First, there were educational or training requirements. Second, candidates had to pass an examination.

The methodology for the examinations was taken largely from the Chinese civil service procedures. They tended to be performance-based, for example, requiring surgeon candidates to operate on an animal. A major methodological problem was inconsistency in scoring, and so in the 20th century, multiple-choice items replaced or supplemented essay and performance-based questions in many credentialing programs. In recent years, there has been a trend back to performance-based items as multiple-choice exams have been criticized for being unrealistic and unable to measure accurately some important professional skills. In addition, professional organizations, such as the National Board of Medical Examiners for medicine, arose to oversee the credentialing process.

1.5.3 Measuring Intelligence

In the late 1800s, psychology developed into a new discipline, distinct from philosophy. Early on, psychologists tried to apply the idea of measuring physical variables, such as height and velocity, to the measurement of constructs. The first attempts focused on intelligence. I will outline this history in some detail because it illustrates some of the controversies and abuses of testing. For an excellent history of intelligence testing, I refer the reader to Stephen J. Gould's *The Mismeasure of Man* (1996).

One of the first theories about intelligence was based on craniometry: the idea that smarter people had larger brains. An early proponent of this theory was Samuel G. Morton, a physician from Philadelphia. To be honest, Morton set out to show that racial groups differed in intelligence and that these differences were inherited. He hoped to support this view by exhuming bodies from different parts of the world and measuring their cranial capacities. Unfortunately, as Gould (1996) shows, Morton manipulated his data in order to come to the conclusion he desired.

Alfred Binet was a French psychologist who directed the Laboratory of Physiological Psychology at the Sorbonne at the turn of the 20th century. His research with his student Theodore Simon focused on child development. In 1904, the French government appointed a commission to study broadly the education of at-risk children and specifically to develop a test to identify these children. As members of this commission, Binet and Simon worked to develop the first intelligence test. At the time, craniometry was still the most prominent theory of intelligence. However, Binet knew that this approach would not work for their test (craniometry would recommend simply lining up the children and picking the smallest). Binet had earlier conducted some research on cranial capacity. He found that there were extremely small differences in head size between children identified as the brightest and slowest by teachers. The brightest children's heads were slightly larger, but this difference could be attributed to better nutrition and health. As a result, he gave up on physical measurement and decided to measure reasoning more directly. In 1905, he and Simon created a short series of tasks, related to everyday life but not explicitly taught in school (i.e., no mathematics or reading). These tasks included things such as repeating sentences and sequences of numbers and stating the difference between pairs of things. The score on the test was a child's mental age, or the average chronological age of children who performed the same tasks correctly as the respondent. Binet thought of his test as measuring different types of intelligence with mental age as an average of these intelligences. The test succeeded in its mission, identifying children with special educational needs.

The success of the Binet–Simon test attracted the attention of Henry H. Goddard, the Director of the Vineland (NJ) Training School for Feeble-minded Girls and Boys. In 1913, he translated the Binet–Simon test into English and used it at the Vineland School to identify and rank students. However, unlike Binet, Goddard subscribed to the idea that intelligence is inherited and fixed. It is interesting to note that he coined the technical terms moron, imbecile, and idiot to classify increasingly lower levels of intelligence. Furthermore, he thought the United States would be a better nation if it could reduce the number of low-intelligence people. Goddard promoted two ways to accomplish this. First, he proposed to sterilize low-intelligence people and was one of the founders of the eugenics movement. Second, the test could be used to prevent low-intelligence people from immigrating. To this end, Goddard established an intelligence testing program at Ellis Island.

At the same time, Lewis Terman, a psychologist at Stanford University, made several major revisions to the last (1911) version of the Binet–Simon test. He added adult-level items and developed an alternate scoring method, the intelligence quotient, or IQ. This revised version became the Stanford–Binet Intelligence Test, which is still used today by psychologists. He and his colleagues used the test in his famous longitudinal study of gifted individuals and their offspring. The Stanford–Binet became widely used and ushered in the field of testing as a business. On the other hand, Terman, like Goddard, believed that intelligence was a fixed, inherited trait and promoted the test as a measure of personal worth. He became an active participant in the eugenics movement.

In 1917, as the United States entered World War I, the army faced a serious problem. Who among the new recruits could serve as officers? In other words, the army wanted to find the most intelligent recruits. The problem was that, because the Stanford–Binet was individually administered and took over an hour to complete, it was unfeasible to test nearly two million recruits quickly. The US Army hired a team of psychologists, led by Robert Yerkes and including Goddard and Terman, to develop large-scale group-administered intelligence tests. They developed two tests, the Alpha, administered to literate recruits, and the Beta, administered to recruits who could not read or speak English. The exams used methods that are common in practice today, including objectively scored item formats such as multiple-choice and analogies. The exams were administered to nearly 1.75 million recruits in a short period of time. The US Army was satisfied with the results, in terms of classifying the recruits for various positions.

In addition to supporting the war effort, the Army Alpha and Beta had enormous consequences for the testing industry, government policy, and the discipline of psychometrics. First of all, the development team was still steeped in the concept of intelligence as a fixed, inherited trait. As a result, the team conducted numerous statistical analyses and used these to advance the policy agenda of Goddard, Terman, and others. For example, Table 1.1 shows a set of results reported by Yerkes (1921) in which Alpha scores were analyzed in terms of years of residence in the United States. Many, if not most, US citizens were immigrants from other nations. The table appears to show a relationship between how long a recruit has lived in the United States and intelligence, with a longer time associated with greater intelligence. Further analysis showed that longer-term recruits tended to come from northern and western Europe while more recent recruits came from southern and eastern Europe. Yerkes

TABLE 1.1 ● Yerkes's (1921) Table for Average Mental Age by Years of Residence in United States	
Years of Residence	**Mean Mental Age**
0–5	11.29
6–10	11.70
11–15	12.53
16–20	13.50
20–	13.74

concluded that northern and western Europeans were more intelligent than southern and eastern Europeans. Analyses such as these led to the Immigration Restriction Act of 1924, which set immigration quotas based on nation of origin. And fourteen years later, before World War II, when Jews wanted to escape to the United States from Germany and other parts of Europe, the United States used the 1924 Act to justify turning them away. Not our finest hour.

Of course, today we come to a far different interpretation of the Yerkes results. Many of the Alpha items required some familiarity with American culture and geography. Plus, the test was in English. Recruits who had been here longer simply had more time to learn English literacy skills and more time to be familiar with the American environment.

Similarly, much intelligence research was originally intended to discover differences in intelligence among race/ethnic groups, the results of which were used to promote discrimination. An examination of peer-reviewed journal articles from the 1930s into the 1960s shows that many researchers considered IQ differences between subgroups a legitimate question for inquiry. Things changed in 1969 with the publication of Arthur Jensen's (Jensen, 1969) article in which he promoted research that he believed suggested racial differences in intelligence. He was widely criticized (and threatened) for his article. Since then, researchers have largely viewed subgroup differences as resulting from environmental factors. However, there is still a small group of scholars, most notably Richard J. Hernstein and Charles Murray (1994) in *The Bell Curve*, who, in the face of severe public pressure and sanctions, persist in promoting genetic differences in intelligence.

Secondly, the Army tests also spurred the development of other large-scale tests, many of which are still in use. Among these are:

- Otis Group Intelligence Scale (1918): Arthur Otis, a student of Terman, created a group intelligence test modeled on the Alpha. This was the first commercial group-administered psychological test.

- ACE's Psychological Examination (1924): Sponsored by the American Council on Education, this was a test developed by L. L. Thurstone (see Chapter 11 on dimensionality), for college admissions. Patterned on the Alpha and Beta, respectively, it had two scores, linguistic and quantitative. As the SAT became more widely used, the Psychological Examination gradually faded.

- Scholastic Aptitude Test (SAT) (1926): The SAT began as Harvard College's test for awarding scholarships. Its two parts were patterned after the Alpha and Beta, but it was designed for entering college students. It became Harvard's admissions test and before long was adopted by all the Ivy League colleges, and then more widely as a nationwide college admissions test. This necessitated the formation of the College Entrance Examination Board, now called simply The College Board, to oversee its development and administration.

- Weschler Intelligence Scales (1939): David Weschler worked on the Army tests. The Weschler scales report two IQs, a Verbal IQ based on the Alpha and a Performance IQ based on the Beta. The Weschler scales are a competitor to the Stanford–Binet and are widely used in psychological assessments.

Finally, the Army tests led to the formation of large-scale testing as an academic and professional discipline as well as a major industry, as distinguished by the following:

- Professional organizations: Psychometric Society (1935), National Council on Measurement in Education (NCME) (1938), and the American Psychological Association (APA) Division 5 (1945).

- Peer-reviewed journals: *Psychometrika* (1936) and *Educational and Psychological Measurement* (1941).

- Textbooks by Kelley (1927) and Guilford (1936).

- Test publishers: Psychological Corporation, California Test Bureau, and the Iowa Testing Programs.

- Guidance in the development and use of tests:

  - *Standards for Educational and Psychological Testing* (AERA, APA, & NCME, 2014).

  - *Code of Fair Testing Practices* (Joint Committee on Testing Practices, 1988).

  - *Educational Measurement* (4th Ed.) (NCME, ACE, 2006).

  - *Handbook of Statistics Volume 26: Psychometrics* (Rao & Sinharay, 2007).

  - The International Test Commission has published numerous guidelines on its website: for test use, computer-based testing, test security and disposal, translating and adapting tests, assessment of diverse populations, a test-taker's guide, and using tests for research (https://www.intestcom.org/page/28).

1.5.4 Educational Achievement

Before 1845, educational achievement as an indicator of school quality was measured by exhibitions—public, well-rehearsed demonstrations of skills, such as recitations of facts and figures and speeches about topics like bravery and loyalty. These were done primarily to secure funding and recruit students for schools and to earn awards and recognition for students. Actual examinations were sometimes administered, but not every student was tested, often only the best students. In addition, what examinations that were given were often of dubious quality. Here is one sample item (reported by Reese, 2013, p. 89):

If 11 young men can become fools by drinking 6 bottles of wine, at $3 a bottle, what would it cost a dinner party of 25, to become fools in the like manner?

As a result, there was no way to compare schools directly. In 1845, legislators from Boston and New York began a lively debate on which city had the better schools. To be able to compare schools and school systems, a common achievement test was needed. And so, a movement was begun in Boston, led by Horace Mann, the Secretary of the new state Board of Education, to create a central examination administered to all students. Several years before, Mann had visited the United Kingdom and Europe and was impressed by their standardized civil service exams. Mann's ulterior motive for achievement testing was that he thought US schools were falling behind those from other nations. He viewed a central examination program as an agent of wholesale reform. To that end, he led a committee to develop the first standardized achievement tests in the United States. These were administered first to students in Boston and consisted of sections on reading, mathematics, writing, and geography.

Mann's vision for achievement tests largely came true in the form of school reform: superintendents were hired for centralized school districts, classrooms were graded, and female teachers were hired. And yet, controversies arose, debates about which are still relevant today. For one thing, teacher quality was evaluated using test scores. And in a statement easily found in today's media:

> *Is it not a wonder that so many of our American boys and girls survive the almost continual examinations to which they are subjected? America is gripped by examination mania, turning pupils into walking encyclopedias and threatening to send teachers to an early grave.*
>
> (Charles Parker, high school principal, 1878, in Reese, 2013, p. 1)

However, achievement testing caught on. By the 1870s, most city school districts used written examinations to evaluate student achievement and school and teacher quality. By 1990, achievement tests were administered in nearly all public school districts. In the 1920s, on the business side, achievement testing intersected with the Army Alpha exam. As mentioned earlier, the methodology developed for the Alpha led to the creation of corporations devoted to large-scale testing. In the 1920s, corporations and organizations were developed to administer and score achievement tests, including the Stanford Achievement Test (1923) and those from the Iowa Testing Programs (1925). What these larger entities made possible were achievement test batteries that enabled comparisons across states and with the nation as a whole.

1.5.5 Personality

Unlike tests for personnel selection, credentialing, intelligence, and educational achievement, in which respondents are instructed to do their best, group-administered tests intended to measure personality constructs instead ask respondents to report their *typical* behavior. As a result, one criticism often made against these tests is that it is uncertain how honest respondents really are.

Ironically, the first personality tests were actually selection tests designed to identify respondents with personality or behavior disorders. The stakes were then quite high. Like the Army Alpha, the first formal personality test was developed during World War I where American military leaders were concerned about the emotional stability of soldiers, many of whom experienced long-term traumatic symptoms, such as nausea, night shakes, and heart palpitations. These symptoms, called "shell shock," are now called post-traumatic stress disorder (PTSD). The US Army commissioned Robert S. Woodworth (1919) to develop a test that would identify soldiers who were emotionally unstable and unfit for further combat service. The test was called the scale of Psychoneurotic Tendencies (PT). The Army used the PT to screen soldiers for further psychiatric intervention. After the war, Woodworth adapted the test for industrial research and renamed it the Woodworth Personal Data Sheet (WPDS).

Many personality tests followed the WPDS, through the 1940s. Nearly all of them focused on maladaptive aspects of personality, such as "emotional instability" and "lack of emotional control." The prevailing view was that emotional problems would cause problems at the workplace, and so, these tests were designed to assist employers in identifying individuals with such problems.

The focus on maladaptive behavior began to change in the 1940s. Katherine Briggs and Isabel Briggs Meyers developed the Myers–Briggs Type Indicator (MBTI). Based on the theory of personality types of Carl Jung, the MBTI has become today the most popular personality test. Its primary appeal is that the sixteen personality types of individuals are presented as having strengths and weaknesses which can explain much human behavior. No stigma is placed on any of the types. As a result, respondents can learn their type, be proud of it, and not worry about being labeled as maladaptive. The MBTI ushered in a new type of personality test for respondents seeking greater self-knowledge and self-awareness.

Beginning in the 1940s, personality tests began to include inventories designed to assist in clinical diagnoses in psychiatric and medical settings. These included the Minnesota Multiphasic Personality Inventory (MMPI) and the Sixteen Personality Factor (16PF) Questionnaire. These tests did attempt to identify maladjustment but in a different way. Their purpose was to identify serious psychopathology.

More recently, personality tests have been used in research settings in an attempt to explain human behavior more broadly. Applications of the MBTI have expanded greatly to include work settings, personal life, relationships, and goal setting. Much research has suggested that many personality variables are changeable in nature, and so respondents' scores on such tests can change over time, challenging their use for high-stakes decisions. The exceptions appear to be the "Big Five" personality traits (Openness, Conscientiousness, Extraversion, Neuroticism, and Agreeableness). Much work has been done in recent decades to explore the explanatory power of other personality constructs, such as self-efficacy, self-concept, locus of control, grit, and motivation. Tests to measure these constructs are often developed by individuals or small teams of researchers.

1.5.6 Current State of Test Development

Test development has exploded in the past two decades for personnel selection, educational achievement, credentialing, and the measurement of cognitive and noncognitive constructs. Some of the work has been undertaken by large testing organizations such as Educational Testing Service, the National Board of Medical Examiners, and programs for statewide educational achievement testing. In addition, however, much work is undertaken by universities and nonprofit organizations, sometimes by small teams or individual faculty and students. These projects often lack the resources of large-scale organizations, but it is still possible for them to develop high-quality tests.

In recent years, four major trends have altered the test development process in fundamental ways.

Norm- Versus Criterion-Referenced Score Interpretations. Until the 1980s, most test scores provided *norm-referenced* information, that is, how respondents compared to a target population. In educational achievement, for example, much emphasis was placed on how far above- or below-average students, schools, and school districts were. More recently, greater emphasis has been placed on how well individuals and groups score compared to performance standards, such as "proficient," resulting in a *criterion-referenced* score interpretation. This distinction is discussed in greater detail in Chapters 3, 4, and 6. Chapter 12 discusses methods for establishing performance standards.

Test Theory. Test theories are conceptions of how to scale and score tests and how to estimate how much measurement error they contain. Until the 1970s, the dominant test theory, now called Classical Test Theory (CTT), was used as the basis for test development. CTT has several drawbacks that were widely known, but until new test theories and corresponding computer applications to implement them were developed, CTT was the best feasible option. One of the modern test theories, Rasch measurement theory, is introduced and implemented in Chapter 9. Many current testing programs use Rasch theory or its relative, Item Response Theory (IRT), to scale and score tests. One of the potential advantages of the modern theories is that test scores are believed to be closer to an interval level measurement than scores developed using CTT.

Technology. One of the critical questions to be addressed in any test development project is how test data are to be collected. For many decades, the best option was a printed test booklet with answers recorded on answer sheets, that is, a paper-pencil format. Initially, the data were transcribed by hand into a storage medium. Later, optically scanned answer sheets greatly speeded up the process. In the past two decades, tests have been increasingly administered by computer. There are several potential benefits to computer-administered tests, including greater data security, instant data entry, and instant score results to the respondent. In the past ten years, advances in computer technology have increased capacity to the point where new item formats are possible, including various types of "technology-enhanced" items that allow the measurement of skills not possible with traditional item formats. Some of these advances are discussed in Chapter 6.

By the same token, advances in artificial intelligence (AI) have supported the automation of many aspects of test development and scoring (NCME, 2020). For example, scoring engines have been *trained* to identify and score salient features of essays, to the point that these engines can operationally score essays with the same degree of accuracy as human raters. Another area enhanced by AI is automated item generation. This technology is aimed at writing items from a template model and can support the large number of items needed for some forms of computer-based test administration.

Distancing From IQ. For many decades, IQ tests and their cousins were used widely to make decisions such as personnel selection and placement and college admissions. IQ is known to correlate positively with almost any cognitive construct. More recent test development frameworks have focused on the specific knowledges, skills, and processes that underlie more global constructs, such as intelligence and achievement. These are discussed in Chapter 5.

1.6 SOME DESCRIPTIVE STATISTICS (CENTRAL TENDENCY, VARIATION, CORRELATION)

Many of you reading this book have had coursework in introductory statistics and/or quantitative research methods in which you studied some of the basic descriptive and inferential statistics. For you, this section will constitute a review. If you are completely new to statistics, then this section serves as an introduction to the statistics that feature prominently in test development and validation.

Statistics are numbers that summarize or characterize some property of the data. For example, statistics that measure central tendency attempt to find the value of a variable that best represents the dataset, while statistics that measure dispersion look for a number that indicates how spread out cases are on variables of interest. Additionally, formulas for statistics that are written in English indicate sample statistics, or values calculated on a sample of respondents from a target population. Formulas written using Greek letters are for *parameters* of the target population, calculated from all cases, that is a *census*, from an entire population. Such datasets are extremely rare. Greek versions of formulas are also frequently used to express theoretical concepts.

Summation Operator. Many statistical formulas require summing various quantities. To express this, an upper-case sigma is used. Consider the following scores for six respondents on a test measuring self-concept:

i	Self-concept (x)
1	7
2	5
3	3
4	8
5	9
6	10

The sum of these six scores is:

$$\sum x_i = 7 + 5 + 3 + 8 + 9 + 10 = 42$$

If you wanted to add only the second and third scores, you can limit the summation operator as follows:

$$\sum_{i=2}^{3} x_i = 5 + 3 = 8$$

For some formulas, the order of operations is important. For example, summing a set of squares is not equal to the squared sum:

$$\sum x^2 = 7^2 + 5^2 + 3^2 + 8^2 + 9^2 + 10^2 = 328$$
$$\left(\sum x\right)^2 = 42^2 = 1,764$$

Central Tendency. By far, the most popular statistic for measuring central tendency is the mean, or average. The sample and population means are shown below. The formulas in this case are identical. The calculation of the sample mean for the above six self-concept scores is shown. N is the population size, and n is the sample size.

Sample	Population
$\bar{X} = \dfrac{\sum x_i}{n}$ $\bar{X} = \dfrac{7 + 5 + 3 + 8 + 9 + 10}{6} = \dfrac{42}{6} = 7$	$\mu_x = \dfrac{\sum x_i}{N}$

Another popular statistic for central tendency is the median. The median is defined as the midpoint of the scores, half below, half above. Sample and population versions of the median are also identical. If there are an odd number of scores, the median is simply the middle score. If there are an even number of scores, the median is the mean of the middle two scores. The self-concept scores are first arranged in ascending order: 3, 5, 7, 8, 9, 10. Since there is an even number of them, we locate the middle two scores, 7 and 8. The median is then 7.5. The median is preferred to the mean when scores are highly skewed. For example, the median salaries of professional athletes and home prices are often reported instead of the mean because of a small number of extremely high salaries and home prices. If Bill Gates were to enroll in a college course, then the average student is a billionaire!

Dispersion. The most frequently used statistics to characterize dispersion are the variance and standard deviation. The variance can be described as the mean of squared deviations from the mean. The standard deviation is simply the square root of the variance. Its major advantage is that it is expressed in the original score units. Sample and population formulas differ, as shown below. Additionally, if a variable is dichotomous, that is, it can take only two values, such as a test item scored correct or incorrect, the formulas for variance and standard deviation are simplified.

	Sample	Population
Variance	$s^2 = \dfrac{\sum(x_i - \bar{X})^2}{n - 1}$ $s^2 = \dfrac{(7-7)^2 + (5-7)^2 + (3-7)^2 + (8-7)^2 + (9-7)^2 + (10-7)^2}{6-1}$ $= \dfrac{34}{5} = 6.8$ For a dichotomously scored variable: $s^2 = p(1-p)$, where p = proportion of one of the possible scores	$\sigma^2 = \dfrac{\sum(x_i - \mu_x)^2}{N}$
Standard Deviation	$s = \sqrt{\dfrac{\sum(x_i - \bar{X})^2}{n - 1}}$ $s = \sqrt{6.8} = 2.61$ For a dichotomously scored variable: $s = \sqrt{p(1-p)}$,	$\sigma = \sqrt{\dfrac{\sum(x_i - \mu_x)^2}{N}}$

Relationship Between Variables. Relationships between two quantitative variables (i.e., variables measured at the interval or ratio levels) are usually described by two related statistics, covariance and correlation coefficient.[1] Both are based on the cross-products between two variables. A cross-product for a single respondent multiplies the deviation from the mean on one variable with the deviation from the mean of the other variable. If these deviations are both positive (i.e., both scores are above the mean) and negative (i.e., both scores are below the mean), their cross-products will be positive, indicating a positive relationship. If one score is above the mean while the other is below the mean, the cross-product will be negative. If most cross-products are negative, a negative relationship results. The covariance is conceptually the mean of the cross-products. The correlation is the covariance divided by the standard deviations of the two variables. Formulas for the covariance and correlation are shown below. As an example, the sample covariance and correlation are computed on the following data:

i	Self-concept (x)	Statistics Anxiety (y)
1	7	10
2	5	9
3	3	13
4	8	9
5	9	11
6	10	14

In this case, statistics anxiety has a sample mean of 11.0 and standard deviation of 2.10. The covariance can range from very large negative values to very large positive values. Its main deficiency as a descriptive statistic is that it is difficult to judge how large a covariance is indicative of a strong relationship. The correlation coefficient solves this problem by dividing the covariance by the product of the two standard deviations. This limits correlations to values between -1.00 and $+1.00$. In this example, the covariance coincidentally is 1.0, but the correlation is 0.11, indicating a positive but weak relationship between self-concept and statistics anxiety.

---

[1]The correlation coefficient presented here is officially the Pearson product-moment correlation coefficient.

	Sample	Population
Covariance	$$S_{xy} = \frac{\sum(x-\bar{x})(y-\bar{y})}{n-1}$$ $$S_{xy} = \frac{(7-7)(10-10)+(5-7)(8-10)+(3-7)(13-10)+(8-7)(9-10)+(9-7)(11-10)+(10-7)(14-10)}{6-1}$$ $$= \frac{5}{5} = 1.0$$	$$\sigma_{XY} = \frac{\sum(X-\mu_X)(Y-\mu_Y)}{N}$$
Correlation Coefficient	$$r_{xy} = \frac{s_{xy}}{s_x s_y}$$ $$r_{xy} = \frac{1.0}{(2.61)(2.10)} = 0.11$$	$$\rho_{XT} = \frac{\sigma_{XT}}{\sigma_X \sigma_T}$$
Point biserial correlation	If x is the dichotomous variable, then: $$r_{pbis} = \frac{\bar{y}_1 - \bar{y}_0}{s_y} \sqrt{\frac{n_1 n_0}{n(n-1)}}$$	
Phi coefficient	Let the sample sizes of each value of each variable are noted as: 			

Phi coefficient table:

	$y = 1$	$y = 0$	Total
$x = 1$	n_{11}	n_{10}	$n_{1.}$
$x = 0$	n_{01}	n_{00}	$n_{0.}$
Total	$n_{.1}$	$n_{.0}$	n

Then,

$$\varnothing = \frac{n_{11}n_{00} - n_{10}n_{01}}{\sqrt{n_{1.}n_{0.}n_{.0}n_{.1}}}$$

As you will see later in this book, there are several versions of the correlation coefficient that simplify the formula for its calculation. If one of the variables being correlated can take only two possible values, often 0 and 1, then the correlation simplifies to the *point biserial correlation coefficient*, as shown above. If both variables can take only two values, then the correlation reduces to the *phi* coefficient. The important thing to note about the phi coefficient is that, even though it is still a Pearson correlation, its value depends entirely on sample sizes, or proportions, of each variable that are 1's and 0's, and not on means, standard deviations, or covariances.

1.7 SAMPLE DATASETS: TIMSS AND CIRP

To do the data analyses suggested in this book requires specialized software (actually, much of it could be done with standard applications such as EXCEL, but it would be quite laborious). In keeping with the assumption that you are either working alone or in a small group and that your resources are limited, I will use only free and open-sourced software. One application is jMetrik (https://itemanalysis.com/), which carries out a wide variety of psychometric analyses necessary for test development. I will also use several R packages (https://www.r-project.org/): psych, mirt, and lavaan. While jMetrik is easy to use through its graphical user interface, R packages can be more challenging. As a result, I have placed the code for all the analyses in Appendix B.

I have selected two datasets to illustrate the various analyses. The first dataset comes from the grade 8 mathematics assessment from the *Trends in International Mathematics and Science Study (TIMSS) Assessment 2003 for Grade 8 Mathematics*. This dataset consists of item response data for 20 multiple-choice items from one booklet of the US sample. The second dataset comes from a series of 18 items measuring political viewpoint from the *1999 CIRP Freshman Survey* (Higher Education Research Institute, 1999). The questionnaire and data come from a random sample of students preparing to attend a large public university. These datasets were selected to illustrate the development of a cognitive construct (mathematics skill) and a noncognitive construct (political viewpoint) and data from items scored dichotomously (correct versus incorrect) and polytomously (varying degrees of agreement). These datasets can be found on the accompanying website.

1.8 CHAPTER SUMMARY

This chapter introduced several terms used throughout the book, the most important being measurement. The measuring devices covered in the book go by a variety of names, including tests, examinations, inventories, and scales, but I will refer to them more broadly as tests. I outlined a brief history of test development in five areas: personnel selection, credentialing, intelligence, educational achievement, and personality. Some of the key principles in test development, such as standardization, go back thousands of years. Despite the vast differences in purpose and design, all of these types of tests use much the same methodology in their development. Finally, although it is likely that many readers have had some familiarity with statistics, I introduced some of the descriptive statistics that are widely used in the context of test development.

1.9 EXERCISES AND ACTIVITIES

Test Development Project

In the chapters to follow, this book will guide you in the development of a new test. For now, begin to think about a construct you would like to measure and how a test measuring that construct would be used. Write a concise definition of this construct.

Questions for Discussion

1. Why is standardization a key characteristic of test development?

2. What is the key difference between a test and a survey questionnaire?

3. How does Stevens's definition of measurement differ from the classical concept of measurement?

FURTHER READING

American Educational Research Association, American Psychological Association, & National Council on Measurement in Education. (2014). *Standards for educational and psychological testing*. Washington, DC: American Educational Research Association.

Elman, B. A. (2013). *Civil examinations and meritocracy in late imperial China*. Cambridge, MA: Harvard University Press.

Emre, M. (2018). *The personality brokers: The strange history of Myers-Briggs and the birth of personality testing*. New York, NY: Doubleday.

Gibby, R. E., & Zichar, M. J. (2008). A history of the early days of personality testing in American industry: An obsession with adjustment. *History of Psychology*, 11(3), 164–184.

Gierl, M. J., & Lai, H. (2013). Using automated processes to generate test items. *Educational Measurement: Issues and Practice*, 32(3), 36–50. NCME ITEM http://ncme.org/publications/items/

Gould, S. J. (1996). *The mismeasure of man: Revised and expanded*. New York, NY: W. W. Norton.

Joint Committee on Testing Practices (1988). *Code of fair testing practices in education*. Washington, DC: Author.

Michell, J. (1999). *Measurement in psychology: A critical history of a methodological concept*. Cambridge, UK: Cambridge University Press.

National Council on Measurement in Education. (2006). In R. L. Brennan (Ed.), *Educational measurement* (4th ed.). Westport, CT: Praeger.

National Council on Measurement in Education (2020). *Digital module 18: Automated scoring*. Mt. Royal, NJ: Author.

Reese, W. J. (2013). *Testing wars in the public schools: A forgotten history*. Cambridge, MA: Harvard University Press.

REFERENCES

Crocker, L., & Algina, J. (1986). *An introduction to classical and modern test theory*. Belmont, CA: Wadsworth Publishing.

Guilford, J. P. (1936). *Psychometric methods*. New York, NY: McGraw-Hill.

Heath, T. L. (1908). *The thirteen books of Euclid's Elements* (Vol. 2). Cambridge, UK: Cambridge University Press.

Hernstein, R. J., & Murray, C. (1994). *The bell curve: Intelligence and class structure in American life*. New York, NY: The Free Press.

Jensen, A. R. (1969). How much can we boost IQ and scholastic achievement? *Harvard Educational Review*, 39, 1–123.

Kelley, T. L. (1927). *Interpretation of educational measurements*. Yonkers-on-Hudson, NY: World Book Company.

Merriam-Webster. (2014). Measurement. In *Merriam-Webster's Collegiate Dictionary* (11th ed., p. 769).

Rao, C. R., & Sinharay, S. (Eds.) (2007). *Handbook of statistics, volume 26: Psychometrics*. Amsterdam: Elsevier North-Holland.

Stevens, S. S. (1946). On the theory of scales of measurement. *Science*, 103, 677–680.

Thorndike, E. L. (1918). The nature, purposes, and general methods of measurement of educational products. In G. M. Whipple (Ed.), *Seventeenth Yearbook of the National Society for the Study of Education* (Vol. 2, pp. 16–24). Bloomington, IL: Public School Publishing.

Woodworth, R. S. (1919). Examination of emotional fitness for warfare. *Psychological Bulletin, 16*, 59–60.

Yerkes, R. M. (Ed.). (1921). *Psychological examining in the United States army: Memoirs of the National Academy of Science* (Vol. 15). Washington, DC: U.S. Government Printing Office.

THE EVOLUTION OF VALIDITY

2.1 FIRST AND CURRENT DEFINITIONS OF VALIDITY

The *Merriam-Webster Dictionary* defines validity as "a) the state of being acceptable according to law," or "b) the quality of being well-grounded, sound, or correct" (https://www.merriam-webster.com/dictionary/validity). The second definition is more applicable in the context of the validity of test scores. An early definition of validity is the "degree to which a test measures what it purports to measure," a definition initially proposed by Garrett (1937, p. 324). In one of the first peer-reviewed articles on validity, Rulon (1946) criticized this definition in connection with educational achievement tests as not being useful "because under it the validity of a test may be altered completely by arbitrarily changing its purport" (p. 290). Rulon's argument against the notion of validity as the degree to which a test measures what it's purported to measure is that this definition does not account for the variety of potential applications. For example, a test measuring high school algebra might be used as a graduation requirement or as a formative assessment of a student's strengths and weaknesses. In both cases, it is important to determine that the algebra skill is indeed what is being measured. On the other hand, these two instruments are likely to be designed differently to meet their purposes. As a result, the evidence to support validity in these two applications of the same content would very likely be different. It is interesting to note that although standardized tests have been in existence for over 4,000 years, notions of validity have arisen only in the last hundred years. And even then, Garrett's writing on the topic was published forty years after the first modern psychological test, Binet's intelligence scale, was implemented. Until then, the user of any test was responsible for demonstrating that the test was actually useful for its intended purpose.

By contrast, the current version of the *Standards* (AERA, APA, & NCME, 2014) offers this definition of validity:

> *Validity refers to the degree to which evidence and theory support the interpretations of test scores for proposed uses of tests. (p. 11)*

In other words, validity is about the interpretation of test scores and the evidence that supports that interpretation, not the test itself. Clearly, views on validity have changed dramatically over the past 77 years. In the next sections, I describe the evolution of thinking about validity. Knowing about this evolution is important because validity and validation will continue to evolve as the methods for test development, delivery, and scaling likewise evolve.

2.2 CRITERION MODEL OF VALIDITY

In the first half of the 20th century, psychometricians tended to view validity from a practical standpoint. Garrett (1937) wrote that "A test is valid for a particular purpose or in a particular situation—it is not *generally* valid" (p. 324). For example, Garrett reports on the use of the Army Alpha exam to select applicants for clerical positions. The test turned out to be a poor predictor of workplace performance. As a result, a test could be valid for one purpose but invalid for another. Most of the first standardized psychological tests were selection tests, such as the Binet intelligence scale and the Army Alpha and Beta Tests. Their validity depended on test scores doing what was intended, selecting at-risk students or selecting recruits for officer training. Pearson's (1896) correlation coefficient offered a statistical approach to validation and was used widely. For example, in one of the first measurement textbooks, Guilford (1946) wrote that "in a very general sense, a test is valid for anything with which it correlates" (p. 429).

This pragmatic view of validity came to be known as *predictive* validity. Validity was expressed by Cureton (1951), in the validity chapter of the first edition of *Educational Measurement*, as "how well a test does the job it is employed to" (p. 621). If this job is selection, a criterion is usually available, such as job performance for a personnel selection test or college GPA for an admissions test. Cureton went to write that a way to validate a test score is:

> to give the test to a representative sample of the group with whom it is to be used, observe and score performances of the actual task by the members of this sample, and see how well the test performances agree with the task performances. (p. 623)

At the same time, the concept of *concurrent* validity was introduced as a separate type of validity (APA, AERA, & NCME, 1954). Here, the test and criterion scores are obtained at the same point in time. This type of validity usually involved correlating test scores with another widely accepted measure of the same construct, although, as Kelley (1927) pointed out, just because two tests measure the same construct by name, they do not necessarily measure the same construct. Still, concurrent validity was considered to be an important source of validity evidence. Eventually, these two types of validity were combined into a single type—criterion-related validity (APA, AERA, & NCME, 1966).

Kane (2006) points out two major advantages of the criterion model of validity. First, the criterion is directly related to the test score and therefore clearly relevant to test score interpretation and use. Second, a quantifiable indicator of validity appears, at least on the surface, to be objective. On the other hand, Cureton (1951) and Anastasi (1986) noted several difficulties measuring the criterion. For one thing, the criterion may not be measured on a quantitative scale. For example, Binet's scale was intended to identify at-risk children. One possible criterion would be teacher judgments on the appropriateness of an educational intervention made as a result of the Binet test score (which originally was a comparison of mental age to chronological age). Such a criterion would be subject to measurement error, such as bias or imprecision on the part of the teachers. Additionally, even for quantitative criteria, some degree of measurement error is likely.

2.3 CONTENT-BASED VALIDITY MODEL

At the same time that the criterion model gained wide acceptance, during the 1940s and 1950s, other psychometricians noted the weaknesses of the criterion model and argued for a validity model based on test content (Rulon, 1946). An initial content-based validity concept was "face validity," defined as the degree to which a test's content appeared to be measuring the intended construct. For example, the item "I am sad most of the time" would appear to be measuring depression, but an arithmetic problem would not. Face validity is still a term occasionally found in use today, but it is one not taken seriously by psychometricians. Angoff (1988) wrote that "the effort to make a test face valid was, and probably is today, regarded as a concession, albeit an important one, to gain acceptability rather than a serious psychometric effort" (p. 24).

Instead, a view arose that, for many tests, particularly those for measuring educational achievement or for credentialing purposes, the criterion model was inadequate. For one thing, there was likely to be no infallible criterion against which to compare test scores. Furthermore, the focus of test score interpretation rested on the measurement of the specific knowledge and skills represented by the test items. This requirement led to the idea of claiming that the test content and associated item format is a representative sample of the universe of all possible items so that the test score is an unbiased estimate of overall performance. If the sample is large enough, that is if the test is long enough, then sampling error can be minimized.

For a time, content validity was challenged by psychometricians who found statistical evidence more convincing. For example, Loevinger (1957) argued that, on most tests, item formats such as multiple-choice were written to measure only some of the processes deemed important, and they were selected to represent particular levels of difficulty and discriminating power. In other words, a representative sample of content is usually impossible to achieve. However, when the relevant content domain has been carefully specified, items have been written that are representative of that domain, and they have been scored appropriately, then content evidence came to be seen as important, particularly for tests that measure mastery of a specific set of knowledge and skills, as in credentialing exams.

2.4 CONSTRUCT VALIDITY MODEL

The criterion and content models worked well for selection and achievement tests and tests measuring cognitive constructs, but they were not as applicable for tests of noncognitive constructs, such as personality tests, whose purpose was to provide psychological interpretations often used by counselors and clinical psychologists. For these tests, no specific criterion is available except for other tests claiming to measure the same construct, and no definitive content is often found. Operational definitions of constructs can vary among tests of the same construct (see Chapter 6), leading to vastly different content. To address this shortcoming, psychometricians in the 1940s explored the idea of construct validity for the validation of tests measuring theoretical constructs. Construct validity appeared for the first time in the *Technical Recommendations* (1954) as a new type of validity to go along with predictive, concurrent, and content validities.

Cronbach and Meehl (1955) published a seminal paper on construct validity that transformed validity into a much different concept, one that has led to modern models of validation. For psychological constructs, Cronbach and Meehl argued that while criterion and content evidence were insufficient for many constructs, those constructs often came with a theory of what they were and a set of hypothesized relationships with other constructs. For example, while a test of emotional intelligence has no definitive criterion or content, one can predict certain relationships to hold true. For example, one theory of emotional intelligence (Goleman, 1995) holds that people high in emotional intelligence have more stable marriages and are more productive at work. Furthermore, emotional intelligence is theorized to be a set of skills on which people can be trained. If these relationships are observed, then support for both the test and theory is found. If not, then either the test or the theory, or both, are suspect.

One implication of their construct validity model is that validation is a process that unfolds over time, not from a single study or data collection effort. Cronbach and Meehl (1955) used the concept of nomothetic span to indicate the network of relationships proposed by the theory of the construct. These relationships can be investigated by the traditional methods of science. For a test measuring depression, these could include experimentation (therapy as a treatment group), comparison of groups (high versus low depression subgroups) on various outcomes, and correlational/regression studies (depression predicting outcomes such a job productivity and stability of long-term relationships). As a result, theories are never proven, but enough evidence accumulates over time that the theory is widely accepted. The same goes for tests. Validation is never completed. Any collection of data from the test can be considered validity evidence.

Another implication of Cronbach and Meehl's (1955) model is that the focus of validation is not on the test but on the interpretation of test scores. Any evidence, including content and criterion-related evidence, bears on construct validity. In this regard, Campbell and Fiske (1959) distinguished between convergent and discriminant validity. Convergent validity consists of correlations between tests measuring the same construct, while discriminant validity consists of correlations between tests measuring different constructs. Multitrait-multimethod matrices (MTMMs) became a popular method for investigating construct validity. Table 2.1 shows an MTMM for two constructs, grit and self-concept, and two methods, objectively scored test scores and ratings by the respondents' colleagues. The entries in the matrix are correlations (I should note here that these correlations are fictitious, not from real data). The numbers in parentheses in the diagonal of the matrix are reliability

TABLE 2.1 ⬡ Example of a Multitrait-Multimethod Matrix		Grit		Self-concept	
		Test	**Self-rating**	**Test**	**Self-rating**
Grit	Test	(.91)			
	Ratings	0.68	(0.85)		
Self-concept	Test	0.66	0.16	(0.79)	
	Ratings	0.35	0.31	0.75	(0.76)

coefficients that indicate the degree of precision of scores (see Chapter 4). The correlations between the same construct by different methods indicate convergent validity. These show relatively strong positive correlations. The correlations between different constructs by the same or different methods show discriminant validity. These are expected to be noticeably weaker than the convergent validity coefficients. Note that this is not the case for the correlation between grit and self-concept test scores. This suggests a correlation due to a common method, using an objectively scored test. Such a correlation undermines the validity of scores on both tests because it suggests that test format can bias scores the same way on both the test and the ratings.

2.5 THE HOLY TRINITY

After the publication of the 1966 *Standards*, validity came to be viewed as a "toolkit." There were three types of validity, each to be used differently for tests with different purposes. For example, typical of many technical reports at the time, the first edition of the *GED Technical Manual* (Auchter, Sireci, & Skaggs, 1993) contained a chapter on validity organized as follows:

> *Content validity:* Showing that the GED Tests measure the typical American high school program of study in each subject area, it's the most important piece of validity evidence. Here, the program shows the steps in developing test specifications and blueprints in consultation with instructional leaders and how the tests reflect high school coursework and workplace skills.

Criterion-related validity: This section shows correlations between GED scores and high school GPA, ACT scores, and other achievement tests. This section also included comparisons of high school seniors and GED candidates on GED scores and analyses showing how GED scores map onto high school letter grades.

Construct validity: This section included any other evidence that did not fall clearly into the previous two sections. This included studies of the relationship of GED passing scores to taking specific high school courses, correlations among the five GED tests, and a comparison of high school seniors and GED candidates on higher education and employment outcomes.

The GED Testing Service planned their validation around these three types of validity; that is, planning to have some evidence to report about each type, even though clearly for this testing program, content and criterion-related validities were the most important.

Not all psychometricians embraced the toolkit approach to validation. Guion (1980) derisively referred to the three types as "something of a holy trinity representing three different roads to psychometric salvation" (p. 386). Cronbach (1971) complained that for some testing programs, construct validity evidence amounted to "haphazard accumulations of data rather than genuine efforts at scientific reasoning" (p. 483).

Unlike criterion-related or content validity, which did not offer a specific set of procedures, construct validity embraced a general scientific approach in which a variety of research methods could be used to provide evidence relevant to test score interpretation. As a result, construct validity came to acquire increasing importance compared to the other two types. This trend led to two ideas. First, a test measures a construct, and any evidence related to that measurement is part of construct validity. Second, there really is only one type of validity, construct validity, and that criterion-related and content validity were types of evidence under the construct validity umbrella. Loevinger (1957) was one of the first psychometricians to argue for considering different types of evidence instead of different types of validity. She divided construct validity into three types: substantive (content validity focused on a theoretical perspective of the construct), structural (internal structure of the test), and external (relationships between test scores and other variables). She was also the first to articulate the view that "construct validity is the whole of validity from a scientific point of view" (p. 636). By the 1980s, this model of construct validity became widely accepted by psychometricians even as many testing programs still used the toolkit model of validity. Then, in 1989, Sam Messick published his landmark chapter on validity in the third edition of *Educational Measurement* (Messick, 1989), in which he introduced an expansion of the unitary model of construct validity, a model that still dominates current thinking.

2.6 MESSICK'S VALIDITY FRAMEWORK

Messick (1989) offered this somewhat dense definition of validity:

> Validity is an integrated evaluative judgment of the degree to which empirical evidence and theoretical rationales support the *adequacy* and *appropriateness* of *inferences* and *actions* based on test scores or other modes of assessment.
>
> (p. 13, italics in original)

Messick means, first of all, that validity is about the meaning or interpretation of test scores and is not a property of a test. In other words, we would never say that a test is valid. Instead, we try to make the case that a particular interpretation and use of a test score is valid. Second, validity is a matter of degree. Like most theories in education and the social sciences, test score validity is never proven. Evidence is collected over time that supports or undermines a test score interpretation. How evidence is collected is much like how research in general is conducted, that is, using the methods of science, such as experimentation, group comparisons, and correlational/ regression studies.

Additionally, because validity has to do with test score interpretations, these inter-pretations need to be specified before validity can be addressed. Messick stressed the need to investigate alternative interpretations of test scores. For example, does a decrease in reading test scores indicate lower achievement? Or, does that decrease result from contextual factors, such as changes in the order of items or how they are presented (see mention of the NAEP Reading anomaly in Chapter 4)? Probably the most controversial aspect of Messick's unified view of validity is the emphasis given to consequential evidence. In other words, the application of a test may result in value labels, such as retarded, depressed, or suicidal, that have consequences for respondents. There may also be social consequences for groups of respondents. Messick argues that value labels and social consequences can affect score interpretations and the way respondents answer test questions and, as a result, are an important part of the validity framework.

Messick sought a unified framework for construct validity that didn't overly rely on specific types of evidence for a particular use. He considered two interconnected *facets* of validity, as shown in Table 2.2. One facet is the outcome of testing, an interpretation of a test score and/or its use. The other facet is the justification for test interpretation or use, based on evidence or consequences. Test interpretation based on evidence is the construct validity conceptualized by Cronbach and Meehl (1955). However, justification for a particular use of a test may require additional evidence to support that use. For example, an interpretative score report from a test measuring emotional intelligence may provide valuable insight to respondents. But if that same test is used to make a decision about a respondent, such as entry to emotional intelligence training, then that use of the test requires additional supporting evidence.

In this framework, there are two basic types of threats to construct validity. The first is *construct underrepresentation*, in which the test does not include important parts of the construct. An example is a high school science test that does not contain any items about biology, and thus the construct "high school science knowledge" is underrepresented. The other main threat is *construct-irrelevant variance*, where a secondary construct contaminates score interpretation. An example is test preparation strategies for multiple-choice items that lead to higher scores.

TABLE 2.2 ◆ Messick's Facets of Validity		Outcome of Testing	
		Test Interpretation	**Test Use**
Justification for Testing	**Evidential Basis**	Construct validity	Construct validity + relevance/ utility
	Consequential Basis	Value implications	Social consequences

To counter these threats, Messick identifies six types of evidence, later called aspects of construct validity (Messick, 1995). These are not types of validity to be chosen as needed for a particular test purpose, but a complete set of evidence types, all of which together answer the two types of validity threats.

2.6.1 Content Evidence

Content validity evidence is similar to but subtly different than the original content validity. Psychometricians have long debated the importance and relevance of content validity for many years. They argued whether judgments of test content were an actual property of a test while other types of validity were the properties of responses to items. In Messick's framework, content evidence is considered to be necessary but not sufficient for a unified evaluation of score validity. That is, content is viewed in conjunction with other types of evidence. Consider, for example, the Iowa Tests of Basic Skills (ITBS) Spelling subtest. The multiple-choice items on this test ask students to identify a misspelled word among four different words. Subject matter experts might not consider this task to be measuring spelling skill, preferring instead to ask students which choice is the correct spelling of a specific word. However, as former ITBS senior author H. D. Hoover once pointed out (1987, personal communication), the item format appearing on its Spelling subtest shows much stronger validity evidence of other types, including stronger correlations with other measures of spelling skill and stronger internal consistency, than the pick-the-correct-spelling format.

Test content is defined by the 2014 *Standards* as "the themes, wording and format of the items, tasks, or questions on a test" (p. 14). Sources of test content vary considerably according to the intended purpose of the test. For a credentialing exam or job selection test, content may be developed by professional judgments and observations of key behaviors. For an educational achievement test, content may be determined by state curricular standards. For tests measuring personality and other noncognitive constructs, a theory of the construct can guide content. A critical component of content evidence in all tests is evaluating the degree of *alignment* between test content and the sources used to develop the content. Alignment is threatened if the content of the test is not representative of the entire construct, in other words, there is construct underrepresentation (e.g., if a certification test of accounting does not include tax law), or if the content is not directly relevant to the construct (e.g., a test measuring motivation includes items related to self-concept).

Content evidence also includes decisions about test design including item format, time limits and test length, mode of administration, and so forth. The main question here is whether these decisions insert construct-irrelevant variance into scores. For example, many tests use multiple-choice items exclusively. There are logical reasons for this, as enumerated in Chapter 7, but since respondents have a chance of guessing the correct answer, scores may be inflated. Furthermore, some components of the construct, such as some higher-level thinking skills, may be difficult to measure with multiple-choice items.

All of this evidence is often offered in the test specifications that appear in technical manuals or reports. For example, in the current *GED Technical Manual* (GEDTS, 2018), there is an extensive discussion of the rationale for moving the GED Tests in the direction of making the high school credential align with "college and career readiness," the primary focus of the Common Core State Standards that have been widely adopted by state assessment programs. What follows in the manual is an extensive discussion of how this overarching goal drives the content specifications of each GED Test. The manual goes on to describe item formats, time limits, administration technology, and other issues.

Finally, content evidence also refers to item technical quality. As discussed in Chapter 8, items undergo some form of pilot testing. How this is carried out varies widely across testing programs. Messick argues that ambiguous or flawed items elicit construct irrelevant variance that undermines test score validity.

2.6.2 Substantive Evidence

Substantive evidence is "a confrontation between content coverage and response consistency" (Messick, 1989, p. 43). As described above, content is guided by subject matter expert judgment, analysis of behavioral indicators, and/or by a theory of the construct. The question here is the degree to which item responses reflect those content considerations. For example, if an item intended to be high in difficulty in fact turns out to be quite easy, construct validity is undermined. Or, a "Strongly Agree" response is intended to indicate a higher level of the construct than a "Strongly Disagree" response, but item response data suggest the opposite. Is the construct being measured in the way desired by the test developers? Messick's later writing (Messick, 1995) and the 2014 *Standards* described substantive evidence as the degree to which respondents' thought processes while answering questions are consistent with the intent of the test developers.

Compared to the other types of evidence, substantive evidence is one of the least collected types because it can be difficult to access. At this time, substantive evidence can come from three potential sources. First, "think-aloud" and cognitive labs protocols can reveal respondents' thought processes. Think-alouds and cognitive labs are one-on-one interviews with respondents who reveal their thought processes while answering test questions. For example, for a mathematics item thought to be difficult, a respondent might reveal that after two or three of the distractors were obviously incorrect, the answer choice became a guess between two options, thereby making the item seem easier than it really was. Cognitive labs became useful during the aborted efforts to create the Voluntary National Test (VNT) during the late 1990s. When Congress delayed funding of the VNT, the test's developers used cognitive labs to analyze item quality on a very small scale. This method uncovered flaws in many items, thereby avoiding more extensive data collection. Further discussion of these two methods are provided in Chapter 7.

A second potential source of substantive evidence comes from recent technological advances in test administration. Many large-scale tests are administered on the computer. As a result, data such as eye tracking, response time, and log files have the potential to be used to reveal respondents' thought processes. Research on "big data analysis" is a current hot topic, and definitive results are not yet available. A third source comes from recent psychometric developments of tests designed to measure cognitive processes. These are called collectively cognitive diagnostic models and have led to the development of tests targeted at measuring the thought processes that lead to a final answer. These are mentioned briefly in Chapter 5 in the section on Evidence-Centered Design.

2.6.3 Structural Evidence

The conceptual basis for the construct includes an explicit or implied internal structure. This structure can take many forms and is closely aligned with the test scores. Many, if not most, tests report a single score. This implies that the construct can be viewed primarily as a single continuum ranging from low to high; that is, as a *unidimensional* construct. There may be components of the content, but these are viewed as being strongly enough correlated that they are considered to be a single dimension. Examples include many tests measuring psychological constructs, such as grit (Duckworth, Peterson, Matthews, & Kelly, 2007) which has two components (passion and perseverance) but a single score. Alternatively, *multidimensional* constructs contain content components that are different enough to justify multiple scores, such as the Myers–Briggs Type Indicator (MBTI) and NAEP Mathematics. There are points in between these two, such as tests that are primarily unidimensional but also report subscale scores. TIMSS is an example of this approach.

Structural evidence seeks to uncover support for the underlying structure. This evidence tends to be highly data driven, most commonly through some form of *factor analysis*. Discussed in greater detail in Chapter 11, factor analysis can take two broad forms. Exploratory factor analysis uses the correlation matrix between items or parts of the test to form an internal structure based on the data. Hopefully, this structure is consistent with the intended structure. Confirmatory factor analysis determines how well an item response dataset conforms to the intended internal structure.

An additional piece of structural evidence is an analysis of *differential item functioning* (DIF). DIF analyses of individual items or groups of items are intended to uncover potential item bias for or against target population subgroups. DIF methods are discussed in Chapter 10. DIF is included as structural evidence because its presence signals that the proposed internal structure may be different for different population subgroups.

2.6.4 External Evidence

External evidence is about the relationships between test scores and scores on other variables. Messick (1989) distinguished between two types of external evidence: *trait validity* and *nomological validity*. Trait validity emphasizes convergent and discriminant validity coefficients, which were mentioned above in relation to Cronbach and Meehl's (1955) presentation of construct validity. As shown above, MTMMs are a common way of demonstrating convergent and discriminant relationships.

Nomological validity focuses on a network of theoretical relationships hypothesized to exist between the construct and other variables. As discussed by Cronbach and Meehl (1955), a theory of the construct often includes hypothesized relationships to other variables. For example, in developing her Grit Scale, Duckworth et al. (2007) hypothesized that grit is strongly related to educational achievement but weakly related to IQ. That these relationships were supported by research strengthened score validity and supported the underlying theory. If these relationships had not been supported, then either score validity, construct theory, or both would have been undermined.

Methods for obtaining external evidence can vary as widely as the methods for conducting research. These include predictive or concurrent test/criterion relationships, as used in the old criterion model of validity. These may also include experimentation and group comparisons. For example, Goleman's (1995) theory of emotional intelligence posits that the construct consists of skills that can be taught. To test that hypothesis, an experiment could be designed with emotional intelligence training as a treatment group. Similarly, individuals who are high in emotional intelligence, as measured by the test, are hypothesized to have more stable relationships and to be more productive at work than those with low emotional intelligence. These relationships can be investigated through group comparisons or regression analysis.

2.6.5 Consequential Evidence

The preceding types of evidence deal with the first row of Table 2.2 and are an integration of earlier types of validity (criterion-related, content, and construct). The second row of the table concerns test consequences as a source of validity evidence. The first column then addresses the value implications of test score interpretations. If respondents receive a score report, they will imbue the interpretation of their score(s) with value. For example, a score report that informs respondents that they lack grit, are low in emotional intelligence, are depressed, or that they have a positive self-concept, are high achieving, or have musical or artistic ability conveys values to respondents. As it pertains to validity, the consequential concern is whether the value labels affect respondents' scores. If a test score leads to a decision about a respondent or a label placed on the respondent, the respondent may provide misleading answers to items. Suppose a company offers motivational training to individuals who score low on a test measuring that construct. Low levels of motivation are often attached to undesirable value labels, such as "lazy," "unambitious," and "withdrawn." As a result, a respondent could be motivated to answer in such a way as to avoid those labels. In other words, an invalid score results. Even if a score report is not provided, as in the case of a research study, participants may still anticipate what the researchers are looking for and respond accordingly.

The second column of Table 2.2 points to test use. Here, Messick was concerned with social consequences. Tests have intended uses, and it is important to evaluate whether those outcomes have occurred. Does a professional licensure test actually promote qualified individuals? Does a personnel selection test pick the best candidates? If not, there is a validity problem in that score interpretation (the individual is qualified, competent), and test use is compromised. Additionally, there may be unintended consequences. There has been widespread criticism that state educational assessment programs, while promoting rigorous achievement, have the unintended consequence of narrowing the curriculum ("If it's not on the test, it's not taught."). One particular unintended outcome is an adverse impact on population subgroups. Accusations of cultural test bias have been leveled against standardized tests for decades. And certainly, an investigation by test developers of potential bias is warranted. However, the adverse impact can occur more subtly. Test preparation services are quite popular for tests such as the SAT, GRE, GED tests, and credentialing exams. These can be quite expensive, thereby favoring candidates with higher income, a variable closely related to gender and race/ethnicity. This impact becomes a validity issue: if individuals with and without test preparation achieve the same score, do their scores mean the same thing?

Consequential evidence has been controversial since Messick introduced it, mainly because it is not clear who should investigate unintended consequences. The 2014 *Standards* offer the following advice:

> *Standard 1.25: When unintended consequences result from test use, an attempt should be made to investigate whether the consequences arise from test's sensitivity to characteristics other than those it is intended to assess or from the test's failure to fully represent the intended construct. (p. 30)*

2.6.6 Generalizability

All tests are samples of items and tasks chosen to be representative of the universe of all possible items and tasks. Data for scaling, scoring, and providing validity evidence come from samples of respondents selected to be representative of the test's target population. It is reasonable to ask then how well scores generalize beyond the specific set of chosen items and samples of respondents.

For items, test reliability is a major piece of evidence, including test-retest coefficients (administration at different times), alternate forms coefficients (different sets of items), and internal consistency coefficients (relationships between items or parts within a test) (see Chapter 4). There is a particular concern for item formats that require human judgment for scoring. Different raters scoring different tasks at different times present different sources of measurement error. As a result, generalizability evidence includes interrater training methods and interrater reliability.

Generalizability to other populations (population generalizability) and settings (ecological generalizability) also come under this type of evidence. Consider the Graduate Record Exam (GRE) whose purpose is to predict academic performance of students in graduate studies. Originally developed for American undergraduates, the GRE is now available internationally in many countries. The generalizability question for the GRE is the degree to which score meaning is consistent across different countries and across different administration conditions.

2.6.7 Integrating Validity Evidence

Messick intended for the six types of validity evidence to be integrated into a rationale for test score validity. He argued that the six types applied to all mental measurements. "Taken together, they provide a way of addressing the multiple and interrelated validity questions that need to be answered to justify score interpretation and use" (Messick, 1995, p. 746). Additionally, alternative interpretations of test scores should be investigated through the possibility of construct underrepresentation and construct irrelevant variance. Together, evidence of all six types and ruling out alternative explanations can provide comprehensive support for test score interpretation.

2.6.8 *Standards* and Messick's Framework

The influence of Messick's unified framework for validity clearly guided the 1999 and 2014 *Standards*. The definition of validity shown at the beginning of this chapter, from the 2014 edition, is an adaptation of Messick's definition from his 1989 chapter and other writings. Furthermore, both the 1999 and 2014 editions discuss types of validity evidence that are similar to Messick's. Table 2.3 compares Messick's six types with the *Standards'* five types of evidence. The primary difference, besides labeling, is that the *Standards* combine external and generalizability evidence into a single type

TABLE 2.3 ◆ Comparison of Types of Validity Evidence: Messick Versus *Standards*

Messick (1989, 1995)	Standards (1999, 2014)
Content relevance	Test content
Substantive theories and process modeling	Response processes
Structural fidelity	Internal structure
External and generalizability	Relations to other variables
Consequences of testing	Consequences of testing

called "Relations to other variables." Within this type, generalizability is called validity generalization.

2.7 KANE'S ARGUMENT-BASED VALIDITY FRAMEWORK

Since Messick's unified framework was introduced and supported in the *Standards*, test developers have expressed some dissatisfaction in applying the framework. This dissatisfaction comes from two primary concerns. First, although integrating validity evidence into a coherent argument is recommended, Messick offered no specific guidance on how to do this. As a result, validation has tended to consist of sorting evidence into each of the distinct types without any prioritization of the evidence. Second, the framework focuses on the construct being measured. Much of the content, structural, and external evidence relies on a coherent theory of the construct. In many applications, such a theory either does not exist or the construct is so complex (e.g., "college and career readiness") that it is difficult to define what evidence is needed.

In recent years, Michael Kane (2001, 2006) has addressed these shortcomings through an argument-based validity framework. Kane defines validity as "the extent to which evidence supports or refutes the proposed interpretations and uses" of test scores and validation as "the process of evaluating the plausibility of proposed interpretations and uses" of those scores (Kane, 2006, p. 17). In this model, much of the same evidence is collected as in the Messick framework, but instead of compiling lists of evidence, validation is organized around the proposed interpretations and uses. In Kane's framework, there are two types of arguments. The *interpretative* argument specifies a network of inferences that lead from responses to test items to the proposed interpretation and use of test scores. The *validity* argument is the evaluation of the interpretative argument, including evidence to support or undermine each of the inferences in the interpretative argument.

In this framework, a test is developed alongside an interpretative argument. First, the interpretative argument is outlined along with test specifications. The test is then developed to be consistent with the interpretative argument. As much as possible, the interpretative argument is evaluated to reveal any weaknesses. Following this procedure necessitates that test score interpretations and intended uses are clearly defined ahead of time, as well as the line of reasoning from test specifications to test scores.

The interpretative argument consists of a series of inferences that result in a claim being made about each inference. This claim then becomes the input for the next inference in the chain. Kane uses the work of Toulmin (1953) to provide a general structure for an inference. This structure is shown in Figure 2.1. As an example, the initial inference for most tests is the scoring inference by Kane. Scoring refers to the process of translating the data, i.e., observed responses to items, to an observed test score. The *warrant* is the set of rules for scoring the observed responses. The *backing* is the evidence supporting the warrant, or in this case the scoring rules. Depending on the item formats, the backing consists of demonstrating that the scoring rules are appropriate and are applied consistently. If the scoring requires human judgment, as is likely needed for performance-based items, then the quality of that scoring would also be a part of the backing. There is room in this structure for exceptions that may qualify the claim. An example of a *qualifier* is the case where a respondent has not answered enough items to produce an accurate observed score.

FIGURE 2.1 ● Toulmin's Structure of an Inference

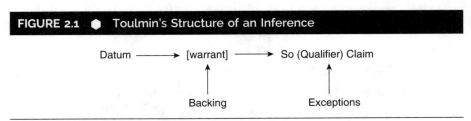

Source: Adapted from Kane (2006, p. 28).

In his validity chapter in the fourth edition of *Educational Measurement*, Kane (2006) discussed six inferences. The first three—scoring, generalization, and extrapolation—are common to most test development projects. The last three—implication, theory-based interpretation, and decision—can vary depending on the intended interpretation and use of test scores.

2.7.1 Scoring Inference

The scoring inference moves validation "from observed performance to the observed score" (Kane, 2006, p. 34). In other words, observed performance is usually responses to items. The scoring inference asserts that items are scored appropriately and accurately, and that scoring is free of bias. Also, implicit in the scoring inference is that the items themselves have sufficient technical quality.

The validity argument for the scoring inference includes any evidence pertaining to item scoring. Many item formats are scored objectively, including multiple-choice, true-false, Likert, and semantic differential items. For these, subject matter experts' review of item quality and pilot test item analyses can support the scoring inference. For item formats that require human judgment, such as constructed response, essay, and performance items, additional evidence from scoring rubrics, demonstrations of rater training, interrater reliability, and quality checks of rater effects are needed to support the scoring inference. Furthermore, item scores are aggregated to test scores in a way that needs to be justified. For example, if some items are weighted more heavily than others, the rationale for such weighting needs to be presented.

2.7.2 Generalization Inference

The generalization inference moves validation "from observed score to universe score" (Kane, 2006, p. 34). That is, does the observed score estimate the universe score, the hypothetical score that would be obtained if individuals responded to all possible items and tasks? The key question here is the degree to which the items and tasks chosen for the test are a representative sample from the universe of items and tasks. If that is the case, then the observed score interpretation expands beyond the specific set of items and tasks to the broader universe of generalization.

The validity argument to support the generalization inference includes test specifications and the rationale for the balance of content domains and processes. The specifications ensure that alternate forms are as identical as possible. Statistical sampling theory applied to the selection of items also plays a role in the validity argument. Reliability coefficients indicate the degree of consistency of repeated measurements (see Chapter 4). Standard errors of measurement indicate the precision of observed scores.

2.7.3 Extrapolation Inference

The extrapolation inference moves validation "from universe score to target score" (Kane, 2006, p. 34). This inference is about the relationship between the observed score, now the universe score, and the target domain for the construct being measured. In other words, does the universe score really measure the construct? If so, then implications or interpretations associated with the construct apply to test scores.

Evidence to support the extrapolation inference can come from both analytical and empirical sources. Analytically, the congruence between the universe of generalization and the target domain can be examined. Extrapolation could be undermined if there are parts of the target domain that are systematically excluded from test specifications. For example, if the test uses multiple-choice items only, then aspects of the domain that require an alternate format to be measured, such as an essay to measure writing skill, extrapolation would be challenged. That is, construct underrepresentation could be an issue. Another type of supporting analytical evidence is what Messick called substantive evidence. Think-aloud and cognitive lab protocols could be used to evaluate whether individuals are responding in a way consistent with how the target domain is conceptualized. Empirical evidence can also be obtained in the form of test-criterion relationships, or convergent validity correlations between test scores and scores on measures of the same or similar constructs. Studies that collect these data can come from different populations and settings.

These first three inferences are set as a series of steps. Most of the work establishing the validity argument is done during test development. If the first inference, scoring, is not supported, say if the items are not technically sound, then the interpretative argument breaks down and there is no need to move to the generalization inference. If the extrapolation inference is supported, then there is support for the intended meaning of test scores. The inferences that follow focus on the intended uses of test scores.

2.7.4 Implication Inference

The implication inference moves from the target score (from the extrapolation inference) "to any implications suggested by the construct label or description" (Kane, 2006, p. 43). This inference addresses implications beyond a description of the meaning of test scores. These could include expected relationships with other variables, an expectation of score stability over time, and predicted group differences. Evidence to support such implications can vary widely, such as discriminant coefficients for different constructs, and MTMMs, while construct underrepresentation and construct irrelevant variance can undermine predicted implications. Finally, implications can come in the form of intended and unintended consequences. As discussed above with the Messick framework, unintended consequences, including negative value labels and adverse impact, can affect test score validity.

2.7.5 Theory-Based Interpretation Inference

Theory-based interpretations represent an inference moving from the target score to the construct as defined by theory and any claims associated with the theory. For example, the MBTI was originally developed to support Carl Jung's theory of personality types. As a result, not only did a respondent receive a description of their personality type, but Jung's theory made broad predictions of how someone with that personality type would behave in specific situations.

Both analytic and empirical evidence are needed to support theory-based inferences. Analytically, one can examine the relationships between the items and tasks in the test and the theory behind them. That is, the theory should provide guidance to test development. Empirically, evaluating the test is closely tied to evaluating the theory. A theory may make predictions that can be investigated. Jung's theory predicts that people of a certain personality type will not work well with individuals of a different personality type. That prediction can be tested using scores from the MBTI. The theory behind the construct may also hypothesize nomological networks of a collection of variables. It is possible then to investigate whether data support such networks through various methodologies, including multiple regression, experimental manipulations, path analysis, and structural equation modeling.

2.7.6 Decision Inference

Many tests are used to make decisions about respondents. These include personnel selection and credentialing tests, college admissions exams, and psychological diagnostic tests. In addition, to an interpretation of test scores, validity evidence is also needed for the decision process.

The most common method for determining how scores relate to decisions is *standard setting*. Standard setting is a group decision-making process that attempts to determine one or more test scores, called *cut scores*, that form the boundaries between decision points, such as pass/fail, selected/not selected, and referred for intervention/not referred. Also, tests that provide a criterion-reference score interpretation typically use standard setting to recommend the cut scores that divide performance levels. Kane (1994) provides a framework for evaluating the validity of the standard setting process. Standard setting methods and their validation are discussed in Chapter 12.

Additional evidence to support the decision inference can come from an evaluation of consequences. Incorrect decisions can have severe consequences. Tess Neal and her colleagues examined the use of psychological tests in legal proceedings (Neal, Slobogin, Saks, Faigman, & Geisinger, 2019). They found that about 60 percent of the tests used in court cases had unfavorable reviews of their psychometric properties while at the same time legal challenges to test score validity were relatively rare (about 2.5 percent of the cases). There may also be adverse impact on population subgroups. For example, in state educational achievement testing programs, there is social pressure to have more students achieve the "proficient" performance level. That can lead to "teaching to the test" preparation practices that raise test scores, but the validity of those score increases could be suspect.

As discussed above, a major issue regarding consequential evidence is: who should be responsible for collecting it? The 2014 *Standards* (see Standard 1.25 above) are not clear on this question. Kane (2006) suggests that test developers should be responsible for any claims about the interpretation of test scores for its intended uses, while test users who decide to use a test for some other purpose are responsible for evaluating consequential evidence.

2.8 CURRENT STATE OF VALIDITY AND VALIDATION

Psychometricians continue to debate theories of validity, and we have surely not reached an end state. At present, the best advice is to follow the guidelines in the 2014 *Standards* because this framework for validity has achieved the consensus of three prominent professional organizations associated with test development and use. Those *Standards* are largely based on the Messick validity framework that centers validity around five (or six) types of evidence to support test score interpretations and uses. In the Instrument Development and Validation course I teach, I ask students to create a validation plan for a new test and give them the choice of designing their plan around either the Messick/*Standards* or Kane's framework. To date, every student has chosen the Messick/*Standards* framework. I'm not sure why, but it may be that it is easier for them to conceptualize types of evidence than an interpretative argument. At the same time, many new testing programs, particularly ones measuring cognitive constructs, are using Kane's framework for a validation plan. These include the GED Tests (GEDTS, 2018) and the Test of English as a Foreign Language (TOEFL) (Chapelle, Enright, & Jamieson, 2010), and the Tripod Student Survey of teacher effectiveness (Kuhfeld, 2017). These programs have developed interpretative arguments that include inferences in addition to the ones Kane suggests. Further examples of validation plans are provided in Chapter 13.

By contrasts, older tests may still be using the "toolkit" approach described above. I continue to work with professionals and organizations whose views of validity lie at different points along the evolutionary continuum. I suspect that part of the reason is that what individuals learned in their graduate programs is what they use today. A personal anecdote here: my own doctoral program in the early 1980s professed the trinitarian view of validity. When I taught courses in psychometrics for the first time in the early 2000s, Messick's 1989 chapter and the 1999 *Standards* had been published. I hadn't followed these developments, so I had some (embarrassing) catching up to do.

2.9 CHAPTER SUMMARY

This chapter describes the evolution of the concept of validity from "the degree a test measures what it's supposed to measure" to "the extent to which evidence supports or refutes the proposed interpretation and uses." This process moved validity from a criterion model to the content model to the construct model to the three types of validity (criterion-related, content, and construct) to the current unified view of validity to the possibly near-future argument-based approach. It is as important to understand this evolution as different tests use different models of validation. As students, researchers, and practitioners who work with tests measuring educational and psychological constructs, you are likely to confront all of these validity models at some point.

2.10 EXERCISES AND ACTIVITIES

1. Why is validity a property of the test score and not the test itself?

2. Why have some large-scale credentialing and educational achievement testing programs been drawn to Kane's validity framework?

3. What is the major difference between the "Holy Trinity" validity types and Messick's unified construct validity framework?

4. What responsibilities do you think the test developer has to ensure that adverse unintended consequences from test scores do not occur?

5. Locate the technical manual, validity studies, and/or website of a published test. What validity information is provided by the test developer? Compare that to Messick's and Kane's framework. Is there any important evidence that has not been yet collected?

FURTHER READING

American Educational Research Association, American Psychological Association, & National Council on Measurement in Education (2014). *Standards for educational and psychological testing*. Washington, DC: American Educational Research Association.

Cronbach, L. J., & Meehl, P. E. (1955). Construct validity in psychological tests. *Psychological Bulletin*, 52, 281–302.

Messick, S. (1989). Validity. In R. L. Linn (Ed.), *Educational measurement* (3rd ed., pp. 13–103). New York, NY: American Council on Education and MacMillan.

Kane, M. T. (2006). Validation. In R. L. Brennan (Ed.), *Educational measurement* (4th ed., pp. 17–64). Westport, CT: Praeger.

REFERENCES

American Psychological Association, American Educational Research Association, & National Council on Measurement Used in Education (1954). Technical recommendations for psychological tests and diagnostic techniques. *Psychological Bulletin*, 51(2, Pt. 2), 1–38.

American Psychological Association, American Educational Research Association, & National Council on Measurement in Education (1966). *Standards for educational and psychological tests and manuals*. Washington, DC: American Psychological Association.

Anastasi, A. (1986). Evolving concepts of test validation. *Annual Review of Psychology*, 37, 1–15.

Angoff, W. H. (1988). Validity: An evolving concept. In H. Wainer, & H. Braun (Eds.), *Test validity* (pp. 19–32). Hillsdale, NJ: Lawrence Erlbaum.

Auchter, J. C., Sireci, S. G., & Skaggs, G. (1993). *The tests of general educational development: Technical manual*. Washington, DC: American Council on Education.

Campbell, D. T., & Fiske, D. W. (1959). Convergent and discriminant validation by the multitrait-multimethod matrix. *Psychological Bulletin*, 56, 81–105.

Chapelle, C. A., Enright, M. K., & Jamieson, J.(Spring 2010). Does an argument-based approach to validity make a difference? *Educational Measurement: Issues and Practice*, 29(1), 3–13.

Cronbach, L. J. (1971). Test validation. In R. L. Thorndike (Ed.), *Educational measurement* (2nd ed., pp. 443–507). Washington, DC: American Council on Education.

Cureton, E. E. (1951). Validity. In E. F. Lindquist (Ed.), *Educational measurement* (1st ed., pp. 691–694). New York, NY: American Council on Education and MacMillan.

Duckworth, A. L., Peterson, C., Matthews, M. D., & Kelly, D. R. (2007). Grit: Perseverance and passion for long-term goals. *Journal of Personality and Social Psychology*, 92(6), 1087–1101.

Garrett, H. E. (1937). *Statistics in psychology and education*. New York, NY: Longmans, Green.

GED Testing Service (2018). *Technical manual: GED Test* (Updated 2018 Edition). Washington, DC: Author.

Goleman, D. (1995). *Emotional intelligence*. New York, NY: Bantam Books.

Guilford, J. P. (1946). New standards for test evaluation. *Educational and Psychological Measurement*, 6, 427–438.

Guion, R. M. (1980). On trinitarian conceptions of validity. *Professional Psychology*, 11, 385–398.

Kane, M. (1994). Validating the performance standards associated with passing scores. *Review of Educational Research*, 64(3), 425–461.

Kane, M. T. (2001). Current concerns in validity theory. *Journal of Educational Measurement*, 38(4), 319–342.

Kelley (1927). *Interpretation of educational measurements.* Yonkers-on-Hudson, NY: World Book Company.

Kuhfeld, M. (2017). When students grade their teachers: A validity analysis of the Tripod Student Survey. *Educational Assessment*, 22(4), 253–274.

Loevinger, J. (1957). Objective tests as instruments in psychological theory. *Psychological Reports*, 30, 635–694 (Monograph Suppl. 9).

Messick, S. (1995). Validity of psychological assessment: Validation of inferences from persons' responses and performances as scientific inquiry into score meaning. *American Psychologist*, 50, 741–749.

Neal, T. M. S., Slobogin, C., Saks, M. J., Faigman, D. L., & Geisinger, K. F. (2019). Psychological assessments in legal contexts: Are courts keeping "Junk Science" out of the courtroom?. *Psychological Science in the Public Interest*, 20(3), 135–164.

Pearson, K. (1896). Mathematical contributions to the theory of evolution. III. Regression, heredity and panmixia. *Philosophical Transactions of the Royal Society of London*, 187, 253–318.

Rulon, P. J. (1946). On the validity of educational tests. *Harvard Educational Review*, 16, 290–296.

Technical recommendations for psychological tests and diagnostic techniques. (1954). *Psychological Bulletin Supplement*, 51(2 Part 2), 1–38.

Toulmin, S. (1953). *The philosophy of science.* London: Hutchinson's Universal Library.

TEST SCALING AND SCORING

As discussed in Chapter 1, measurement is about the assignment of numbers according to rules. In this case, we are creating a test to measure a construct, a variable that we cannot observe directly. The goal then is to translate responses to questions into numbers and those numbers into a measurement of an individual on the construct of interest. This chapter first introduces ways to convert responses to questions into item scores and then shows how to transform the item scores into a score on the entire test.

3.1 SCORING ITEMS

First, what exactly is an item? An item is a test question with a scoring rule. A number of item formats and how to write items in those formats are introduced in Chapter 7. The formats often differ in terms of what type of construct they are intended to measure, say cognitive versus noncognitive constructs, and what is required of the respondent. In this chapter, the focus is on how to score them. Roughly, there are two types of items in terms of how they are scored—dichotomously and polytomously scored items. How items are scored plays a role later on in deciding what measurement theory to use and how to score the entire test.

Dichotomously scored items have two possible scoring outcomes. These can be anything—1 and 2, 0 and 10—but the most common and convenient scoring is 0 and 1. For items with answer choices such as Yes or No, True or False, Agree or Disagree, a score of 0 is assigned to one answer, and a score of 1 is assigned to the other. Dichotomous scoring can also be applied to items with more than one answer choice. Multiple-choice items may have four or more choices, but only one of them, the correct answer, is scored 1, with the other choices scored 0. Essays or other items in which the respondent supplies a written answer can be scored 1 for a correct answer and 0 for an incorrect answer.

Polytomously scored items have three or more score points. A Likert item, in which a respondent is presented with a statement followed by answer choices, such as Strongly Disagree, Disagree, Neutral, Agree, and Strongly Agree, is usually scored on a 1–5 or 0–4 basis. Each response choice is given a score, and a higher score is intended to mean a higher level of the construct being measured. Essays, performances, Likert, constructed response, and other such item formats are typically scored polytomously, but they can also be scored dichotomously. I should point out that multiple-choice items can be scored polytomously if there is one correct answer and other answers that are given partial credit. For these reasons, we refer to items that are dichotomously or polytomously scored, not dichotomous or polytomous items.

3.2 RAW SCORES FOR A TEST

One of the simplest and most commonly used test scores is the raw score, also referred to as a summed score or observed score. Raw scores are obtained by summing the item scores. A dichotomously scored 30-item multiple-choice test would have a raw score range of 0–30. A test that consisted of 10 polytomously scored items, each of which has 5 score points, would have a raw score range of 10–50, if each item was scored 1–5, or 0–40, if each item was scored 0–4. A variation on the summed score is the weighted sum score, where some items are given specific weights to give them greater or lesser importance than other items. Additionally, average item scores are a form of raw score. For dichotomously scored items, the average item score becomes the proportion or percent correct (or the proportion of items with a score of 1). For polytomously scored items, on a 1–5 scale, the average item score can range from 1 to 5.

Some psychometric analyses differ depending on whether the items are scored dichotomously or polytomously. I will use two datasets mentioned in Chapter 1 to illustrate a variety of analyses using jMetrik and the psych R package. The first dataset comes from Booklet 1 of the US sample of the 2003 TIMSS Mathematics. This dataset consists of 20 multiple-choice items measuring Grade 8 Mathematics. These data can be found in the EXCEL file, TIMMS 2003 Math data.xlsx, on the online website. The pdf file T03_RELEASED_M8.pdf (https://timss.bc.edu/PDF/T03_RELEASED_M8.pdf) contains information about each item including its content specifications, item format, and correct answer. Additionally, this file contains the actual items themselves.

Before running any analyses, it is important to investigate how the data are coded in the EXCEL file. A good place to start is to run simple frequencies of the item response codes for all items. jMetrik and the psych package can perform this. For now, I will use jMetrik. Both data files should be imported into jMetrik, as described in the Quick Start Guide on the website (https://itemanalysis.com/jmetrik-quick-start/). Table 3.1 shows the codes for the first item, M012001, using jMetrik. The values 1–5 correspond to answer choices A–E, respectively. The TIMSS codebook indicates that a code of 8 means "Not administered," and a code of 9 means "Omitted." Other items contain codes of 6, meaning "Not reached," and 7, meaning "Invalid response." In other words, codes of 6–9 indicate different types of missing or unscorable answers. I'll address how to handle missing data in the next section.

The second dataset comes from a series of 18 items measuring political viewpoint administered to incoming undergraduate freshmen during a summer orientation visit. The data for these items can be found on the website for this book in an EXCEL file

TABLE 3.1 ● Frequencies of Item Codes for TIMSS Item M012001					
Value	Frequency	Percent	Valid Pct.	Cum. Freq.	Cum. Pct.
1.0	446	58.9168	58.9168	446	58.9168
2.0	33	4.3593	4.3593	479	63.2761
3.0	51	6.7371	6.7371	530	70.0132
4.0	73	9.6433	9.6433	603	79.6565
5.0	150	19.8151	19.8151	753	99.4716
8.0	3	0.3963	0.3963	756	99.8679
9.0	1	0.1321	0.1321	757	100.0000
Valid Total	757	100.0000	100.0000		
Missing	0				
Grand Total	757				

named poliview.xlsx. (https://www.heri.ucla.edu/researchers/instruments/CIRP/1999 SIF.pdf) The entire questionnaire itself can be found in the pdf file 1999SIF.pdf. The items are named View9901 to View9918 and are each scored 1–4, for responses of Disagree Strongly, Disagree, Agree, and Agree Strongly, respectively. The 18 items are shown in Figure 3.1. I have used these items and data in class numerous times, and there is always disagreement on some items as to whether or not they should be reverse scored. So, here I will use the scoring from my most recent class as of this writing. With high item scores indicating a conservative viewpoint, the following items were reverse scored: View99 02, View9903, View9904, View9905, View9908, View9909, View9913, View9914, and View9918. Table 3.2 shows the frequency distribution for the first item, View9901.

Some descriptive statistics and a histogram are shown in Figures 3.2 and 3.3 for the TIMSS and political viewpoint tests, respectively, using jMetrik. In jMetrik, the TIMSS items must be scored prior to any analysis. The easiest way to do this is by using Basic Item Scoring (as described on the jMetrik website). Then, the test scoring utility should be used to calculate raw scores (called summed or average scores by jMetrik). The TIMSS items have a mean of 12.43, out of a possible 20, or about 61 percent correct. The raw score distribution is also somewhat negatively skewed. This is a typical distribution for educational achievement tests, which are usually designed to have a percent correct greater than 50 percent.

FIGURE 3.1 ● Political Viewpoint Items From 1999 CIRP Questionnaire

Item Name	
view9901	There is too much concern in the courts for the rights of criminals.
view9902	Abortion should be legal.
view9903	The death penalty should be abolished.
view9904	If two people really like each other, it's all right for them to have sex even if they've known each other for only a very short time.
view9905	Marijuana should be legalized.
view9906	It is important to have laws prohibiting homosexual relationships.
view9907	Employers should be allowed to require drug testing of employees or job applicants.
view9908	Just because a man thinks that a woman has "led him on" does not entitle him to have sex with her.
view9909	The federal government should do more to control the sale of handguns.
view9910	Racial discrimination is no longer a major problem in America.
view9911	Realistically, an individual can do little to bring about changes in our society.
view9912	Wealthy people should pay a larger share of taxes than they do now.
view9913	Colleges should prohibit racist/sexist speech on campus.
view9914	Same-sex couples should have the right to legal marital status.
view9915	Material on the Internet should be regulated by the government.
view9916	The activities of married women are best confined to the home and family.
view9917	Affirmative action in college admissions should be abolished.
view9918	People have a right to know about the personal lives of public figures.

TABLE 3.2 ● Frequency Distribution for View9901

Value	Frequency	Percent	Valid Pct.	Cum. Freq.	Cum. Pct.
1.0	42	3.6269	3.6745	42	3.6745
2.0	245	21.1572	21.4348	287	25.1094
3.0	656	56.6494	57.3928	943	82.5022
4.0	200	17.2712	17.4978	1,143	100.0000

(Continued)

TABLE 3.2 (Continued)

Value	Frequency	Percent	Valid Pct.	Cum. Freq.	Cum. Pct.
Valid Total	1,143	98.7047	100.0000		
Missing	15	1.2953			
Grand Total	1,158	100.0000			

FIGURE 3.2 ● Descriptives and Histogram for TIMSS Raw Scores

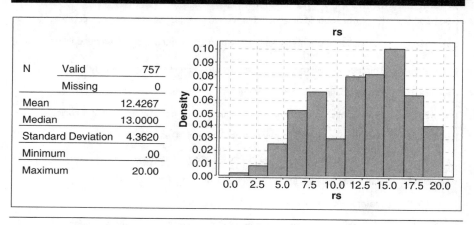

FIGURE 3.3 ● Descriptives and Histogram for Political Viewpoint Raw Scores

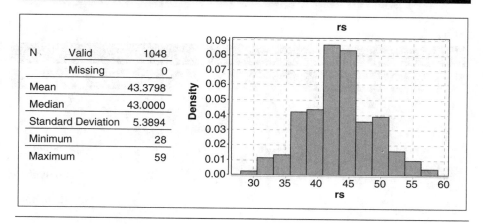

In jMetrik, I recommend using the advanced item scoring utility to score and reverse score the items for the political viewpoint test. Then, the test scoring utility can again be used to calculate raw scores. The raw score mean is 43.4 where the possible range is 18–72. This mean is near the center point of 45. If political viewpoint is theorized to be a normally distributed construct in a population of interest, then this distribution is a good approximation.

3.3 HANDLING MISSING DATA

Missing data, from respondents who do not answer every item, have been the focus of much statistical research. Little and Rubin (1987) identified three types of missing data. Data that are *missing completely at random* refer to the idea that the missing data are unrelated to the completed data, that is, respondents randomly omit the answers to items. If this is the case, then raw scores using the available data are unbiased estimates of the raw score from a completed dataset. When data are *missing at random*, the missing values are dependent on other variables in the dataset, for example, demographic variables, time limits. A third type of missing data is *nonignorable missing values*. These occur when there is a specific reason for the missing responses, such as deliberately skipping the most difficult items or those inquiring about sensitive topics.

There are different ways missing data can be handled by statistical and psychometric software. Two options are widely available. *Listwise deletion* means that the analysis is carried out only for respondents with complete datasets, that is, they have answered every item. If there is a lot of missing data, listwise deletion can reduce the sample size to an unacceptably small number. For *pairwise deletion*, respondents with missing data are excluded only if the missing values include the variables on which the analysis is run. For example, a correlation matrix could be run with different numbers of respondents contributing to the calculation of each correlation. By contrast, pairwise deletion could result in different sample sizes for each item. These sample sizes will likely be larger than the listwise sample size, but if there is a substantial amount of missing data, it will be difficult to compare item statistics because they will be based on different samples of respondents.

In general, both methods are effective for data that are missing completely at random but not for missing at random or nonignorable values. In the latter two situations, which are considered to be much more likely to happen with responses to test items, these methods can produce biased estimates of raw scores from complete datasets. To overcome this problem, a number of methods have been developed to substitute a value, called imputing a value, for the missing response. These range from simple, such as substituting the mean item response, to highly sophisticated, called single or multiple imputation methods. A discussion of these methods is beyond the scope of this book, but the interested reader is referred to several key sources (Dillman, Eltinge, Groves, & Little, 2002; Enders, 2001, 2003; Roth, 1994). Psychometric software typically does not offer these methods within the application. The imputations must occur prior to importing the dataset into the application.

How missing data are handled can also vary by the application. For example, in SPSS Reliability, if missing value codes are used for each item, then the application will run an analysis only on complete data cases, or *listwise deletion*. In jMetrik, missing data are handled differently for different analyses. By default, a missing value is coded as zero. For the TIMSS data, missing data will be considered as not correct. This will make jMetrik and the psych package agree because there will be in effect no missing data with all responses either missing or incorrect coded as zero. The psych package, like jMetrik, handles missing data differently for each analysis, but missing responses are not coded 0 by default.

For the original political viewpoint data, missing item responses were indicated by blank cells. As mentioned above, for jMetrik, the default option for missing data is an item score of 0. This means that a raw score could include some zeros. This would be misleading. For example, a respondent answering in a conservative fashion on a small number of items could appear to be liberal. For this book, the data supplied for your use contain only complete cases, that is, listwise deletion was carried out. I will note that over ninety percent of the original cases contained responses to all items.

Finally, missing data might be mitigated to some degree by the instruction given to respondents. For multiple-choice items, respondents can be encouraged to guess if they can eliminate one or more of the response choices. For Likert items, a neutral response choice can be available. This issue is discussed in greater detail in Chapter 7.

3.4 RAW SCORES VERSUS SCALE SCORES

In many large-scale testing programs, raw scores are not by themselves reported to respondents. When they are reported, they are usually accompanied by scale score, a transformation of the raw score into something that has additional meaning. This is because raw scores have several serious disadvantages. First, they are really ordinal data, not interval. Consider the following test measuring geographic knowledge:

1. *What is the name of this planet?*

2. *What is the name of the continent on which the United States is located?*

3. *What is the tallest mountain in the world?*

4. *What country has the largest population?*

5. *What is the depth of the Atlantic Ocean 100 miles east of Boston?*

Possible raw scores range from 0 to 5, but no one could argue that these scores are equal interval. In terms of the geographic knowledge construct, there is a huge difference between a raw score of 4 and a raw score of 5. If mapped out onto a continuum of geographic knowledge, the five items would likely be placed approximately as shown in Figure 3.4. The first four items are extremely easy; the last one is quite difficult (unless you are a New England fisherperson). An equal interval score scale would give us values that are reflected in the figure.

A second disadvantage of raw scores is that they have little inherent meaning. A raw score of 45 on the political viewpoint items indicates a viewpoint more conservative than a raw score of 35, but how *big* of a difference is that? Plus, what can you say about an individual respondent's political viewpoint? A score of 45 lies in the middle of the raw score scale, but you cannot really say that this represents a middle-of-the-road viewpoint. If all of items had been worded to reflect extreme conservative views (e.g., "I believe in the death penalty for shoplifting."), then a score in the middle of the range would actually indicate a relatively conservative viewpoint. Likewise, a raw

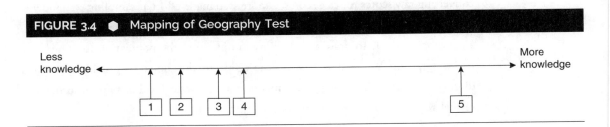

FIGURE 3.4 ● Mapping of Geography Test

Less knowledge ← ——————————————————————————— → More knowledge

1 2 3 4   5

score of 15 out of 20 mathematics items would suggest a high level of math skill if all the items were calculus problems or a low level if all the items were arithmetic operations with integers.

Finally, multiple versions, or forms, of tests are often created. For example, the forms could be intended to be as similar as possible for security purposes, as pretest and posttest forms in an experimental study in order to avoid a practice effect, or long and short versions to serve different purposes. Despite the best efforts of test developers and item writers, it is extremely difficult to produce forms that are exactly equal in difficulty. As a result, it would be misleading to compare raw scores on different forms. To be fair, there is a statistical adjustment, called test equating, which is designed to overcome form differences. This procedure will be discussed briefly later in this chapter.

As a result of these problems, raw scores are typically converted to *scale scores* to aid in the interpretation of score meaning for respondents and test users. To this end, there are two frames of reference for score interpretation: *norm-referenced* and *criterion-referenced* score interpretations. These were briefly mentioned in Chapter 1. Norm-referenced scale scores indicate how a respondent compares to others in a specific population. These types of scale scores can be used to select the best (or worst) cases or rank order respondents or groups of respondents. By contrast, criterion-referenced scale scores compare a respondent's score to a performance standard, such as pass/fail, basic/proficient/advanced, licensed or certified, whether a psychological intervention is needed. Some testing programs provide both types of score interpretations, but one of these two types is usually the primary purpose of the test.

Implicit in the conversion of raw scores to scale scores is that item response data have been collected in a systematic way from a population of interest. In Chapter 8, *pilot testing* is discussed as a way to evaluate item quality in the development of a test. For converting raw scores to scale scores, a more systematic effort at sampling respondents is needed. Many testing organizations refer to this effort as a *field test*. In a field test, an attempt is made to draw a probability sample from the population for which the test is targeted. While it is beyond the scope of this book to provide a detailed discussion of sampling plans, I will mention a few strategies. For more information, several references are listed at the end of this chapter.

A probability sample is one in which the probability of a respondent being selected is known in advance. This property makes it possible for scale scores to provide norm-referenced and criterion-referenced score interpretations. Several types of probability samples include:

- *Simple random sample:* Every member of the target population has an equal probability of being selected. Each selection is independently made.

- *Systematic sample:* Every kth member is selected. This will produce a sample nearly as efficient as a simple random sample.

- *Stratified sample:* The target population is classified into subgroups or strata based on one or more variables, such as geographic region or socioeconomic status. Then, a simple random sample is taken within each stratum so that the final sample is exactly representative of the target population on the variables being stratified.

- *Cluster sample:* Instead of sampling individuals, a simple random sample is taken of clusters, or groups, of individuals, such as institutions, schools, or census tracts.

- *Multistage sampling:* Sampling is done in stages. This is usually needed for nationally representative samples or samples from very large target populations. For example, the first stage could be a stratified sample of schools or school districts in primary sampling units. In stage 2, a simple random sample is taken within each unit selected in the first stage. Such a strategy has been used for survey programs such as NAEP and TIMSS.

The data from samples selected in these ways form the basis for developing scale scores.

3.5 SCALING FOR NORM-REFERENCED SCORE INTERPRETATIONS

3.5.1 Percentiles and Percentile Ranks

It's common for many testing programs to report percentiles, with a statement such as "A score of 30 is at the 55th percentile". This means that 55 percent of the population (calculated from the field test data described above) scored a 30 or less. An alternative way to say the same thing is "A score of 30 has a percentile rank of 55." Percentiles are easily understood by respondents. They let them know where they stand in relation to a specific population. For the political viewpoint test, a raw score of 45, which sits in the middle of the raw score range, actually has a percentile rank of 66, indicating that 66 percent of the target population, incoming college freshmen, are just as or more liberal than the respondent who scores 45 (higher scores mean more conservative).

The concept is straightforward, but to actually calculate percentile ranks involves a technicality. For example, part of the TIMSS Book1 raw score distribution is shown in Table 3.3, calculated by jMetrik. It would be tempting to think that a raw score of 15 has a percentile rank of 70.54, but it's a score of 15.5 that has a percentile rank of 70.54. This is because a raw score of 15 is considered to span an interval between 14.5 and 15.5, which are referred to as the lower and upper real limits, respectively. A raw score of 14.5 has a percentile rank of 16.62, and 15.5 has a percentile rank of 70.54. The percentile rank of a score of 15 is halfway between 62.6 and 70.5, or 66.58, as illustrated in Figure 3.5 and calculated as follows:

$$\text{PR}_x = \text{PR}_{ll} + \frac{\text{PR}_{ul} - \text{PR}_{ll}}{2} = 62.6156 + \frac{70.5416 - 62.6156}{2} = 66.5786 \quad (3.1)$$

where PR_{ul} and PR_{ll} are the upper and lower real limits. Note that it is impossible to receive a percentile rank of either 0 or 100. Perfect scores are usually reported as a percentile rank of 99, and scores of 0 are reported as a percentile rank of 1. Percentile ranks calculated in this fashion are called *midpoint percentile ranks*.

TABLE 3.3 ● Section of Raw Score Distribution for TIMSS Book1				
	Frequency	**Percent**	**Valid Pct.**	**Cum. Pct.**
14.00	57	7.5297	7.5297	62.6156
15.00	60	7.9260	7.9260	70.5416
16.00	79	10.4359	10.4359	80.9775

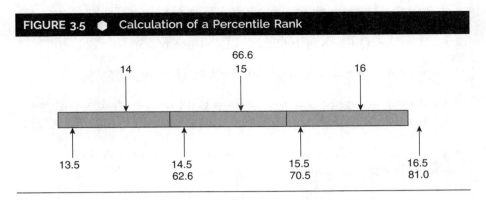

FIGURE 3.5 ● Calculation of a Percentile Rank

3.5.2 Linear Transformations of Raw Scores

Another way to obtain a norm-referenced score interpretation is to linearly transform raw scores into z-scores, which will have a mean of 0 and a standard deviation of 1. As mentioned in Chapter 1, a z-score for a raw score X is calculated as follows:

$$z_X = \frac{X - \bar{X}}{s_X} \tag{3.2}$$

From Table 3.1 above, this sample of TIMSS Book1 raw scores has a mean of 12.43 and a standard deviation of 4.37. A raw score of 14 converts to a z-score of $(14-12.43)/4.37=0.36$. Z-scores indicate how many standard deviations away from the mean a raw score is, that is, how far from average a respondent is. So, a raw score of 14 is 0.36 standard deviations above the mean.

The main disadvantage of reporting z-scores to respondents is that most people do not like receiving negative numbers for their score, which everyone below the mean will get. As a result, a number of score scales have been developed as linear transformations of z-scores:

$$SS_z = z \times S_{ss} + \bar{SS} \tag{3.3}$$

where $\bar{SS}$ and S_{ss} are the mean and standard deviation, respectively, of the new scale score. Some popular score scales include the following:

- College Board score (mean of 500, standard deviation of 100)

- T scores (mean of 50, standard deviation of 10)

- Weschler IQ (mean of 100, standard deviation of 15)

- Stanford–Binet IQ (mean of 100, standard deviation of 16)

- Stanines (mean of 5, standard deviation of 2): stanines range mostly from 1 to 9

- Normal Curve Equivalents (NCE) (mean of 50, standard deviation of 21.06): NCEs range mostly from 1 to 99.

Table 3.4 shows the raw scores of 14–16 transformed to z-scores and then to scale scores. All of these transformations are intended to tell the respondent how he or she compares to the population mean.

3.5.3 Nonlinear Transformations of Raw Scores

One disadvantage of the above linear transformations is that, if you created a histogram of the frequency distribution of scale scores, these scale scores would have the same shape as the raw scores. For TIMSS Book1, this means a negatively skewed distribution. However, through nonlinear transformations of z-scores, the resulting scale scores can assume any desirable shape. The most common target shape is the normal distribution. L. L. Thurstone (1925) suggested a way to transform raw scores into scale scores that follow a normal distribution:

1. Find the midpoint percentile rank corresponding to each raw score.

2. Find the z-score in a standard normal distribution that corresponds to each midpoint percentile rank, as shown in Figure 3.6. For example, a percentile

TABLE 3.4 ● Linear Transformations into Scale Scores for TIMSS Book1							
Raw score	**z**	**College Board**	**T**	**W IQ**	**S-B IQ**	**Stanine**	**NCE**
14	0.360	536	53.6	105	106	6	58
15	0.590	559	55.9	109	109	6	62
16	0.819	582	58.2	112	113	7	67

FIGURE 3.6 ● Determination of Normalized z-Score

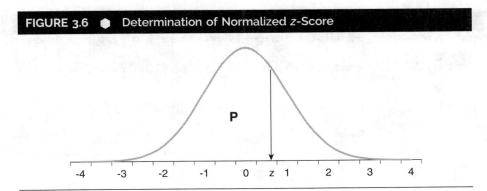

rank of 50 corresponds to a *z*-score of 0. A percentile rank of 84 corresponds to a *z*-score of 1.0. These *z*-scores, referred to as normalized *z*-scores, now have a normal distribution no matter the distribution of raw scores.

3. Apply a linear transformation of these *z*-scores, as above, to transform them into a desired score scale.

Table 3.5 shows the normalized *z*-scores and scale scores for the same raw scores on TIMSS Book1. In some cases, the scale scores are quite different from the above scale scores created through linear transformation. These scale scores have two advantages. First, many hypothesis tests, such as *t*-tests and ANOVA, assume that dependent variables are normally distributed. This nonlinear transformation ensures that this is the case. Second, as mentioned earlier, many constructs are theoretically assumed to be normally distributed in a population. Normalized *z*-scores are intended to be equal-interval in nature and a closer approximation to their actual spacing on the construct than raw scores. Thus, normalized z-scores would result in the spacing of scores as suggested in Figure 3.4 above for the geography test.

jMetrik can calculate raw scores, percentile ranks, and normalized *z*-scores. Select Analyze/Test Scaling. Select the items to be scaled. Select the type of score: sum score or average score (raw score), percentile rank, or normalized score.

TABLE 3.5 ● Normalized Scores for TIMSS Book1								
Raw score	midpt PR	Norm-z	College Board	T	W IQ	S-B IQ	Stanine	NCE
14	58.9	0.224	522	52.2	103	104	5	55
15	66.6	0.428	543	54.3	106	107	6	59
16	75.8	0.699	570	57.0	110	111	6	65

3.6 SCALING FOR CRITERION-REFERENCED SCORE INTERPRETATIONS

A major shortcoming of norm-referenced score interpretations is that respondents can be substantially above average but still not considered to be competent on the construct being measured. This is why educational achievement has transitioned from norm-referenced scores such as percentiles to criterion-referenced scores that indicate what a student knows and can do. As a result, a respondent discovers how she or he compares to predetermined performance levels. From raw or scale scores, cut scores are determined that divide the score scale into performance levels. For example, NAEP in some subject areas reports scale scores on a 0–500 scale. This scale is divided into performance levels, called achievement levels by NAEP, as follows for 12th grade science (https://nces.ed.gov/nationsreportcard/science/achieve.aspx):

- 0–141: below basic

- 142–178: basic

- 179–221: proficient

- 222–500: advanced

NAEP describes what each performance level means. For example, proficient generally means "solid academic performance and competency over challenging subject matter (NCES, https://nces.ed.gov/nationsreportcard/NDEHelp/WebHelp/achievement_levels.htm)." For 12th grade science (and for all other grades and subject areas), there is a detailed description of the knowledge, skills, and processes mastered by students at that performance level. How the cut scores are determined is through a method called *standard setting*. A variety of standard setting methods are discussed in Chapter 12.

3.7 EQUATING/LINKING ALTERNATE TEST FORMS

Earlier, I mentioned the problem of comparing raw scores on different forms of a test. It is nearly impossible for professional item writers to construct alternate forms that are equivalent in all respects. On lengthy multiple-choice forms of educational achievement tests, it is common to find up to three- or four-point differences in mean raw scores between forms intended to be equally difficult. One way to address this problem is through a procedure called *test equating*. Kolen and Brennan (2004) define equating as follows:

> *Equating is a statistical process that is used to adjust scores on test forms so that scores on the forms can be used interchangeably. Equating adjusts for differences in difficulty among forms that are built to be similar in difficulty and content. (p. 2)*

The outcome of equating one form to another is that equivalent raw scores for one form are calculated for each possible raw score on the other form.

Equating makes sense only if the forms measure the same construct and are built from the same set of test specifications. Situations where equating is required include:

- Alternate forms are needed for security purposes.

- Different forms are needed for pretests and posttests in a research study in order to avoid practice effects.

- Short and long forms of a test are used for different purposes, e.g., screening versus diagnosis.

- Groups to be compared are administered different forms.

- Forms are deliberately different in difficulty, such as grade levels for educational achievement.

It should be noted here that the latter two situations are better described as *linking* rather than equating because the forms are systematically different, but the goal is the same—to make scores on different forms interchangeable. Furthermore, there is an extensive literature on linking and equating. Some of the primary references are provided at the end of this chapter. My purpose here is to introduce the concept of equating and provide several examples. For operational applications of equating and linking, the reader is advised to use one or more of the many equating applications. These include those offered by the University of Iowa and several R packages (see NCME's software database: https://www.ncme.org/resources/database).

In addition to the requirement that the forms measure the same construct, there are three additional requirements to be met for an equating to occur:

1. *Equity:* "It is a matter of indifference to a respondent which form she or he takes (Lord, 1980, p. 195)." This means that an individual would be expected to receive the same raw score on each form, after equating, with the same degree of precision.

2. *Invariance:* The equating function should be the same for any sample from the target population. For example, the equating relationship should be the same for all subgroups, such as those based on gender, race/ethnicity, geographic region, SES, etc.

3. *Symmetry:* If the two forms to be equated are labeled X and Y, then equating Form Y to Form X should be the same as equating Form X to Form Y. (Note that this rules out regression as a possible equating method.)

3.7.1 Data Collection Designs for Equating

One way in which equating methods differ is how the data to perform the equating are collected. Data for these analyses should come from the field test or from a special data collection. In either case, it is important that the equating results apply to a clearly defined population. That said, there are three data collection designs that can permit equating to take place. They are:

- *Single group design:* Individuals have responded to both forms in one administration.

- *Random, or equivalent, groups design:* One group of individuals responds to one form, while a second group responds to the second form. Through careful sampling, the two groups are considered equal on the construct being measured. This is assured by randomly or systematically assigning forms to individuals. One popular way to do this in a group test administration is called *spiraling*, where forms are assigned in systematic order, e.g., form1, form2, form1, form2, etc.

- *Common-item nonequivalent groups design:* There are two groups of individuals. Each group is assigned one of the forms, but the groups' equivalence cannot be assured. For example, a group of 8th graders in one year is assigned one form, and the following year's 8th grade is assigned the other form. To ensure that form differences are not due to group differences, a set of common items is given to both groups. The common items, sometimes referred to as an anchor test, can either be part of both forms or a separate set of items.

3.7.2 Three Classical Methods for Equating

Classical methods for equating attempt to find, for each possible raw score on one form, its equivalent raw score on the other form. Three common classical methods are mean, linear, and equipercentile equating. For a practical example, suppose that we wish to divide the TIMSS Book1 into two half-length forms, divided into even- and odd-numbered items. The odd-numbered items will be called Form X, and the even-numbered items will be called Form Y. The task is to equate Form Y (even items) to Form X (odd items), that is, for every possible raw score on Form Y, in this case 0–10, find its equivalent raw score on Form X. It is important to note that this is the single group design. The methodology would be the same for the random groups design but not the common-item nonequivalent groups design. Descriptive statistics on both forms are shown in Table 3.6.

Mean equating. The simplest equating method is mean equating, in which the difference in raw score means is calculated. That difference is then added to each raw score on Form Y:

TABLE 3.6 ⬤ Descriptive Statistics for Raw Scores on TIMSS Half-Length Book 1		
	Form Y (even)	**Form X (odd)**
Mean	6.2413	6.1836
Median	6.000	6.000
Standard deviation	2.3052	2.4714
Minimum	0	0
Maximum	10	10

$$Y_X = Y + \left[\bar{X} - \bar{Y} \right] = Y + [6.1836 - 6.2413] = Y - 0.059 \qquad (3.4)$$

In other words, Form X is slightly more difficult than Form Y. Therefore, 0.059 is subtracted from every possible Form Y raw score to make it equivalent for Form X. For example, a raw score of 8 on Form Y (even-numbered items) is equivalent to a raw score of 7.941 on Form X (odd-numbered items). It is important to note that one consequence of mean equating is that the mean of Form Y after equating is equivalent to the mean of Form X.

Linear equating. The basic idea behind linear equating is that the raw scores corresponding to the same z-score are equivalent:

$$\frac{X - \bar{X}}{s_X} = \frac{Y - \bar{Y}}{s_Y} \qquad (3.5)$$

For example, a Form Y score that is one standard deviation above the mean is equivalent to the Form X raw score that is also one standard deviation above the mean. To equate Form Y to Form X, raw scores on Form Y are linearly transformed as follows:

$$Y_X = AY + B \qquad (3.6)$$

where $A = s_X/s_Y$ and $B = \bar{X} - A\bar{Y}$.

To continue the above example, $A = 2.4714/2.3052 = 1.072$. Then, $B = 6.1836 - (1.072*6.2431) = -0.510$. Then, the equating function, and for a Y score of 8, is as follows:

$$Y_X = AY + B = 1.072*Y - 0.510 = 1.072*8 - 0.510 = 8.067$$

Like mean equating, linear equating results in the two means being equal. Furthermore, Form X and its Form Y equivalents will have the same mean and standard deviation. However, if the shapes of the two raw score distributions differ, they will still differ after equating. For the two distributions to also have the same shape, equipercentile equating is needed.

Equipercentile equating. For this method, raw scores on the two forms that have the same percentile rank are deemed equivalent (this means the midpoint percentile rank, as described above). To find, for example, the Form X equivalent of a raw score of 8, first find its percentile rank. Then, find the Form X raw score with the same percentile rank. A technical issue is that Form X integer score with that exact percentile is usually not found. The midpoint percentile rank on Form Y of a score of 8 is 72.919. For Form X, a score of 7 has a percentile rank of 59.115, and a score of 8 has a percentile rank of 73.250. So, the equivalent score must lie somewhere between 8 and 9. To obtain the equivalent, linear interpolation is used:

$$Y_X = 8 + \frac{72.919 - 59.115}{73.250 - 59.115} = 7.973$$

Table 3.7 shows the Form Y raw score equivalents to Form X. The three methods produced similar equating results.

The rationale for the three methods described above are easy enough to understand, but as you can see, the technical details can be somewhat complex. Furthermore, applying these methods to the common-item nonequivalent groups design adds an additional level of complexity. As a result, to implement an equating, I strongly recommend using one of the software applications for the particular data collection design at hand. Finally, these equating methods are intended to be applied to raw scores, not scale scores. Once the equating of raw scores has been completed, then the scale scores can be calculated on the raw score equivalents, as described above.

TABLE 3.7 ● Form *X* Equivalents for Form *Y* Raw Scores			
Form *Y* RS	Mean	Linear	Equipercentile
0	−0.059	−0.510	0.000
1	0.941	0.562	0.692
2	1.941	1.635	1.557
3	2.941	2.707	2.573
4	3.941	3.779	3.662
5	4.941	4.851	4.888
6	5.941	5.923	6.032
7	6.941	6.995	6.930
8	7.941	8.067	7.973
9	8.941	9.139	9.234
10	9.941	10.211	9.981

3.8 CHAPTER SUMMARY

This chapter introduced a number of methods for scoring and scaling tests. First, a distinction was drawn between scoring items dichotomously or polytomously. Raw scores on a test, or summed or observed scores, are the simple sum (or average) of the item scores. There are several disadvantages to reporting raw scores to respondents or using them for research or policy studies. They are ordinal data and don't have any inherent meaning. For this reason, raw scores are transformed into scale scores that have a norm-referenced or criterion-referenced interpretation. Finally, this chapter introduced test equating as a statistical method for adjusting raw scores on alternate forms of tests so that they can be directly compared.

3.9 EXERCISES AND ACTIVITIES

1. Describe a multistage sampling plan for obtaining a nationally representative sample of high school science teachers.

2. Suppose you are attending a professional meeting when a colleague proposes, "I know how we can raise raw scores on our test. Add more items!" How do you respond to this proposal?

3. For the political viewpoint items,

   a. Use jMetrik to calculate raw scores, percentile ranks, and normalized z-scores.

   b. By hand, calculate the percentile ranks for a raw scores of 40 and 50. Use Analyze/Frequencies to obtain the cumulative percent for raw scores.

   c. By hand, calculate the normalized z-score for raw scores of 40 and 50.

   d. Compare histograms of raw scores and normalized z-scores. Histograms can be created with Graph/Histogram.

4. Divide the political viewpoint items into two halves, View9901 to View9909 as Form X and View9910 to View9918 as Form Y. Use mean, linear, and equipercentile equating to determine the Form X equivalent of a raw score of 20 on Form Y. (Use jMetrik Analyze/Frequencies to obtain percentile ranks for the two half-length forms and Analyze/Descriptives for means and standard deviations.)

FURTHER READING

Sampling Plans for Field Testing

Trochim, W. M. K. (2006). *Research methods knowledge base. Retrieved from:* http://www.socialresearchmethods.net/kb/sampling.php.

Scaling and Scoring

Kolen, M. J. (2006). Scaling and norming. In R. L. Brennan (Ed.), *Educational measurement* (4th ed., pp. 155–186). Westport, CT: Praeger.

Equating and Linking

Dorans, N. J., Pommerich, M., & Holland, P. W. (Eds.) (2007)., *Linking and aligning scores and scales.* New York, NY: Springer.

Gonzalez, J., & Wiberg, M. (2017). *Applying test equating methods using R*. Cham, Switzerland: Springer International.

Holland, P. W., & Dorans, N. J. (2006). Linking and equating. In R. L. Brennan (Ed.), *Educational measurement* (4th ed., pp. 187–220). Westport, CT: Praeger.

Kolen, M. J., & Brennan, R. L. (2004). *Test equating, scaling, and linking: Methods and practices* (2nd ed.). New York, NY: Springer-Verlag.

REFERENCES

Dillman, D. A., Eltinge, J. L., Groves, R. M., & Little, R. J. A. (2002). Survey nonresponse in design, data collection, and analysis. In R. M. Groves, D. A. Dillman, J. L. Eltinge, & R. J. A. Little (Eds.), *Survey nonresponse* (pp. 3–26). New York, NY: Wiley.

Enders, C. K. (2001). A primer on maximum likelihood algorithms for use with missing data. *Structural Equation Modeling: A Multidisciplinary Journal, 8,* 128–141.

Enders, C. K. (2003). Using the EM algorithm to estimate coefficient alpha for scales with item level missing data. *Psychological Methods, 8,* 322–337.

Little, R., & Rubin, D. B. (1987). *Statistical analysis with missing data*. New York, NY: Wiley.

Lord, F. M. (1980). *Applications of item response theory to practical testing problems*. Hillsdale, NJ: Erlbaum.

Roth, R. L. (1994). Missing data: A conceptual review for applied psychologists. *Personnel Psychology, 47,* 537–560.

Thurstone, L. L. (1925). A method of scaling psychological and educational tests. *Journal of Educational Psychology, 16,* 433–451.

4

CLASSICAL TEST THEORY

Unlike measurement in the physical sciences, measuring constructs requires serious attention to measurement error. Test theories are theories about how to measure constructs and estimate the degree of measurement error. Anyone who develops a test will have to decide which measurement theory will be used to develop the scores and evaluate their precision. This chapter presents Classical Test Theory (CTT), in practice for the past one hundred years or so but still widely used. Chapter 9 introduces Rasch Measurement Theory, a modern approach widely used in new test development projects.

4.1 THE CONCEPT OF MEASUREMENT ERROR

One recent morning, I stood on my bathroom scale. It measured my weight at 203.0 pounds, a disappointing number for me. I resolved to eat better and get more exercise, which I did for the next week. A week later, at the same morning hour, I once again weighed myself—203.0 pounds. No change, all that hard work for nothing! Then, I realized something. I could have actually lost (or gained) nearly half a pound. The digital readout on my scale gives me my weight in half-pound increments. The first time I weighted myself, my true weight could have been 203.24 pounds, and the scale would have read 203.0. A week later, I could have weighed 202.76, but the scale would have still given me 203.0. (Of course, my real weight could have just as easily increased from 202.76 to 203.24, but I won't go there.)

The culprit? *Measurement error.* My bathroom scale is *precise* only to the nearest half pound. Differences smaller than that cannot be detected by my scale. The scale at my doctor's office is precise to the nearest tenth of a pound. That would provide a more precise measurement of my weight change and be precise enough for my own needs. In fact, there are scales that can measure weight with sufficient precision for any purpose at hand so that we don't have to worry about measurement error. This is true for most measurements of directly observed variables in the physical world: height, weight, length, speed, reaction time, etc.

However, in educational and social science research and applications, we don't have this luxury. Measurement error is present and large enough that we need to estimate how much measurement error we have and decide what to do about it. Tests that we develop will always have some nontrivial amount of measurement error. In class, I often ask how many students took the SAT or GRE more than once, and of those students, how many received the exact same score each time. In 20 years of teaching, only one student raised their hand the second time. And yet, these tests claim to measure what is thought to be a relatively stable construct, one's likelihood of doing well in college. Differences in scores could be due to numerous sources of measurement errors: test anxiety, greater test preparation, practice effect of the first testing occasion, or simply a better night's sleep.

This brings us to an important distinction between two types of measurement error: *systematic* and *random*. Systematic measurement errors are biasing factors that consistently mismeasure something in a predictable way. For example, the clock on the dashboard of my car runs fast. If I set the correct time, a month later, the clock is ten minutes fast. In a measurement context, the National Assessment of Educational Progress (NAEP) noticed a sharp decline in reading scores in 1986, in what has become known as the 1986 Reading Anomaly. An investigation suggested that the decline was due in part to changes in the order of items and the contexts in which they appeared (Zwick, 1992).

On the other hand, random measurement errors are the chance effects that have nothing to do with the construct being measured. A professional swimmer or runner, for example, will record a range of times for the same event. In responding to a test, an individual may have different feelings, moods, attitudes, distractions, or may guess and mistakenly fill in the wrong answer choice. These are random errors. So, too, are simply good days and bad days. It is important to note here that test theories deal almost exclusively with random measurement error. Systematic errors are errors that should be investigated and accounted for (I reset my car's clock once a month), but random errors point to the *precision* of test scores, and that is what we want to estimate.

Notice that I have not actually defined the term measurement error. That is because there are different views of measurement error encapsulated in *test theories*. These are not the theories typically found in education and the social sciences, such as learning theory, theory of personality types, and so forth. Test theories are visions of what measurement is and how to estimate how much measurement error is present in a test. At present, there are three primary test theories: Classical Test Theory (CTT), Rasch Measurement Theory, and Item Response Theory (IRT). In addition, Generalizability Theory is an outgrowth of CTT and is often used to design performance-based tests. Generalizability is briefly described later in this chapter. These theories differ not only in how they estimate measurement error but also in their underlying assumptions and how they go about developing and validating tests. CTT has been around for over a hundred years and was the dominant test theory until the 1970s and 1980s, when Rasch Theory, IRT, and Generalizability Theory became practical to implement. Rasch Theory and IRT are very similar mathematically, and some psychometricians treat them as a single theory, but their philosophical orientations are quite different. Of the two, I recommend Rasch Theory for developing new tests. It is simpler to implement and, from a practical point of view, test scores from Rasch Theory and IRT tend to be highly correlated.

4.2 THE CONCEPT OF RELIABILITY

CTT revolves around the idea of test score *reliability*. To return again to the encounter with my bathroom scale, I admit that my first thought when I saw 203 pounds was: something must be wrong with this scale. That number can't be right. So, I stepped off, waited a minute, and then stepped back on. I got the same number. Then, I went down the hall to another bathroom that contained an older scale. Unfortunately, the same number, 203, showed up. The scales are what we call *reliable*. I wasn't happy to see reliability here, but with tests that you want to use for research, credentialing, or other purpose, reliability is essential.

Most of us think of something reliable as being dependable and trustworthy. The measurement of my weight is dependable and trustworthy, and so I can count on my bathroom scale to be reliable. *Merriam-Webster's Collegiate Dictionary* defines reliability as "the extent to which an experiment, test, or measuring procedure yields the same results on repeated trials" (11th Edition, 2014, p. 1051). In the context of measuring constructs, being reliable incorporates the idea of *consistency*, that is, when I measure something more than once, I get the same result each time, which in turn implies that I can depend on and trust the score. If, for example, my weight the second time was 210, 197 a third time, 201 a fourth time, and so forth, then there is little reliability and I would have little confidence in the measurement. That in turn would make me doubt the validity of my weight score. This is how several well-known measurement resources define reliability:

> *...desired consistency (or reproducibility) of test scores is called* reliability.
>
> (Crocker & Algina, 1986, p. 105)

...reliability is concerned solely with how the scores resulting from a measurement procedure would be expected to vary across replications of that procedure.

(Haertel, 2006, p. 65)

...the more general notion of consistency of the scores across instances of the testing procedure....

(AERA, APA, & NCME, 2014, p. 33)

4.3 THEORY OF TRUE AND ERROR SCORES

CTT is based on the idea of a *true score*, that for any person at a specific moment in time and occasion, there is a true score on the construct being measured. In class, before the advent of smartphones and computers tied to an atomic clock (and a digital clock on the wall), I used to ask my students what time was shown on their watches. I would write these on the whiteboard. These are fallible measurements of time, called *observed scores* of time. I would also check the government's atomic clock for the true time, or the true time score. The differences between the true time and students' observed times are the *measurement errors*. Typically, students' watch times ranged plus or minus five minutes around the true time. No wonder I often had trouble starting class on time!

To estimate how much measurement error we have with a test, we must first introduce a conceptual sleight of hand. With my bathroom scale, I could weigh myself repeatedly, an infinite number of times. My true weight could then be conceptualized as the average (or expected value) of my observed weights across repeated measurements. Of course, practically speaking, this would not be correct because as time passes, my true weight could change. Similarly, one's true score on a test measuring a construct could be considered as the expected value of an observed score on repeated administrations of the test. Here again, there is a practical problem, namely, a practice effect of responding over and over again. As a result, we idealize the situation by hypothesizing repeated administrations of a test, followed each time by erasing the respondent's memory of the occasion to make each administration independent of what came before, a kind of psychometric *Groundhog Day*.

If we symbolize an observed score as X, the true score as T, and the measurement error as E, we come to the core equation of CTT:

$$X = T + E \qquad (4.1)$$

And now, since we desire to put numbers to these scores, CTT from this point on becomes a statistical theory. The true score of person p is T_p. Person p's observed score on a specific instance i of measurement is X_{pi}. Person p's measurement error on this occasion is E_{pi}. A specific instance of measurement refers to a particular administration of a test. Then, the core equation becomes:

$$X_{pi} = T_p + E_{pi} \qquad (4.2)$$

Based on our hypothesized ideal of an infinite number of repeated and independent measurements of a construct, another way to define person p's true score, T_p, is as the average, or expected value, of all possible observed scores, or:

$$T_p = \mu_{X_{pi}} \qquad (4.3)$$

This means that an observed score X is an unbiased estimate of the true score T. In addition, since we are dealing with random measurement errors only, we expect positive and negative errors to cancel each other out and average to zero:

$$\mu_{E_{pi}} = 0 \qquad (4.4)$$

For a population of respondents, the following "principles" can be derived, assuming the above definitions of a true score and random measurement errors:

$$\mu_X = \mu_T. \qquad (4.5)$$

This principle means that in a population, the mean of observed scores estimates the mean of true scores, which is an indication that observed scores are unbiased.

$$\mu_E = 0. \qquad (4.6)$$

The second principle reiterates the lack of bias, or absence of systematic measurement errors. Errors look like random deviations from true scores.

$$\rho_{TE} = 0. \tag{4.7}$$

The third principle is that true scores and measurement errors are uncorrelated. If this correlation were positive, then higher true scores would be associated with larger measurement errors, and vice versa. The opposite would be true for a negative correlation. This state of affairs would in turn mean that the precision of observed scores would depend on the true score. In effect, this principle means that all true scores are measured with the same degree of precision.

$$\rho_{E_1 E_2} = 0. \tag{4.8}$$

This principle indicates that measurement errors are uncorrelated. If a population of respondents is measured twice, their measurement errors are uncorrelated. This indicates that measurement error on the first occasion does not influence the measurement error on the second occasion.

The above assumptions and principles form what psychometricians call a *random error model*. Everything that follows is based on this model. At this point, it is a good thought exercise to ask if this model is a reasonable approximation to real data—the responses of individuals to the items in a test. For example, I often ask students if they have experienced going into a class exam and scoring worse than they thought they should. A number of hands get raised here. I'll then ask who has experienced doing better than expected. Usually, some hands get raised but not as many. However, CTT says that both under- and overachieving are equally likely, challenging the experience of most students. The same students will often say that their true score on a high-stakes test such as the GRE is their highest score!

In trying to calculate how much random measurement error we have in a test, two types of statistics are important: *reliability coefficients* and absolute *estimates of error*. Reliability coefficients seek to calculate how much of the total amount of variation in observed scores is due to random measurement error. Absolute estimates indicate in score units how precise an observed score is. The primary absolute estimate is called the *Standard Error of Measurement* (SEM). We'll discuss reliability coefficients first.

4.4 RELIABILITY COEFFICIENTS

One of the first statistics for estimating reliability was the *reliability index* and was defined as the correlation between true and observed scores:

$$\rho_{TX} \tag{4.9}$$

This makes intuitive sense in that if everyone's observed score were actually their true score, this correlation would be 1.00. If this correlation were equal to 0.00, then there would be no relationship between true and observed scores. This would be akin to a respondent's score being a random number. Furthermore, by using the assumptions and principles introduced above, the following can be derived:

$$\rho_{TX} = \frac{\sigma_T}{\sigma_X} \tag{4.10}$$

As we shall see shortly, a better statistic is the reliability coefficient, defined as the squared correlation between true and observed scores. The reliability coefficient describes the proportion of observed score variation that is attributable to true scores. Again, the following result can be easily derived:

$$\rho_{TX}^2 = \frac{\sigma_T^2}{\sigma_X^2} \tag{4.11}$$

Both of these statistics would be simple enough to calculate if not for the inconvenient fact that no one knows respondents' true scores, only the observed scores. To get around this problem, additional assumptions are required. Dozens of reliability coefficients have been developed over time. These are chiefly differentiated by the nature of these additional assumptions.

4.4.1 Reliability Coefficients Based on Parallel Measures

The earliest set of assumptions, and ones still widely in use, involves the concept of *parallel* measures. The idea behind parallel measures is that they are interchangeable measurements, such as my two scales measuring weight. I could use either one and get the same result. Another example would be two tape measures to measure length. For educational and psychological tests, parallel measures essentially mean assuming that two observed scores are interchangeable. These two scores could come from alternate forms of the test, repeated measurements from the same test, or alternate parts from the same test. Formally, parallel measures require two assumptions:

1. Each respondent has the same true score on the two measures: $T_1 = T_2 = T$. In other words, a respondent expects the same score on each measure, but the actual observed scores could be different due to measurement error.

2. The variances of measurement errors on the two measures are equal. This means that the measures have the same degree of precision.

From these two assumptions, it follows that the two sets of observed scores will have the same mean and variance. Additionally, the two sets of observed scores will correlate equally well with any other variable.

Using the additional assumptions of parallel measures along with the original assumptions and principles and a bit of algebra, the following can be derived:

$$\rho_{X1,X2} = \frac{\sigma_T^2}{\sigma_X^2} = \rho_{XT}^2 \qquad (4.12)$$

In other words, the correlation between two parallel observed scores estimates the *squared* correlation between true and observed scores, which is the reliability coefficient. Taking the square root of this correlation estimates the reliability index, which is inconvenient. And this is why the reliability coefficient is a more useful statistic than the reliability index. The above derivation suggests two widely used ways for estimating reliability coefficients from test response data.

Test/retest Reliability Coefficient. Consider administering the same test twice to a group of respondents, then correlating the two sets of observed scores. This correlation is then a test/retest reliability coefficient. On the positive side, the assumption of parallel measures is clearly met. It's the same test! Test/retest is also close to the conceptual definition of reliability, that is, consistency across replications of the measure of the measurement procedure, as in Haertel's definition shown above. This coefficient taps into measurement errors related to the stability of observed scores over time and is sometimes referred to as a coefficient of stability.

However, an important practical question is how long to wait between the two administrations. Too soon, such as immediately after the first administration, creates the possibility of a practice effect. Too long raises the question of whether the respondents' true scores may have actually changed. There is no simple answer to how long of a break between the two administrations. If the construct being measured is considered to be relatively stable, such as some ability and personality constructs, then a longer interval is appropriate, such as several weeks or months. On the other hand, for constructs that are expected to change more quickly, such as those measuring maturational or knowledge constructs, the interval needs to be relatively short, a single day or a week. Additionally, there is one logistical problem with test/retest coefficients, which is the difficulty of measuring the same group of respondents twice. There will likely be some degree of attrition, and who does not return for the second administration may not be representative of the whole sample. The longer the interval, the greater the attrition. This is why test/retest coefficients, while highly valued by psychometricians, are calculated relatively infrequently.

Alternate Forms Reliability Coefficient. One way to avoid both the interval dilemma and attrition is to administer alternate versions, or forms, of the same test at the same time, carefully counterbalancing the order of the two forms. The correlation between the two sets of scores is the alternate forms reliability coefficient. This coefficient makes sense only if the two forms are constructed to be as similar as possible. That is, they are developed from the same set of test specifications (see Chapter 6). As a result, the alternate forms reliability coefficient estimates random measurement errors due to form equivalence and is often called a coefficient of equivalence.

There are also potential problems implementing the alternate forms coefficient. First and foremost, developing more than one form takes considerable resources. Second, the two forms may not be truly parallel despite them being constructed from the same specifications. Finally, there could be a logistical problem in asking respondents to provide data for two forms. If the forms are lengthy, respondent fatigue could present a source of systematic measurement error. As a result, like the test/retest coefficients, alternate forms coefficients are found relatively infrequently.

Reliability of a Composite Score. At this point, you may be wondering: can we estimate reliability by administering a single test to a single group of respondents? The answer is yes. To accomplish this, we need to think of an observed score on a test as a composite of observed scores on individual parts of the test. These parts could be sections of the test, or even individual items. Thought of this way, an observed total score, C, on a test is a composite of its parts:

$$C = X_1 + X_2 + X_3 + X_4 + \cdots + X_k \tag{4.13}$$

where k is the number of parts. The X's are the observed scores on each part. Then, by definition, the reliability of this composite score is:

$$\rho_{CC'} = \rho_{CT}^2 = \frac{\sigma_{T_C}^2}{\sigma_C^2} \tag{4.14}$$

If all of the parts are assumed to be parallel, the reliability of the composite can be derived by knowing the reliability of each part (they are assumed to be equally reliable) and the number of parts:

$$\rho_{CC'} = \frac{k\rho_{XX'}}{1 + (k-1)\rho_{XX'}} \tag{4.15}$$

This equation is called the Spearman–Brown Prophecy Formula (Brown, 1910; Spearman, 1910). This formula has an important implication: longer tests are more reliable. Suppose you have a test composed of 30 items with an estimated reliability of 0.80. If you were to double the length of this test, that is, adding an additional 30 items that are parallel to the original 30, then the double-length test would have a reliability of:

$$\rho_{CC'} = \frac{2(0.80)}{1 + (2-1)80} = 0.88$$

The Spearman–Brown formula also means that in order to compare the reliabilities of different tests, you need to account for the length of each one, that is, the number of parts. Consider, an alternative test with a reliability of 0.85 but composed of 60 items. Its reliability is higher than the first test only because of its greater length. In deciding which one to use for a research study, the crucial question is whether the increment in precision is worth the additional response time.

I think most people intuitively realize the importance of test length. I've often imagined what it would be like to play a tennis match against Serena Williams. Because her true tennis score is ridiculously higher than mine, I would welcome lots of measurement error and want the match to be exactly one point in length. Who knows? Maybe she'll double fault. As the match gets longer, our tennis true scores will be measured more precisely, and I will be certain to lose. Another implication of the Spearman–Brown formula is that it suggests another way to estimate reliability by administering a single test to a single sample of respondents.

Split-half Reliability Coefficient. Suppose you divide a test into two halves. For these two halves to be parallel, they should be as similar as possible in content and difficulty. A number of schemes have been proposed to divide a test into two parts. One could randomly divide the items, or match the items in terms of content and difficulty. Probably the most common method is to separate the odd-numbered and even-numbered items. One method that should *not* be used is to divide the first half of the test from the second half. Once this is done, then the correlation between scores on the two halves is calculated. However, this correlation is now the reliability coefficient for one of the halves, or a test that is half as long as the actual one. Therefore, the Spearman–Brown formula is applied where $k = 2$ to calculate the split-half reliability coefficient.

As an example, consider the responses of eight persons to five items, as shown in Table 4.1 (Please note that these data are totally made up numbers). Each item is scored on a one to five scale. The odd-numbered items are 1, 3, and 5, while 2 and 4 are the even-numbered items. It does not matter here if there are an equal number of items.

The correlation between the odd and even halves is 0.041, which would be the estimated reliability of a test consisting of two and a half items. Using the Spearman–Brown formula to double the test length, the split-half reliability coefficient is:

$$\rho_{CC'} = \frac{2(0.041)}{1 + (2 - 1)0.041} = 0.078$$

Since reliability can range from 0.0 to 1.0, this reliability is awful but not surprising, given that these are random data to begin with.

	Item Scores						Odd	Even
Person	1	2	3	4	5	Total	Odd Total	Even Total
1	5	3	4	4	3	19	12	7
2	5	3	5	1	2	16	12	4
3	4	2	4	3	3	16	11	5
4	4	4	2	4	4	18	10	8
5	5	1	1	3	2	12	8	4
6	4	3	4	3	4	18	12	6
7	4	1	4	3	4	16	12	4
8	5	2	4	3	3	17	12	5

TABLE 4.1 ● Example of Split-half Reliability Coefficient

The split-half method for estimating reliability is quite popular. Again, it's convenient to calculate this coefficient from a single administration of a test to a single sample. The primary challenge of this coefficient is being able to assume that the two halves are really parallel. Furthermore, since there are many ways the two halves can be formed, there are many possible split-half coefficients that can be calculated from the same data, and they could be quite different.

4.4.2 Reliability Coefficients Based on Other Models of Part-Test Similarity

At this point, it is reasonable to ask, can reliability be estimated without having to assume parallel measures or parts? The answer again is yes. There are other models of how the parts of a test are related that relax in some way the rigid assumptions of parallel measures. Three widely used models are tau-equivalent, essentially tau-equivalent, and congeneric measures. In all three cases, the correlation between true scores on the parts is assumed to be 1.0.

Tau-equivalent measures. The parallel measures model required two assumptions: equal true scores and equal error variances. If the second assumption is relaxed, we now have tau-equivalent measures:

1. Each respondent has the same true score on the two measures: $T_1 = T_2 = T$.

2. The variances of measurement errors on the two measures are not necessarily equal. This means that the measures do not have to have the same degree of precision. They can be unequally reliable.

The classic example of tau-equivalent measures is one where they differ only in length, but the observed scores are in a common metric, such as proportion correct. Observed scores may have different variances, but both measures are expected to have equal correlations with other variables.

Essentially tau-equivalent measures. The assumptions can be relaxed even further by not requiring true scores to be equal. In particular:

1. True scores on the two measures differ by a constant: $T_1 = T_2 + c_2$. In other words, there is a constant difference between true scores.

2. The variances of measurement errors on the two measures are not necessarily equal. This means that the measures could have different reliabilities.

An example of essentially tau-equivalent measures is two forms that differ in difficulty. This situation is especially likely in the case of parts within a test. The parts need not be equally precise, and observed scores could differ in variance, but correlations with other variables will be equal.

Congeneric measures. Congeneric measures represent the weakest form of part similarity:

1. True scores on the two measures are linearly related: $T_1 = b_2 T_2 + c_2$. That is, they don't need to be in the same units of measurement.

2. The variances of measurement errors on the two measures are not necessarily equal. This means that the measures do not have to have the same degree of precision and could have different reliabilities.

The two measures could differ in difficulty and length, such as short and long forms of a test. They could also be in different units of measurement, such as inches and centimeters.

Reliability coefficients have been developed for each of these models of part-test similarity. Additionally, they are nested, meaning that each model is less restrictive, and the more restrictive models are special cases of the more relaxed ones. Again, there are many reliability coefficients, but I will focus on the most popular one, coefficient alpha.

Coefficient alpha. The above reliability coefficients rely on the correlation of two observed scores, either an entire test or parts of a test. Cronbach's coefficient alpha (Cronbach, 1951) estimates reliability by using more than two scores or parts that are summed to obtain a composite score. Again, the total score on the test is the sum of the observed scores on the parts. Usually, alpha is calculated with the parts being the individual items. Additionally, alpha was derived by assuming that the parts are essentially tau-equivalent. If the assumptions of essential tau-equivalence do not hold, which is to say the parts are congeneric, then alpha will be a *lower bound* estimate of reliability. For this reason, alpha is often lower than other reliability coefficients. The formula for coefficient alpha is as follows:

$$\alpha = \rho_{CC'} = \frac{k}{k-1}\left[1 - \frac{\sum \sigma_{x_i}^2}{\sigma_C^2}\right] \tag{4.16}$$

As before, k is the number of parts, usually the number of items. The summation of variances in the numerator is the sum of the variances of each part or item. The variance in the denominator is the variance of total test scores. The calculation can be illustrated with the same data used to compute the split-half coefficient, as shown in Table 4.2.

$$\alpha = \rho_{CC'} = \frac{5}{5-1}\left[1 - \frac{\sum 0.29 + 1.13 + 1.71 + 0.86 + 0.70}{4.57}\right] = -0.029$$

This, like the split-half coefficient, shows atrocious reliability, actually a bit worse than assigning scores randomly.

If the parts, or items, are scored dichotomously, that is 0 or 1, then each item's variance is equal to the proportion correct (p) times the proportion incorrect (q). In

	Item Scores					
Person	**1**	**2**	**3**	**4**	**5**	**Total**
1	5	3	4	4	3	19
2	5	3	5	1	2	16
3	4	2	4	3	3	16
4	4	4	2	4	4	18
5	5	1	1	3	2	12
6	4	3	4	3	4	18
7	4	1	4	3	4	16
8	5	2	4	3	3	17
Mean	4.50	2.38	3.50	3.00	3.13	16.50
Variance	0.29	1.13	1.71	0.86	0.70	4.57
SD	0.53	1.06	1.31	0.93	0.83	2.14

TABLE 4.2 ⬣ Calculation of Coefficient Alpha

this case, coefficient alpha simplifies to a reliability coefficient, KR_{20}, proposed by Kuder and Richardson (1937)[1]:

$$KR_{20} = \rho_{CC'} = \frac{k}{k-1}\left[1 - \frac{\sum p_i q_i}{\sigma_C^2}\right] \quad (4.17)$$

Neither of these formulas looks remotely like the correlation-based coefficients above. It is instructive, when faced with formulas that are not obviously logical, to ask what makes the results larger or smaller. For alpha, the larger the total test score variance, σ_C^2, the larger the alpha will be. This implies that you will tend to obtain higher alphas from heterogenous samples of respondents than from more homogenous samples. Second, although it is not obvious from the formula, large positive correlations between the parts will produce higher alphas. Large interpart or interitem correlations suggest that the parts are all measuring the same construct. For this reason, coefficient alpha is often referred to as an *internal consistency* reliability

---

[1]There is also a KR_{21}, in which all items are assumed to have the same difficulty, i.e., equal p and q values.

coefficient. Coefficient alpha is by far the most frequently used reliability coefficient for both logistical and theoretical reasons. It is relatively easy to collect data from a single administration to a single sample. Alpha also does not require assuming that the parts are parallel, merely essentially tau-equivalent, which is considered to be more realistic of the parts of a test, especially individual items.

Despite its popularity, alpha has been criticized in several ways as an estimate of composite score reliability. First, it may not be reasonable in some situations to assume that parts are essentially tau-equivalent, for example, with early drafts of a test. Second, we still assume that the four derived principles apply here, but if random measurement errors are correlated, then alpha will be less than true composite reliability.

4.4.3 Other Reliability Coefficients

As mentioned above, there are many reliability coefficients. The basic difference between them lies the assumptions required for their derivation. I will briefly mention here several of them that are provided with jMetrik and the R psych package, the applications used to exemplify the analyses in this book:

Standardized Alpha (Osburn, 2000). Standardized alpha is coefficient alpha calculated by converting item or part scores to *z*-scores. This means that all items or parts will have the same variance, and it means that standardized alpha is the reliability of a test in which items or parts are scored this way.

Guttman's Lambdas (λ_1–λ_6) (Guttman, 1945). These six coefficients were derived as lower bounds for test reliability. Of these, λ_2 is the most widely used and will always be equal to or greater than coefficient alpha. λ_3 is equivalent to coefficient alpha.

Gilmer–Feldt (1983) assumes congeneric parts and parts of unequal length.

Feldt–Brennan (1989) assumes *classical* congeneric parts and parts of unequal length. For classical congeneric parts, the true score variances of parts are proportional to the lengths of the parts.

Raju's Beta (1977) assumes essential tau-equivalence and parts of unequal length.

4.4.4 What Is Good Reliability?

There is no single cutoff value that divides a reliable test from one that isn't. Most psychometricians would agree that, in general, a reliability coefficient of 0.90 or higher indicates strong reliability and one less than 0.50 means weak reliability. How to characterize reliability coefficient values in between is a matter of some disagreement. Partly, this is due to the abovementioned impact test length has on reliability. In the above example, where the split-half reliability was 0.078, a reliability of 0.90 could be actually reached if the test were lengthened to 1,050 items! Additionally, some types of constructs, such as multiple-choice tests measuring cognitive constructs, tend to produce higher reliabilities than noncognitive constructs. For example, it is common to find reliabilities greater than 0.90 for educational achievement tests. At the same time, reliabilities of 0.70–0.90 are common in tests measuring psychological constructs. My best advice would be to compare reliability coefficients to those from tests of similar lengths and constructs.

4.4.5 Reliability Coefficients for Real Data

Reliability coefficients for the TIMSS and political viewpoint tests were calculated using two applications: jMetrik and the R psych package. The R code for the psych package is provided in Appendix B. The calculation of reliability coefficients is tied to the item analysis programs of each application. The specifics of implementing each application are discussed in Chapter 8.

Table 4.3 shows the reliability coefficients for the TIMSS data. Reassuringly, estimates of coefficient alpha are identical. The psych package also provides Guttman's λ_6 and standardized alpha. jMetrik provides Guttman's λ_2, Feldt–Gilmer, Feldt–Brennan, and Raju's Beta reliability coefficients. Regardless of their theoretical differences, all of these coefficients produce virtually identical estimates of reliability, from 0.80 to 0.84, which I would argue is adequate reliability.

The reliability coefficients for the political viewpoint data are shown in Table 4.4. Two differences from the TIMSS data are apparent. First, the reliabilities are disappointingly low. Second, there is greater variability in the coefficients themselves. The reasons for this are discussed in Chapters 8 and 11. Essentially, the degree to which the assumptions of some of the coefficients are met is questionable. In particular, the parts (items) are not always strongly correlated with each other.

TABLE 4.3 ● Reliability Coefficients for TIMSS Booklet 1		
	jMetrik	**R Psych**
Alpha	0.8123	0.81
Standardized Alpha		0.81
Lambda 2	0.8155	
Lambda 6		0.82
Feldt–Gilmer	0.8149	
Feldt–Brennan	0.8140	
Raju's Beta	0.8123	

TABLE 4.4 ● Reliability Coefficients for Political Viewpoint Test		
	jMetrik	**R Psych**
Alpha	0.5070	0.50
Standardized Alpha		0.47
Lambda 2	0.5590	
Lambda 6		0.55
Feldt–Gilmer	0.5498	
Feldt–Brennan	0.5182	
Raju's Beta	0.5070	

4.5 STANDARD ERROR OF MEASUREMENT

Reliability coefficients are estimates of the proportion of observed test variation that can be attributed to true score variation. By themselves, they do not provide any indication of how precise test scores are. As an absolute indicator of score precision, a reliability coefficient can be used to estimate the standard deviation of random measurement errors. This statistic is called the *Standard Error of Measurement* (SEM). It can be shown that for $X = T + E$:

$$\sigma_X^2 = \sigma_T^2 + \sigma_E^2 \qquad (4.18)$$

Observed test score variance is the combination of true score variance and measurement error variance, keeping in mind that error means random measurement error. Solving this equation for σ_E gives the following formula for the SEM[2]:

$$\text{SEM} = \sigma_E = \sigma_X \sqrt{1 - \rho_{XX'}} \qquad (4.19)$$

For example, if score reliability is 0.90, using one of the above coefficients, and observed test scores have a standard deviation of 5.0, then $\text{SEM} = 5.0\sqrt{1 - 0.90} = 1.58$. Typically, the SEM is used to form a 95 percent confidence interval around a *true* score, $T \pm 1.96$ SEM, or plus or minus approximately two SEMs. In this example, if a respondent has a true score of 10 on the test, then we would expect this respondent's observed score to range from $\pm 1.96{*}1.58$, or 6.9–13.1, 95 percent of the time. In practice, this confidence interval is often placed around an observed score to indicate its precision, with an accompanying interpretation that there is a 95 percent chance of the true score being in this interval. However, this is backwards. A correct interpretation is: if this observed score were the actual true score, then there is a 95 percent chance that the observed score will fall in this range.

It is important to note that this use of the SEM requires two assumptions. First, measurement errors are assumed to follow a normal distribution; this allows us to use 1.96. Second, measurement errors are assumed to be *homoscedastic*, meaning that the SEM is the same for every observed score. This second assumption is in keeping with the four principles of CTT which posit that all observed scores are equally precise.

4.6 RELATIONSHIP BETWEEN RELIABILITY AND VALIDITY

Before leaving Classical Test Theory, it is important to point out that there is a relationship between reliability and validity. To be sure, both the Messick and Kane validity frameworks consider reliability to be a form of validity evidence. If there is zero reliability, there can be no validity because test scores would essentially be random draws out of a hat, and then nothing is being measured.

---

[2] σ_X is the standard deviation of observed scores. These are most likely composite scores comprised of item scores. Hence, σ_C that was used earlier could also be used here.

However, there is more to be said about the impact of reliability on the correlations between variables. Specifically, the lack of perfect reliability in two tests limits the size of the correlation between them in this way:

$$|\rho_{XY}| \leq \sqrt{\rho_{XX'}}\sqrt{\rho_{YY'}} \qquad (4.20)$$

So, if the test measuring variable X has a reliability of 0.60, and the test measuring variable Y has a reliability of 0.70, then the strongest the two tests could actually correlate is $\sqrt{\rho_{XX'}}\sqrt{\rho_{YY'}} = \sqrt{0.60}\sqrt{0.70} = |0.65|$. Of course, they may not correlate that strongly, but this is the upper limit on their correlation. Consider the political viewpoint test, which had a reliability of approximately 0.50. In the same dataset, there is an item, called polivw99, which asks: How would you characterize your political views? Far left to Far right on a 1–5 scale. That item should correlate strongly with the 18-item political viewpoint test. However, the correlation is only 0.47. Because the test's reliability is only 0.45–0.50 (depending on which reliability coefficient is used), it is unsurprising to find that this test does not correlate strongly with other variables with which it would be expected to correlate.

A more subversive application of this relationship between reliability and correlations between tests can be found in what's called the *correction for attenuation*. Rather than the observed correlation between two tests, most researchers are really interested in the correlation between true scores on the two tests, in other words, what the correlation would be if both tests were perfectly reliable or contained no measurement error. This true score correlation can be estimated as follows:

$$\rho_{T_X T_Y} = \frac{\rho_{XY}}{\sqrt{\rho_{XX'}}\sqrt{\rho_{YY'}}} \qquad (4.21)$$

For example, suppose that the observed correlation between scores on tests X and Y is 0.76, and the tests have reliabilities of 0.85 and 0.92, respectively. Then, the estimated correlation between true scores on both tests is:

$$\rho_{T_X T_Y} = \frac{\rho_{XY}}{\sqrt{\rho_{XX'}}\sqrt{\rho_{YY'}}} = \frac{0.76}{\sqrt{0.85}\sqrt{0.92}} = 0.86$$

0.86 looks stronger than 0.76, and the former is often reported in research articles with an asterisk or footnote that says, "correlation corrected for attenuation" or "disattenuated correlation." I should note that there is potential for abuse here. An observed correlation can be overinflated. For instance, a correlation of 0.20 can become a disattenuated correlation of 0.50 if the reliabilities are both 0.40. It is also possible for a disattenuated correlation to be greater than 1.0! Theoretically, this is not possible, but if the reliabilities are obtained from a different dataset, this result can occur.

$$\frac{0.75}{\sqrt{0.80}\sqrt{0.60}} = 1.08$$

4.7 GENERALIZABILITY THEORY

Hoyt (1941) devised a way to estimate reliability from an Analysis of Variance (ANOVA) design. Consider the data from Tables 4.1 and 4.2, copied here as Table 4.5. You could view these data as a two-way repeated measures design, eight persons by five items, with one observation per cell (the effects are both random). If you run this analysis in a statistical program (SPSS was used here), you obtain the results in Table 4.6.

Hoyt's focus was on the values of the mean squares, not the significance tests. Each mean square is an estimate of the variance attributable to each factor in the design.

TABLE 4.5 ● Data for Hoyt's ANOVA

Person	Item Scores				
	1	2	3	4	5
1	5	3	4	4	3
2	5	3	5	1	2
3	4	2	4	3	3
4	4	4	2	4	4
5	5	1	1	3	2
6	4	3	4	3	4
7	4	1	4	3	4
8	5	2	4	3	3

TABLE 4.6 ⬡ Results of ANOVA					
Source	**Sum of Squares**	**df**	**Mean Square**	**F**	**Sig.**
Item	19.650	4	4.913	5.220	0.003
Person	6.400	7	0.914	0.972	0.471
Item * Person	26.350	28	0.941		

The expected values of the mean squares for persons (p), items (i), and persons by items interaction (pi) are:

$$\text{EMS}(p) = \sigma^2_{pi} + n_i\sigma^2_p \tag{4.22}$$

$$\text{EMS}(i) = \sigma^2_{pi} + n_p\sigma^2_i \tag{4.23}$$

$$\text{EMS}(pi) = \sigma^2_{pi} \tag{4.24}$$

Recall that reliability under CTT has been derived as:

$$\rho_{XX'} = \frac{\sigma^2_T}{\sigma^2_X} = \frac{\sigma^2_T}{\sigma^2_T + \sigma^2_E} \tag{4.25}$$

Hoyt translated that concept into the ANOVA framework as:

$$\rho_{XX'} = \frac{\sigma^2_p}{\sigma^2_p + \sigma^2_E} \tag{4.26}$$

Using the expected mean squares above to solve for σ^2_p and σ^2_E:

$$\sigma^2_p = \frac{(\text{MS}_p - \text{MS}_{pi})}{n_i} = \frac{0.914 - 0.941}{5} = -0.005$$

$$\sigma^2_E = \frac{\text{MS}_{pi}}{n_i} = \frac{0.941}{5} = 0.188$$

$$\rho_{XX'} = \frac{\sigma^2_p}{\sigma^2_p + \sigma^2_E} = \frac{-0.005}{-0.005 + 0.188} = -0.027$$

It turns out that this value (with rounding error) is equal to coefficient alpha.

Hoyt's ANOVA led to the development of a broad approach to reliability, called generalizability theory. The basic idea is that the test score is the dependent variable, and the independent variables are persons and items, and could be any other factor that may contribute to measurement error, such as different raters, different occasions, and different forms. Additionally, a variety of ANOVA designs can be used, including fully crossed designs such as above as well as nested designs.

A generalizability analysis consists of two parts. In the G study, the variance components are estimated from the ANOVA design used to obtain data. In the D study, reliability coefficients, now called generalizability coefficients, are calculated from the current design but can also be estimated for other designs. What results is a powerful system of estimating how many items, forms, raters, occasions, and so forth are needed to achieve a desired reliability for different data collection designs. This allows test developers to design measurement systems for optimal reliability.

Even though generalizability could be carried out using traditional statistical software for ANOVA, it can be extremely complex and time consuming. There are software applications to conduct generalizability analyses that are much more efficient and less painful. These include the long standing GENOVA program from the University of Iowa (https://education.uiowa.edu/centers/center-advanced-studies-measurement-and-assessment/computer-programs) and the gtheory R package. Generalizability is used primarily in complex test designs involving raters, occasions, and/or alternate forms.

4.8 CHAPTER SUMMARY

This chapter introduced the concepts of Classical Test Theory (CTT). Its central idea is that there is a true score for any individual on a test at that specific point in time. The actual, or observed, score that she or he receives could differ from the true score due to measurement error. Measurement errors can be systematic or random, but CTT refers only to random error. From several basic assumptions and principles derived from those assumptions, reliability coefficients are developed as estimates of the proportion of observed score variation that is due to true score variation. This proportion can range from 0.0 (no reliability; observed scores are essentially random data) to 1.0 (perfect reliability; no measurement error). A large number of reliability coefficients have been developed based on assumptions of how the parts, or items, of a test are related to each other. The most popular of these is coefficient alpha. The standard error of measurement (SEM) is used to indicate in raw score terms how precise a score is. A lack of reliability limits how strongly variables can correlate with each other. Lastly, generalizability theory, an important outgrowth of CTT and ANOVA methodology, was briefly described. Its main application currently is in designing complex tests.

4.9 EXERCISES AND ACTIVITIES

1. Which of the following are likely to produce systematic measurement and which are likely to produce random measurement error?

   a. To save money, a testing program decides to contract with a new publisher who can deliver tests with smaller fonts and fewer pages.

   b. A respondent oversleeps and rushes to be at the testing site on time.

   c. A contestant tries to estimate the number of jelly beans in a glass jar.

   d. A respondent has an argument with her/his significant other immediately before taking a test.

2. The following is a snippet of data from the political viewpoint data.

Person	view9902	view9903	view9904	view9905
1	2	3	1	2
2	2	1	1	3
3	2	2	2	2
4	4	2	3	3
5	1	1	1	1
6	4	2	3	1
7	2	2	2	1

   1. Calculate the split-half and alpha reliability coefficients (I suggest using an excel worksheet for this).

   2. What assumptions have been made for each reliability coefficient?

3. Suppose you are a guest on the *Daily Show*. Trevor Noah asks you, "So, what's this thing called reliability all about?" How would you answer him in a nontechnical way?

4. What kinds of random measurement errors are test/retest, alternate forms, split-half, and coefficient alpha intended to estimate?

5. Describe a complex testing system in which generalizability would be useful in its design.

FURTHER READING

The 2014 *Standards* provide a nontechnical (i.e., no equations) conceptual overview of reliability. The references by Crocker and Algina, Haertel, and Raykov, and Marcoulides are more technical/statistical. These references are all influenced by the classic (but difficult) book by Lord and Novick. Brennan's work is a compact introduction to generalizability theory.

American Educational Research Association, American Psychological Association, & National Council on Measurement in Education. (2014). *Standards for educational and psychological testing.* Washington, DC: American Educational Research Association.

Brennan, R. L. (1992). Generalizability theory. *Educational Measurement: Issues and Practice*, 11(4), 27–34. Also issued as NCME's ITEM Module 14 https://ncme.elevate. commpartners.com/

Crocker, L., & Algina, J. (1986). *Introduction to classical and modern test theory.* Belmont, CA: Wadsworth Publishing.

Haertel, E. H. (2006). Reliability. In R. L. Brennan (Ed.), *Educational measurement* (4th ed., pp. 65–110). Westport, CT: Praeger.

Lord, F. M., & Novick, M. R. (1968). *Statistical theories of mental test scores.* Reading, MA: Addison-Wesley.

Merriam-Webster. (2014). Measurement. In *Merriam-Webster's Collegiate Dictionary* (11th ed., p. 1051).

Raykov, T., & Marcoulides, G. A. (2011). *Introduction to psychometric theory.* New York, NY: Routledge.

REFERENCES

Brown, W. (1910). Some experimental results in the correlation of mental abilities. *British Journal of Psychology*, 3, 296–322.

Cronbach, L. J. (1951). Coefficient alpha and the internal structure of tests. *Psychometrika*, 16, 151–160.

Feldt, L. S., & Brennan, R. L. (1989). Reliability. In R. L. Linn (Ed.), *Educational measurement* (3rd ed., pp. 105–146). New York, NY: American Council on Education; Macmillan.

Gilmer, J. S., & Feldt, L. S. (1983). Reliability estimation for a test with parts of unknown length. *Psychometrika*, 48, 99–111.

Guttman, L. A. (1945). A basis for analyzing test-retest reliability. *Psychometrika*, 10, 255–282.

Hoyt, C. J. (1941). Test reliability estimated by analysis of variance. *Psychometrika*, 6, 153–160.

Kuder, G. F., & Richardson, M. W. (1937). The theory of the estimation of test reliability. *Psychometrika*, 2, 297–334.

Osburn, H. G. (2000). Coefficient alpha and related internal consistency reliability coefficients. *Psychological Methods*, 5, 343–355.

Raju, N. S. (1977). A generalization of coefficient alpha. *Psychometrika*, 42, 549–565.

Spearman, C. (1910). Correlation calculated from faulty data. *British Journal of Psychology*, 3, 271–295.

Zwick, R. (1992). Chapter 7: Statistical and psychometric issues in the measurement of educational trends: Examples from the National Assessment of Educational Progress. *Journal of Educational Statistics*, 17(2), 205–218.

TECHNICAL APPENDIX: DERIVATIONS OF SOME CTT PRINCIPLES

For the technically inclined reader, this appendix offers derivations of several of the important principles of CTT.

Recall that in the beginning of this chapter, CTT started with the following assumptions:

$$X = T + E \tag{A.1}$$

For an individual p:

$$X_{pi} = T_p + E_{pi} \tag{A.2}$$

Define person p's true score as:

$$T_p = \mu_{X_{pi}} \tag{A.3}$$

And, since measurement errors are random:

$$\mu_{E_{pi}} = 0 \tag{A.4}$$

Furthermore, these initial assumptions lead to the derivation of the following four "principles":

$$\mu_X = \mu_T \tag{A.5}$$

$$\mu_E = 0 \tag{A.6}$$

$$\rho_{TE} = 0 \tag{A.7}$$

$$\rho_{E_1 E_2} = 0 \tag{A.8}$$

Estimating reliability for many coefficients requires some additional assumptions. The assumptions for parallel measures are:

$$\text{True scores are equal:}\quad T_1 = T_2 = T \qquad (A.9)$$

$$\text{Error variances are equal:}\quad \sigma_{E1}^2 = \sigma_{E2}^2 \qquad (A.10)$$

A.1 ESTIMATING THE RELIABILITY COEFFICIENT UNDER PARALLEL MEASURES

The correlation between parallel measures is:

$$\rho_{X_1 X_2} = \frac{\sigma_{X_1 X_2}}{\sigma_{X_1} \sigma_{X_2}} = \frac{\sum (X_1 - \mu_1)(X_2 - \mu_2)/N}{\sigma_{X_1} \sigma_{X_2}} \qquad (A.11)$$

To reduce the algebra, let $x_1 = X_1 - \mu_1$ and $x_2 = X_2 - \mu_2$. Since $\sigma_{X_1} = \sigma_{X_2}$ and $\sigma_{X_1} \sigma_{X_2} = \sigma_x^2$, then,

$$\rho_{X_1 X_2} = \frac{\sum x_1 x_2 / N}{\sigma_X^2} \qquad (A.12)$$

$$\rho_{X_1 X_2} = \frac{\sum (t_1 + e_1)(t_2 + e_2)/N}{\sigma_X^2} \qquad (A.13)$$

Since $t_1 = t_2 = t$,

$$\rho_{X_1 X_2} = \frac{\sum (t^2 + e_1 t + e_2 t + e_1 e_2)/N}{\sigma_X^2} \qquad (A.14)$$

$$\rho_{X_1 X_2} = \frac{\sum t^2 / N}{\sigma_X^2} + \frac{\sum e_1 t / N}{\sigma_X^2} + \frac{\sum e_2 t / N}{\sigma_X^2} + \frac{\sum e_1 e_2 / N}{\sigma_X^2} \qquad (A.15)$$

Because measurement errors correlate 0 with true scores and errors, the last three terms drop out.

$$\rho_{X_1 X_2} = \frac{\sum t^2 / N}{\sigma_X^2} = \frac{\sum (T - \bar{T})^2 / N}{\sigma_X^2} = \frac{\sigma_T^2}{\sigma_X^2} \qquad (A.16)$$

A.2 RELIABILITY OF A COMPOSITE (SPEARMAN–BROWN FORMULA)

If a test is composed of k parts, and a composite score is formed by adding the observed scores for the parts:

$$C = X_1 + X_2 + X_3 + X_4 + \cdots + X_k \qquad (A.17)$$

The reliability of composite score C is:

$$\rho_{CC'} = \rho_{TC}^2 = \frac{\sigma_{TC}^2}{\sigma_C^2} \qquad (A.18)$$

The denominator here can be expressed as a sum of all part covariances, k of which are variances and the rest are covariances between all possible pairs of parts:

$$\sigma_C^2 = \sum \sigma_{X_i X_j} = \sum \sigma_{X_i}^2 + \sum_{i \neq j} \sigma_{X_i X_j} \qquad (A.19)$$

Since X_i's are parallel, all part variances and covariances are equal, σ_X^2, and have the same reliability, $\rho_{XX'}$.

$$\sigma_C^2 = k\sigma_X^2 + (k-1)\rho_{XX'}\sigma_X^2 \qquad (A.20)$$

$$\sigma_C^2 = k\sigma_X^2[1 + (k-1)\rho_{XX'}] \qquad (A.21)$$

For the numerator,

$$\sigma_{T_C}^2 = \sum \sigma_{T_i T_j} = \sum \sigma_{T_i}^2 + \sum_{i \neq j} \sigma_{T_i T_j} \qquad (A.22)$$

Since X_i's are parallel, all part true variances and covariances are equal, σ_T^2. Then,

$$\sigma_{T_C}^2 = k\sum \sigma_T^2 + k(k-1)\sigma_T^2 = k^2 \sigma_T^2 \qquad (A.23)$$

Putting it all together:

$$\rho_{CC'} = \frac{\sigma_{T_C}^2}{\sigma_C^2} = \frac{k^2 \sigma_T^2}{k\sigma_X^2[1 + (k-1)\rho_{XX'}]} \qquad (A.24)$$

Since $\rho_{XX'} = \frac{\sigma_T^2}{\sigma_X^2}$, the final result is the Spearman–Brown formula.

$$\rho_{CC'} = \frac{k\rho_{XX'}}{1 + (k-1)\rho_{XX'}} \tag{A.25}$$

A.3 STANDARD ERROR OF MEASUREMENT

Starting with $X = T + E$,

$$\sigma_X^2 = \sigma_T^2 + \sigma_E^2 + 2\sigma_T\sigma_E\rho_{TE} \tag{A.26}$$

Since the correlation between true and error scores is 0,

$$\sigma_E^2 = \sigma_X^2 - \sigma_T^2 \tag{A.27}$$

$$\frac{\sigma_E^2}{\sigma_X^2} = \frac{\sigma_X^2}{\sigma_X^2} - \frac{\sigma_T^2}{\sigma_X^2} \tag{A.28}$$

$$\frac{\sigma_E^2}{\sigma_X^2} = 1 - \rho_{XX'} \tag{A.29}$$

$$\sigma_E^2 = \sigma_X^2(1 - \rho_{XX'}) \tag{A.30}$$

$$\text{SEM} = \sigma_E = \sigma_X\sqrt{1 - \rho_{XX'}} \tag{A.31}$$

TEST
DEVELOPMENT

5

FRAMEWORKS FOR TEST DEVELOPMENT

Quite often, individuals and organizations want to begin the test development process by writing items. This is understandable in that initial thinking about the test often includes those specific pieces of content that are most important to the developer. For example, a credentialing program may wish to revise an existing certification test because there is new knowledge that it sees as critical to someone attaining certification. Or, clinicians concerned about the mental health of adolescents likely already have in mind some behaviors that suggest the severity of risk is high enough to warrant immediate intervention.

However, beginning the process with item writing is akin to building a house without a blueprint. While different resources may vary somewhat on the details on their recommended process for test development, they all agree that item writing is not the first step. As in construction, some type of test design, called a test blueprint, is essential in order to assure that the test is developed soundly and will achieve its purpose, that is, that score interpretations and uses are valid.

5.1 *STANDARDS* FRAMEWORK FOR TEST DEVELOPMENT

Depending on the purpose and intended uses of a test, the specific steps for its development can vary to some extent. As a result, the 2014 *Standards* (pp. 75–84) offer a generic process consisting of the following steps:

1. *Develop Test Specifications.* These are the decisions and activities that should be undertaken prior to writing the items. The *Standards* tend to focus on large-scale test development rather than development by individuals or small groups of researchers. As a result, some of the activities listed below are beyond the resources of small-scale development.

    a. *Statement of purpose and intended uses.* This beginning of the development process consists of a number of decisions. What is being measured and for what purpose? What are the intended uses of the test? What is the target population for this test? Are accommodations or alternate forms needed for specific subgroups? Is the test score interpretation primarily intended to be norm-referenced or criterion-referenced?

    b. *Content specifications, or frameworks.* Given the purpose of the test, the actual content of what is going to be asked of respondents must be determined.

    c. *Format specifications.* Given the purpose and content, the format of the test must be decided, including item format, e.g., multiple-choice, essay, performance, etc., reading level, accessibility by respondents, and technology requirements.

d. *Test length.* Logistical issues and item formats together determine the length of the test. For example, administration time may be limited by external constraints, such as a class period in school. The number of items is likewise limited by their format. Fewer essay items can be administered in the same time period than multiple-choice or true-false items. Based on content and format specifications, a test blueprint, sometimes called a table of specifications, is developed. This blueprint specifies how many items of a particular item format are needed to measure each content area and how many items in each content area are intended to measure the construct at specific depths of understanding.

e. *Psychometric specifications.* Scaling and scoring the test are guided by the psychometric framework, or test theory. Each test theory rests on assumptions about the structure of the test. For example, classical test theory, discussed in the previous chapter, rests on an assumption of equal precision for all scores, while Rasch measurement theory, discussed in Chapter 9, bases item selection on score precision where it is most needed.

f. *Scoring specifications.* Each item format includes one or more possible models for scoring them. Some formats can be objectively scored, while others, such as constructed response and performances, need to be scored by raters. Raters then have to be trained.

g. *Test administration specifications.* Decisions need to be made about what administration procedures are permissible, paper–pencil or computer-based, what instructions and materials are needed for respondents and test users, what security procedures are needed.

h. *Refinement of test specifications.* The above activities are related to each other. Development of the content specifications may refine administrative and format specifications, and vice versa.

i. *Considerations for adaptive testing.* Adaptive tests have become increasingly popular in recent years. They are computer administered where the next item a respondent receives is determined by the answers to previous items. Items continue to be administered until a respondent's score can be determined with a predetermined degree of precision. Rather than an intact fixed-length test, adaptive tests require the development of large item banks.

j. *Systems supporting item and test development.* Technology to support test development has advanced rapidly in recent years. This includes software for efficient test assembly, item scoring, item banking, and item and test analysis.

2. *Item Development and Review.* Only after all or most of the above-listed activities are completed should item writing begin. In large-scale development efforts, the above specifications are delivered to professional item writers. In small-scale projects, the same individual or small group that determined the specifications also writes the items. In both cases, this includes developing an item pool, reviewing drafts of items, and pilot testing them for quality. The blueprint directs the development of items in specific formats for each targeted content area and the level of understanding in each content area for each item format. Considerably more items than needed are written for each content area/level of understanding combination.

After the first drafts of items are written, several types of item review are conducted, including reviews for item technical quality, copy editing, and fairness and bias. Following this, the first data collection effort, called pilot testing, is carried out. The purpose of pilot testing is to analyze items for their statistical quality.

3. *Assembling and Evaluating Test Forms.* Based on the results of item reviews and item analysis from *pilot testing*, items are identified as flawed and thus discarded, in need of further revision (and pilot testing), or of sufficient quality to be considered for the final test. One or more test forms are then assembled for a second data collection effort, commonly called a *field test.* A field test is larger in scale and scope than the pilot test. Its goal is to collect statistical information on the form as a whole and contribute data to be used for validity evidence, such as internal structure and content evidence.

4. *Developing Procedures and Materials for Administration and Scoring.* The specificity and breadth of these materials is determined by their purpose and intended use. If, for example, the test is to be used solely for research purposes, then these materials may be minimal, particularly if respondents never receive their scores. On the other hand, if respondents are to receive score reports, if individuals or organizations other than the test developers are to use the test, or if the test is to be a commercial product, then an infrastructure around the test needs to be developed. This includes documents to support administration and scoring, hardware and software requirements for computer-based administration, procedures to assure test security, and technical documentation of validity evidence (such as a technical report).

5. *Test Revisions.* Procedures for updating any aspect of test development and administration may be necessary. For some tests, particularly those designed for credentialing or measuring achievement, the content may need to be revised. Additionally, technology requirements may change over time and necessitate revision.

5.2 WILSON'S FRAMEWORK FOR TEST CONSTRUCTION

The process outlined in the *Standards* is intended to support the validation of test scores regardless of the validity framework that is used: *Standards*, Messick, Kane, or other framework. However, you will notice that defining the construct to be measured is mentioned but not particularly stressed in the *Standards* framework. This lack of emphasis is consistent with other descriptions of the development process that come from educational measurement sources (e.g., Crocker & Algina, 1986; Millman & Greene, 1989; Schmeiser & Welch, 2006). The emphasis in these sources is on tests that measure cognitive constructs and that are used for credentialing, personnel selection, college admissions, or assessing educational achievement purposes. Additionally, as pointed out in Chapter 2, Kane's validity framework places less emphasis than the Messick framework on what construct is measured and more emphasis on the claims that are made about test scores.

On the other hand, for tests measuring noncognitive constructs, particularly psychological variables, the nature of the construct being measured is of central importance in the test development process. Several authors (e.g., McCoach, Gable, & Madura, 2013; Wilson, 2005) have recognized this imbalance and devoted considerably more thought to defining the construct and mapping its definition into the development process than for tests measuring cognitive constructs. This duality also corresponds to the two basic directions for educational and psychological measurement discussed in the history section of Chapter 1: tests for high-stakes uses, for decisions made about respondents and in which respondents seek the highest score possible versus tests with low stakes and for which respondents seek the typical score.

Mark Wilson, in his 2005 book *Constructing Measures*, describes test development in terms of four building blocks as shown in Figure 5.1.

Construct Map. A construct is graphically visualized as a single dimension between two extremes, e.g., positive self-concept/negative self-concept, liberal/conservative political viewpoint, advanced science knowledge/below basic science knowledge. Between these extremes, both individuals and items can be located. Construct maps describe how individuals at different locations on the construct continuum are different from each other, such as high and low emotional intelligence, and how items at different locations are likewise different from each other, such as more or less difficult items or content areas.

Items Responses. Items are designed to be strongly related to the construct. Furthermore, responses to items are thought to be caused by the *amount* of a construct that a

FIGURE 5.1 ● Wilson's Four Building Blocks for Test Development

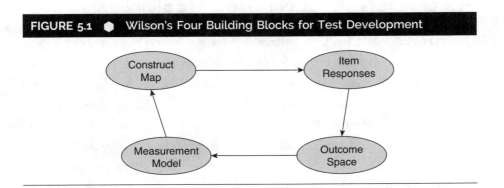

respondent has. The task of the test developer is to design items in such a way as to be sensitive to differences in the construct. For example, which item format is better at measuring mathematics problem solving skills, multiple-choice or constructed response?

Outcome Space. Items need to be scored in a way that promotes the validity of score interpretation. Items may be objectively scored dichotomously, 0 and 1, as incorrect and correct, respectively, or polytomously, as in 1–5, strongly disagree to strongly agree. Alternatively, scoring rubrics could be developed to score open-ended item formats.

Measurement Model. A measurement model summarizes item scores into a single scale score. Wilson proposes using Rasch models, but a variety of measurement models is possible.

A unique feature of Wilson's framework is that the development process can in fact be cyclical. If the measurement model results in a scale different than one visualized by the construct map, then the construct map itself may be revisited and revised.

Compared to the process outlined in the *Standards*, Wilson's framework places greater emphasis on the upfront work prior to item writing by encouraging clarity on the construct to be measured. Additionally, Wilson addresses the process of converting item responses to item scores and then ultimately to test scores, a topic the *Standards* do not address in their development process. This topic is typically covered in references focused more on test theory and psychometrics.

5.3 EVIDENCE-CENTERED DESIGN

In recent years, there has been an increased interest in developing tests to measure more complex constructs, such as higher-level thinking skills and skills diagnosis, and the use of item formats made possible by recent technology. As a result, Robert J. Mislevy and his colleagues have developed a framework for the development for such tests (Mislevy & Haertel, 2006; Mislevy, Steinberg, & Almond, 2003; Mislevy, Steinberg, Almond, & Lukas, 2006). This framework, called evidence-centered design (ECD), has been applied mostly by large-scale testing organizations to develop computer-based, interactive tests measuring cognitive processes. In ECD, a test's intended use results in a claim made about its score(s). For example, "an individual receiving a score of ___ becomes licensed to practice ___" is a claim that needs to be supported by evidence. Test development activities are organized around collecting this evidence and presenting it in a clear argument.

Although ECD could be used to guide the development of the tests measuring simpler unidimensional constructs that are the focus of this book, it has to this author's knowledge yet to be used this way. I believe this is due to two primary reasons. First, ECD uses a language based on Toulmin's (1958) framework for structuring arguments. This language may seem arcane to traditional test developers. Second, for simpler tests, the actual activities in which the developer engages are not notably different than for the *Standards* and Wilson frameworks. However, several aspects of ECD are worth noting and incorporating into any test development. First, while the activities may not be different, ECD organizes these activities into a coherent narrative that serves to validate the test's score meaning. ECD stresses response processes/substantive validity evidence much more than is usually done. As pointed out in Chapter 2, this type of validity evidence tends to be one of the least collected. Second, ECD follows Kane's validity framework in emphasizing the claims that are made about test scores and their uses. Both ECD and Kane utilize Toulmin's argument structure.

The ECD framework consists of five steps, called layers, that are roughly sequential in nature. They are domain analysis, domain modeling, the conceptual assessment framework, assessment implementation, and assessment delivery.

Domain Analysis. This is an analysis of the content to be measured. In this layer, research and theories related to the construct are gathered. Indicators of the characteristics of individuals with varying degrees of the construct and situations in which these indicators are observed are initially proposed. This layer is similar to Wilson's construct map approach. For cognitive constructs, such as knowledge and skills, there is often an extensive body of research and thinking about what is to be measured. For noncognitive constructs, the evidence is sometimes less plentiful, or there are competing theories about the construct. For example, creativity is viewed by some as a personality construct and by others as a cognitive skill. As will be shown in the next chapter, these two views result in vastly different tests.

Domain Modeling. This layer seeks to translate the work of domain analysis into a claim about a respondent. The claim is a narrative argument that an individual's response to tasks (items) and potential observations lead to an interpretation of the individual's measurement on the construct. This layer is similar to an explication of the intended uses of the test but is much more detailed in how responses to items lead to a particular interpretation. It lays out the connections between an individual's measurement on the construct, task features, and responses and observations.

Conceptual Assessment Framework. This layer corresponds roughly to test specifications but is likewise much more detailed and argument-based. Here, specifications are developed for the tasks/items (task models), how they are to be scored and how they will be scaled to provide the desired interpretation (evidence models), and the outcome variables (student models). This layer includes the measurement models to be used, such as CTT, Rasch models, IRT models, or cognitive diagnostic models.

Assessment Implementation. This layer addresses the construction and preparation of all the models specified in the conceptual assessment framework. It's the actual work of developing, revising, piloting, and field testing the test.

Assessment Delivery. This final layer is the test in action, including respondents' interactions with tasks/items, scoring, scaling, and reporting results.

As mentioned above, ECD is a complete framework that can be applied in arguably every test development application. For traditional unidimensional tests, ECD represents a process that echoes the activities found in the *Standards* and Wilson's approaches outlined above. The development activities are much the same. What is different is the organization and integration of those activities into a narrative argument that supports the claim(s) (i.e., score interpretations). Furthermore, ECD provides a way to collect and synthesize substantive/response processes evidence, evidence that is often minimally collected. On the other hand, ECD has been developed and proposed primarily for educational achievement purposes. To this author's best knowledge, it has not been applied to tests measuring noncognitive constructs.

However, the true innovation of ECD lies in guidance for nontraditional tests, including those that measure more than one construct, provide diagnostic information to respondents, or enable the use of recently developed technology-enhanced item formats. Consider, for example, a test designed to measure high school mathematics skills for a high-stakes purpose, such as a graduation requirement or teacher/school/district evaluation. Instead of a fixed-length test composed of multiple-choice items measuring content areas such as fractions, geometry, and number operations, a test could be designed to be computer adaptive, so that students' scores are updated after each item is administered. Furthermore, items could measure underlying mathematics skills and processes that may undergird more than one content area, thereby providing diagnostic information. Finally, computer-administered technology-enhanced items could enable students to interact with the test delivery system in order to demonstrate directly reasoning and problem-solving skills. ECD provides a framework for developing such a test.

5.4 FRAMEWORK FOR THIS BOOK

In this book, I utilize features from all three of the above frameworks. This approach is targeted for small-scale test development projects, such as those used by graduate students, faculty, and small organizations. The development steps will be explored in the next chapter. Here is a brief outline:

1. Definition of the purpose and intended uses of the test: This includes a statement of purpose and/or a claim that is to be made about test scores.

2. Early decision-making: The context for the use of the test may determine the outcome of several upfront important decisions, such as time limits, test delivery system, and data handling.

3. Construct map: A construct map is created showing how respondents and items vary along different locations of the construct continuum.

4. Internal structure model: Based on the construct map, a model is developed for the internal structure of the test.

5. External relationship model: Based on theory and research of the construct, a model is developed to show how the construct is expected to be related to other constructs and variables.

6. Operationalization of the construct: Based on the construct map and internal model, the construct is operationalized, showing what behaviors, knowledge, and thought processes indicate some amount of the construct.

7. Test specifications: Using all of the above, a blueprint and related specifications are developed.

8. Item writing and review.

9. Pilot testing of items for quality.

10. Development of the final version of the test.

11. Field test of the final version.

12. Score items and scale the test: This step includes preparing any needed score reports, documentation, and support systems.

13. Prepare validation plan for future work.

5.5 CHAPTER SUMMARY

This chapter reviewed three frameworks for developing tests. These frameworks list the steps or describe the process of development. It is important to realize that the specific process may vary across projects depending on the type of construct being measured and its intended use(s). The 2014 *Standards* provide a general framework applicable to most projects. Wilson's construct mapping approach emphasizes a complete understanding of the construct. Wilson provides examples primarily in educational achievement, but his framework is well-suited for measuring noncognitive constructs. ECD is a comprehensive framework that can accommodate multidimensional constructs, measurement of cognitive processes, technology-enhanced item formats, and test delivery systems. The test development process used in this book takes features from all three frameworks.

5.6 EXERCISES AND ACTIVITIES

Consider the *Standards*, Wilson, and ECD frameworks that were discussed in this chapter.

1. What features do they have in common?

2. What are some important differences between them?

FURTHER READING

For Further Reading on the Test Development Process, the Reader is Referred to the Following References

AERA, APA, & NCME. (2014). *Standards for educational and psychological testing*. Washington, DC: American Educational Research Association.

Mislevy, R. J., & Haertel, G. D. (2006). Implications of evidence-centered design for educational testing. *Educational Measurement: Issues and Practice*, 25, 6–20.

Mislevy, R. J., Steinberg, L. S., & Almond, R. G. (2003). On the structure of educational assessments. *Measurement: Interdisciplinary Research and Perspectives*, 1, 3–62.

Wilson, M. (2005). *Constructing measures: An item response modeling approach*. Mahwah, NJ: Erlbaum.

REFERENCES

Crocker, L., & Algina, J. (1986). *Introduction to classical and modern test theory*. Belmont, CA: Wadsworth Publishing.

McCoach, D. B., Gable, R. K., & Madura, J. P. (2013). *Instrument development in the affective domain: School and corporate applications*. New York, NY: Springer.

Millman, J., & Greene, J. (1989). The specification and development of tests of achievement and ability. In R. L. Linn (Ed.), *Educational measurement* (3th ed., pp. 335–366). New York, NY: American Council on Education; Macmillan.

Mislevy, R. J., Steinberg, L. S., Almond, R. G., & Lukas, J. F. (2006). Concepts, terminology, and basic models of evidence-centered design. In D. M. Williamson, I. I. Bejar, & R. J. Mislevy (Eds.). *Automated scoring of complex tasks in computer-based testing* (pp. 15–48). Mahwah, NJ: Erlbaum.

Schmeiser, C. B., & Welch, C. J. (2006). Test development. In R. L. Brennan (Ed.), *Educational measurement* (4th ed., pp. 307–353). Westport, CT: Praeger.

Toulmin, S. (1958). *The uses of argument*. Cambridge, UK: Cambridge University Press.

6

TEST SPECIFICATIONS

6.1 DEFINING THE PURPOSE AND INTENDED USES

The first step in the test development process is to create a statement that defines what is being measured and what are the intended purposes of the test. For individual and small-group development projects, the best statement is a simple direct sentence or two. For example, consider the following purpose statement from the *Tests of General Educational Development* (GED Tests):

> *The GED test certifies the high school-level academic achievement of national and international non-high school graduates.*
>
> (GED Testing Service, 2018)

This purpose statement indicates what is being measured, high school–level academic achievement, and for what purpose, certification of a level of achievement commensurate with national and international high schools. All decisions related to the development of the GED Tests, from test specifications to item writing to test administration to score reporting, are made to support this purpose.

Another example comes from the Grit Scale, developed by Angela Duckworth and her colleagues (Duckworth, Peterson, Matthews, & Kelly, 2007). They define grit as:

> *perseverance and passion for long-term goals. (p. 1087)*

The purpose of the Grit Scale is to test several hypotheses regarding the importance of grit: "grit may be as essential as IQ to high achievement," and "grit, more than self-control or conscientiousness, may set apart the exceptional individuals who … made maximal use of their abilities" (p. 1089). In other words, its primary intended use is for research.

For some larger-scale test programs, there is more than one purpose. In Virginia, the state-mandated curriculum in grades three through eight and in high school is called the *Standards of Learning* (SOL). Virginia has a state assessment program to measure achievement of the SOLs in a series of tests. One purpose of the SOL tests is stated as follows:

> *The **Standards of Learning (SOL)** for Virginia Public Schools establish minimum expectations for what students should know and be able to do at the end of each grade or course in English, mathematics, science, history/social science and other subjects.*

SOL tests in reading, writing, mathematics, science and history/social science measure the success of students in meeting the Board of Education's expectations for learning and achievement.

(http://www.doe.virginia.gov/testing/index.shtml)

In other words, this purpose is to measure student learning. How well have students mastered the SOL curriculum in a variety of subject areas and grade levels? However, another part of the Virginia Department of Education website states:

Results from these tests—which most students take online—are used by the commonwealth to identify schools in need of assistance and to inform parents and the public about the progress of schools through the awarding of annual accreditation ratings.

(http://www.doe.virginia.gov/statistics_reports/school_report_card/
accountability_guide.pdf)

The SOL tests have a second purpose, which is to evaluate school and school district quality and report this evaluation to the public. Additionally, there has been some discussion and controversy about using SOL test scores to evaluate teachers. This dual purpose is common to many (if not most) state educational achievement testing programs.

When there is more than one purpose, it is possible that the optimal test design for one purpose is at cross-purposes with the other ones. For example, the purpose of measuring student achievement leads to the development of tests that contain a representative sampling of content in a particular subject area. All students would take the same test, or equivalent versions of the same test. This is how the SOL tests are currently designed. However, for evaluating schools and districts, a different design could be implemented in which a much broader, more in-depth, sampling of content is measured through a large number of test booklets. Students would not take enough of the assessment to receive individual scores, but schools and districts could receive detailed reports of subcontent areas or even specific parts of the curriculum. Tests developed for the NAEP and TIMSS are currently designed this way.

Another example of a purpose statement comes from the popular *Myers–Briggs Type Indicator* (MBTI):

> *The purpose of the Myers-Briggs Type Indicator® (MBTI) personality inventory is to make the theory of psychological types described by C. G. Jung understandable and useful in people's lives. The essence of the theory is that much seemingly random variation in the behavior is actually quite orderly and consistent, being due to basic differences in the ways individuals prefer to use their perception and judgment.*

> *In developing the Myers-Briggs Type Indicator [test], the aim of Isabel Briggs Myers, and her mother, Katharine Briggs, was to make the insights of type theory accessible to individuals and groups. They addressed the two related goals in the developments and application of the MBTI test:*

> *The identification of basic preferences of each of the four dichotomies specified or implicit in Jung's theory.*

> *The identification and description of the 16 distinctive personality types that result from the interactions among the preferences.*
>
> (http://www.myersbriggs.org/)

This is straightforward. What is measured is each individual's personality type. The test was initially a tool for investigating and validating Jung's theory. If respondents' types could be measured, and hypothesized relationships predicted by the theory occurred, then both the validity of personality type scores and Jung's theory would be supported. If not, then either the test or the theory or both would be suspect.

Intended uses of the MBTI have greatly expanded to include applications to work life, career choices, relationships, and personal growth. In the armed forces, mission creep refers to an expansion of a military mission beyond its original purpose. Similarly, many tests, including the MBTI, have created applications beyond their initial purpose, a situation I call "purpose creep." Given the resources needed to develop new tests, it is understandable for developers to maximize their use. However, new uses of existing tests need to be supported by additional validity evidence.

6.2 SEVERAL EARLY DECISIONS TO MAKE

After defining the purpose and intended uses, but before proceeding further, several decisions need to be made: determining the primary frame of reference and identifying constraints.

Frame of Reference. As mentioned in Chapter 3, there are two basic ways of interpreting test scores, norm-referenced and criterion-referenced. Norm-referenced score interpretations provide respondents with information about how their scores compare to a target, or norming, population, and whether and to what extent they are below average, average, or above average in relation to the norming population. Norm-referenced interpretations are usually important in research studies when the goal is to investigate the relationship of test scores to other variables. Criterion-referenced score interpretations let respondents know how they compare to a particular performance standard, such as pass/fail, basic/proficient/advanced, or whether an educational or psychological intervention is needed/not needed. Whenever decisions are made about respondents on the basis of test scores, a criterion-referenced interpretation is important. Both interpretative frames can be met with the same test, but one of these is typically more important for meeting the test's purpose. For example, the GED Tests' first and foremost result is a decision about the respondent, whether or not to award a high school equivalency certificate, in others words a criterion-referenced interpretation. However, respondents also receive normative information in the form of percentile ranks, or the percentage of graduating high school seniors who had the same or lower score than the respondent.

Constraints. Some limitations are evident from the outset. For example, there is often a time constraint on the maximum amount of time it can take to complete the test. If a test is to be administered in a school setting, completion time may be restricted to a class period. Given the resources of the test developer, the modality for collecting data may be limited to paper/pencil and/or computer-based administration. There may be limits to the number of respondents that can access the test at a given time, from one to a small group to an unlimited number. Finally, whether the test is developed by an individual or an organization, there are constraints on financial and personnel resources. These can dictate the length of time to develop the test and the extent of data collection.

An example of these early decisions can be found in the development of NAEP. The general purpose of NAEP is:

> *NAEP is the largest nationally representative assessment of what America's students know and can do. Since NAEP assessments are administered uniformly using the same sets of test booklets across the nation, NAEP results serve as a common metric for all states and selected urban districts. The assessment stays essentially the same from year to year, with only carefully documented changes. This permits NAEP to provide a clear picture of student academic progress over time.*
>
> (http://nces.ed.gov/nationsreportcard/about/)

Its intended uses are: (1) compare achievement across states, (2) provide a picture of academic progress over time, (3) provide a check on state assessment programs, (4) disaggregate achievement results by demographic variables (sex, race/ethnicity, type of community, geographic region), and (5) provide a research base. Policy decisions for NAEP are determined by the National Assessment Governing Board (NAGB). Among these decisions are:

- NAEP is administered to nationally representative samples of students in grades 4, 8, and 12.

- Reading and mathematics are assessed every other year. Other subjects—writing, science, history, geography, civics, economics, foreign languages, and arts are assessed less often.

- Results reported in terms of percents of students in four different achievement levels: below basic, basic, proficient, advanced. This means that a criterion-referenced score interpretation is to be used. The advanced level should indicate a "world class" standard.

- No results will be reported for individual students, classrooms, or schools.

- Tests will be administered in paper/pencil mode using machine-scorable answer sheets.

These policy decisions guide and constrain the development of assessment tests.

6.3 CREATING A CONSTRUCT MAP

Most constructs that we would like to measure can be thought of as lying on a continuum, or a single dimension, between two extremes. Wilson's (2005) construct map is a useful tool for explaining the meaning of a construct. Figure 6.1 shows a generic construct map. The construct itself is visualized as a line between large and small amounts of the construct. Below the line are the various indicators of different amounts of the construct. Above the line are the respondents at different levels of the construct. This map could be quite detailed, but at this stage of test development, two or three levels (high, medium, or low) of the construct may be all that is needed. Several examples of construct maps follow. The maps below were reconstructed from the development process described in their lead article or test framework. What they all have in common is that they describe how respondents who score high on the construct are different from respondents who score low on the construct.

School Counselor Self-Efficacy Scale (SCSE) (Bodenhorn & Skaggs, 2005). This test measures the construct of self-efficacy, defined as "beliefs about one's own ability to successfully perform a given behavior" (Bodenhorn & Skaggs, 2005, p. 14). Self-efficacy is described within Bandura's social cognitive theory as "a generative capability in which component cognitive, social, and behavioral skills must be organized into integrated courses of action to serve innumerable purposes" (Bandura, 1986, p. 122). The test was developed with this theoretical perspective in mind.

FIGURE 6.1 ● Generic Construct Map

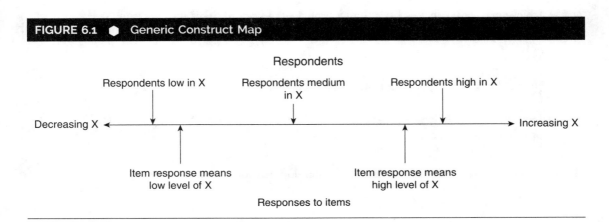

The initial purpose for the SCSE was to conduct research to support or refute predicted relationships between self-efficacy and other variables, such as job performance evaluation, social desirability, state-trait anxiety, and self-concept. Ultimately, however, the SCSE is intended to support the training of school counselors by identifying areas of strength and weakness. As a result, there is a total test score and a series of subscale scores.

Figure 6.2 shows a construct map for the SCSE. This map was not explicitly shown in the 2005 article, but was constructed (no pun intended) from the description of the test's development. Several important features of this construct map are worth noting. First, the continuum for the self-efficacy construct illustrates three locations: high, medium, and low degrees of self-efficacy. Below the continuum are a list of indicators of the types of skills that can differentiate levels of self-efficacy among school counselors. These indicators are shown at all three levels, meaning that all of these indicators are important across the self-efficacy continuum. Second, what differentiates the three levels is the degree of self-confidence for performing the indicators. Also, there is the implicit assumption that these indicators are strongly correlated. That is, a mix of strengths and weaknesses in the middle of the continuum is not considered. Nor is there a belief that these indicators are ordered in difficulty in any way.

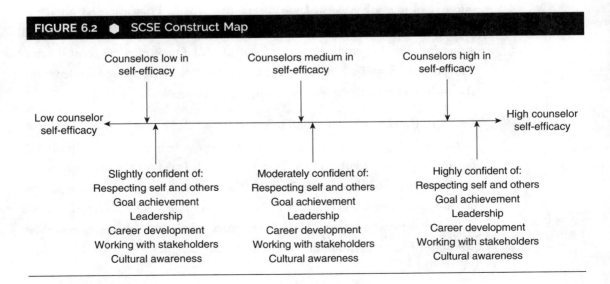

FIGURE 6.2 ● SCSE Construct Map

NAEP Geography Assessment. The specific purpose of the NAEP Geography Assessment is:

> *For more than a generation, geography has been badly neglected in American schools. The consequence is wide-spread ignorance of our own country and of its place in the world. (p. v)*

> *The purpose of geography education is to foster the development of citizens who will actively seek and systematically apply the knowledge and skills of geography in life situations. (p. vii)*

> *This framework (NAEP Geography) is designed to assess the outcomes of students' education in grades 4, 8, and 12 as part of the National Assessment of Educational Progress (NAEP). (p. vii)*
>
> —NAEP Geography Framework (NAGB, 2010)

There are three broad content areas in the geography assessment: (1) Space and Place, (2) Environment and Society, and (3) Spatial Dynamics and Connections. Each of these areas is assessed at grades 4, 8, and 12. Construct maps could be created for all nine grade/content combinations. Here, in Figure 6.3, I show a construct map for grade 8 Space and Place. As this is a criterion-referenced test, students are classified as into one of four achievement levels: Below Basic, Basic, Proficient, and Advanced. Descriptions of the knowledge, skills, and processes of each level (except Below Basic) were taken directly from the *Framework* (pp. 40–42). One sees in this construct map a progression, from Basic to Advanced levels, not only of increasing knowledge but also increasing cognitive skills from Knowing to Understanding to Applying.

Grit Scale (Duckworth et al., 2007). As mentioned above, Duckworth and her colleagues define grit as "perseverance and passion for long-term goals" (p. 1087). Figure 6.4 shows a construct map for the Grit Scale based on the description of its development provided in the 2007 article. This map indicates two main components of grit: passion, or the consistency of interests over time, and perseverance, or the ability to overcome adversity. What differentiates individuals high in grit from those low in grit is a combination of both of these components.

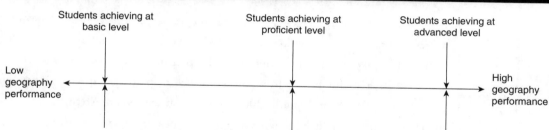

FIGURE 6.3 ● NAEP Geography/Space and Place/Grade 8 Construct Map

Students achieving at basic level | Students achieving at proficient level | Students achieving at advanced level

Low geography performance ← → High geography performance

Students should possess fundamental knowledge and vocabulary of concepts relating to patterns, relationships, distance, direction, scale, boundary, site, and situation; solve fundamental locational questions using latitude and longitude; interpret simple map scales; identify continents and their physical features, oceans, and various countries and cities; respond accurately to descriptive questions using information obtained by use of visual and techn logical tools; explain differences between maps and globes; and find a wide range of information using an atlas or almanac.

Students should possess a fundamental geographic vocabulary; understand geography's analytical concepts; solve locational questions requiring integration of information from two or more sources, such as atlases or globes; compare information presented at different scales;and identify a wide variety of physical and cultural features and describe regional patterns.

Students should possess a fundamental geographic vocabulary; understand geography's analytical concepts; solve locational questions requiring integration of information from two or more sources, such as atlases or globes; compare information presented at differentscales; and identify a wide variety of physical and cultural features and describe regional patterns.

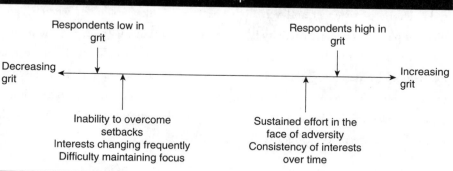

FIGURE 6.4 ● Grit Scale Construct Map

Respondents low in grit | Respondents high in grit

Decreasing grit ← → Increasing grit

Inability to overcome setbacks
Interests changing frequently
Difficulty maintaining focus

Sustained effort in the face of adversity
Consistency of interests over time

These examples reveal a wide variety of ways to create a construct map. They vary in the level of detail at different locations on the construct continuum. More importantly, at this stage of test development, they provide a clear vision of the construct and how individuals at different locations on the map might differ in the ways they behave and think.

6.4 INTERNAL STRUCTURE MODEL

At this point, many large-scale testing programs, especially those measuring achievement and other cognitive constructs, move on to developing test specifications. For smaller-scale test development, the preparation of two construct models can serve as a useful bridge from the construct map to test specifications. First introduced by Wolfe and Smith (2007), internal structure and external relationship models are particularly helpful in developing tests measuring noncognitive constructs. These constructs often do not have clearly defined content, but theories associated with them often describe an internal structure as well as a network of hypothesized relationships with other variables.

The internal structure model describes the components or elements of a construct and the relationships between them. Explication of these components supports content validity evidence that leads to test blueprints, response process/substantive validity evidence, and internal structure validity evidence. An internal model can be specified graphically or simply as a list. Here are some examples.

MUSIC Model of Academic Motivation Inventory (Jones, 2009; Jones & Skaggs, 2016). My colleague Brett Jones developed the MUSIC Inventory to measure academic motivation, defined as "a process that is inferred from actions (e.g., choice of tasks, effort, persistence) and verbalizations (e.g., 'I like biology.'), whereby goal-directed physical or mental activity is instigated and sustained" (p. 272). The primary intended use of the Inventory is to be a tool used by faculty to improve their instruction by designing their classes so that student motivation is increased. A secondary use is for researchers investigating academic motivation. According to Jones's model, motivation can be increased in five different ways, which comprise the internal structure model (Jones & Skaggs, 2016, p. 2):

- e**M**powerment: The extent to which students perceive they have control over their learning environment.

- **U**sefulness: The extent to which students perceive the coursework is useful to their future.

- **S**uccess: The extent to which students perceive they can succeed at the coursework.

- **I**nterest: The extent to which students perceive that the instructional methods and content are interesting.

- **C**aring: The extent to which students perceive that the instructor cares about whether they succeed in the coursework and cares about their well-being.

Jones considers these five components to be highly correlated, and that the more of them that a student perceives to be in effect, the higher academic motivation will be.

SAT-V Reading Comprehension (Sheehan, 1997). Sheehan presented a graphical presentation of the structure of the SAT I Verbal Reasoning test—reading comprehension subsection. The version shown in Figure 6.5 is an adaptation of the one shown as Figure 1 (p. 340) in her 1997 article. Here, reading comprehension consists of four components, three of which further consist of subcomponents. It should be noted that Sheehan intended this hierarchical structure to facilitate skills diagnosis.

Emotional Intelligence. Several theories of emotional intelligence have been proposed in the past two decades. The theory popularized by Dan Goleman (Boyatzis, Goleman, & Rhee, 2000; Cherniss & Goleman, 2001; Goleman, 1998) defined emotional intelligence as a collection of emotional competencies that can be learned. Boyatzis, Goleman, and Rhee developed the initial version of the *Emotional and Social Competence Inventory (ESCI),* based on Goleman's theory. They presented a 2 × 2 framework of emotional competencies as shown in Table 6.1. One dimension

FIGURE 6.5 ● Internal Model for SAT-Verbal Reading Comprehension

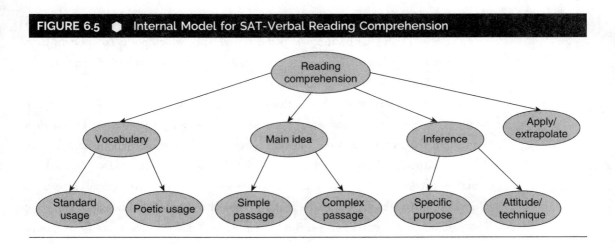

TABLE 6.1 ● Internal Model of Emotional Intelligence Based on Goleman's Theory		
	Self: Person Competence	**Other: Social Competence**
Recognition	Self-awareness	Social awareness
Regulation	Self-management	Relationship management

refers to the self versus others while the other dimension refers to recognizing versus regulating. Goleman's theory posits these four competencies as learned skills.

By contrast, John D. Mayer and Peter Salovey (1997; Mayer, Caruso, & Salovey, 2016) offered an alternative theory of emotional intelligence as a mental ability rather than a learned skill. Their internal structure model posits four "branches":

1. Managing emotions

2. Understanding emotions

3. Facilitating thought using emotion

4. Perceiving emotion

This theory of emotional intelligence was the basis for developing the *Mayer-Salovey-Caruso Emotional Intelligence Test (MSCEIT)* (Mayer, Salovey, Caruso, & Sitarenios, 2003). As will be seen later, these two different internal models of emotional intelligence led to the development of very different tests.

How can an internal model be generated? Guidance may come from several sources. It's helpful if there has been previous theoretical work which posits component parts of the construct. In many cases, these authors develop the test to help validate the theory. This was the case above for the emotional intelligence tests, MUSIC Inventory, and grit scale. Alternatively, in employment settings, information can come from a job analysis, as was the case for the self-efficacy test for school counselors and tests for job satisfaction. Sometimes, however, the test developer is at a loss for how to structure the test. In this case, it's helpful to solicit information from subject matter experts. NAEP, for example, convenes panels of instructional experts to develop the frameworks for each grade and subject area. These frameworks then serve as a guide for test development. Bearss et al. (2016) describe a series of focus groups used to develop an internal model for a test to diagnose autism spectrum disorder (ASD). The participants were a diverse group of parents of children with ASD. They provided indicators of ASD in a variety of settings. The test developers then transcribed and coded the transcripts of the focus groups, resulting in six broad themes that formed the basis for an internal model.

6.5 EXTERNAL RELATIONSHIP MODEL

An external relationship model portrays how the construct is hypothesized to be related to other constructs. While this model does not directly influence the development of the test, it lays the groundwork for external/relations-with-other-variables validity evidence to be collected when the test has been finalized.

MUSIC Inventory for Academic Motivation (Jones, 2009). Jones linked academic motivation to student learning, as shown in Figure 6.6 (Figure 1 from Jones, 2009, p. 273). The components on the left side of the figure show the internal model of the Inventory. Jones hypothesized that if instructors design instruction to increase one or more of the components, then motivation will increase, thereby increasing student achievement. Additionally, MUSIC model components were expected to correlate positively and strongly with related constructs, such as learning climate, utility value, perceived competence, situational interest, teacher support, intrinsic motivation, and instructor ratings.

Emotional and Social Competence Inventory (ESCI) (Boyatzis et al., 2000). Goleman's theory posits a number of constructs to be related to emotional intelligence. These

---

FIGURE 6.6 ● External Model for the MUSIC Inventory

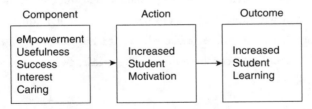

A model, based on a social-cognitive theoretical framework, in which five components lead to increased student motivation, resulting in increased student learning

Component	Action	Outcome
eMpowerment Usefulness Success Interest Caring	Increased Student Motivation	Increased Student Learning

Source: Adapted from Jones (2009).

include productivity and job performance, high achievement in school, successful long-term relationships, greater self-awareness and self-confidence, and a high quality of personal life. Individuals low in emotional intelligence are predicted to be "nerdy," "critical," and "condescending." Those high in emotional intelligence would likely be "poised," "outgoing," "sympathetic," and "caring." Additionally, people who learn emotional intelligence skills would be less likely to engage in disruptive behavior.

Mayer-Salovey-Caruso Emotional Intelligence Test (MSCEIT) (Mayer et al., 2003). Brackett and Salovey (2006) describe external evidence for each of the four abilities underlying the MSCEIT. Perceiving emotions is related to emotional awareness and expressivity, and affect sensitivity. Using emotions to facilitate thought is related to reasoning, problem-solving, and decision-making abilities. Understanding emotions is related to a wide "feelings" vocabulary and an ability to identify the meaning behind emotional experiences. Finally, managing emotion is related to self-efficacy and the ability to help and inspire others. In addition, MSCEIT scores are predicted to be minimally related to intelligence and the Big Five personality traits but are hypothesized to be positively related to psychological well-being and inversely related to depression and anxiety.

Smarter Balanced Assessment Consortium (SBAC). For many large-scale educational achievement and credentialing testing programs, external models are not explicit. The purposes of the testing programs are largely independent of relationships to external variables, which is to certify a level of accomplishment. However, all such testing programs are developed within a larger societal context. There is an implicit assumption in many testing organizations that the testing program itself will promote a higher professional standard or greater student accomplishment. An example of this can be found with the SBAC. The SBAC is an assessment system with three components: summative end-of-year tests that many states use as their criterion-referenced achievement program, interim tests to measure student progress leading to the summative tests, and a library of instructional resources for teachers. The primary purpose of the SBAC system's three components is that students in the states that use the SBAC system will finish high school prepared for higher education or a career. Other external relationships are predicted: (1) teaching effectiveness will improve; (2) school and school district achievement will increase; and (3) student engagement in learning will increase.

6.6 OPERATIONALIZING THE CONSTRUCT

At this point in the development process, by creating the construct map and internal and external models, you have a solid foundation on which to *operationalize* the measurement of your construct. Operationalization here means identifying the ways in which the construct can be observed through the thoughts, feelings, and behaviors of respondents. In other words, a universe of potential indicators of the construct is created for each component of the construct that was identified in the internal model. My advice here is to brainstorm a large list of potential indicators. These are not items, just ideas that could become items. For example, a test measuring marital satisfaction might include these indicators: time spent with friends versus spouse, time spent arguing, stress level, and disagreements over finances, physical attraction, life goals, and temperament.

For an example of an existing test, let's take a look at the *Job Descriptive Index (JDI)* (Lake, Gopalkrishnan, Sliter, & Withrow, 2010), a test that measures job satisfaction. The JDI is comprised of six components. Operationalizing each component consists of the following sample indicators:

1. *People on Present Job:* stimulating, helpful, stupid, responsible, rude, lazy, supportive, stubborn

2. *Job in General:* pleasant, waste of time, worthwhile, superior, makes me content, rotten, enjoyable

3. *Work on Present Job:* interesting, challenging, dull, gives sense of accomplishment, fulfilling, rewarding, uses my abilities

4. *Pay:* underpaid, overpaid, fair, barely live on income, less than I deserve

5. *Opportunities for Promotion:* dead end job, promotion on merit, fairness in promotion, very limited

6. *Supervision:* encouraging, critical, hard to please, tactful, poor planner, around when needed, influential

The indicators for each component consist of things that can be observed or rated by respondents. It is important to note that there are other ways that job satisfaction could be operationalized, such as personal behaviors (e.g., often late for work, willing to work overtime, grouchy while working, calling in sick frequently, etc.). This approach would obviously result in a much different test.

At this point, it's instructive to compare tests that measure the same construct and see how differences in the construct definition, internal model, and operationalization play out in the actual test itself. In this example, I compare the *Khatena-Torrance Creative Perception Inventory (KTPCI)* (Khatena & Torrance, 1976) with the *Profile of Creative Abilities (PCA)* (Ryser & McConnell, 2003). Table 6.2 summarizes the construct definition, internal model, and operationalization for each test.

TABLE 6.2 ◆ Comparison of KTPCI and PCA Tests		
	Khatena-Torrance Creative Perception Inventory (KTPCI)	**Profile of Creative Abilities (PCA)**
Construct definition	The KTPCI consists of two tests: "The first measure is based upon the rationale that the individual has a psychological self, whose structures have incorporated creative and noncreative ways of behaving. The purpose of this measure is to present verbal stimuli to trigger those subselves that would yield an index of the individual's disposition or motivation to function in creative ways. The second measure is based upon the rationale that creativity is reflected in the personality characteristics of the individual, in the kind of thinking strategies he employs, and in the products that emerge as a result of his creative strivings" (Khatena, 1977, p. 517).	The PCA consists of two subtests, Drawing and Categories, and two rating scales, Home and School. According to the publisher's website (https://www.proedinc.com/Products/12245/pca-profile-of-creative-abilities.aspx), the PCA is based on two theories of creativity: Guildford's (1959) Structure of Intellect, and Amabile's (1996) Componential Model of Creativity.
Internal model	The first test, *What kind of person are you?*, consists of five components: acceptance of authority,	Guilford's model of the intellect posits six major creative abilities: sensitivity to problems, fluency,

	Khatena-Torrance Creative Perception Inventory (KTPCI)	Profile of Creative Abilities (PCA)
	self-confidence, inquisitiveness, awareness of others, and disciplined imagination. The second test, *Something about myself*, consists of six components: environmental sensitivity, initiative, self-strength, intellectuality, individuality, and artistry.	flexibility, originality, redefinition, and penetration. Amabile's model of creativity consists of three basic components: domain-relevant skills, creativity-relevant processes, and intrinsic-task motivation.
Operationalization	For the first test, indicators include: courageous in convictions, nonconforming, courteous, socially well-adjusted, self-assertive, adventurous, persistent, energetic, and preferring complex tasks. For the second test, indicators include: openness to others' ideas, producing new products, resourcefulness, imagination, preference for working alone, self-starter, and willingness to take risks.	For Guilford's model, indicators include: drawing "a picture that no one else would think of," scored for sensitivity (number of new elements), originality (uniqueness of picture), redefinition (orientation of the picture), and penetration (respondent can see more than just what's on the surface); naming categories, scored for fluency (number of responses) and flexibility (number of categories). For Amabile's model, how often creative skills are exhibited.
Sample items	For the first test, the respondent chooses between creative and noncreative options: Feels strong emotions/ Reserved Fault finding/Popular. For the second test, the respondent determines if stated characteristics apply to him/her: I am resourceful. I have invented a new product. I can spot the source of a problem and define it.	"Draw a picture that no one else would think of." "From 20 animal pictures and 20 shapes, form categories of at least three objects, name as many categories as possible."

In their construct definition, the KTPCI views creativity as a personality character-istic. By contrast, the PCA views creativity as an intellectual ability. This leads to a series of personality components for the KTPCI's internal model and a series of intellectual abilities in the PCA's. Operationalizing each component then results in two very different tests.

6.7 TEST SPECIFICATION ISSUES

The last step before item writing begins is to use the purpose statement, construct map, internal and external models, and construct operationalization to develop test specifications. These include decisions about any external and internal issues that have not yet been made and a blueprint for the design of the test. In large-scale testing organizations, professional item writers work from these specifications. In small-scale or individual test development projects, where a single author or small team is completing all the steps, it is still a good idea to develop specifications to ensure that the test is developed soundly and to help convince potential test users of the validity of score interpretations.

Decisions about specification issues have been mentioned already (see Section 6.2 and Chapter 5). If not already made, such decisions need to be made at this point. Several issues that are external to the test include:

- *Target population:* What is the intended population of respondents? What is their reading level? Do they have special needs that impact their participation?

- *Time Constraints:* How much time is available for respondents? Longer tests will generally be more reliable (see Chapter 4), but greater length can adversely impact response rates and induce respondent fatigue. Additionally, some tests may have to fit within an institutional structure.

- *Administration method:* Will tests be group or individually administered? Will they be administered by computer, paper/pencil, or both? Where will they be administered, at a specific location or one of the respondent's choosing? Is security a concern?

Other decisions are internal to the test. These include:

- *Test content:* Important content by now is determined by the construct map and internal model, but other questions remain. What is the intended dimensionality of the test, i.e., will there be a single composite score, subscores, or multiple independent scores? How will content be distributed across the different components of the internal model? What is the tradeoff between breadth and depth of coverage of the content areas?

- *Item types and characteristics:* What item formats will be used? Can items be scored objectively or are human raters required? What range of difficulty or location on the construct continuum is desired, spread over a wide range or targeted to a specific point or narrow range? Given the response times for different item formats, how many items of each format are desired? Do items need to be administered in a preset order, administered adaptively, or administered in random order?

- *Scoring criteria and procedures:* Are items to be scored dichotomously or polytomously? Will partial credit scoring be allowed for some items? Do some items need to be weighted in their scoring? If human raters are required, what training methods will be implemented?

The answers to these questions largely derive from the purpose statement and intended uses of the test.

6.8 TEST BLUEPRINTS

All of the work done so far leads directly to the development of a test blueprint, sometimes called a table of specifications. Explicit blueprints tend to be found more often for tests measuring cognitive constructs, particularly educational achievement, but they should be prepared for all tests. Its basic form is a two-way table (Millman & Greene, 1989), in which one axis lists the content areas, as specified in the internal model. The other axis indicates a desired level of cognitive processing.

6.8.1 Content Dimension

Some test blueprints consist of a listing of content areas along with numbers or percentages of items from each area. An example of this type of blueprint is shown in Figures 6.7 and 6.8 for the 2018 NAEP US History Assessment (https://www.nagb. gov/content/dam/nagb/en/documents/publications/frameworks/history/2018-history-framework.pdf). Content for this assessment is a combination of historical themes crossed with historical periods. The figures show percentages of items devoted to each theme and period for the three grade levels that are measured. Three item formats are used: multiple-choice, short, and extended constructed response. Test specifications in

FIGURE 6.7 ● Blueprint for Historical Themes for the 2018 NAEP US History Assessment

Themes grade levels	Change and continuity in American democracy: ideas, institutions, events, key figures, and controversies	The gathering and interactions of peoples, cultures, and ideas	Economic and technological changes and their relationship to society, ideas, and the environment	The changing role of America in the world
Grade 4	25%	35%	25%	15%
Grade 8	30%	30%	20%	20%
Grade 12	25%	25%	25%	25%

FIGURE 6.8 ● Blueprint for Historical Periods for the 2018 NAEP US History Assessment

Periods grade levels	Beginnings–1607	1607–1763	1763–1815	1801–1861	1850–1877	1865–1920	1914–1945	1945–Present
Grade 4	20%	15%	15%	15%	10%	5%	5%	15%
Grade 8	5%	10%	20%	15%	20%	10%	10%	10%
Grade 12	5%	10%	15%	10%	10%	15%	15%	20%

the *Framework* (NAGB, 2018) indicate percentages of each type of item format. Implicit in this blueprint is the idea that each item represents one and only one theme/period content area.

Figure 6.9 shows two sample items from the Change and Continuity in American Democracy theme during the Expansion and Reform Period (1801–1861) (https:// nces.ed.gov/NationsReportCard/nqt/Search#). You can see that the second item is more difficult than the first item, and it measures different cognitive skills. In fact, the NAEP Frameworks address how they want each content to be measured, that is, what cognitive skills are to be measured. The first sample item measures the content at a level called Historical Knowledge and Perspective while the second item is measured at a level called Historical Analysis and Interpretation. Without this distinction, it can be easy for test developers to focus on recall of facts when measuring higher level thinking skills is desired for at least some percentage of the items. For this reason, I

FIGURE 6.9 ● Sample Item From the 2018 NAEP US History Assessment. *Note:* These items are from the 2006 US History Assessment, but the framework is essentially unchanged in the 2018 version.

Question ID: 2006-8H7 #5 H057601

Sojourner Truth said these words in 1852:

I hears talk about the constitution and rights of man. I come up and I takes hold of this constitution. It looks mighty big. And I feels for my rights, but they not there.

What did Sojourner Truth want to communicate with her words?

    A. Poor people did not know what was written in the constitution.
    B. African Americans were not allowed to read the constitution.
    C. The constitution did not talk about the rights of African Americans.
    D. The constitution needed to talk about the rights of Native Americans.

The correct answer is:

    C. The constitution did not talk about the rights of African Americans.

Question ID: 2006-8H8 #8 H034702:

Question refers to the excerpt from the speech below.

. . . we here highly resolve that these dead shall not have died in vain; that this nation, under god, shall have a new birth of freedom; and that government of the people, by the people, for the people, shall not perish from the earth.

— Abraham Lincoln's Gettysburg Address, 1863

Why did Lincoln think that the nation was in danger?

strongly recommend that a test blueprint include desired process levels for each content area.

6.8.2 Process Dimension

Process levels indicate the intended cognitive skills or processes at which the content areas are to be measured. A number of process models have been proposed and used in test blueprints. One of the most popular process models is Bloom's taxonomy for the cognitive domain (Bloom, Englehart, Furst, Hill, & Krathwohl, 1956). The six levels, knowledge, comprehension, application, analysis, synthesis, and evaluation, range from simple recall (knowledge) to a high-level thinking skill (evaluation). An example of a blueprint that uses Bloom's taxonomy is shown in Figure 6.10 from the 2002 Series GED Social Studies Test (GED Testing Service, 2009). The test consisted of 50 multiple-choice items in five content areas and four of Bloom's process levels. The numbers inside the table indicated the number of multiple-choice items for each content/process combination. Again, it is important to note that these two-dimensional blueprints imply that each item measures a single content/process level combination.

Several more recently developed tests, including NAEP and the current GED Tests, may have items that measure more than one content area and/or technology-enhanced item formats that may require more than one cognitive process level.

FIGURE 6.10 ⬢ Blueprints for 2002 Series GED Test for Social Studies

Specifications for the social studies test: Numbers of items, by item content and cognitive level

Item content	Cognitive levels			
	Comprehension 20% (10 items)	Application 20% (10 items)	Analysis 40% (20 items)	Evaluation 20% (10 items)
History: National 26% (13 items)	3	2	6	2
History: World 14% (7 items)	1	2	3	1
Geography 16% (8 items)	1/1	1/1	2/0	1/1
Economics 20% (10 items)	1/1	1/0	4/1	1/1
Civics and Government 24% (12 items)	1/1	2/1	3/1	2/1

Note: The number to the left of the slash (/) indicates the number of items in an operational form that must represent a global perspective. The number on the right represents the number of items that must represent a specific US (or Canadian) perspective.

For these, numbers or percentages of items in each content category or process level are specified without the content/process combinations. For example, the 2010 NAEP Geography Framework (NAGB, 2010) lists, for each grade level, the percentage of items of each format type that covers each of three content dimensions and each of three cognitive process levels, but specific combinations can vary to some degree across forms.

There are models other than Bloom's for specifying process levels. The 2019 NAEP Reading assessment uses three process levels: locate and recall, integrate and interpret, and critique and evaluate. A number of large-scale testing programs, including the current edition of the GED Tests, use Webb's Depth of Knowledge model (1997). This model posits four levels: recall and reproduction, skills and concepts, short-term strategic thinking, and expanded thinking.

In my experience, process levels are rarely defined for tests measuring noncognitive constructs. And yet, I argue that process levels are equally important for validating scores from tests of noncognitive constructs because many constructs are complex and operate at different levels. Consider, for example, a test that measures one's attitude toward abortion. Some respondents' views may be determined by women's health issues or practical concerns. Other respondents may view abortion in moral or religious terms. If a test is developed that addresses only one level, say health issues only, it may well mismeasure individuals who see abortion primarily as a moral issue.

One model that addresses noncognitive process levels is Krathwohl and Bloom's taxonomy for the affective domain (Krathwohl, Bloom, & Masia, 1973). The five levels of this model are shown in Table 6.3, along with examples. In general, the levels progress from concrete to abstract and from external to internal. The examples correspond to a test measuring job satisfaction. This taxonomy works for many noncognitive constructs, but the test developer may find a need for a different model, one that may need to be created.

Many test developers find specifying process levels to be particularly difficult. In this case, one way to proceed is to examine the operationalization of the construct and any potential indicators. They may suggest a breakdown into process levels. For example, for a test measuring "social capital," potential indicators could be organized around individual versus community support. A test measuring "connectedness to nature"

TABLE 6.3 ⬡ Levels of the Krathwohl/Bloom Affective Taxonomy		
Level	**Descriptor**	**Examples**
Receiving	Awareness of an aspect of the construct	All jobs are the same to me. My job is routine. I do the same thing every day.
Responding	Reaction to an aspect of the construct	I find pleasure in the work that I do. When my supervisor gives me a task, I try to find the fastest way to finish it.
Valuing	The worth a respondent places on an aspect of the construct.	I work hard to meet the company's deadlines. My coworkers can depend on me.
Organization	Prioritizing values and resolving conflicts between them	I refuse to follow a direction that violates my religious views. If offered a promotion, the type of work that I will do is more important than the increase in pay.
Characterization	An organized value system that governs behavior	It is important that the work I do benefits society. I would not take a job in a company that harms the environment. My work needs to be fulfilling.

might find a distinction between concrete (feeling and listening) and abstract (beliefs). Or, a test measuring "risk from adverse childhood experiences" could have indicators based on individual, family, and community experiences. The importance of specifying these levels is to ensure that the test developer makes an intentional decision on what levels to tap into in order to validly measure individuals on the construct.

6.9 CHAPTER SUMMARY

This chapter outlined a series of steps to be undertaken before item writing begins. The series progresses from a general purpose statement to test specifications. By working from general to specific, every aspect of development will line up to support the purpose and intended uses of the test. In the next chapter, we turn (finally) to item writing, but the steps outlined in this chapter will ensure that the resulting set of items reflects the developer's intention and supports test score validity.

6.10 EXERCISES AND ACTIVITIES

Test Development Project

For the construct you identified in Chapter 1 (or maybe now there is another one you would prefer to measure), complete the following steps:

1. Write a single statement of purpose and intended uses.

2. Create a construct map.

3. Develop an internal model.

4. Develop an external relationship model.

5. Operationalize the construct.

6. Prepare a test blueprint.

FURTHER READING

Millman, J., & Greene, J. (1989). The specification and development of tests of achievement and ability. In R. L. Linn (Ed.), *Educational measurement* (3rd ed., pp. 335–366). New York, NY: American Council on Education and Macmillan.

Schmeiser, C. B., & Welch, C. J. (2006). Test development. In R. L. Brennan (Ed.), *Educational measurement* (4th ed., pp. 307–353). Westport, CT: Praeger.

REFERENCES

Amabile, T. M. (1996). *Creativity in context*. Boulder, CO: Westview Press.

Bandura, A. (1986). *Social foundations of thought and action: A social cognitive theory*. Englewood Cliffs, NJ: Prentice Hall.

Bearss, K., Taylor, C. A., Aman, M. G., Whittemore, R., Lecavalier, L., Miller, J., ... Scahill, L. (2016). Using qualitative methods to guide scale development for anxiety in youth with autism spectrum disorder. *Autism*, 20(6), 663–672.

Bloom, B. S., Englehart, M. D., Furst, E. J., Hill, W. H., & Krathwohl, D. R. (1956). *Taxonomy of educational objectives: The classification of educational goals. Handbook I: Cognitive domain.* New York, NY: David McKay.

Bodenhorn, N., & Skaggs, G. (2005). Development of the school counselor self-efficacy scale. *Measurement and Evaluation in Counseling and Development*, 38(1), 14–28.

Boyatzis, R., Goleman, D., & Rhee, K. (2000). Clustering competence in emotional intelligence: Insights from the emotional competence inventory (ECI). In R. Bar-On & J. D. A. Parker (Eds.), *Handbook of emotional intelligence*. San Francisco, CA: Jossey-Bass.

Brackett, M. A., & Salovey, P. (2006). Measuring emotional intelligence with the Mayer-Salovey-Caruso Emotional Intelligence Test (MSCEIT). *Psicothema*, 18(Suppl.), 34–41.

Cherniss, G., & Goleman, D. (Eds.). (2001). *The emotionally intelligent workplace*. San Francisco, CA: Jossey-Bass.

Duckworth, A. L., Peterson, C., Matthews, M. D., & Kelly, D. R. (2007). Grit: Perseverance and passion for long-term goals. *Journal of Personality and Social Psychology*, 92(6), 1087–1101.

GED Testing Service. (2009). *Technical manual: 2002 series GED tests*. Washington, DC: American Council on Education.

GED Testing Service. (2018). *Technical manual: GED test* (Updated 2018 Edition). Bloomington, MN: Author.

Goleman, D. (1998). *Working with emotional intelligence*. New York, NY: Bantam.

Guilford, J. P. (1959). Three faces of intellect. *American Psychologist*, 14, 469–479.

Jones, B. D. (2009). Motivating students to engage in learning: The MUSIC Model of academic motivation. *International Journal of Teaching and Learning in Higher Education*, 21(2), 272–285.

Jones, B. D., & Skaggs, G. (2016) Measuring students' motivation: Validity evidence for the *MUSIC Model of Academic Motivation Inventory. International Journal for the Scholarship of Teaching and Learning*, 10(1), Article 7.

Khatena, J. (1977). The Khatena-Torrance Creative Perception Inventory for identification diagnosis facilitation and research. *The Gifted Child Quarterly*, 21(4), 517–525.

Khatena, J., & Torrance, E. P. (1976). *Manual for Khatena-Torrance creative perception inventory*. Chicago, IL: Stoelting.

Krathwohl, D. R., Bloom, B. S., & Masia, B. B. (1973). *Taxonomy of educational objectives, the classification of educational goals, Handbook II: Affective domain*. New York, NY: David McKay Co., Inc.

Lake, C. J., Gopalkrishnan, P., Sliter, M. T., & Withrow, S. (2010). The job descriptive index: Newly updated and available for download. *The Industrial-Organizational Psychologist*, 48(1), 47–49.

Mayer, J. D., & Salovey, P. (1997). What is emotional intelligence? In D. J. Sluyter (Ed.), *Emotional development and emotional intelligence: Educational implications* (pp. 3–34). New York, NY: Basic Books.

Mayer, J. D., Salovey, P., Caruso, D. R., & Sitarenios, G. (2003). Measuring emotional intelligence with the MSCEIT V2.0. *Emotion*, 3, 97–105.

Mayer, J. D., Caruso, D. R., & Salovey, P. (2016). The ability model of emotional intelligence: Principles and updates. *Emotion Review*, 1–11.

Millman, J., & Greene, J. (1989). The specification and development of tests of achievement and ability. In R. L. Linn (Ed.). *Educational measurement* (3rd ed., pp. 335–366). New York, NY: American Council on Education and Macmillan.

National Assessment Governing Board. (2010). *Geography framework for the 2010 National Assessment of Educational Progress*. Washington, DC: Author.

National Assessment Governing Board. (2018). *U.S. History Framework for the 2018 National Assessment of Educational Progress*. Washington, DC: Author.

Ryser, G. R., & McConnell, K. (2003). *Scales for identifying gifted students*. Waco, TX: Prufrock Press.

Sheehan, K. M. (1997). A tree-based approach to proficiency scaling and diagnostic assessment. *Journal of Educational Measurement*, 34(4), 333–352.

Webb, N. (1997). *Criteria for alignment of expectations and assessments on mathematics and science education. Research Monograph Number 6*. Washington, DC: CCSSO.

Wilson, M. (2005). *Constructing measures: An item response modeling approach*. Mahwah, NJ: Erlbaum.

Wolfe, E. W., & Smith, E. V. (2007). Instrument development tools and activities for measure validation using Rasch models: Part I—Instrument development tools. *Journal of Applied Measurement*, 8(1), 1–27.

7

ITEM WRITING AND SCORING

Only after you have completed the steps outlined in the previous chapter—statement of purpose, construct map, internal and external models, and test specifications—is it safe to write items. There are dozens of item types, and it is impossible to discuss all of them is detail. Instead, in this chapter, I offer guidance on writing the most frequently used types:

- Multiple-choice

- Constructed response

- Essay

- Performance

- Likert

7.1 ITEMS AND SCORING MODELS

At the outset, it is important to define the term *item* and to distinguish it from a question. The NCME website contains a glossary (https://www.ncme.org/resources/glossary), in which an item is defined as "a statement, question, exercise, or task on a test for which the test taker is to select or construct a response, or perform a task." This definition implies that a question is a type of item, and not all items ask respondents to answer a question.

Additionally, there is a scoring model attached to an item. A scoring model is a set of rules for interpreting item responses and assigning numerical scores. Scoring models can indicate whether we assign "partial credit" to some responses, use holistic or analytic scoring procedures, or differentially weight the responses of some items over others. The item scores themselves can be considered to be measurements at one of the four levels proposed by Stevens (1946):

Nominal: item scores represent categories

Ordinal: item scores represent rankings

Interval: item scores are equal interval

Ratio: item scores are equal interval with a true zero.

The general English definition of the noun "item" goes something like this: an item "is a distinct part in an enumeration, account, or series" (Merriam-Webster's Collegiate Dictionary, 11th edition, 2014). This definition then specifies another important distinction from a question, namely, that an item is part of a series of items. Most tests are composed of several items, and a score is created by summarizing in some fashion the scores of the items.

7.2 ITEM FORMATS USED MOSTLY FOR COGNITIVE CONSTRUCTS

In this section, I will discuss item types that are typically used to measure cognitive constructs, such as knowledge, skill, reasoning, or response processes. These are used most often for tests, such as for measuring achievement and abilities, credentialing, and personnel selection and placement. This does not mean that they cannot be used to measure noncognitive constructs, but other item types are more popular for those constructs.

7.2.1 Multiple-Choice Items

Nearly all of us have encountered multiple-choice items, on standardized achievement tests, college admissions exams, classroom tests, or certification or licensure exams. For many of us, the experience was not fun and often anxiety provoking. At the same time, we have occasionally faced flawed multiple-choice items in which the correct answer is given away or the intended correct answer is confusing. Multiple-choice items are often thought to be useful only for measuring low-level thinking and knowledge skills. This tends to be true, but not always. Higher-level skills can often be measured by multiple-choice items, and some low-level skills cannot. For example, counting from 1 to 10 is a frequent first grade instructional objective, but asking a student to identify the next number after, say 7 with four answer choices, is not the same as counting.

First, though, some terminology is used by psychometricians to describe the parts of a multiple-choice item. Figure 7.1 shows an item from a test measuring the ability to appreciate humor (Shammi & Stuss, 1999). Although this test at first glance appears to be measuring a personality construct, Shammi and Stuss actually investigated cognitive processes, such as working memory, verbal abstraction ability, and the ability to focus on details, thought to be necessary for a sense of humor. In this item, the beginning of the joke is called the *stem*. The respondent is asked to select the

FIGURE 7.1 ● Example of a Multiple-Choice Item and Component Parts

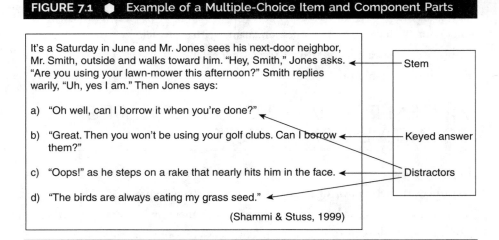

It's a Saturday in June and Mr. Jones sees his next-door neighbor, Mr. Smith, outside and walks toward him. "Hey, Smith," Jones asks. "Are you using your lawn-mower this afternoon?" Smith replies warily, "Uh, yes I am." Then Jones says: ← Stem

a) "Oh well, can I borrow it when you're done?"

b) "Great. Then you won't be using your golf clubs. Can I borrow them?" ← Keyed answer

c) "Oops!" as he steps on a rake that nearly hits him in the face. ← Distractors

d) "The birds are always eating my grass seed."

(Shammi & Stuss, 1999)

answer choice that is the funniest, that is, what we would call the punch line. Here, that's answer choice (b). This is the *correct* or *keyed answer*. The incorrect answers, called *distractors*, are hopefully somewhat plausible but still incorrect. Here, answer choice (a) follows from the stem, but it's not funny. Answer choice (c) might be funny, but it has no relationship to the stem. Answer choice (d) is neither funny nor has anything to do with the stem.

Many professional item writers will tell you that writing high-quality multiple-choice items is an art form and a difficult one at that. It can easily take an entire day to write one or two good items. The most difficult part of writing the items is formulating the distractors. If they are obviously incorrect, no one will select them. For example, consider the two items in Figure 7.2. They have the same stem but different distractors. The item on the left is much more difficult because the distractors on the item to the right are implausible.

Fortunately, there is a large body of research on how to write multiple-choice items, and just as fortunately, Haladyna, Downing, and Rodriguez (2002) compiled an exhaustive review of that research. What follows are 31 multiple-choice guidelines from that article. Admittedly, it is a very difficult task to write items with all 31 guidelines in mind. My personal recommendation is to simply compose (possibly lousy) first drafts of items, just to get the content down, and then use the guidelines as a checklist for revision. If you have met all of the guidelines, chances are that you have an item of at least adequate technical quality. The guidelines are organized (by Haladyna et al.) into major subcategories. Many of them are self-evident. I will make a few comments about some of them.

1. *Each item should reflect specific content and single specific behavior.* This guideline is absolutely essential. Every item must be located somewhere within the test blueprint. This is necessary to support Messick's content validity evidence or Kane's generalization inference.

FIGURE 7.2 ● Different Distractors Affect an Item's Difficulty

Who was Grover Cleveland's Vice President?	Who was Grover Cleveland's Vice President?
a) Elbridge Gerry	a) Daffy Duck
b) William Wheeler	b) Luke Skywalker
c) Thomas Hendricks	c) Thomas Hendricks
d) Charles Curtis	d) Julius Caesar

Content

1. Each item should reflect specific content and single specific behavior.

2. Focus on important content.

3. Use novel material or paraphrased language from the curriculum.

4. Keep item content independent from other items.

5. Avoid over specific and over general content.

6. Avoid opinion-based items.

7. Avoid trick items.

8. Keep vocabulary simple.

---

4. *Keep item content independent from other items.* In other words, the answer to one item should not depend on the answer to a previous item, as in "Based on your answer to item 1, what is…." The validity problem with this is that a respondent can understand the knowledge or skills of the later item but have it scored incorrectly because of the response to the previous item. Furthermore, if a latent variable measurement model, such as the Rasch model, is used to score the test, one of its key assumptions, that item responses are independent of each other, would be violated.

8. *Keep vocabulary simple.* It is important to keep the reading level of the target population in mind. Aim for vocabulary that nearly all respondents will understand.

Format

9. Use question, completion, and best answer versions of MC items, alternative choice, True-False, matching, and context-dependent item formats. *Avoid* complex MC format.

10. Format the response options vertically.

Style

11. Edit and proof items.

12. Use correct grammar, punctuation, capitalization, and spelling.

13. Minimize reading required for each item.

9. ***Avoid*** *complex MC format.* These are often referred to as Type K items. They are often used when there is more than one answer that is deemed correct. For example:

Which of the following are descriptive statistics that measure central tendency?

1. Mean

2. Median

3. Mode

4. Standard deviation

5. Correlation coefficient

    A. 1, 2, and 3

    B. 1 only

    C. 3 and 4

    D. 2, 3, and 5

    E. 4 and 5

In a review of research on Type K items, Albanese (1993) found that they decrease reliability and are more likely to contain content flaws. Furthermore, they can be confusing to respondents.

Stems

14. Ensure that directions in stem are clear.

15. Include the central idea in the stem instead of the response choices.

16. Avoid excessive verbiage.

17. Avoid **NOT** or **EXCEPT**. When used, they should be capped and bolded.

---

15. *Include the central idea in the stem instead of the response choices.* Consider this item:

Politics

A. is a branch of philosophy.

B. is the most popular genre of nonfiction.

C. seeks to understand decision-making by governments.

> The item can be confusing to respondents because the knowledge that the item intends to measure is not clear. An clearer alternative would be "Understanding decision-making by governments is a focus of which profession?"

16. *Avoid excessive verbiage.* Consider this item:

Virginia Tech

A. is a land-grant university located in Southwest Virginia.

B. is a land-grant university affiliated with the Southeastern Conference.

C. is a land-grant university with the nation's largest enrollment.

D. is a land-grant university whose alumni include the current U S President.

> This item requires the respondent to read the same phrase four times. A better approach would be to put that phrase, "is a land-grant university," in the stem. In general, reduce the reading load as much as possible.

Options

18. Three options are adequate, but more can be included.

19. Verify that there is only one correct answer.

20. Vary location of correct option.

21. Place options in logical or numerical order.

22. Keep choices independent and nonoverlapping.

23. Keep choices homogeneous in content and grammatical structure.

24. Keep length of choices about equal.

25. Use NONE OF THE ABOVE carefully.

26. Avoid ALL OF THE ABOVE.

27. Phrase choices positively (avoid NOT).

28. Avoid giving clues to the correct option.

   a. Specific determiners (always, never, completely, absolutely).

   b. Words identical or resembling those in the stem.

   c. Grammatical inconsistencies.

   d. Conspicuous correct choice.

   e. Pairs or triplets of options that clue correct choices.

   f. Implausible options.

29. Make all distracters plausible.

30. Use typical errors for distracters.

31. Use humor carefully.

---

24. *Keep length of choices about equal.* I was once able to nearly pass a certification exam for accountants involved with large defense contracts simply by selecting the longest answer choice. This is a common test-taking strategy.

25. *Use NONE OF THE ABOVE carefully.* This answer choice can be a dumping ground for respondents who do not know the correct answer. As a result, the item can appear easier than its material would suggest. Consider this variation on an earlier sample item:

Who was Grover Cleveland's Vice President?

   a. Daffy Duck

   b. Luke Skywalker

   c. Julius Caesar

   d. None of the above

   This item is still an easy item to answer correctly, even when the respondent does not know the actual answer to the question.

26. *Avoid ALL OF THE ABOVE.* This answer choice is often used when trying to measure content with more than one correct choice. For example:

Which of the following is a major measurement theory paradigm?

A.   Classical Test Theory

B.   Item Response Theory

C.   Rasch Measurement Theory

D.   All of the above

While this is an improvement over the Type K format, research has shown that having items with this response choice reduces test reliability and that this choice, like None of the Above, can become a dumping ground for respondents who are unsure of the correct answer. For instance, if a respondent knows that A and B are correct but is unsure about C, then D has to be the correct answer.

7.2.2 Alternate Multiple-Choice Formats

Haladyna et al. (2002) list several alternate formats in which the respondent selects an answer choice. These are shown in Table 7.1.

In summary, my strong recommendation is to write rough drafts of items first, without serious consideration of their quality, and then to use these guidelines to revise them and improve their quality. If you have met all 31 guidelines, then you probably have a reasonably good item.

7.2.3 Open-Ended Item Formats

There are a number of item formats that require the respondent to supply an answer. Additionally, a human being (or computer) is required to score them. These formats include the following:

- Constructed response: A short written answer, such as a sentence or two, is required.

- Extended constructed response: A longer written response, such as a paragraph or two, is required.

TABLE 7.1 ● Alternate Type of Multiple-Choice Item Formats		
Format	**Description**	**Comments**
Alternate choice	Contains a stem and two choices	This can be used when there is only one plausible distractor.
True-false	An alternate-choice item with the choices being true/false, yes/no, correct/incorrect, etc.	These can be difficult to write. A single questionable word or punctuation mark can make the stem False.
Multiple true-false	Stem with multiple options. Respondent is asked to "Mark all that apply" or "Mark T if true, F if false."	This can be a reasonable alternative to Type K and All or None of the above answer choices.
Matching	Three to 12 options with a group of stems.	Little research has been completed on its properties.
Context-dependent Items	A stimulus, such as a text passage, picture, or graphic followed by a series of multiple-choice items connected to the stimulus.	This format can be useful for measuring higher-level thinking skills, but item responses can be dependent.

- Essay: A coherent longer written response, often an expository or persuasive text, is required.

- Performance assessment: These can include musical or artistic performances, medical procedures, or other performances that are observed and rated.

- Manuscript, project, or portfolio: The most extensive format, requires a large-scale submission, completed over a time frame.

Much of the interest in using these formats on a large-scale basis comes from a movement beginning in the 1980s and 1990s toward *authentic assessment*. There was a growing consensus among educators that relying strictly on multiple-choice items limited the breadth and depth of the knowledge, skills, and processes that educators would like to measure. As a result, research and methods for open-ended item formats intensified. Much of the focus of this research was devoted to the scoring of items and the training of raters, rather than how to write the items, which is often fairly easy (e.g., "What are the major causes of the US Civil War?"). For any of these formats to be used on a large-scale basis, there must be a *scoring rubric* that translates item responses into item scores.

7.2.3.1 Scoring Rubrics

Figure 7.3 shows a constructed-response item from the 2005 NAEP Science along with its scoring rubric, sample scored responses, and an explanation of the scoring.

FIGURE 7.3 ⬡ Constructed-Response Item From 2005 NAEP Science

There are many different kinds of human-made satellites orbiting the Earth. List three things that these satellites are used for.

(NAEP Science, 2005)

Score and Description

2 Complete   Student lists three ways that satellites are used.

1 Partial   Student lists one or two ways that satellites are used.

0 Unsatisfactory/Incorrect   Student does not list any correct ways satellites are used.

Sample Responses:

Complete:

> ① is for your television, ② weather to tell if there's a storm coming, ③ landsat to help make maps to show the elevation.

Partial:

> They are used to predict the weather, watch and take pictures of space so humans can learn about space, and to help know when storms will come.

> When you watch television, they use satellites.

Unsatisfactory/Incorrect:

> The satellites are used for energy. It is also used for electricity and for help.

The first response provides two correct uses of satellites; it discusses weather predictions and a specific way satellites can provide information to study space. The second response provides one correct use of satellites.

You will note that the rubric is very specific. In the development of scoring rubric methodology, great attention was placed on scoring reliability. Since human raters were doing the scoring, it was important to be able to design rubrics and train raters so that they would agree with each other to a great extent.

By contrast, Figure 7.4 shows an example of an extended constructed-response item from the 2001 NAEP Geography, along with the scoring rubric. It's apparent that a much more extensive written response is called for in this format, reflected in the greater number of score points in the rubric. And yet, the scoring is still very specific, and raters can score this item very reliably.

Figure 7.5 shows a scoring rubric for an early version of the GED Writing Test. This test required an expository essay on a topic supplied by the test administrator. These score points are much less specific than those for the constructed-response items. This is an example of *holistic* scoring, in which the score points are based on a combination of several factors. Here, the rubric shows that scores differ on a combination of organizational framework, support for major points, and the conventions of standard English. An alternative to holistic scoring is analytic scoring, in which separate scores could be obtained for each of the three factors described for holistic scoring.

7.2.3.2 Training Raters

Over the past three decades, a well-developed methodology has emerged for training individuals to reliably score items with open-ended formats. The process can be summarized as follows. First, after a scoring rubric has been created, "experts" (the author or subject matter experts) score a large number of answers. It's important here to have a variety of answers at each score point. During this process, some unexpected responses will emerge, and decisions will have to be made on how to score them. Eventually, enough responses will have been scored that novel responses are no longer found. Second, individuals who will score items operationally are trained on the rubric and provided with examples of responses at each score point and explanations for those scores. Third, raters are asked to score responses that have been previously scored by the experts. Any differences are discussed. This work continues until each rater has achieved a certain level of agreement with the experts.

FIGURE 7.4 ● Extended Constructed-Response Item and Scoring Rubric From 2001 NAEP Geography

The shift of the center of population in the United States, 1790–1990

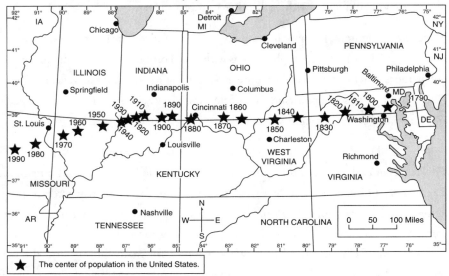

★ The center of population in the United States.

The map above shows the changes in the population center of the United States over a 200-year period of time. Identify and explain some important factors that contributed to the changes in the population center shown on the map.
(NAEP Geography, 2001)

Scoring rubric:

3 Complete	The response states or implies an understanding of the population trend shown on the map. The response explains at least two factors that significantly contributed to the westward movement (or southern movement, if explained correctly). TREND and two factors
2 Essential	The response states or implies an implicit understanding of the trend shown on the map AND the response explains one factor that significantly contributed to the westward movement. TREND and one factor
1 Partial	The response states or implies an implicit understanding of the trend shown on the map. The response does not explain any factors that significantly contributed to the westward movement OR gives at least one significant migration factor, but does not relate it to the westward trend. TREND or one factor
0 Inappropriate	The response does not address the trend shown in the map or give any acceptable reasons contributing to this trend, such as those in the list given. Unacceptable reasons might be such as, people are always moving.

FIGURE 7.5 ◉ Scoring Rubric for the GED Writing Test (1988 Series)

GED ESSAY SCORING GUIDE
Copyright (c) 1987, GED Testing Service

Appendix c

Papers will show <u>some or all</u> of the following characteristics.

Upper-half papers make clear a definite purpose, pursued with varying degrees of effectiveness. They also have a structure that shows evidence of some deliberate planning. The writer's control of the conventions of standard written English (spelling, punctuation, grammer, word choice,and sentence structure) range from fairly reliable at 4 to confident and accomplished at 6.

6   The <u>6 paper</u> offers sophisticated ideas within an organizational framework that is clear and appropriate for the topic. The supporting statements are particularly effective because of their substance,specificity,or illustrative quality. The writing is vivid and precise, although it may contain an occasional flaw in the conventions of standard English.

5   The <u>5 paper</u> is clearly organized with effective support for each of the writer's major points. While the wring offers substantive ideas, it lacks the fluency found in the 6 paper. Although there are some errors, the conventions of standard English are consistently under control.

4   The <u>4 paper</u> shows evidence of the writer's organizational plan. Support, though adequate, tends to be less extensive or effective than that found in the 5 paper. The writer generally observes the conventions of standard English. The errors that are present are not severe enough to interfere significantly with the writer's main purpose.

Lower-half papers either fail to convey a purpose sufficiently or lack one entirely. Consequently, their structure ranges from rudimentary at 3, to random at 2, to absent at 1. Control of the conventions of standard written English tends to follow this some gradient.

3   The <u>3 paper</u> usually shows some evidence of planning, although the development may be insufficient. The supporting statements may be limited to a listing or a repetition of ideas. The 3 paper often demonstrates repeated weaknesses in the conventions of standard English.

2   The <u>2 paper</u> is characterized by a marked lack of organization or inadequate support for ideas, The developement may be superficial or unfocused. Errors in the conventions of standard English may seriously interfere with the overall effectiveness of this paper.

1   The <u>1 paper</u> lacks purpose or development. The dominant feature is the absence of control of structure or the conventions of Standard English. The deficiencies are so severe that the writer's ideas are difficult or impossible to understand.

*   An asterisk code is reserved for papers that are blank, illegible, or written on a topic other than the one assigned. Because these papers cannot be scored, a writing skills Test composite score cannot be reported.   5/87

When raters are tasked with scoring open-ended items operationally, it is important to monitor their scores to determine if any rater effects have occurred. This can be done by having raters occasionally score previously scored responses. Rater effects include *leniency*, the tendency for raters to assign higher scores to the same responses over time, *severity*, the tendency to assign lower scores over time, and *centrality*, the tendency to assign middle scores over time. If such effects are observed in a rater, periodic retraining may be needed.

In small-scale instrument development efforts, large numbers of respondents' answers to open-ended items are not yet available. Some data may have been collected as part of a pilot test (discussed in the next chapter). Additionally, it may just be the instrument developer or the small development team that will score the responses. Is a formal rubric still needed? Absolutely! Documentation of the scoring process is a critical part of content evidence in the *Standards*/Messick validity framework and of the scoring inference in Kane's framework.

The developers should create a draft rubric that is as clear as possible. Then, when response data are available, the developers begin applying that rubric. Quite often, novel responses not anticipated by the developers appear, and a decision needs to be made on how to score them. Once finished, the developers should go back and check the scoring of all respondents to ensure consistency.

7.2.3.3 Interrater Reliability

Whenever there are items that require raters, it is important to investigate interrater reliability to ensure a close correspondence between individuals or computers who score such items. There are three main ways to evaluate interrater reliability: traditional reliability, agreement between raters, and generalizability.

Traditional Reliability. Suppose that you have an essay item on your test. The essay is scored on a 1–4 rubric by two raters, and the two scores are combined to yield an essay raw score. You could calculate a traditional reliability in one of two ways. First, scores from the two raters could simply be correlated and then adjusted using the Spearman–Brown formula. This procedure corresponds to a split-half reliability coefficient. Alternatively, coefficient alpha could be calculated by viewing the two sets of scores as a two-item test.

Agreement Between Raters. A second method looks at the proportion or percent agreement between raters. For example, for the essay scored by two raters, suppose that out of 107 respondents, the raters agreed on 9 essays scored 1, 54 scored 2, 22 scored 3, and 12 scored 4. Then, the proportion agreement is $(9 + 54 + 22 + 12)/107 = 0.907$, or 90.7 percent agreement. This sounds impressive, but there is a certain amount of chance agreement (i.e., if both raters randomly assigned essay scores according to their overall score distribution). As an extreme example, if two raters score a constructed response item 0 or 1, and they both score 90 percent of the items as 0, then there is a 0.81 chance proportion (0.90×0.90) agreement on a score of 0 and a 1 proportion chance agreement on a score of 0.01 (0.10×0.10), for a total of 0.82 chance proportion agreement. This means that there is no way to have less than 0.82 proportion chance agreement. One way to adjust for this problem is to calculate a statistic called Kappa:

$$\text{Kappa} = \frac{P_o - P_e}{1 - P_e} = \frac{0.907 - 0.363}{1 - 0.363} = 0.854 \qquad (7.1)$$

where P_o is the actual proportion agreement and P_e is the proportion of chance agreement. In this example, chance agreement is 0.363. Kappa is 0.854, which can be interpreted as proportion agreement controlling for chance agreement.

For validity evidence, I recommend providing both traditional and agreement interrater reliability evidence because they can contradict each other. Consider Table 7.2. Here, proportion agreement is 1.00, but a reliability coefficient (split-half and alpha give the same answer) is 0.00. Kappa is also 0.00. In Table 7.3, the opposite is true. Proportion agreement and kappa are both 0.00, but reliability is 1.00. Interrater reliability is strongly supported if proportion agreement and kappa and a reliability coefficient are both strong.

Generalizability. As mentioned in Chapter 4, generalizability theory is an outgrowth of CTT. It views persons responding to items as independent variables in a repeated measures experimental design. From this design, a generalizability coefficient can be

TABLE 7.2 ● Perfect Agreement But Zero Reliability

	P	F
P	0	0
F	0	100

TABLE 7.3 ● Zero Agreement But Perfect Reliability				
	1	**2**	**3**	**4**
1	0	25	0	0
2	0	0	25	0
3	0	0	0	25
4	0	0	0	0

calculated. With just items and persons, this coefficient will be equal to coefficient alpha. The power of generalizability is that other independent variables, such as raters, can be added to the design. Generalizability coefficients can be calculated for raters as well as items. Additionally, the design can be altered hypothetically to estimate what generalizability coefficients would be for different numbers of raters, items, and the number of items scored by each rater. As a result, an optimal test design (how many raters scoring how many items on how many different occasions) can be produced with a sufficient degree of reliability. The details of implementing generalizability are quite complex, and special software is needed to conduct the analyses. These include *GENOVA* (http://www.education.uiowa.edu/centers/casma/computer-programs#c074 8e48-f88c-6551-b2b8-ff00000648cd) and the R package *g* theory.

7.3 ITEM FORMATS USED MOSTLY FOR NONCOGNITIVE CONSTRUCTS

Among item formats that are primarily used to measure noncognitive constructs, such as personality or behavioral constructs or attitudes, Likert items (pronounced *Lĭk'ert*, not *Lyk'ert*) appear by far the most often. I will discuss this item format in some detail, then mention several other item formats.

7.3.1 Likert Items

A Likert item consists of a statement to which the respondent is given two or more answer choices. The respondent is asked to select the most appropriate answer choice. Conceptually, Likert items fit nicely into the construct map approach to defining the construct to be measured. For example, Figure 7.6 shows two Likert items that could appear on a test measuring a construct called "attitude toward access to abortion."

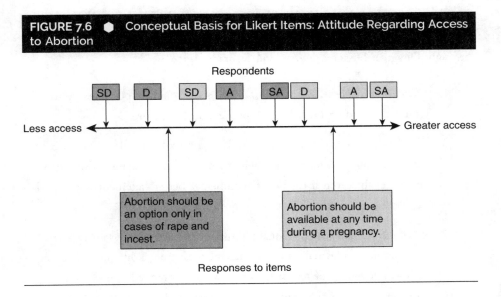

FIGURE 7.6 ⬣ Conceptual Basis for Likert Items: Attitude Regarding Access to Abortion

This construct can be visualized as a continuum between two extremes of greater or lesser access. The two items can be viewed as located at different points on this continuum. The statement "Abortion should be an option only in cases of rape and incest" rests at a point of lesser access than the statement "Abortion should be available at any time during a pregnancy." At the same time, each statement has four answer choices reflecting the degree of agreement or disagreement to the statement on the part of the respondent. These answer choices can also be located on the construct continuum, but there is no reason to believe that these answer choice locations are equally spaced. Usually, Likert items with four answer choices are scored 1–4 or 0–3, but these scores are ordinal data. Additionally, the answer choice locations can overlap. For instance, does Agree with the first statement indicate a greater or lesser access to abortion than Disagree to the second statement? In Chapter 9, we will look at Rasch measurement models that attempt to convert these ordinal scores into an equal interval scale.

7.3.2 Writing Likert Items

A first and necessary requirement is that every item can be located within the test blueprint. For writing high-quality Likert items, Wolfe and Smith (2007) offer a list of guidelines for writing. As was the case with multiple-choice items, I recommend writing rough drafts of items, then using the guidelines as a checklist. If all guidelines have been met, then there is a high likelihood that you have a reasonably good item. For the examples in the following guidelines, consider that the answer choices are: Strongly Disagree, Disagree, Agree, and Strongly Agree.

1. *Write simple, short, clear, direct statements.* As much as possible, try to reduce the reading load. Use simple sentence structure.

2. *Avoid references to the past.* "I felt sad on my sixth birthday." You are asking respondents to rely on their memory of an occasion, which may not be reliable even if they do remember. A better statement may be: "I feel sad on my birthday."

3. *Avoid factual statements.* "Donald Trump was elected President in 2016." Responding to a factual statement may be measuring a different construct, such as knowledge of recent history, than the intended one. A better statement may be: "Donald Trump deserved to be elected President in 2016."

4. *Avoid absolutes.* "Requests for test results should always be granted." Very few things are always or never. A better statement may be: "Requests for test results should be granted," accompanied by answer choices such as Almost always, Frequently, etc.

5. *Avoid interpretative terms.* "I go to the movies regularly." "Regularly" can mean different things to different people, that is, whether the respondent goes to the movies daily, weekly, monthly, or some other regular interval. As a result, respondents who go to the movies with the same frequency could respond differently to this statement because they interpret "regularly" differently. A better statement may be: "I go to the movies about once a week," or "I go to the movies…" with answer choices indicating how often.

6. *Avoid double-barreled items.* "Teachers listen to students' problems, and students feel that they can talk to their teachers about things that are bothering them." Respondents can agree with the first part of the statement but not the second, or vice versa. A better version would be to divide this statement into two separate items.

7. *Avoid slang.* "It's important to beat one's face before a job interview." Some respondents may take "beat" literally. This is also a slang expression that may fade from use. A better version may be: "It's important to look one's best for a job interview."

8. *Avoid suggesting an answer.* "I have great confidence in the country's medical industry leaders." This is an item that appeared in a *Time* article (9/3-10/2018). The article reported that only 34 percent of respondents agreed with this statement, suggesting a lack of confidence. The problem with the statement is the adjective "great." Respondents can have some degree of confidence but yet disagree with the statement because it's not great confidence. A better version may be: "I have confidence in the country's medical industry leaders."

9. *Avoid extreme statements.* "Shoplifters should be shot before a firing squad." This statement is so extreme that no respondent (hopefully) will agree to it, even ones who believe in strong penalties for breaking the law. In general, you want some degree of variation in responses to an item. An item where everyone answers the same way doesn't contribute to distinguishing between respondents. A better version may be: "Shoplifters should be required to pay for the goods they have stolen."

10. *Avoid making statements negative.* "I am not in favor of legalizing marijuana use." It is easy for respondents to miss the word *not*. It is tempting in Likert scales to have statements worded in the opposite direction to most other items in order to reduce a *response set*, or the tendency for respondents to maintain responding in a consistent way, say agreeing to all statements without carefully reading them (see below). But simply inserting the word *not* into a statement doesn't solve the problem. A better version may be: "I believe marijuana use should continue to be illegal."

11. *Make sure the reading level is appropriate.* "I consider myself to be a facetious person." If your target audience has a high degree of education, this statement may work just fine. But why not err on the side of easier reading? A better version may be: "I consider myself to be a funny person."

12. *The response should be logically consistent with the stem.* "I read for an hour every day." Answer choices about agreement or disagreement do not fit this statement. The answer choices should match the statement. A better version would be to have answer choices based on frequency: Almost always, Frequently, etc.

13. *Avoid statements that the respondent cannot answer.* "People in my community are honest." This statement actually appears on a test measuring school climate. The first problem with this statement is that respondents are left to define community, which could range from the respondent's neighborhood to his/her part of the country, or could refer to a social group (e.g., community of fellow musicians). A second and deeper problem is that the respondent cannot possibly know whether people are being honest some or all of the time. A better version may be: "Most of my neighbors seem to be honest."

7.3.3 Likert Item Issues

Apart from writing high-quality statements, there are several other issues to consider when developing a test composed of Likert items. These include the answer choices, the number of answer choices, having a neutral category, and negatively worded items.

Common Answer Choices. By far, the most popular set of answer choices refer to the degree of agreement with a statement: Strongly Disagree, Disagree, Agree, and Strongly Agree. Another set of choices refer to frequency: Almost Never, Rarely, Sometimes, Frequently, Almost Always. Occasionally, answer choices reflect a degree of endorsement of a statement: Very Dissatisfied, Somewhat Dissatisfied, Somewhat Satisfied, and Very Satisfied. Another set of answer choices characterizes the degree to which the respondent identifies with a statement: Very much like me, Mostly like me, Somewhat like me, and Not much like me. A final set of answer choices refers to a degree of severity regarding a statement: Poor, Fair, Good, and Excellent.

Middle or Neutral Answer Choice. Many Likert scales contain a middle answer choice labeled Neutral, Neither/nor, or Undecided. For many statements, a respondent may truly be neutral. On the other hand, this middle category can also become a dumping ground for individuals who are reluctant to indicate a position or for individuals who do not know enough about the issue to take a position. Research on the usefulness of this option is mixed. There is some evidence to suggest that the middle category does not fit in the intended order of other response choices (Smith, Wakely, De Kruif, & Swartz, 2003), that is, neutral does not locate between Agree and Disagree. On the other hand, Alwin (2007) did not find a difference in reliability between Likert scales with four or five answer choices. Sturgis, Roberts, and Smith (2014) found that most respondents who selected neutral did so because they didn't know. An alternative is to provide a NA, or "I don't know enough to answer," option as well as a neutral option. For example, the statement "I support fracking as an energy source" could have the following answer choices:

Strongly Disagree	Disagree	Neutral	Agree	Strongly Agree	NA

Respondents who have little knowledge of fracking could select the NA option, while respondents who are truly neutral, who see both positive and negative aspects of fracking, could select the middle option. That way, test users could distinguish between these groups of respondents.

Negatively Worded Items. In the previous section, I noted problems with inserting a negative word, such as "not," into a statement to make it negative. It is tempting in developing Likert scales to have statements worded in the opposite direction to most other items in order to reduce a *response set*, or the tendency for respondents to maintain responding in a consistent way, say agreeing to all statements, without carefully reading them. Likert (1932) himself recommended balancing statements of agreement with statements of disagreement. The bigger question is: is having negatively worded statements a good idea? Much research has investigated the advantages and disadvantages of using negatively worded items (see Barnette, 2000; Chyung, Barkin, & Shamsy, 2018, for summaries of this literature). While there may be some advantage to reducing response sets, the research suggests that this is more than offset by some serious disadvantages. In particular, negatively worded items can often look like a second construct, or dimension (DiStefano & Motl, 2006; Greenberger, Chen, Dmitrieva, & Farruggia, 2003). On tests with negatively worded items, reliability also tends to be lower (Schriesheim & Hill, 1981), and item means tend to be higher than on tests containing all positively worded items. The best advice then is to avoid negatively worded items whenever possible. The exception to this advice would be statements that are naturally negative: avoid making them artificially positive by adding the word *not*.

Number of Answer Choices. Most Likert scales have between three and seven answer choices, with four or five being the most popular. Research has generally indicated that reliability increases with the number of answer choices (Lissitz & Green, 1975; Weng, 2004), but that little is gained beyond seven answer choices.

Labels of Answer Choices. Weng (2004) recommends labeling of all answer choices, rather than labeling only the end points. Labeling all answer choices often increases reliability over that of endpoint labeling. Additionally, labeling the choices improves the interpretation of scale results.

7.3.4 Other Item Formats

Likert scales are not the only type of format for measuring (mostly) noncognitive constructs. Other options include the Q-sort, paired comparisons, and semantic differential. A brief description is offered for each one.

Q-Sort. First proposed by Stephenson (1953) for measuring personality constructs, the Q-sort begins by constructing a large number of statements that are intended to be as inclusive as possible for the construct to be measured. The respondent then sorts these statements into a small number of discrete piles, according to the perceived relevance to themselves. The piles themselves are ordered from descriptors such as "most like me" to "least like me." The middle categories are restricted to receive the most statements while the extreme categories receive the fewest. Its major advantage is that the large number of statements may provide stronger content validity evidence than shorter Likert tests. Some reliability and validity evidence are available to support the Q-sort format. Buckley, Klein, Durbin, Hayden, and Moerk (2002) developed a Q-sort test to measure temperament in preschool children. They reported adequate reliability and strong external validity evidence.

Paired Comparisons. For this format, a relatively small number of statements are generated. In pairwise fashion, respondents choose which of two statements best applies to them. For example, "I enjoy staying at home and reading a book." or "I like to attend karaoke parties." The respondent chooses between all possible pairs. Ten statements therefore produce 45 paired comparisons. Using Thurstone's (1927) Law of Comparative Judgment, it is relatively simple to develop an approximately equal-interval scale such that preferences that respondents have difficulty deciding are scaled to be close to each other. Paired comparisons have been used for decision-making, interest inventories, and personality tests. One notable example of a paired comparisons test is the MBTI, where the respondent is asked to choose which of two statements is most like the respondent.

Sematic Differential. First proposed by Osgood (Osgood, Suci, & Tannenbaum, 1957), this format has been used widely to measure attitudinal constructs and the connotative meanings of common language expressions. It has also been used in psychological assessment tools. An item consists of two opposite adjectives, such as hot/cold, closed/open, and strong/weak, that reference the construct being measured. These are located as bipolar ends of a continuum, and the respondents indicate their view by locating themselves on the continuum. For example, for measuring an attitude toward a graduate degree:

| Uncertain future | 1 | 2 | 3 | 4 | 5 | 6 | 7 | Promising future |
| Easy | 1 | 2 | 3 | 4 | 5 | 6 | 7 | Difficult |

Several possible issues with semantic differential scales include the necessity of standardizing it within a given culture/language and the ambiguity of answers in the middle of the continuum. On the other hand, Friborg, Martinussen, and Rosenvinge (2006) showed that, compared to Likert scales, the semantic differential may be better at reducing response sets.

7.4 ITEM REVIEWS

Once first drafts of all items have been written, and after the item writer reviews and revises the items, there are still several additional types of item reviews that should be undertaken. These have been outlined by Schmeiser and Welch (2006) and are shown in Figure 7.7.

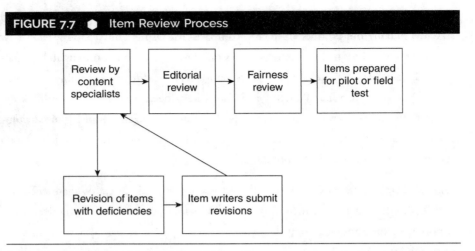

FIGURE 7.7 ● Item Review Process

Review by content specialists → Editorial review → Fairness review → Items prepared for pilot or field test

Review by content specialists → Revision of items with deficiencies → Item writers submit revisions → Review by content specialists

Source: Adapted from Schmeiser and Welch (2006).

Review by Content Specialists. The first review, by content specialists, is intended to support the technical quality of the items. This review should be undertaken by subject matter experts and not the item writers. Subject matter experts should examine the fit of each item to the content and process levels with which the item is associated in the test blueprint. They should also examine the technical correctness and overall clarity of each item. Any item deficiencies are referred back to the item writers for revision and resubmission. This may take more than one iteration.

Use of Cognitive Labs/Think-Alouds. An additional review step that has gained in popularity in recent years is to interview a small number of participants one-on-one as they respond to test items in order to reveal their cognitive processes. Two related types of interviews are cognitive labs and think-alouds. For cognitive labs, the test developer probes the respondent as they answer items. The probes may focus on how well the respondent understands specific terms and directions in the item and what the item is asking the respondent to do. The interviews are recorded and transcribed for a coding analysis. For think-alouds, the probing is more to keep the respondent talking about the cognitive processes she/he is using to answer the item. As a result, cognitive labs are most useful as an exploratory method when the developer does not have a clear understanding of what cognitive processes are needed to answer an item. Think-alouds are most useful to confirm an existing cognitive processing model and are therefore a major piece of substantive/response processes validity evidence. Both methods have the potential to discover flaws of items before any extensive data collection. For an overview of these methods, I recommend the NCME Digital Module on this topic (Leighton & Lehman, 2020).

Editorial Review. The next type of review is an editorial review, sometimes called copyediting. Its purpose is to ensure that item texts are consistent in appearance and that grammar is correct. Any artwork or graphics should be appropriately identified and associated with the correct items. Also, this review ensures that nothing has been omitted, added, or presented in the wrong proportion. It is critical that this review is not done by the item writers. This point was hit home to me painfully on a mathematics test that I helped to develop for a large public school district. After printing and distributing 5,000 test booklets, school personnel pointed out that the first item contained the following answer choices: A, B, B, and D. And the correct answer was B!

Fairness Review. The 2014 *Standards* indicate that fairness "is a fundamental validity issue and requires attention throughout all stages of test development and use" (p. 49). The concept of fairness refers to a level playing field in terms of "responsiveness to individual characteristics and testing contexts so that test scores will yield valid interpretations for intended uses" (p. 50). In Chapter 10, fairness is statistically addressed. Here, I mention fairness in the context of item writing.

Much of the previously discussed item writing guidelines, such as attention to vocabulary and reading level, are aimed at ensuring fairness to all respondents. As it pertains to reviewing items for fairness, four major concerns arise:

1. *Cultural stereotyping:* Are different groups of people treated equally, and are they equally represented? Are they balanced with respect to roles, socioeconomic status, and settings? For example, the statement "Girls are as good at mathematics as boys" may sound fair, but if you turn this statement around to "Boys are as good at mathematics as girls," you can see an implicit bias at work.

2. *Unfair advantage on content:* If some items refer to regional or subgroup geography, culture, or history, an unfair disadvantage could be given to people outside that area or subgroup.

3. *Sensitive topics:* In general, it is best to avoid items that address sensitive topics, such as religion, sex, or other personal behavior. It is possible that

respondents may not provide accurate responses to these items and thus invalidate test scores.

4. *Offensive language:* Likewise, offensive language should be avoided. Such language could also lead to invalid scores.

7.5 CHAPTER SUMMARY

This chapter introduced a number of item formats. Because of the high frequency of their use, I focused on multiple-choice, open-ended, and Likert formats. Guidelines for each format were offered, along with the suggestion of using them as a technical review checklist once rough drafts of items have been written. Finally, several types of item reviews are recommended to address different possibilities of item flaws. Since collecting item response data can be labor- and resource-intensive, it is advantageous to make sure the items are in the best shape possible before pilot testing them.

7.6 EXERCISES AND ACTIVITIES

Test Development Project

1. For each cell (content by process level combination) in the test blueprint, write rough drafts of items in the number of items and format specified in the blueprint.

2. Conduct an item review by a content expert.

3. Conduct a think-aloud interview for an item by a potential respondent.

4. Conduct a fairness review.

FURTHER READING

Arter, J. A., & Spandel, V. (1992). Using portfolios of student work in instruction and assessment (Module 11). Instructional Topics in Educational Measurement (ITEMS). Madison, WI: NCME. Retrieved March 01, 2009, from http://www.ncme.org/pubs/items/ITEMS_Mod_11.pdf

Greenberger, E., Chen, C., Dmitrieva, J., & Farruggia, S. P. (2003). Item-wording and the dimensionality of the Rosenberg self-esteem scale: Do they matter? *Personality and Individual Differences*, 35(2003), 1241–1254.

Haladyna, T. M., Downing, S. M., & Rodriguez, M. C. (2002). A review of multiple-choice item-writing guidelines for classroom assessment. *Applied Measurement in Education*, 15(3), 309–334.

Hogan, T. P., & Murphy, G. (2007). Recommendations for preparing and scoring constructed-response items: What the experts say. *Applied Measurement in Education*, 20(3), 427–441.

Schmeiser, C. B., & Welch, C. J. (2006). Test development. In R. L. Brennan (Ed.), *Educational measurement* (4th ed., pp. 307–353). Westport, CT: Prager Publishers.

Stiggins, R. J. (1987). Design and development of performance assessments (Module 1). Instructional Topics in Educational Measurement (ITEMS). Madison, WI: NCME. Retrieved March 01, 2009, from http://www.ncme.org/pubs/items/ITEMS_Mod_1_Intro.pdf

Wolfe, E. W., & Smith, E. V., Jr (2007). Instrument development tools and activities for measure validation using Rasch models: Part I—Instrument development tools. In E. V. Smith Jr, & R. M. Smith (Eds.), *Rasch measurement: Advanced and specialized applications* (pp. 202–242). Maple Grove, MN: JAM Press.

REFERENCES

Albanese, M. A. (1993). Type K and other complex multiple-choice items: An analysis of research and item properties. *Educational Measurement: Issues and Practice*, 12(1), 28–33.

Alwin, D. (2007). *Margins of error. A study of reliability in survey measurements*. Hoboken, NJ: John Wiley.

Barnette, J. (2000). Effects of stem and Likert response option reversals on survey internal consistency: If you feel the need, there is a better alternative to using those negatively-worded stems. *Educational and Psychological Measurement*, 6, 361–370.

Buckley, M. E., Klein, D., Durbin, C. E., Hayden, E., & Moerk, K. C. (2002). Development and validation of a Q-Sort procedure to assess temperament and behavior in preschool-age children. *Journal of Clinical Child and Adolescent Psychology*, 31(4), 525–539.

Chyung, S. Y., Barkin, J. R., & Shamsy, J. A. (2018). Evidence-based survey design: The use of negatively worded items in surveys. *Performance Improvement*, 57(3), 16–25.

DiStefano, C., & Motl, R. (2006). Further investigating method effects associated with negatively-worded items on self-report surveys. *Structural Equation Modeling*, 13, 440–464.

Friborg, O., Martinussen, M., & Rosenvinge, J. H. (2006). Likert-based vs. semantic differential-based scorings of positive psychological constructs: A psychometric comparison of two versions of a scale measuring resilience. *Personality and Individual Differences*, 40, 873–884.

Leighton, J. P., & Lehman, B. (2020). Think-aloud interviews and cognitive labs (Digital ITEMS Module 12). *Educational Measurement: Issues and Practice*, 39(1), 96–97.

Likert, R. (1932). A technique for the measurement of attitudes. *Archives of Psychology*, 140, 4–55.

Lissitz, R. W., & Green, S. B. (1975). Effect of the number of scale points on reliability: A Monte Carlo approach. *Journal of Applied Psychology*, 60, 10–13.

Merriam-Webster. (2014). Item. In *Merriam-Webster's Collegiate Dictionary* (11th ed., p. 666).

Osgood, C., Suci, G., & Tannenbaum, P. (1957). *The measurement of meaning*. Urbana, IL: University of Illinois Press.

Schriesheim, C. A., & Hill, K. D. (1981). Controlling acquiescence response bias by item reversals: The effect on questionnaire validity. *Educational and Psychological Measurement*, 41, 1101–1114.

Shammi, P., & Stuss, D. T. (1999). Humour appreciation: A role of the right frontal lobe. *Brain: A Journal of Neurology*, 122(4), 657–666.

Smith, E. V., Jr, Wakely, M. B., De Kruif, R. E., & Swartz, C. W. (2003). Optimizing rating scales for self-efficacy (and other) research. *Educational and Psychological Measurement*, 63, 369–391.

Stephenson, W. (1953). *The study of behavior: Q-technique and its methodology*. Chicago, IL: University of Chicago Press.

Stevens, S. S. (1946). On the theory of scales of measurement. *Science*, 103, 677–680.

Sturgis, P., Roberts, C., & Smith, P. (2014). Middle alternatives revisited: How the neither/nor response acts as a way of saying "I don't know". *Sociological Methods and Research*, 43(1), 15–38.

Thurstone, L. L. (1927). A law of comparative judgment. *Psychology Review*, 34(4), 273–286.

Weng, L.-J. (2004). Impact of the number of response categories and anchor labels on coefficient alpha and test-retest reliability. *Educational and Psychological Measurement*, 64(6), 956–972.

8

PILOT TESTING AND ITEM ANALYSIS

8.1 PILOT TESTING

In large-scale testing programs, there are typically two or three rounds of item response data collection during the test development process: (1) pilot testing, (2) field testing, and sometimes (3) validation/norming/standard setting/equating special studies. These data collection efforts serve different purposes. The purpose of pilot testing is to evaluate the quality of individual items. Here, poorly performing items are identified and eliminated or revised, and the best performing items are selected for a final, or next, version of the test. The field test collects data on the final version for the purpose of developing score scales (as discussed in Chapter 3), establishing test reliability, and collecting additional validity evidence on the test as a whole. Occasionally, sponsoring organizations conduct special studies for the purposes of validation, norming, standard setting, and/or equating alternate forms. An example of this is the 1988–2010 forms of the GED Tests. In those studies, which they called Standardizations, data were collected on alternate forms of the GED Tests with nationally representative samples of graduating high school seniors, who were the norming population. These studies were used to equate the forms, establish percentile ranks, and determine passing scores.

8.1.1 Methods

There are three primary methods used by testing organizations for pilot testing new items:

Use Piloted Items as the Operational Test. Poorly performing items are not counted in the scoring. This method is popular when there is no opportunity to do a separate pilot test, for example, when the test cannot be revealed ahead of its use or when time and/or financial constraints exist. This is the least desirable of the three methods. The major risk is finding out that there are too many poor items and, as a result, some of them do need to count in the scoring. The poor items may also be concentrated in specific cells of the test blueprint.

Embed Items Within an Operational Test Form. These items do not count in the scoring, and respondents don't know which ones they are. This method is attractive to many large-scale testing programs because a separate pilot test is not required, and respondents answer these items under standardized conditions. The method is designed to pilot test items for new forms of an existing test. The main disadvantage is that test length is increased. As a result, only a small number of new items, say 5–10, can be pilot tested within a single operational form. That, in turn, means that this method requires that a number of operational test forms already exist. In other words, this option works only for large-scale testing programs.

Pilot Test Items in a Separate Administration. That is, a special data collection is planned to pilot test a large number of items. This is arguably the best method for a new test and the one I will focus on below. Its major disadvantage is that respondents know (or should know) that this administration is for item tryouts only and will not count for any decisions.

8.1.2 Samples

In planning a pilot test, one important consideration is the sample to which the items will be administered. For some large-scale testing organizations, some form of probability sampling is used to obtain a representative sample. Most individuals or small teams developing tests for research purposes obtain a convenience sample from their target population. Every effort should be made to make this convenience sample as representative as possible. Table 8.1 shows the target sample size for several large-scale testing programs. These range from approximately 250–800. The primary consideration here is a target sample size large enough to produce stable estimates of item difficulty and discrimination statistics.

Another way to view target sample size is by constructing a desired confidence interval and calculating the sample size needed for that interval. For example, suppose that you would like your item mean (for a dichotomously scored item) to vary no more than 0.1 across samples. For detecting a mean item difference of 0.1 from a mean of 0.5 (SD = 0.25), a 95 percent confidence interval of ± 0.1 requires a sample size of only 25. For item discrimination (i.e., the correlation between item and test scores), let's suppose that you would like a correlation between an item and the test

TABLE 8.1 ⬢ Pilot Test Sample Sizes for Several Testing Programs	
Testing Program	**Target Sample Size per Item**
National Assessment of Educational Progress (NAEP)	500
Smarter Balanced Assessment Consortium (SBAC)	300
Norway National Reading Test	250
2017 eTIMSS	800
MUSIC Academic Motivation Inventory (Jones & Skaggs, 2016)	400

raw score to vary by no more than 0.1 from a true value. A 95 percent confidence interval for this degree of precision requires a sample size of 387. If you can tolerate a difference of 0.2, only 96 respondents would be required. Clearly, much larger samples are required for the same degree of precision for item discriminations than for item difficulties. For individually developed tests, I suggest a target sample size of at least 100 with the caveat that this sample needs to be as representative as possible of the target population. If population subgroups need to be analyzed separately, then a larger sample, ideally at least 100 from the smallest subgroup, is needed. This recommendation is intended for a pilot test in which the primary goal is to evaluate item quality. This sample size would likely not be sufficient for a field test that results in test reliability, item scoring and test scaling, and applying a CTT or Rasch measurement model.

8.1.3 Test Length

How many items should you pilot test? Thorndike (1982) famously suggested "50 percent more than you will need." My recommendation is 100 percent, or twice as many as specified on the test blueprint, for several reasons. It can be difficult to write items for some cells in the blueprint, particularly those that involve higher process levels. These cells will often turn out to have a higher percentage of poorly performing items. In addition, a set of items connected to a common stimulus, such as a reading passage, graph, or picture, are at risk. If enough of these items perform poorly, the entire set may have to be discarded. If your test is intended to provide a criterion-referenced score interpretation, then some items need to be located near a particular level of difficulty or location. For these, it may be desirable to pilot test additional items.

8.1.4 Design

For both pilot and field testing, whether the test is to be administered paper–pencil or by computer, it is important to present the test to respondents in such a way as to promote the validity of the item response data. A typical test will include some or all of the following at the beginning of the test:

1. Title of the test

2. Directions

3. Introduction: This can include any information about the intended purpose of the test, how much time is needed, how personal data are handled, how to interpret results, or other information not given to the respondent elsewhere

4. How data will be handled

5. Sample items

Below are some examples from published tests. Figure 8.1 shows an example of directions to respondents for the Grit Scale. It's important to note that these directions ask the respondent to answer how he or she perceives themselves to be typically compared to other people, rather than try to achieve a high score.

Figure 8.2 shows the cover page for the School as Caring Community Profile-II, a test measuring school climate as it pertains to character education. This introduction explains what construct is being measured (the degree to which schools are caring communities), the Profile's intended use (evaluation of character education), the target population (teachers, students, etc.), and a description of the test.

Figure 8.3 shows part of the cover page for the questionnaires of the Education Longitudinal Survey of 2002 (https://nces.ed.gov/surveys/els2002/pdf/StudentQ_baseyear.pdf). This section details how data will be used, how confidentiality will be ensured, and that responding is voluntary. For many tests, this information is not often provided to respondents at the time of testing. It is sometimes given to respondents at the time they register for the test or when respondents are recruited for participation. In any case, from an ethical point of view, respondents need to know how data will be handled, how their identity will be protected, and that their participation will be voluntary (excepting for credentialing or other high-stakes situations).

FIGURE 8.1 ● Grit Scale (Duckworth, Peters, Matthews, & Kelly, 2007)

Grit Scale

Here are a number of statements that may or may not apply to you. There are no right or wrong answers, so just answer honestly, considering how you compare to most people. At the end, you'll get a score that reflects how passionate and persevering you see yourself to be.

FIGURE 8.2 ● School as a Caring Community-II (Lickona & Davidson, 2003)

SCHOOL AS CARING COMMUNITY PROFILE-II (SCCP-II)

A good community will have a high degree of congruence in its perception of itself.
— Douglas Heath, *Knowledge Without Goodness Is Dangerous*

In ***Eleven Principles of Effective Character Education*** by the Character Education Partnership, Principle 4 states:

> *The school must be a caring community. The school itself must embody good character. It must progress toward becoming a microcosm of the civil, caring, and just society we seek to create as a nation.*[1]

The School as a Caring Community Profile-II (SCCP-II) is an instrument developed by the Center for the 4th and 5th Rs (Respect and Responsibility) to help schools assess themselves as caring communities. The SCCP may be administered at any point (ideally at the beginning) of a character education initiative and then at later points to assess progress. Its validity as a measure of caring community is enhanced if it is given to varied constituencies that make up the school:

* **teachers**
* **administrators**
* **non-teaching professional staff**
* **other staff**
* **parents**
* **students (Items 1-20)**
* **school board members**

The School as a Caring Community Profile-II (SCCP-II) is a 42-question survey. The first 25 items relate to perceptions of students; the final 17 items relate to perceptions of adults. Younger children may be asked to answer only items 1 through 34. (For most items, a high rating is positive; for a few items, the reverse is true.) The SCCP-II identifies areas of strength and areas for improvement. Areas of relatively low ratings, and areas where there are significant discrepancies between ratings by different groups, can then become the focus of efforts to strengthen the experience of the school as a caring community.

Note: The items in this survey seek to gather the perceptions of all members of the school community. In order to validly assess the strength of community in a school, it is important to assess how both students and adults are perceived. Data analysis, however, should protect the anonymity of all individuals, students and adults. An individual teacher may wish to look at the data for his/her classroom, but those data should be recoded and/or entered into a school-wide data pool that does not link classroom data to particular faculty.

FIGURE 8.3 ● Data Uses and Confidentiality From Education Longitudinal Study of 2002

USES OF THE DATA
The data from this survey will be used by educators and by federal and state policy makers to address important issues facing the nation's schools: educational standards, high school course-taking patterns, dropping out of school, the education of the disadvantaged, the needs of language minority students, and the features of effective schools.

ASSURANCE OF CONFIDENTIALITY
The collection of information in this survey is authorized by Section 404(a) of the National Education Statistics Act of 1994, Title IV of the Improving America's Schools Act of 1994, Public Law 103-382 and continued under the auspices of the Education Sciences Reform Act of 2002, Public Law 107-279. Participation is voluntary. You may skip questions you do not wish to answer; however, we hope that you will answer as many questions as you can. All responses that relate to or describe identifiable characteristics of individuals may be used only for statistical purposes and may not be disclosed, or used, in identifiable form for any other purpose, unless otherwise compelled by law. Information will be protected from disclosure by federal statute (20 USC 9003a-9007, as amended). Data will be combined to produce statistical reports. No individual data that links your name, address, telephone number, or identification number with your responses will be reported.

According to the Paperwork Reduction Act of 1995, no persons are required to respond to a collection of information unless such collection displays a valid OMB control number. The valid OMB control number for this information collection is 1850-0652. The time required to complete this information collection is estimated to average 45 minutes per response, including the time to review instructions, search existing data resources, gather the data needed, and complete and review the information collection. **If you have any comments concerning the accuracy of the time estimate(s) or suggestions for improving this form, please write to:** U.S. Department of Education, Washington, D.C. 20202-4651. **If you have comments or concerns regarding the status of your individual submission of this form, write directly to:** National Center for Education Statistics, ESLSD, 1990 K Street, N.W., Washington, D.C., 20006.

Following the introductory information, the actual items of the test can be ordered in several ways:

1. *Random ordering:* Items are arranged in random order without regard to content, item format, or process level. Random ordering requires respondents to shift their cognitive processes on an item-by-item basis. This generally makes the test more taxing and longer to complete.

2. *Content grouping:* Items measuring the same content are grouped together. This practice reduces cognitive shifting. Additionally, items with a common stimulus (e.g., passage, map, graph, chart, picture) should be grouped together and if possible on the same page.

3. *Item format grouping:* Items using the same format are grouped together. Again, this reduces cognitive shifting by respondents. One possible problem is that item format grouping may provide clues to correct answers. For example, for math word problems, examinees might be able to identify the algorithms for solution if problems are structured the same way.

4. *Ordering by difficulty:* Items arranged according to their difficulty level. Often, test developers will begin with a relatively easy item for respondents to answer with the intent that test anxiety will be reduced.

A number of researchers have investigated the degree to which the ordering of items affects both item characteristics and overall test scores. This research has been motivated by several concerns regarding test development and administration. First, items that have been pilot tested may appear in a different position on the final version of the test. Second, some online versions of tests have been configured to administer items in a random order to increase security. Third, some measurement models, such as Rasch models, assume that item responses are independent of each other, that is, there is no context effect due to item order.

The results of this research have been mixed. Leary and Dorans (1985) reviewed research and found that, under power conditions (i.e., when respondents are given ample time), no item position effects or effects on scores were observed. However, under speeded conditions, items arranged from most to least difficult produced lower scores than the same items arranged from least to most difficult. A number of studies have examined item position effects for specific testing programs, including NAEP (Zwick, 1991), PISA (Adams & Wu, 2000; Debeer & Janssen, 2013), ACT (Brennan, 1992; Harris, 1991; Kolen & Harris, 1990; Pommerich & Harris, 2003), SAT (Eignor & Stocking, 1986), TOEFL (Way, Carey, & Golub-Smith, 1992), and state assessment programs (Meyers, Miller, & Way, 2009). In general, items administered late in a test appeared to be more difficult than when administered earlier, but there were numerous exceptions to this general finding.

What are the implications of item position during pilot testing? First, if the operational version of the test will administer items in random order, then any position effects would seem to be the same for all respondents. Similarly, if there is to be a single fixed-order form, then any position effects would be the same. As mentioned above, trouble could occur if item positions during pilot testing are considerably different than those for the operational form. The best advice then is to develop form(s) for pilot testing that are as similar as possible in terms of item ordering and organization as they will be in the operational forms.

What about the tests related to the datasets used in this book? The items in the TIMSS Booklet 1 appear to be randomly ordered by content and process level. The first item measures Numbers/Using concepts, followed by Algebra/Using concepts and Measurement/Knowing facts and procedures. The political viewpoint items within the larger questionnaire are all grouped together, with the reverse-scored items appearing randomly. You can find examples of highly successful tests of each type of item ordering.

8.1.5 Mode of Administration

In a pilot or field test, one major decision is whether to administer it in paper/pencil, a computer-based format, or both. In recent years, there has been a significant trend toward computer-based testing. For example, for the 2011 *National Survey of Student Engagement* (NSSE), where institutions were permitted their choice of paper/pencil or online administration, 86 percent chose online only, 3 percent chose paper/pencil only, and 11 percent chose both. In my test development class, almost all students conduct pilot testing using an online survey platform, such as Qualtrics or SurveyMonkey.

If a test is intended to be administered through both methods, it is important to investigate whether scores from both methods are comparable. A large amount of research has been conducted comparing administration methods. Kingston (2009) conducted a meta analysis of 81 comparisons of educational achievement tests for which both paper/pencil and computer-based administrations were conducted. Overall, he found very small differences between the two methods. These small differences included an advantage of computer-based tests in language arts and social studies, and paper/pencil tests in mathematics. For some tests, there were no differences at all, but for a few tests, there were substantial differences. There is much less research comparing methods for noncognitive constructs. However, the major conclusion from this research is that if both administration methods are to be used, then their equivalence needs to be investigated rather than assumed.

If the mode of administration is a choice to be made by the test developer, then there are advantages and disadvantages to each method. For paper/pencil administration, one of the main considerations is how to handle the data. If respondents answer directly in a booklet, then the data need to be hand-entered into a file, a practice ill-advised due to frequency of data-entry errors. Alternately, machine-scorable booklets can be printed, or respondents can answer on scannable answer sheets. However, these options do involve some expense.

By contrast, computer-based administration has the advantage of obtaining item response data automatically. For example, many online survey platforms permit data to be downloaded into an EXCEL spreadsheet. On the other hand, the appearance of the test may vary across different devices, and respondents could see the test in different ways. This can be particularly pronounced if some items are technology-driven. One of the purposes of pilot testing, in addition to evaluating item quality, is to evaluate the mode of administration by observing any technology issues that may emerge. For example, one state educational assessment program developed online versions of its tests but found that they did not work well because some schools were still using 386 computers with Windows 95!

The overriding consideration with regard to mode of administration is standardization. Respondents need to be measured in the same way to ensure score validity. This is particularly important for a high-stakes test. One common standardizing procedure is to have a time limit. Test developers often refer to speededness, or the effect of a time limit on test performance. If respondents are running out of time, they may change their response strategy, e.g., resorting to random guessing. Some evidence for this can be found if you find that a large number of respondents are omitting the answers at the end of the test. A real consequential validity aspect of this can occur if the speededness effects vary by target population subgroups. For most tests, speed is not part of what is to be measured, and so the intent is for respondents to have sufficient time to respond. However, some sort of time constraint is often needed to prevent a few people from taking an extremely long time to complete a test. During pilot testing, you should note how long it takes for respondents to complete the test. Then, a rough guide is to have a time limit so that 90–95 percent of the pilot test respondents have finished.

The flip side of speededness is a test that takes too much time to complete. Tests that include large numbers of extended constructed-response items can be exhausting for respondents. This can result in a reduced response rate and/or large numbers of omitted items. Again, it is important during the pilot test to observe the response time and make revisions to the test so that the target time is reached.

8.2 ITEM ANALYSIS

In this section, we examine various indicators of item quality for identifying those items that are performing poorly and to select adequately performing items for a field test, or final, version of the test. There are two primary item quality indicators: *difficulty/location* and *discrimination*.

Item difficulty characterizes the difficulty level of an item measuring a cognitive construct. A calculus problem is more difficult than a multiplication problem. For noncognitive constructs, such as self-efficacy or motivation, it doesn't make much sense to talk about how difficult an item is. Instead, we refer to the item's *location* on the construct map. For example, an item such as "I can climb any mountain" indicates a location at one end of the self-efficacy construct, while "I can't do anything right" can be located at the other end of the construct map.

Item discrimination is an important item characteristic that we typically don't think about as much as difficulty/location. Item discrimination refers to the degree to which an item can discriminate between individuals with different levels of a construct. For example, an item that is answered similarly by individuals with low and high levels of intrinsic motivation does not discriminate well. There are a variety of statistical indicators of item discrimination. The ones most commonly used are based on correlations between item scores and test scores.

Because the analyses of dichotomously and polytomously scored items look quite different, we will treat them separately. Furthermore, our item analyses will be based on classical item statistics rather than ones based on modern test theories, which usually require larger samples.

8.2.1 Item Analysis for Dichotomously Scored Items
8.2.1.1 Item Quality Indicators

Item Difficulty. For dichotomously scored items, item difficulty is usually reported as the *p-value*, or the proportion of respondents who answered the item correctly (or responded in such a way as to receive a score of 1). This index is bounded by 0 and 1 with smaller values indicating a more difficult item (i.e., a small proportion of respondents answered correctly) and larger values indicating an easier item. An obvious problem with *p*-values is the fact that their interpretation is sample-dependent—if the average skill level of the sample changes, the *p*-values will change. The *p*-value for item *i* is calculated as follows:

$$p_i = \bar{x}_i = \frac{\sum_{j=1}^{n} x_j}{n} \text{ where } x_j = \{0, 1\} \tag{8.1}$$

Notice that the *p*-value is actually the mean of an item in which the possible scores are 0 and 1. The variance and standard deviation of item *i* are

$$s_i^2 = p_i(1 - p_i) \text{ and } s_i = \sqrt{p_i(1 - p_i)} \tag{8.2}$$

If $p = 0.50$ (i.e., 50 percent scored 1), the item's variance is $0.25 = 0.5$ (1–0.50) and its standard deviation is 0.50. As *p* approaches 0 or 1, the item's variance and standard deviation become smaller. At $p = 0$ or 1, item variance and standard deviation both equal 0. At this point, all respondents have received the same score, 0 or 1, resulting in no variance. This means that the item contributes nothing to total test raw score variance.

As a result, items with *p*-values near 0 or 1 (and standard deviations near 0) are probably not beneficial for tests intended to provide a norm-referenced score inter-pretation because such items cannot differentiate between respondents. By the same token, items with *p*-values near 0.50 and variances near 0.5 are the most desirable items for norm-referencing. For criterion-referenced score interpretations, *p*-values near 0 or 1 may be desirable if what they measure is considered important for the criterion being measured, and the criterion itself is located near one end of the construct map (e.g., admission to an elite music school).

Item Discrimination. The most widely used index of item discrimination is the item-total score correlation (also known as the *point-biserial correlation*), which is simply the Pearson correlation between a dichotomously scored item and the raw score on the entire test. A positive correlation means that respondents who answer an item correctly tend also to receive higher scores on the test, which suggests that the item is measuring what the test measures. If the correlation is near 0, then responses to the item are not related to test scores, an indication that the item may be measuring something different. If the correlation is negative, then respondents who answer this item correctly tend to get a lower overall test score, a strong indicator of a poor item, or one that has been scored incorrectly.

One modification often made to this correlation is the exclusion of the item being studied from the test score. Using the item score as part of the test score inflates the size of the correlation. Item analysis software refers to this modification as Correction for Spuriousness (jMetrik), Corrected Item-Total Correlation (SPSS), or r.drop (psych R package). Table 8.2 below shows how this works. Instead of correlating the first and second columns, the correction correlates the first and third columns. Essentially, the corrected item-total correlation is the correlation between scores on the item and scores on the *remainder of the test*.

Research conducted on the point-biserial correlation has revealed two major problems with its use. First, it's not a particularly stable statistic. In other words, its value can vary considerably from one random sample to another. This is the reason that point-biserials require larger sample sizes than *p*-values for the same level of precision. Second, as the *p*-value approaches 0.0 or 1.0, the point-biserial's range becomes restricted and closer to 0.0. As a result, the point-biserial can be low because of item difficulty, not necessarily poor item discrimination.

To overcome these problems, a popular alternative is the *biserial correlation*. This correlation assumes that the underlying construct is normally distributed in the target

TABLE 8.2 ⬡ Correction for Spuriousness for Item-Total Correlation		
Item Score	Test Score	Corrected Test Score
1	25	24
1	22	21
0	15	15
1	18	17
0	20	20

population, a reasonable assumption for many constructs. Statistically, the point-biserial and biserial correlations are related as follows:

$$r_{bis} = r_{pt-bis}\frac{\sqrt{p(1-p)}}{Y} \tag{8.3}$$

where p is the p-value and Y is the ordinate of the normal distribution, whose value is commonly found in tables of the standard normal distribution, or can be calculated by

$$Y = \frac{1}{\sqrt{2\pi}}\exp\left(-\frac{z^2}{2}\right) \tag{8.4}$$

Table 8.3 shows the point-biserial to biserial conversion factors for different p-values, from 0.1 to 0.9. As you can see, the biserial correlation is always larger than the point-biserial correlation, but the conversion factor increases as the item p-value becomes closer to 0 or 1. This means that the biserial will be increasingly larger relative to the point-biserial as the item becomes less or more difficult.

Distractor Analysis. An important analysis specific to multiple-choice items is an examination of the distractors, or incorrect answers. Many problems with multiple-choice items can be traced to problems with distractors rather than the correct answer. Item difficulty and discrimination indicators can be calculated for each answer choice.

p-Values for the distractors indicate the proportion of respondents who selected each distractor. Distractors that have been chosen by a small proportion or not at all are distractors that have no contribution to item quality, but this may not indicate a flaw of the item. As mentioned in Chapter 7, it is often exceedingly difficult to construct three or four attractive distractors. Replacing an unattractive distractor with a more appealing one will have the effect of making the item more difficult. However, an

TABLE 8.3 ● Conversion Factors From Point-Biserials to Biserials

p-Value	0.1	0.2	0.3	0.4	0.5	0.6	0.7	0.8	0.9
Conversion factor	1.71	1.43	1.32	1.27	1.25	1.27	1.32	1.43	1.71

item could be extremely easy because all of the distractors are obviously incorrect. Additionally, distractors that attract more respondents than the correct answer may indicate an item flaw and are worth investigating.

Point-biserial or biserial correlations of distractors can also reveal potential item flaws. We would expect these correlations to be negative, that is, respondents who picked these incorrect answers to tend to have lower test scores than respondents who did not select them. If these correlations are positive, then that distractor is attractive to high scoring respondents, suggesting a potential item flaw.

Table 8.4 demonstrates the calculations of item p-values, standard deviations, and point-biserial and biserial correlations for a made-up set of dichotomously scored items. The first item has a p-value of 1.0, which means that the standard deviation, and discriminations all have values of 0.0. By contrast, item 5 has a point-biserial of -0.52 (and biserial of -0.70). Respondents who score 1 on this item tend to score lower on the remainder of the test.

TABLE 8.4 ◗ Item Analysis Calculations for Dichotomously Scored Items

			Item Scores			
Person	1	2	3	4	5	Total
1	1	1	1	0	0	3
2	1	1	0	0	0	2
3	1	0	0	0	0	1
4	1	0	1	0	1	3
5	1	1	1	1	0	4
6	1	1	1	1	0	4
7	1	0	0	0	1	2
8	1	1	0	1	0	3
p-Value	1.000	0.625	0.500	0.375	0.250	2.750
SD	0.000	0.518	0.535	0.518	0.463	1.035
r_{pt-bis}	0.000	0.124	0.378	0.325	−0.516	
r_{bis}	0.000	0.158	0.474	0.489	−0.704	

8.2.1.2 Item Analysis of TIMSS Booklet 1

To demonstrate an item analysis, we will use data from the TIMSS Booklet 1. I will demonstrate the item analysis using two applications: jMetrik and the psych R package. A quick mention of SPSS is in order. It is possible to conduct the item analysis with this package, but it is cumbersome and somewhat laborious. First, item responses need to be recoded to 0 and 1. Second, item difficulty and discrimination will be provided by the Reliability program, while distractor information will come from the Frequencies and Correlations applications. These will not agree unless care is taken to use listwise deletion with Frequencies. SPSS Reliability does work well with polytomously scored items.

The R code for the psych package is provided in Appendix B. For jMetrik, the item analysis was run by checking the following options: (1) Compute item statistics, (2) Item deleted reliability, (3) All response options, and (4) Correct for spuriousness. Clicking on Pearson correlation will produce point-biserial correlations, while clicking on the Polyserial correlation will result in biserial correlations.

Figures 8.4 and 8.5 show the jMetrik and psych item statistics for the first item, M012001. The two applications organize the analyses in different sets of tables and

FIGURE 8.4 ● Item Analysis for M012001 From jMetrik

Item	Option (Score)	Difficulty	Std. Dev.	Discrimin.
m012001	Overall	0.5892	0.4923	0.5460
	1.0(1.0)	0.5892	0.4923	0.5460
	2.0(0.0)	0.0436	0.2043	-0.1806
	3.0(0.0)	0.0674	0.2508	-0.2708
	4.0(0.0)	0.0964	0.2954	-0.2905
	5.0(0.0)	0.1982	0.3989	-0.4371

Item	Option (Score)	Difficulty	Std. Dev.	Discrimin.
m012001	Overall	0.5892	0.4923	0.6907
	1.0(1.0)	0.5892	0.4923	0.6907
	2.0(0.0)	0.0436	0.2043	-0.3991
	3.0(0.0)	0.0674	0.2508	-0.5208
	4.0(0.0)	0.0964	0.2954	-0.5018
	5.0(0.0)	0.1982	0.3989	-0.6258

RELIABILITY IF ITEM DELETED

Item	L2	Alpha	F-G	F-B	Raju
m012001	0.7975	0.7947	0.7969	0.7960	0.7947

FIGURE 8.5 ● Item Analysis for M012001 From the Psych R Package

```
           vars  n   mean   sd  median  trimmed  mad  min  max  range  skew  kurtosis
M012001     1   757  0.59  0.49    1      0.61    0    0    1     1   -0.36   -1.87

Reliability if an item is dropped:
          raw_alpha  std.alpha  G6(smc)  average_r  S/N  alpha se
M012001      0.79       0.80     0.80       0.17    3.9   0.0108

Item statistics
            n   raw.r  std.r  r.cor  r.drop  mean   sd
M012001    757  0.62   0.62   0.61    0.55   0.59  0.49
```

with different sets of headings. For jMetrik, the first table shows point-biserial item discriminations, while the second table shows the same analysis for biserial correlations. For the psych package, raw.r is the uncorrected point-biserial, std.r is the uncorrected item-total correlation when all items are standardized, that is, converted to z-scores, r.cor is the item-total correlation corrected for both item overlap and scale reliability, and r.drop is the item-total correlation without the item as part of the test score. R.drop is therefore comparable to the item-total correlation corrected for spuriousness from jMetrik.

For this item, both applications show the same results: M012001 has a *p*-value of 0.59, standard deviation of 0.49, corrected point-biserial of 0.54 (or biserial of 0.69), and an alpha of 0.79 if the item were to be deleted. The distractor analysis provided by jMetrik also provides information about the other response options. Nearly 20 percent of the respondents chose answer E, while only 4 percent chose B. The point-biserials or biserials for the distractors are all negative, a good sign in that respondents who chose any distractor tended to score lower on the rest of the items. This item therefore seems to be functioning well.

For this booklet, item *p*-values ranged from 0.25 to 0.82. Corrected point-biserials ranged from 0.21 to 0.54, or biserials from 0.28 to 0.69. All of the distractor point-biserials were negative. If any item were to be deleted, test reliability would be reduced. In other words, none of the indicators point to flaws in any of the items. So, what would suspicious items look like? If item M012001 were incorrectly scored by designating E instead of A as the correct answer, the jMetrik item analysis would appear as in Figure 8.6. As you can see, numerous red flags are now prominent. First,

FIGURE 8.6 ● Item M012001 Item Analysis If Incorrectly Keyed

```
 Item        Option (Score)   Difficulty    Std.Dev.    Discrimin.
---------    ----------------  ----------    ----------  ----------
 m012001           Overall       0.1982       0.3989      -0.4515
                  1.0(0.0)       0.5892       0.4923       0.5052
                  2.0(0.0)       0.0436       0.2043      -0.3925
                  3.0(0.0)       0.0674       0.2508      -0.5219
                  4.0(0.0)       0.0964       0.2954      -0.4965
                  5.0(1.0)       0.1982       0.3989      -0.4515

                        RELIABILITY ANALYSIS
=================================================================================
 Method             Estimate        95%Conf. Int.                    SEM
---------------------------------------------------------------------------------
 Guttman's L2        0.7777       (0.7950, 0.8331)                  2.1126
 Coefficient Alpha   0.7675       (0.7869, 0.8266)                  2.1537
 Feldt-Gilmer        0.7768       (0.7940, 0.8324)                  2.1173
 Feldt-Brennan       0.7733       (0.7918, 0.8305)                  2.1289
 Raju's Beta         0.7675       (0.7869, 0.8266)                  2.1537

                     RELIABILITY IF ITEM DELETED
=================================================================================
 Item        L2       Alpha      F-G       F-B       Raju
---------------------------------------------------------------------------------
 m012001    0.7975    0.7947    0.7969    0.7960    0.7947
```

the item biserial is negative, meaning that respondents who answer this item "correctly" tend to score lower on the remainder of the booklet. Second, the biserial for answer A is positive, indicating that those who score higher prefer this answer. Third, coefficient alpha will be higher if this item is deleted. As a result, an item analysis with results like these strongly suggests checking the answer key. If the item has been scored correctly, then some evaluation by subject matter experts is needed to determine why high scoring respondents prefer answer choice A.

To see what the item analyses of some poorly performing items look like, let's look at several items from another test, in this case a pilot test of a high school literacy exam from a large public school district. The purpose of this exam is to prepare students for the state exam. The state exam is criterion-referenced in that a certain score is necessary for high school graduation. This pilot test form consisted of 85 multiple-choice items. Because this was a first data collection of these items, it is not surprising that some of them did not perform as desired. It is also important to point out that items should not be dropped strictly due to their item statistics. Instead, when items seem to perform poorly, they should be investigated for content to try to pinpoint the sources of the problems. It is quite possible for items with questionable statistics to turn out to be good items or items that can be fixed with minor revisions. Below, I will review item analyses for five potentially problematic items (Figure 8.7).

Item 4 looks extremely easy with a *p*-value of 0.94. None of the distractors was picked by more than 3 percent of the respondents. On the other hand, the biserial correlation is a strong positive value of 0.63, and all of the distractors' biserials are negative. In other words, although easy, this item does discriminate between high and low scorers. This item asks students to identify the key elements of a drama. When reviewed by high school English instructional specialists, no one could think of more attractive distractors from their instruction. Additionally, although identifying the key elements of a drama is a basic concept, the specialists nevertheless felt that it was an important one. As a result, this item was retained as is.

Item 22 was somewhat difficult with a *p*-value of 0.47, but it also had a positive discrimination of 0.30. The distractors also had negative biserials. This item was

FIGURE 8.7 ● Item Statistics From Five High School English Literacy Items

Item	Option (Score)	Difficulty	Std. Dev.	Discrimin.
i4	Overall	0.9421	0.2336	0.6257
	A(0.0)	0.0154	0.1231	-0.7613
	B(0.0)	0.0262	0.1599	-0.4077
	C(1.0)	0.9421	0.2336	0.6257
	D(0.0)	0.0145	0.1195	-0.6327
i22	Overall	0.4087	0.4918	0.3041
	A(0.0)	0.5081	0.5002	-0.1340
	B(1.0)	0.4087	0.4918	0.3041
	C(0.0)	0.0425	0.2018	-0.5486
	D(0.0)	0.0380	0.1912	-0.5918
i36	Overall	0.4747	0.4996	-0.0440
	A(0.0)	0.0552	0.2284	-0.2726
	B(0.0)	0.1193	0.3243	-0.2395
	C(0.0)	0.3264	0.4691	0.1934
	D(0.0)	0.0208	0.1428	-0.2783
	E(1.0)	0.4747	0.4996	-0.0440
i38	Overall	0.1944	0.3959	0.4272
	A(0.0)	0.7459	0.4355	-0.2713
	B(0.0)	0.0253	0.1572	-0.3089
	C(0.0)	0.0163	0.1266	-0.4237
	D(0.0)	0.0163	0.1266	-0.4730
	E(1.0)	0.1944	0.3959	0.4272

flagged for further review because answer A was selected by more respondents than the correct answer B. This item asked respondents to categorize poetry that was unrhymed iambic pentameter. Answers A and B were free and blank verse, respectively. The other two distractors were obviously incorrect. This is an example of an item that has only one good distractor. The instructional specialists maintained that, although free versus blank verse was a fine distinction, it was taught in all schools and was a state content objective. The item was retained.

The remaining two items utilized a format in which a sentence was presented to the respondents. They were then asked to identify where there might be grammatical, punctuation, or spelling errors in the sentence. A fifth option was "no error." For item 36, no error was the correct answer, but this choice had a biserial near zero. However, answer C had a positive biserial, meaning this option tended to be preferred by high scorers. A closer examination of the item revealed that what was intended to be a comma may have appeared to be a period due to the bottom portion of the comma being overwritten by underlining.

Item 38 was extremely difficult with a *p*-value of 0.19, or roughly what you would expect from random guessing. However, answer A was selected by 75 percent of the respondents. Answer A consisted of the following beginning of the sentence, "George and he went…." This is technically correct, but not typical of conversational English. The instructional specialists deleted this item.

These examples illustrate the importance of using the item statistics to flag suspicious items but then looking closer at the content of the item to decide if the item is flawed in some way. For this test, it turned out that most of the flagged items were of the Find-the-error item format. Besides potential problems with the printing, the No error option functions like a None-of-the-above option. It can become a dumping ground for respondents who don't know the correct answer.

8.2.1.3 Selecting Multiple-Choice Items

After pilot testing and item analysis, items that are not performing well and need revision or elimination have been identified. It's important to note that a revised item needs to be pilot tested again. Even a seemingly minor revision can significantly alter an item's statistical properties (and you want this to happen). Since you have hopefully pilot tested more items than you need, a set of items that appear to be functioning well remains. How do you decide which ones to select for the final version of your test? The answer to this question depends to some extent on the test's primary purpose, whether your most important score interpretation is norm- or criterion-referenced.

If the test is intended to provide a norm-referenced score interpretation, that is, the goal is to rank respondents or inform them where they stand in relation to a target population, it is desirable to select the items with higher discriminations. Additionally, items that nearly everyone answers correctly or incorrectly are not useful. As a result, look for items with moderate difficulties, p-values in the 0.40–0.70 range, and with high positive biserials or point-biserials.

For a criterion-referenced score interpretation, items that discriminate well are still desirable. As a result, select items with high positive biserials or point-biserials. Easy or difficult items may be also useful if the content they measure is deemed critical to interpreting the performance standard. However, it is important to match item difficulties to the performance standard. For example, if the standard is located at the high end of the construct, say to identify the top scorers, then more difficult items are desired. The very best items will be highly discriminating ones whose difficulty matches the performance level.

As an example, let's say that the pilot test of TIMSS Booklet 1 has identified all 20 items as high quality items, but only 10 are needed for the final version of the test. Which items do you select for each cell of the test blueprint? For a norm-referenced interpretation, the most and least difficult items would be less desirable. As a result, items such as M022251 ($p = 0.25$) and M012014 ($p = 0.82$, $r_{bis} = 0.63$) would not be selected, even though they appear to be good items. Items such as M012001 ($p = 0.59$, $r_{bis} = 0.69$) and M012042 ($p = 0.65$, $r_{bis} = 0.69$) are highly desirable because of their moderate level of difficulty combined with high discrimination.

For a criterion-referenced interpretation, item selection will depend on the location of the performance standard. If, for instance, the purpose of the test is to screen for students who need additional instructional support, then items with high p-values and high discriminations are the most desirable. In this case, M012014 would be an excellent choice. If instead, the test is intended to identify students for a mathematics honors program, then an item like M012004 ($p = 0.47$, $r_{bis} = 0.57$) would be a useful one to select. Note here that the primary purpose of TIMSS is norm-referenced (i.e., to rank nations), but it does this by categorizing students into performance levels. Booklet 1 does not contain many very easy or very difficult items because of its norm-referenced purpose and because the performance levels themselves are not extreme.

8.2.2 Item Analysis for Polytomously Scored Items
8.2.2.1 Item Quality Indicators

For polytomously scored items, we are still concerned with item difficulty and discrimination, but the indicators take on different forms. As mentioned above, for noncognitive constructs, such as self-concept, alienation, and political viewpoint, it does not make much sense to talk about how difficult an item is. Instead, we can point to an item's *location* on the construct. For instance, to repeat the example from Chapter 7, two items measuring attitude toward access to abortion can be located in different places on the construct map, as shown in Figure 8.8. The item "Abortion should be available at any time during a pregnancy" can be located toward the more access end of the construct map, while "Abortion should be an option only in cases of rape and incest" is located closer to the less access end. Depending on the polarity of the scoring, i.e., whether more access is scored higher or lower, item difficulty/location will be higher or lower in value.

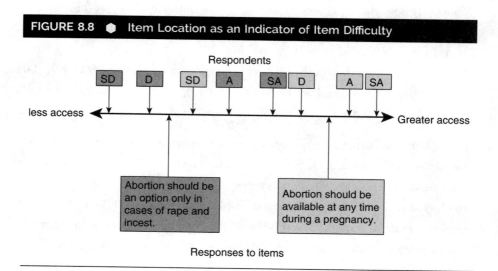

FIGURE 8.8 ● Item Location as an Indicator of Item Difficulty

One commonly used indicator of item difficulty/location is the simple item mean. For item i, this is

$$\bar{x}_i = \frac{\sum_{j=1}^{n} x_{ij}}{n} \tag{8.5}$$

The item mean will range between the lowest and highest possible item scores. An alternative difficulty/location indicator is

$$p_i = \frac{\sum_{j=1}^{n} x_{ij}}{nK}, \text{ where } X_{ij} = 0, 1, 2, \ldots, K \tag{8.6}$$

This indicator ranges from 0.0 to 1.0 and is interpreted as the average of the proportion of total points. Interpretation is similar to p-values for dichotomously scored items. An item mean near the minimum or maximum item score, or a p-value near 0.0 or 1.0, indicates an item with little variance, respondents have largely answered the same way regardless of their overall test score.

Item discrimination for polytomously scored items is conceptualized as the correlation between item and total test scores. As in the case of dichotomously scored items, this correlation should be "corrected" or "adjusted" by excluding the studied item from the total test score. Because this correlation is more stable than the point-biserial correlation, the Pearson correlation is often used, although the polyserial correlation could also be used. Interpretation is the same as for dichotomously scored items. It's desirable for these to be positive. A negative item-total correlation questions whether the item should have been reverse scored. A zero correlation suggests that the item may be measuring something different than the rest of the test.

Table 8.5 demonstrates the calculated values of the item mean, standard deviation, p-values, and item-total correlations for the brief dataset used in Chapter 3. The adjusted item-total correlations were calculated by subtracting the studied item score from the total. These results show that item 1 is "easy," thus reducing its standard deviation compared to other items. Its item-total correlation is strongly negative, meaning that persons who score high on this item tend to score low on the remainder of the test. If this item were reverse-scored, its discrimination would be 0.46.

TABLE 8.5 ● Example of Item Difficulty/Location and Discrimination Statistics						
Item Scores						
Person	1	2	3	4	5	Total
1	5	3	4	4	3	19
2	5	3	5	1	2	16
3	4	2	4	3	3	16
4	4	4	2	4	4	18
5	5	1	1	3	2	12
6	4	3	4	3	4	18
7	4	1	4	3	4	16
8	5	2	4	3	3	17
Mean	4.50	2.38	3.50	3.00	3.13	16.50
SD	0.53	1.06	1.31	0.93	0.83	2.14
p	0.90	0.48	0.70	0.60	0.63	0.66
$r_{item-tot}$	−0.46	0.31	−0.12	−0.08	0.25	

8.2.2.2 Item Analysis of Political Viewpoint Data

To demonstrate the item analysis of a set of polytomously scored items, we will use the 18 political viewpoint items. It is important to point out that the authors of the questionnaire intended for each item to be reported as a separate variable. However, a common endeavor in educational and social science research is to explore the possibility that a set of items from a large-scale survey could be used as if it were a test measuring a construct. If that were possible, then a variety of analytical methods, such as structural equation and multilevel modeling, would be possible. For these items, let's suppose that the 18 items are intended to comprise a test that measures overall political viewpoint, ranging from conservative to liberal.

The item analysis will be run using jMetrik and R psych package. Table 8.6 shows the frequency distribution of the first item, using jMetrik. To show the results, I have

TABLE 8.6 ● Frequency Distribution of View9901					
Value	**Freq.**	**Percent**	**Valid Pct.**	**Cum. Freq.**	**Cum. Pct.**
1	39	3.7249	3.7249	39	3.7249
2	214	20.4394	20.4394	253	24.1643
3	609	58.1662	58.1662	862	82.3305
4	185	17.6695	17.6695	1,047	100.0000
Valid	1,047	100.0000	100.0000		
Missing	0	0.0000			
Grand Total	1,047	100.0000			

collapsed the relevant results into single tables for each application. For all three applications, coefficient alpha is a disappointing 0.507 or 0.500. Psych and jMetrik results are shown in Tables 8.7–8.9, respectively.

Although there are no differences in the results of the two applications, there could be some differences if there were missing data. jMetrik uses listwise deletion for missing data, while for the R psych package, each item statistic is based on those respondents who answered that item, resulting in different sample sizes for each item and larger ones than for jMetrik. If there were a great deal of missing data, listwise deletion would present the problem of a much reduced sample size, while use of all available data would undermine comparisons between items because they would be based on different samples. There is no easy solution to the problem of a large amount of missing data. The psych package allows the user to impute an item's mean or median for a missing response.

jMetrik provides additional item analyses for each answer choice. This is shown in Table 8.9 for the first item. The Option column lists each answer choice and in parentheses how each choice is scored. The Difficulty column shows the proportion of respondents that selected each choice. Like the other 17 items, this frequency distribution is essentially unimodal, that is, a single highest proportion surrounded by decreasing proportions in either direction. A bimodal distribution, high proportions at both ends, would suggest a polarizing item (e.g., approval rating for the current US President), which should be investigated.

TABLE 8.7 ● R Psych Package Results for Political Viewpoint Item Analysis					
Item	n	Mean	SD	r.drop	raw_alpha
View9901	1,047	2.90	0.72	0.228	0.48
View9902	1,047	2.33	1.11	0.303	0.46
View9903	1,047	3.13	0.90	0.170	0.49
View9904	1,047	2.66	0.95	0.200	0.48
View9905	1,047	2.83	1.00	0.260	0.47
View9906	1,047	2.01	0.99	0.501	0.41
View9907	1,047	3.11	0.86	0.133	0.50
View9908	1,047	1.44	0.76	0.085	0.50
View9909	1,047	1.87	0.95	0.164	0.49
View9910	1,047	2.06	0.77	0.179	0.49
View9911	1,047	2.09	0.81	0.116	0.50
View9912	1,047	2.47	0.91	−0.100	0.54
View9913	1,047	2.31	0.97	−0.047	0.53
View9914	1,047	2.44	1.05	0.507	0.41
View9915	1,047	2.10	0.94	−0.009	0.52
View9916	1,047	1.93	1.02	0.265	0.47
View9917	1,047	2.82	0.92	0.122	0.50
View9918	1,047	2.90	0.82	−0.174	0.55

The Discrimination column shows the corrected item-total correlation for each answer choice. As the item score increases, these run from negative to positive. This is an expected result, showing that as an item score increases, the correlation between selecting that answer choice, with its associated item score, and the remainder of the test tends to increase. Note that the psych package can provide these results, but it is somewhat laborious to set up.

Looking at the results of the item analyses gives one the impression of an overall problematic test. Item means can range between 1 and 4. Fortunately, these item means range from 1.9 to 3.1. So, there do not appear to be any extreme items.

Item	Difficulty	Std. Dev.	Discrimin.	Alpha If Deleted
View9901	2.8978	0.7212	0.2276	0.4805
View9902	2.3314	1.1088	0.3029	0.4558
View9903	3.1270	0.8951	0.1695	0.4884
View9904	2.6590	0.9466	0.1997	0.4821
View9905	2.8329	0.9989	0.2595	0.4686
View9906	2.0057	0.9942	0.5006	0.4126
View9907	3.1108	0.8642	0.1329	0.4953
View9908	1.4413	0.7612	0.0848	0.5029
View9909	1.8730	0.9490	0.1637	0.4896
View9910	2.0602	0.7694	0.1787	0.4876
View9911	2.0860	0.8053	0.1159	0.4981
View9912	2.4699	0.9093	−0.1002	0.5390
View9913	2.3114	0.9721	−0.0467	0.5321
View9914	2.4384	1.0503	0.5068	0.4064
View9915	2.0955	0.9431	−0.0093	0.5237
View9916	1.9284	1.0178	0.2645	0.4671
View9917	2.8176	0.9183	0.1218	0.4978
View9918	2.8988	0.8188	−0.1740	0.5463

TABLE 8.8 ● jMetrik Results for Political Viewpoint Item Analysis

However, as mentioned above, coefficient alpha is only about 0.50, and very few of the item-total correlations are strongly positive. Only three discriminations were above 0.30. Does this mean that 15 of the 18 items are flawed? Not necessarily. Items View9902, View9906, and View9914 ask about legal issues surrounding abortion or same-sex relationships. Two items, View9912 and View9918, have negative discriminations, suggesting that maybe they should have been reverse-scored. Two other items, View9913 and View9915, have negative discriminations near zero. All four of these items ask generally about the government's role in people's lives. The remaining items, with positive but weak discriminations, seem to be about a variety of social issues,

TABLE 8.9 ⬢ jMetrik Item Analysis of 9901 for Each Score Point				
Item	**Option (Score)**	**Difficulty**	**Std. Dev.**	**Discrimin.**
View9901	Overall	2.8978	0.7212	0.2276
	1.0 (1.0)	0.0372	0.1895	−0.1904
	2.0 (2.0)	0.2044	0.4035	−0.2860
	3.0 (3.0)	0.5817	0.4935	−0.0725
	4.0 (4.0)	0.1767	0.3816	0.2151

including gender, race, and justice. Therefore, it is possible that political viewpoint is not a single construct but at least three separate and minimally related constructs. We call this situation *multidimensionality*, an issue that will be explored in Chapter 11. The items themselves may be perfectly fine. Remember that these items were created by the survey authors to be used as separate variables, not collectively as a test.

8.2.2.3 Selecting Among Polytomously Scored Items

Guidelines for selecting among well-functioning items are much the same as discussed above for dichotomously scored items. For a norm-referenced score interpretation, it is desirable to have item difficulty/locations near the middle of the item score scale. For items on a 1–4 scale, such as the political viewpoint items, that means 2.5, or items roughly in 2.0–3.0 range. It is also desirable to have strong positive item discriminations. For a criterion-referenced score interpretation, it is desirable to have a range of item difficulties/locations with some located near the performance standard. Item discriminations should be positive, but it is more important for the strongest discriminations to be for the items whose difficulty/ location are near the performance standard. For example, for political viewpoint, if the purpose is to identify strongly liberal or conservative students, then one would choose items with difficulty/locations closer to 1 and 4, respectively. Among these items, select those with the highest discriminations. One caveat, as demonstrated with the political viewpoint items, is that a multidimensional test may result in weak discriminations. An alternative strategy would be to create separate tests for each dimension and conduct item analyses separately for each dimension. This approach is discussed in Chapter 11.

8.3 CHAPTER SUMMARY

This chapter presented concepts and methods related to pilot testing and item analysis. As with all other aspects of test development, the primary driver behind test development decision-making is validity. After one has written and revised items to be in the best shape possible, it is necessary to collect data to evaluate their quality statistically. This is the purpose of pilot testing. Hopefully, more items than needed are pilot tested, from which poorly performing items can be eliminated and the best items selected for a final version. In preparing a test for pilot testing, this chapter discussed test design issues, delivery methods, and sampling considerations.

Once pilot test data have been collected and screened, this chapter presented methods for item analysis using two popular item analysis applications. Two primary types of item quality statistics were discussed: difficulty/location and discrimination. Item difficulty is generally described as its location on a construct map. Item discrimination measures how strongly related item responses are to scores on the total test (minus the score on the studied item). This chapter also drew a distinction between item analyses for dichotomously scored and polytomously scored items. Finally, the results for the TIMSS Booklet 1 mathematics test and a potential test for measuring political viewpoint were presented for jMetrik and the R psych package. Each application presents a common set of item statistics, but each one has some unique aspects. With complete data, both applications produced identical results. With missing data, the psych package results would differ from jMetrik due to differences in how missing data are handled.

It is important to emphasize that items should not be automatically rejected due to weak item statistics, especially item discrimination. The political viewpoint data demonstrate that, if the construct being measured is multidimensional, discriminations for good items may appear to be near zero or even negative. Finally, once poorly performing items have been eliminated, how to select among the remaining items was discussed. Although positive discriminations are always desired, item selection depends somewhat on whether a norm-referenced or criterion-referenced score interpretation is most important.

8.4 EXERCISES AND ACTIVITIES

Test Development Project

1. Develop a pilot test form that begins with what the test measures and what are its intended uses, how confidentiality and respondent identity will be protected, directions for responding, and one or two sample items.

2. Administer the pilot test form to a convenience sample that is as representative as possible of the test's target population.

3. Run an item analysis of pilot test data.

4. Use the item analysis results to make a decision for each item: keep as is, revise and pilot test again, or eliminate.

Questions for Discussion

a. Suppose you have developed and pilot tested a test measuring "health risk behavior." Its purpose is to screen for respondents who have a high risk score to be referred for a psychological intervention. What statistical characteristics of items are most desirable for this test?

b. For a multiple-choice item, why is a positive discrimination for a distractor an indicator of a possible item flaw? Why is a p-value of near 0.00 or 1.00 an indicator of a possible item flaw?

c. For the TIMSS and political viewpoint data, run the item analyses in both jMetrik and the R psych package. You should get the same results as shown in this chapter.

FURTHER READING

Computer-based Versus Paper-and-Pencil Administration

Kingston, N. M. (2009). Comparability of computer- and paper-administered multiple-choice tests for K-12 populations: A synthesis. *Applied Measurement in Education*, 22(1), 22–37.

Designing and Administering Tests

Colton, D., & Covert, R. W. (2007). *Designing and constructing instruments for social research and evaluation*. San Francisco, CA: Jossey-Bass.

Dillman, D. A., Smyth, J. D., & Christian, L. M. (2008). *Internet, mail, and mixed-mode surveys: The tailored design method* (3rd ed.). Hoboken, NJ: Wiley.

Item Analysis

Meyer, J. P. (2014). *Applied measurement with jMetrik*. New York, NY: Routledge.

REFERENCES

Adams, R. J., & Wu, M. L. (2000). *PISA 2000 technical report*. Paris, France: OECD.

Brennan, R. (1992). The context of context effects. *Applied Measurement in Education*, 5, 225–264.

Debeer, D., & Janssen, R. (2013). Modeling item-position effects within an IRT framework. *Journal of Educational Measurement*, 50(2), 164–185.

Duckworth, A. L., Peterson, C., Matthews, M. D., & Kelly, D. R. (2007). Grit: Perseverance and passion for long-term goals. *Journal of Personality and Social Psychology*, 92(6), 1087–1101.

Eignor, D. R., & Stocking, M. (1986). *An investigation of possible causes for the inadequacy of IRT pre-equating ETS RR-86-14*. Princeton, NJ: Educational Testing Service.

Harris, D. (1991). Effects of passage and item scrambling on equating relationships. *Applied Psychological Measurement*, 8, 147–154.

Jones, B. D., & Skaggs, G. (2016). Measuring students' motivation: Validity evidence for the MUSIC Model of Academic Motivation Inventory. *International Journal for the Scholarship of Teaching and Learning*, 10(1). Article 7.

Kolen, M. J., & Harris, D. (1990). Comparison of item pre-equating and random groups equating using IRT and equipercentile methods. *Journal of Educational Measurement*, 27(1), 27–39.

Leary, L., & Dorans, N. (1985). Implications for altering the context in which test items appear: A historical perspective on an immediate concern. *Review of Educational Research*, 55, 387–413.

Lickona, T., & Davidson, M. (2003). *School as a Caring Community Profile-II Cortland, NY: Center for the 4th and 5th Rs (Respect and Responsibility)*. Washington, DC: Character Education Partnership.

Meyers, J. L., Miller, G. E., & Way, W. D. (2009). Item position and item difficulty change in an IRT-based common item equating design. *Applied Measurement in Education*, 22, 38–60.

Pommerich, M., & Harris, D. J. (2003). Context effects in pretesting: Impact on item statistics and examinee scores. Paper presented at the Annual Meeting of the American Educational Research Association, New Orleans, LA.

Thorndike, R. L. (1982). *Applied psychometrics*. Boston, MA: Houghton Mifflin.

Way, W. D., Carey, P., & Golub-Smith, M. (1992). *An exploratory study of characteristics related to IRT parameter invariance with the Test of English as a Foreign Language TOEFL Technical Report No. 6*. Princeton, NJ: Educational Testing Service.

Zwick, R. (1991). Effects of item order and context on estimation on NAEP reading proficiency. *Educational Measurement: Issues and Practice*, 10, 10–16.

9

INTRODUCTION TO RASCH MEASUREMENT THEORY

9.1 PROBLEMS WITH CLASSICAL TEST THEORY

Chapter 4 introduced the concepts of Classical Test Theory (CTT). These included reliability and reliability coefficients, the standard error of measurement (SEM), and item characteristics such as difficulty and discrimination. Despite its widespread use over the past one hundred years, measurement experts have long noted a number of problems with CTT. Here are the main ones:

1. Reliability is a single property of the test, applied to the entire test. This implies that all scores are equally precise. This may be unwarranted. In particular, scores at the high and low ends of the score scale are likely to be less precise than scores in the middle.

2. The calculation of reliability coefficients themselves requires some assumptions about the relationships between parts of a test, assumptions which may not be realistic.

3. The SEM is a test property and likewise implies equal precision of all scores. To be fair, this limitation can be mitigated by the use of Conditional SEMs (CSEMs) that provide varying degrees of precision for each possible true score. Reporting CSEMs is recommended in the 2014 *Standards*.

4. The random error model of CTT excludes systematic measurement errors, such as context effects and measurement bias, which may in fact be larger than random errors.

5. Item statistics, such as difficulty and discrimination, are sample-dependent. For example, if 90 percent of a sample of respondents can answer an item correctly, does this mean that the item is easy or the sample is highly knowledgeable?

6. The calculation of reliability coefficients, SEMs, and item statistics are based on raw scores, or composites of observed scores on the parts of a test, usually the individual items. As pointed out in Chapter 3, raw scores have numerous limitations. Conversion to scale scores, as discussed also in

Chapter 3, can alleviate some of these problems, but reliability coefficients and SEMs are not well developed for scale scores.

7. Related to number 6 above, CTT has some difficulty being applied to tests composed of different item formats, such as a test composed of both multiple-choice and essay sections.

Consider the brief geography test from Chapter 3:

1. *What is the name of this planet?*

2. *What is the name of the continent on which the United States is located?*

3. *What is the tallest mountain in the world?*

4. *What country has the largest population?*

5. *What is the depth of the Atlantic Ocean 100 miles east of Boston?*

If mapped out onto a continuum of geographic knowledge, the five items would likely be placed approximately as shown in Figure 9.1. In contrast to classical raw scores, *Rasch Measurement Theory* attempts to create an equal interval measurement scale that would reflect the unequal distances between raw score points.

9.2 DEVELOPMENT OF PROBABILITY MODELS

The above limitations of CTT have been known to psychometricians for a long time. Alternatives have generally focused on the idea of the probability that a respondent will select a particular answer to an item or will earn a specific score on an item. That probability is modeled as a consequence of a person's measurement on the construct and the properties of the item. A number of probability models have been developed

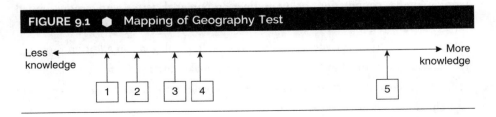

FIGURE 9.1 ● **Mapping of Geography Test**

in recent decades. The one presented here was proposed by the Danish mathematician Georg Rasch (1960) and is called the binary Rasch model.

Consider a game of chess, a tennis match, or other contest in which you are competing against someone who is exactly as good as you are. What is your probability of winning? About 0.50. In other words, your winning is a 50/50 proposition. If you play someone more skilled than you, you have a less than 50 percent chance of winning. And if your opponent is less skilled, your chances of winning are greater than 50 percent.

Rasch Measurement Theory aims to use this idea about probability to develop a measurement system designed to achieve two major goals:

1. An *equal interval score scale* on which person scores, unlike raw scores, will indicate equal units of measurement.

2. *Objectivity* in which the measurement of a construct does not depend on the specific items in the test. This means that a person will receive the same score regardless of the items. In other words, a different set of items measuring the same construct should result in the same score. By the same token, although we don't think about it as much, the calibration of test items, or the estimation of their difficulties, should not depend on the specific sample of respondents.

9.3 BINARY RASCH MODEL

This same reasoning can be applied to items in a test. To simplify things, let's assume that all items are dichotomously scored, that is, 0 or 1, incorrect or correct. In keeping with standard notation, item i has a difficulty level of β_i, and person s has a skill level of θ_s. It is important to note that many Rasch Theory references refer to the construct being measured as *ability*, a measure of a person's level on the construct as *person ability*, and the test score as an *ability estimate*. Unfortunately, the use of the term ability has connotations of IQ and person potential, terms with a more limited meaning than is intended here. Likewise, the term item *difficulty* makes sense only for a cognitive construct. A calculus problem is more difficult than an addition problem. However, as mentioned in Chapter 8, the term makes little sense for a noncognitive construct, such as motivation or self-concept. A better term is item location, or where an item is located on a construct map.

Figure 9.2 depicts three possible outcomes on a construct map when person s responds to item i. The top line shows the situation in which a person's construct level exactly matches the difficulty of the item. In other words, $\theta_s - \beta_i = 0$, and the probability of a correct answer is 0.50, or $P(X_{is} = 1) = 0.50$. The second line shows the situation in which the person's ability is greater than the item's difficulty, or $\theta_s - \beta_i > 0$. As a result, the probability of a correct response is greater than 0.50, or $P(X_{is} = 1) > 0.50$. The bottom line shows the opposite situation, in which the item's difficulty is greater than the person's ability, or $\theta_s - \beta_i < 0$, and $P(X_{is} = 1) < 0.50$.

To go a step further, as person ability becomes greater than the item difficulty, the probability of a correct response approaches 1.0. Likewise, as item difficulty becomes increasingly larger than person ability, the probability approaches 0.0. The difference $\theta_s - \beta_i$ can be plotted against the probability of a correct response, as shown in Figure 9.3. Notice that this line is not straight. Since no probability can be greater than 1.0, the graph tapers off at the higher end. Likewise, since probability cannot be less than 0.0, the graph bottoms out at 0.0.

Georg Rasch developed the binary Rasch model to represent the probability of a score of 1 on a dichotomously scored item:

FIGURE 9.2 ● Probability of a Correct Response by Person s to Item *i*

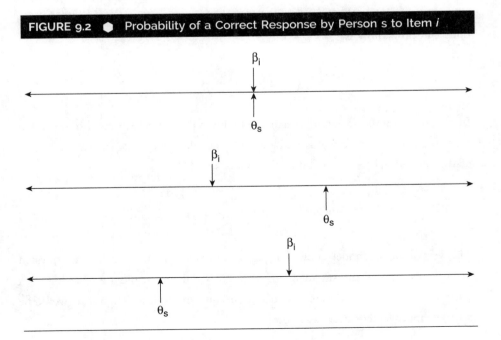

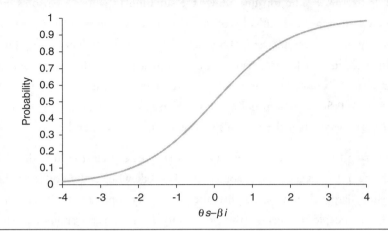

FIGURE 9.3 ● Probability of a Correct Response According to $\theta_s - \beta_i$

$$P(X_{is} = 1 | \theta_s, \beta_i) = \frac{e^{(\theta_s - \beta_i)}}{1 + e^{(\theta_s - \beta_i)}} \qquad (9.1)$$

The value of this formula can range between 0.0 and 1.0, and when graphed, follows the ogive shape in the above figure. Another version of this model comes in terms of the odds rather than the probability of a correct response. The relationship between odds and probability is

$$\text{odds} = \frac{P}{1 - P} \qquad (9.2)$$

In casinos and horse racing, the chances of winning are often expressed in odds. For example, if the probability of winning is 0.50, the odds of winning are 1.0, or 1:1. By taking the natural log of the odds, the model simplifies to

$$\ln(\text{odds}) = \ln\left[\frac{P}{1 - P}\right] = \theta_s - \beta_i \qquad (9.3)$$

This version of the model shows that person ability and item difficulty are expressed in log odds units of measurement, or logits. It is difficult to picture what log odds units mean, but these units are intended to be equal interval, which, if true, would be a major improvement over raw scores.

As an example, suppose there is a five-item test measuring "enjoyment of lawn mowing." Each item is dichotomously scored, 0 or 1, for Disagree or Agree, respectively. Suppose also that the difficulties of these five items are −2.0, −1.5, 0.0, 0.5, and 2.0. Item 1 could be "I can only bring myself to mow the lawn when the grass gets two feet tall." Item 5 might be "Lawn mowing is my favorite thing to do on a hot summer afternoon." The five items can be graphed together, as shown in Figure 9.4, one response curve for each item. These curves are also called item response functions, item characteristic curves, or trace lines depending on the software application. Notice that each item's difficulty can be located at the point of inflection, above the horizontal axis where the probability is 0.50.

For a respondent with a lawn mowing enjoyment "ability" of −4.0 (i.e., someone who really hates to mow their lawn), the probability that this person will Agree to the first item is

$$P(X_{is} = 1|\theta_s, \beta_i) = \frac{e^{(-4.0 - (-2.0))}}{1 + e^{(-4.0 - (-2.0))}} = \frac{0.135}{1 + 0.135} = 0.12$$

In other words, not very likely. The probabilities that this person will Agree to the remaining items are 0.08, 0.02, 0.01, and 0.002, increasingly less likely because the items' difficulties/locations increase. If a person with a lawn mowing enjoyment ability of −2.0 responds to item 1, the probability of agreement is

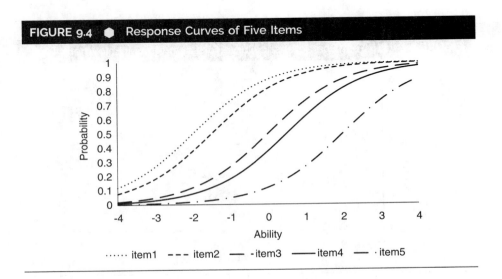

FIGURE 9.4 ● Response Curves of Five Items

$$P(X_{is} = 1|\theta_s, \beta_i) = \frac{e^{(-2.0 - (-2.0))}}{1 + e^{(-2.0 - (-2.0))}} = \frac{1}{1 + 1} = 0.50$$

This is just like competing against someone with your exact skill level. That person's probabilities of agreement with the other four items are 0.38, 0.12, 0.08, and 0.02.

9.4 SCALING AND SCORING WITH THE RASCH MODEL

Once item difficulties are estimated from data, respondents can be scored. One scoring option is to calculate a person's *estimated true score*, that is, the raw score to be expected from someone with a specific ability level, found by adding the probabilities of a score of 1 across all items:

$$\hat{T} = \sum P_i \tag{9.4}$$

If the above-mentioned person has a lawn mower enjoyment ability of -4.0, the sum of the probabilities of agreement is $\sum P_i = 0.12 + 0.08 + 0.02 + 0.01 + 0.002 = 0.23$. That is, on a 0–4 raw score scale, this person is expected to obtain a score of 0.23. Likewise, the person with an ability of -2.0 is expected to obtain a raw score of $\sum P_i = 0.50 + 0.38 + 0.12 + 0.08 + 0.02 = 1.09$. By plotting the expected raw scores for each ability value, the *test characteristic curve* is obtained, as shown in Figure 9.5.

FIGURE 9.5 ● Test Characteristic Curve for Lawn Mower Enjoyment Test

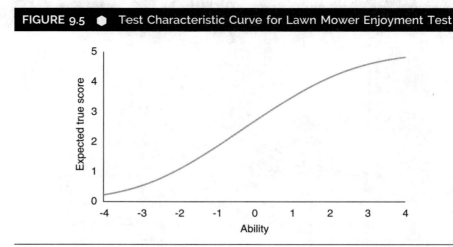

Note that there is a nonlinear relationship between ability and raw score. As ability changes by a logit unit, the expected true score changes by different amounts depending on the ability level. The biggest change occurs in the middle of the logit scale, while the smaller change occurs at the extremes.

On the other hand, when using the Rasch model, one typically wants a test score in logit units because they are assumed to be equal interval. Again, using item response probabilities, an ability estimate can be obtained for each response pattern. Suppose a respondent agrees with the first four items in the above lawn mower test but disagrees with the fifth item, in other words, a response pattern of 11110. For any ability level, the probability of this response pattern is the product of the five probabilities, that is, $P(X_{1s} = 1|\theta_s, \beta_1) \times P(X_{2s} = 1|\theta_s, \beta_2) \times P(X_{3s} = 1|\theta_s, \beta_3) \times P(X_{4s} = 1|\theta_s, \beta_4) \times P(X_{5s} = 0|\theta_s, \beta_5)$. Note that, for item 5, $P(X_{5s} = 0|\theta_s, \beta_5) = 1 - P(X_{5s} = 1|\theta_s, \beta_5)$. This product is called the *likelihood* of the response pattern and has this general formula:

$$L = \prod P(X_{is} = 1 \text{ or } 0|\theta_s, \beta_i) \tag{9.5}$$

For the respondent with an ability of -4.0, the likelihood of the response pattern 11110 is

$$L = \prod P(X_{is} = 1|\theta_s, \beta_i) = 0.12 \times 0.08 \times 0.02 \times 0.01 \times (1 - 0.002) = 0.000002$$

In other words, it is highly unlikely that this respondent will answer the items that way. For the respondent with an ability of -2.0, the likelihood of the same response pattern is

$$L = \prod P(X_{is} = 1|\theta_s, \beta_i) = 0.50 \times 0.38 \times 0.12 \times 0.08 \times (1 - 0.02) = 0.002$$

This probability is still fairly unlikely to occur but is more probable for this respondent than the first one.

The likelihood values can be plotted across all ability levels. For this response pattern, the graph is shown in Figure 9.6. Visually, the high point of the likelihood function is above an ability of about 1.80 (an exact ability will require some specialized software). That means that a person with an ability of 1.80 has the highest probability of

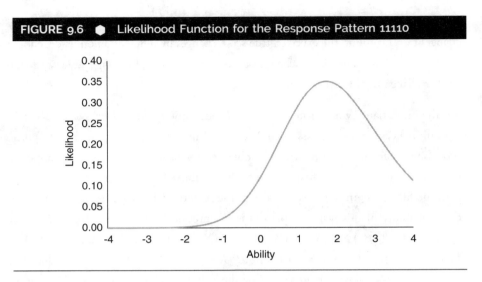

FIGURE 9.6 ● Likelihood Function for the Response Pattern 11110

answering with this response pattern, that is, agreeing with the first four items, disagreeing with the fifth item. Consequently, a respondent with this pattern will be assigned a logit ability estimate of 1.80. This method of estimating person ability is descriptively called *maximum likelihood*.

This method can be used to assign an ability estimate for any response pattern. For example, a pattern of 11001 (Agree with items 1, 2, and 5; Disagree with items 3 and 4) would show the likelihood function shown in Figure 9.7. The maximum likelihood ability estimate for this pattern is about −0.48. Note also that this likelihood function is much lower than the one above. This is because this is overall a much less likely response pattern because the respondent has agreed to an item with a higher difficulty/location, while disagreeing with items with a lower difficulty/location. Imagine someone disagreeing with the statement "I can only bring myself to mow the lawn when the grass gets two feet tall," while agreeing with "Lawn mowing is my favorite thing to do on a hot summer afternoon." That would be odd.

There is one important point to be made about using maximum likelihood to estimate person ability. Note that there are five different ways a respondent could Agree with four items and Disagree with one item: 01111, 10111, 11011 11101, and 11110. If the likelihood functions for all five were plotted on the same graph, the following would result, as shown in Figure 9.8. All five have the same maximum

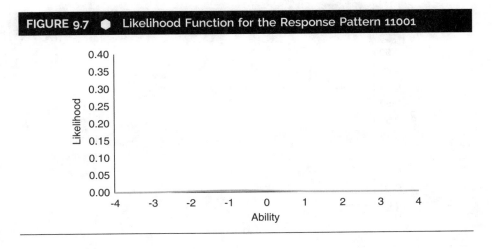

FIGURE 9.7 ● Likelihood Function for the Response Pattern 11001

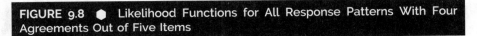

FIGURE 9.8 ● Likelihood Functions for All Response Patterns With Four Agreements Out of Five Items

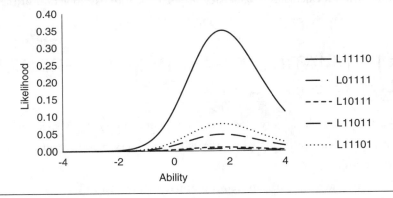

likelihood value. In other words, everyone with the same raw score will receive the same ability estimate, regardless of the pattern of item responses.

Finally, what about response patterns of 11111 or 00000: Agree or Disagree with all five items? These patterns are tantamount to zero and perfect raw scores. These are graphed in Figure 9.9. Note that there is no maximum likelihood for either pattern (they are actually minus and plus infinity, respectively). This means that we cannot estimate ability using maximum likelihood for zero and perfect scores. Practically,

FIGURE 9.9 ⬡ Likelihood Functions for Zero and Perfect Scores

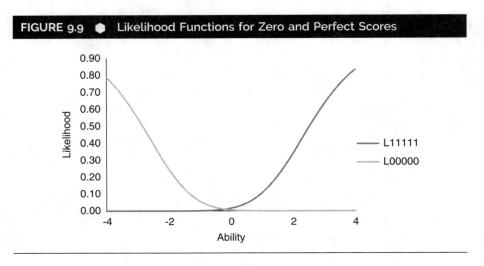

different software applications adopt rules of thumb for these respondents. For example, jMetrik calculates a value that approximates an extrapolation of the ability estimates for raw scores near to zero and perfect scores.

9.5 ESTIMATING MEASUREMENT ERROR WITH THE RASCH MODEL

Unlike CTT, Rasch Theory does not assume that everyone is measured equally precisely. Error can be estimated separately for each person ability value. The vehicle for accomplishing this is the concept of item and test *information*. For the binary Rasch model, each item has an item information function as follows:

$$I_i(\theta) = P_i(\theta)(1 - P_i(\theta)) \tag{9.6}$$

In other words, the information value of item i is simply the probability of a correct response (or score of 1) times the probability of an incorrect response (or score of 0). These probabilities vary according to ability. For item 1 of the lawn mower test, the information function is shown in Figure 9.10. This item has a difficulty of -2.0. As a result, the information function peaks at an ability of -2.0. This is where a respondent with an ability of -2.0 has a 0.50 probability of answering Agree. The item information value here is $0.50 \times (1-0.50) = 0.25$. As ability becomes higher or

FIGURE 9.10 ● Information Function for Item 1

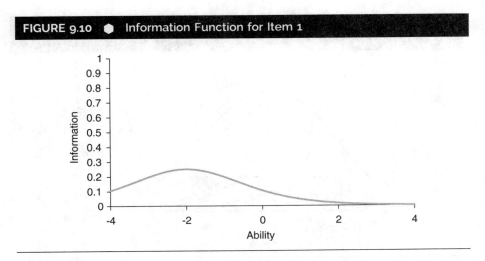

lower than -2.0, the item information value becomes less than 0.25. The item information value itself does not have much meaning. What to look for is the location on the ability scale where the values are the highest and lowest. This item has the highest information at an ability of -2.0, meaning that it provides the most measurement precision for respondents with an ability of -2.0, less so as respondents' abilities deviate from -2.0.

Each item has its own information function. The test as a whole has a test information function that is the sum of the item information functions at each ability level:

$$TI(\theta) = \sum I_i(\theta) \qquad (9.7)$$

For the lawn mower test, the five item information functions and the test information function are graphed in Figure 9.11. The test information function has a maximum value, and the greatest precision, for a person ability of about -0.40. Precision decreases as ability increases or decreases away from that point.

The test information function has implications for test development. Knowing that measurement precision varies by ability level, the developer of a test can sketch a target test information function to ensure that precision is highest where it's needed the most. For example, Figure 9.12 shows three possible target test information

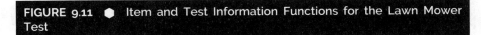

FIGURE 9.11 ● Item and Test Information Functions for the Lawn Mower Test

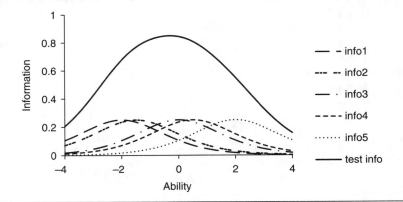

FIGURE 9.12 ● Three Sample Target Test Information Functions

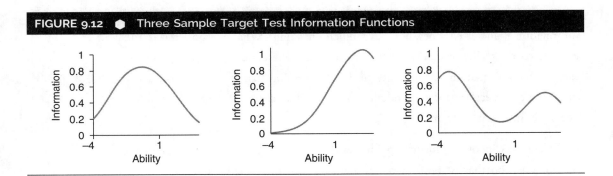

functions. The function on the left could be used for a test for which the greatest precision is desired at lower ability levels, such as identifying a minimal level of skill or referring an individual for intervention for low levels of motivation, self-concept, or emotional intelligence. The middle figure shows a function for a test where the greatest desired precision is at a high level of ability, such as a selection test for a gifted/talented program. The function on the far right is ideal for a test where the most precision is desired at two levels, such as identifying basic and proficient levels of performance. For any target information function, item selection will be guided by using items whose item information functions will add up to the target test information function. This means finding items whose difficulties are near the high points of the target information function.

An indicator of absolute measurement precision can be found by using the *standard error of ability*. This statistic can be calculated as the reciprocal of the square root of the test information function:

$$SE_\theta = \frac{1}{\sqrt{TI}} \tag{9.8}$$

For the lawn mower test, a graph of the SE_θ is shown in Figure 9.13. The smallest standard error and greatest precision is, like the test information function, at an ability of about -0.40. The standard error of ability can be used in a manner similar to the SEM from CTT, to form a confidence interval around an ability estimate. For example, for a respondent with an ability of -0.40, $SE_\theta = \frac{1}{\sqrt{0.85}} = 1.09$. This person would be expected to obtain an ability estimate in the range $-0.40 \pm 1.96 \times 1.09$ about 95 percent of the time. By contrast, a respondent with an ability of 3.0 would be expected to have a 95 percent chance of obtaining an ability estimate in the range of $3.0 \pm (1.96 \times 1.74)$. The ability of the latter respondent will be estimated with much less precision than the former respondent.

9.6 ASSUMPTIONS AND MODEL FIT

As mentioned in Section 9.2, the two goals of Rasch Measurement Theory are an equal interval scale and objectivity. The equal interval scale is obtained by using logits as the units of measurement. Objectivity is achieved because item difficulties

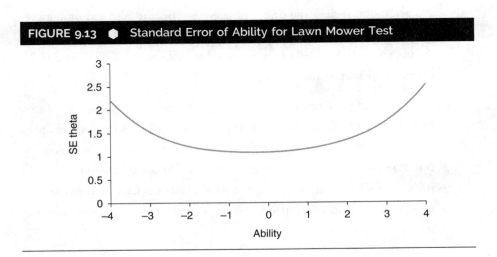

FIGURE 9.13 ● Standard Error of Ability for Lawn Mower Test

and person abilities are measured on the same logit scale. An item with a difficulty of 1.1 has that difficulty no matter who responds to it. It will be difficult for persons with abilities less than 1.1 but easy for persons with abilities greater than 1.1. Likewise, a respondent will obtain the same ability estimate no matter the difficulties (within reason) of the items. What will change across different sets of items is the degree of precision of item difficulties and person abilities. Rasch Theory replaces CTT reliability with test information and the SEM with the standard error of ability.

However, all this great stuff comes at a price, coming in the form of assumptions. Like CTT, the validity of Rasch Theory is based on the viability of its assumptions. For the binary Rasch model, three assumptions were required to derive the likelihood and information functions. These assumptions are also necessary to develop the software needed to estimate item difficulties and person abilities from actual item response data:

1. *Unidimensionality.* In the binary Rasch model, there is one ability to be estimated for each person. This means that the test is assumed to measure one and only one construct. There are methods for determining how well this assumption holds given a set of response data. These methods are discussed in Chapter 11.

2. *Fit of the data to the model.* In the binary Rasch model, items are identified by just one characteristic, item difficulty. Items could vary on other characteristics, such as the degree of guessing (for true-false and multiple-choice items) or discrimination, which is not part of the Rasch model. A number of statistics have been proposed to evaluate model fit. These will be discussed later in this section.

3. *Local item independence.* Responses to items by individuals are assumed to be independent of each other. In other words, a person's response to any item is not affected by the items that came before it. This assumption could be challenged, for example, by a set of items with a common stimulus, such as a reading passage or graph. Statistics have been proposed to measure local item independence. These will also be discussed later in this section.

When using the Rasch model, we assume that the mathematical formulation of the model is a realistic representation of the responses of individuals to the items. If people or items do not respond as the model suggests, a situation called person or item *misfit*, then there is reason to question the validity of person ability or item difficulty estimates. Some reasons why respondents misfit the Rasch model include:

1. Lucky guesses on difficult items

2. Carelessness on easy items

3. Test security breeches/cheating

4. Specialized knowledge or deficiencies

Likewise, some items may not fit the Rasch model because of:

1. Multidimensionality

2. Poor item quality

3. Miskeying or incorrect data entry

4. Guessing

5. Items varying in discrimination

To evaluate model fit, a number of fit statistics have been developed. They are intended to detect unusual response patterns, such as those described above for the geography knowledge and lawn mower tests. It is important to state that it is unwise to delete an item based solely on a fit statistic. The test developer should explore possible explanations for the fit statistic flagging items or persons.

Rasch model fit statistics are based on the idea of residuals, which are the differences between actual item responses and the probabilities of those responses according to the Rasch model. Consider the following dataset in Table 9.1, in which ten individuals responded to five dichotomously scored items. Also suppose that the difficulties for these five items are known to be 1.0, −1.5, 0.0, −0.5, and 2.0. Table 9.2 shows the abilities of the ten respondents and their probabilities of a score of 1 on each item, based on the binary Rasch model.

TABLE 9.1 ⬡ Item Responses for a Five-Item Test					
Person	Item 1	Item 2	Item 3	Item 4	Item 5
1	1	1	1	1	1
2	0	0	0	0	1
3	0	1	1	1	0
4	0	1	1	1	0
5	1	1	1	1	0
6	1	1	1	1	1
7	0	1	1	1	0
8	0	0	0	1	0
9	1	1	1	1	0
10	1	1	1	1	1

TABLE 9.2 ⬡ Probabilities of Scoring a 1 on Each Item by the Respondents						
Person	Ability	Item 1	Item 2	Item 3	Item 4	Item 5
1	1.1	0.525	0.931	0.750	0.832	0.289
2	−0.6	0.168	0.711	0.354	0.475	0.069
3	−0.5	0.182	0.731	0.378	0.500	0.076
4	0.1	0.289	0.832	0.525	0.646	0.130
5	2.0	0.731	0.971	0.881	0.924	0.500
6	2.4	0.802	0.980	0.917	0.948	0.599
7	−0.3	0.214	0.769	0.426	0.550	0.091
8	−0.8	0.142	0.668	0.310	0.426	0.057
9	0.6	0.401	0.891	0.646	0.750	0.198
10	1.6	0.646	0.957	0.832	0.891	0.401

The residuals can be found by subtracting the probability in Table 9.2 from the corresponding response of 0 or 1 in Table 9.1. These are shown in Table 9.3. For example, for Person 1 responding to Item 1, the residual is 1–0.525 = 0.475. The larger the residual, the larger the difference between the observed and expected values

Person	Item 1	Item 2	Item 3	Item 4	Item 5
TABLE 9.3 ⬠ Residuals: Observed Response Minus Probability					
1	0.475	0.069	0.250	0.168	0.711
2	−0.168	−0.711	−0.354	−0.475	0.931
3	−0.182	0.269	0.622	0.500	−0.076
4	−0.289	0.168	0.475	0.354	−0.130
5	0.269	0.029	0.119	0.076	−0.500
6	0.198	0.020	0.083	0.052	0.401
7	−0.214	0.231	0.574	0.450	−0.091
8	−0.142	−0.668	−0.310	0.574	−0.057
9	0.599	0.109	0.354	0.250	−0.198
10	0.354	0.043	0.168	0.109	0.599

of an item response, but it is difficult to know how large is really large. Therefore, residuals are standardized by squaring them and then dividing by their information function, $P(1 - P)$. Each squared standardized residual is now a chi-square statistic with one degree of freedom. These are now shown in Table 9.4.

The critical value for a significantly large standardized residual is 3.84. Now, we can see that the response to item 5 by person 2 significantly misfits. This is someone with an ability of −0.6 scoring a 1 on an item with a difficulty of 2.0. Unlikely, but it happened. One advantage of this chi-square fit statistic is that it can be summed across items to obtain a fit statistic for each person, and it can be summed across persons to give a fit statistic for each item. This shows significant misfit for item 5 and for person 2 (highlighted in bold), but it's really the person 2/item 5 combination (also bolded) that is driving the misfit. A major disadvantage of chi-square fit statistics in general is that they are sensitive to sample size. With a reasonably large sample size and a test of typical length, an unrealistically high percentage of residuals will be significant even though their magnitude is of moderate size.

To get around this problem, other fit statistics are more widely used. For Rasch models, the most popular are mean squares and standardized mean squares. Mean

Person	Item 1	Item 2	Item 3	Item 4	Item 5	Chi-square
TABLE 9.4 ● Standardized Residuals						
1	0.905	0.074	0.333	0.202	2.460	3.973
2	0.202	2.460	0.549	0.905	**13.464**	**17.579**
3	0.223	0.368	1.649	1.000	0.082	3.322
4	0.407	0.202	0.905	0.549	0.150	2.212
5	0.368	0.030	0.135	0.082	1.000	1.615
6	0.247	0.020	0.091	0.055	0.670	1.083
7	0.273	0.301	1.350	0.819	0.100	2.843
8	0.165	2.014	0.449	1.350	0.061	4.039
9	1.492	0.122	0.549	0.333	0.247	2.743
10	0.549	0.045	0.202	0.122	1.492	2.410
Chi-square	4.829	5.637	6.211	5.417	**19.725**	41.818

squares are calculated by dividing the chi-square value by the degrees of freedom. According to Bond and Fox (2007), mean squares have an expected value of 1.0, and a range of 0.8–1.2 is considered to indicate good fit to the Rasch model. Values greater than that indicate lack of fit. Values less than that suggest overfit, that the data fit the model too well. Fitting too well seems counterintuitive, but it can suggest that the test is of higher quality than it really is. For example, if a test consisted of the same item repeated many times, the item mean squares would show overfit.

Standardized mean squares are found by converting mean squares to a statistics that can be interpreted like z-scores. They have an expected value of 0.0 and a standard deviation of about 1.0. Meyer (2014) recommends a value greater than 3.0 to indicate misfit, and a value less than -3.0 to indicate overfit. Both mean squares and standardized mean squares can be weighted by the item information values. These are called *infit* mean squares. Residuals for persons near an item's difficulty value count more than those farther away. Unweighted mean squares are called *outfit* mean squares.

Residuals can also be used to investigate the assumption of local item independence. A widely used statistic to detect local item dependence (LID) is Yen's Q_3

(Yen, 1984). Q_3 is defined as the correlation between residuals of two items. If this assumption of local item independence holds true, these correlations are expected to be zero. A common use of Q_3 is to flag residual correlations greater than 0.2 or less than -0.2 as showing LID between two items.

9.7 EXAMPLE USING TIMSS BOOKLET 1 DATA

Applying the Rasch model to a dataset requires the use of specialized software. WINSTEPS (Linacre, 2021), IRTPRO (Vector Psychometric Group, 2020), and several R packages including mirt (Chalmers et al., 2017) are among the many applications that can carry out Rasch analyses. For this example, I will use jMetrik and the TIMSS Book1 data to illustrate the binary Rasch model. This is mostly a matter of convenience because jMetrik was already set up for this data in Chapters 3 and 8. I am also intentionally skipping the technicalities of item difficulty and person ability estimation. Conceptually, item difficulties and person abilities are estimated using the maximum likelihood method described above. However, the maximum of the likelihood function is determined through an iterative algorithm called *joint maximum likelihood estimation* (JMLE). First, item difficulties are estimated. Then those difficulty estimates are used to estimate person abilities, which in turn are used to reestimate item difficulties, and so on until a solution converges.

The analysis was run as follows:

1. Select the table containing the data for TIMSS Book1. In the Analyze menu, select Rasch Models (JMLE).

2. Select all items. Leave all selections in the Global tab as is.

3. In the Item tab, select Correct UCON bias and Save Item Estimates. Create a new table name for the item difficulty estimates.

4. In the Person tab, select Save person estimates, Save person fit statistics, and Save residuals. Next to Save residuals, create a new table name for the residuals.

5. Select Run.

Two tables from the jMetrik output are shown below. First is a table showing the item difficulty estimates and item fit statistics. The easiest item is M022040 (-1.21), and the most difficult is M022251 (2.03) (Table 9.5).

TABLE 9.5 ● Item Parameter Estimates for TIMSS Book1

Item	Difficulty	Std. Error	WMS	Std. WMS	UMS	Std. UMS
M012001	0.20	0.08	0.82	−5.45	0.76	−4.61
M012002	−0.54	0.09	1.04	0.95	1.13	1.54
M012003	−0.24	0.09	0.93	−1.9	0.89	−1.53
M012004	0.78	0.08	0.92	−2.37	0.91	−1.76
M012005	0.39	0.08	1.16	4.44	1.18	3.14
M012006	−0.53	0.09	1.10	2.29	1.15	1.74
M012037	−0.21	0.09	1.08	2.18	1.16	2.18
M012038	−0.50	0.09	0.96	−1.05	0.98	−0.18
M012039	0.88	0.08	1.11	3.13	1.14	2.53
M012040	−1.21	0.10	0.91	−1.65	0.74	−2.22
M012041	−0.67	0.09	0.89	−2.43	0.89	−1.20
M012042	−0.12	0.09	0.83	−4.95	0.74	−4.17
M032570	−0.44	0.09	0.99	−0.28	0.88	−1.49
M032643	0.73	0.08	0.95	−1.55	0.92	−1.50
M012013	0.46	0.08	1.05	1.48	1.03	0.67
M012014	−1.23	0.10	0.85	−2.67	0.73	−2.36
M012015	−0.28	0.09	0.93	−1.78	0.91	−1.19
M012016	0.28	0.08	1.11	3.07	1.10	1.74
M012017	0.22	0.08	1.01	0.43	1.03	0.61
M022251	2.03	0.10	1.18	3.50	1.39	3.84

Table 9.6, called the Score Table, shows the ability estimate associated with each raw score, from 0 to 20. As mentioned above, the maximum likelihood ability estimate is the same for all persons with the same raw score, regardless of which items were answered correctly. Additionally, scores of 0 and 20 do not actually have ability estimates. These were created by jMetrik to be reasonable values given the other raw score to ability estimate conversions. However, for reporting and research

TABLE 9.6 ⬢ Raw Score to Rasch Ability Estimate Conversion Table		
Score	**Theta**	**Std. Err**
0	−4.42	1.85
1	−3.16	1.04
2	−2.39	0.76
3	−1.91	0.64
4	−1.54	0.58
5	−1.23	0.54
6	−0.96	0.51
7	−0.70	0.49
8	−0.47	0.48
9	−0.24	0.47
10	−0.02	0.47
11	0.21	0.48
12	0.44	0.48
13	0.68	0.50
14	0.93	0.52
15	1.22	0.55
16	1.54	0.59
17	1.92	0.66
18	2.43	0.77
19	3.22	1.05
20	4.50	1.86

purposes, logit ability estimates, or linear transformations of those ability estimates to prevent negative scores, are the primary test scores of interest. These ability estimates, by checking for Save person estimates, are now part of the Booklet 1 data table. Additionally, the person fit statistics, same as the ones for item difficulties, can be used to identify misfitting persons.

Examining the item fit statistics in the first table shows that item M022251 displays misfit from three of the four fit statistics, and one item, M012005 shows misfit for both standardized mean squares. Some possible explanations for the misfit can be suggested here. First, these are multiple-choice items, and it is possible for respondents to guess the correct answer. This would show up as misfitting low ability respondents the most. Second, the Rasch model assumes equal discrimination. But as we saw previously in Chapter 8, item biserials for this data indicate that these items do not discriminate equally well. Finally, using the table of residuals, jMetrik can calculate Q_3 statistics by correlating all possible pairs of residuals. All of these correlations were in the -0.2 to $+0.2$ range, indicating no evidence of LID.

Finally, an item map is a useful graph from jMetrik (Graph/Item Map). Shown in Figure 9.14, the item map indicates how well items are matched to respondents. The histogram on the left shows the distribution of estimated person abilities, while

FIGURE 9.14 ● Item Map of TIMSS Booklet 1

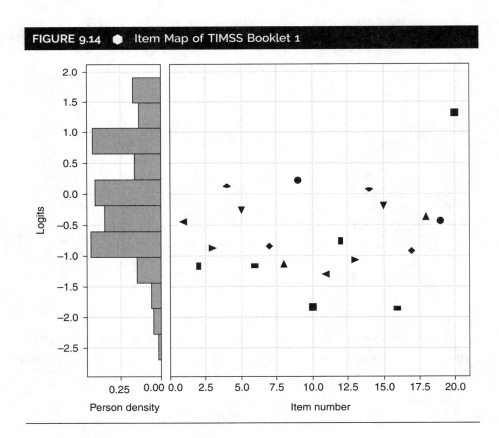

the points on the right show the 20 item difficulties. Both persons and items are graphed on the logit metric. If you were to turn this graph ninety degrees, it would look like an empirical construct map with estimated person abilities and item difficulties inked in.

9.8 POLYTOMOUS RASCH MODELS

The binary Rasch model discussed above applies to items that are dichotomously scored. Rasch models have been developed for other item formats, particularly items that are polytomously scored. Alternately, the polytomous Rasch models discussed here could be applied to essay scores or scores for constructed-response items. Writing these items was discussed in Chapter 7. The common thread among these item formats is that the score points are ordered in terms of their location on a construct map.

Consider again the two Likert items measuring one's attitude on the availability of abortion. Figure 9.15 (repeated from Figure 7.6) shows how the two items and their answer choices could be located on the construct map. However, it is not clear whether a Strongly Disagree response to the right-hand statement indicates a less or more positive attitude than an Agree response to the left-hand statement. Furthermore, a classical approach to scoring here would be a one to four scoring that implies an equal interval between the response choices and an equal weight to each item. Both of these implications are questionable.

FIGURE 9.15 ● Representation of Likert Item Choices Onto Construct Map

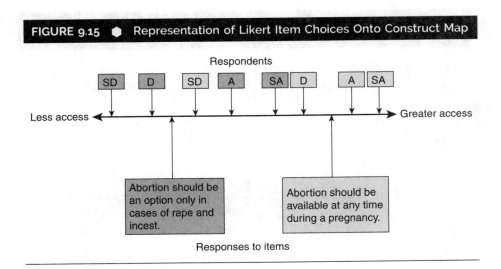

Two Rasch models have been popular for polytomously scored items in which the answer choices are ordered. With these models, there is a response curve for each answer choice. Figure 9.16 shows what this might look like for the right-hand item ("available at any time during a pregnancy"). The curve labeled P_0 indicates the response curve for the Strongly Disagree response choice. If someone is strongly opposed to any access to abortion, there is a high probability that this answer choice will be the one selected. The probabilities of picking one of the other choices is quite low. However, as an individual's attitude toward access becomes more positive, the probability of selecting Strongly Disagree diminishes, and the probability of the next choice, Disagree, increases. The point at which the response curves intersect is the point on the ability scale where the two choices are equally likely to be picked. As attitude becomes even more positive, the probability of choosing Disagree decreases, and the probability of choosing Agree increases. Likewise, as attitude becomes even more positive, the probability of Agree decreases, and the probability of Strongly Agree increases. The two Rasch models presented below attempt to model this situation. Note that with four answer choices, there are three points where the response curves intersect. Where these points are located on the ability scale are called category intersection parameters, or step difficulties. In other words, this four-choice item will have three item difficulty parameters instead of just one, as was the case of the binary Rasch model.

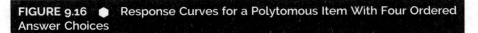

FIGURE 9.16 ● Response Curves for a Polytomous Item With Four Ordered Answer Choices

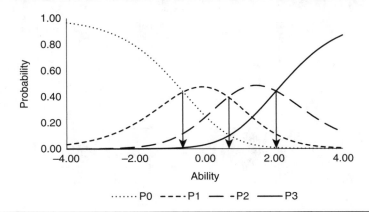

9.8.1 The Partial Credit Model

The Partial Credit Model (PCM) (Masters, 1982) was originally conceived as a model for items, such as often found in mathematics or science, for which partial credit could be earned for achieving steps along the way to a final answer but not the final answer itself. It has been used, however, for any item in which response choices are ordered. Each item is scored 0 to one less than the number of answer choices. So, an item with five response choices would be scored 0–4. Masters's original model had the step difficulties, as shown in Figure 9.16 as the item difficulties. Some software applications, such as WINSTEPS (Linacre, 2021), estimate the three β_{ij}'s, or step difficulties. Modern uses of the model, such as found in jMetrik, tend to set up the item parameters differently, so that $\beta_{ij} = \beta_i + \tau_{ij}$. The model shows the probability that person s with ability θ_s will select answer choice j from item i is

$$P_{six}\left(x = j \mid \theta_s, \beta_i, \tau_{ij}\right) = \frac{\exp\left[\sum_{j=0}^{x}\left(\theta_s - \beta_i - \tau_{ij}\right)\right]}{\sum_{r=0}^{m_j}\left[\exp\sum_{j=0}^{x}\left(\theta_s - \beta_i - \tau_{ij}\right)\right]} \tag{9.9}$$

In this model, β_i is the overall item difficulty, similar to the location of the statement, as shown in Figure 9.15. Additionally, there are a series of τ_{ij}'s that are the distances from the overall item difficulty to the response category intersection points, with the restriction that the τ_{ij}'s sum to zero. These are called category threshold parameters. This model is mathematically complex, but it will produce a graph like the one shown in Figure 9.16. The item in this figure can be represented by the following item parameters: $\beta_i = 0.71$, $\tau_{ij} = -1.33$, -0.03, and 1.36. For this item, the lowest category intersection point is $0.71 - 1.33 = -0.62$, the middle intersection point is $0.71 - 0.03 = 0.68$, and the highest intersection point is $0.71 + 1.36 = 2.07$.

9.8.2 Rating Scale Model

The second Rasch model is the Rating Scale Model (RSM) (Andrich, 1978). Its form is very similar to the PCM:

$$P_{six}\left(x = j \mid \theta_s, \beta_i, \tau_{ij}\right) = \frac{\exp\left[\sum_{j=0}^{x}\left(\theta_s - \beta_i - \tau_j\right)\right]}{\sum_{r=0}^{m_j}\left[\exp\sum_{j=0}^{x}\left(\theta_s - \beta_i - \tau_j\right)\right]} \tag{9.10}$$

The major difference is that the category threshold parameters are the same for all items. This model was designed for items in which the response choices were the same, such as Likert items with all answer choices being Strongly Agree to Strongly Disagree. This means that the RSM is simpler than the PCM because there is the strong assumption that the differences between category intersections are the same across all items. On the other hand, there are fewer item parameters to estimate with data. For example, for a 10-item test with four response choices, the PCM requires estimation of 10 items times 3 parameters per item for a total of 30 parameters. The RSM requires only 13 parameters, 10 item difficulties, and 3 thresholds. Much of the discussion below revolves around how to choose between these two models.

9.8.3 Example Using Political Viewpoint Data

The PCM and RSM were applied to the 18-item political viewpoint data using jMetrik. Some of the items were reverse scored due to the way they are written, as was done in Chapters 3 and 8. For both models, the item responses need to be recoded from 1–4 to 0–3. For any dataset, the first score point must be 0. To run the PCM in jMetrik:

1. Select the table containing the data for political viewpoint. In the Analyze menu, select Rasch Models (JMLE).

2. Select all items. Leave all selections in the Global tab as is.

3. In the Item tab, select Correct UCON bias and Save Item Estimates. Create a new table name for the item parameter estimates.

4. In the Person tab, select Save person estimates, Save person fit statistics, and Save residuals. Next to Save residuals, create a new table name for the residuals.

5. Select Run.

This is the same setup that was used for the TIMSS Booklet 1 data. For the RSM, switch to the Variable screen. In the Group column, enter the same number or letter in the row next to all 18 items. Then, run the analysis using the same five steps listed above for the PCM. Tables 9.7 and 9.8 show the item difficulties and fit statistics for the PCM and RSM, respectively.

TABLE 9.7 ● Item Difficulties for the Partial Credit Model						
Item	Difficulty	Std. Error	WMS	Std. WMS	UMS	Std. UMS
View9901	−0.62	0.04	0.94	−1.25	0.95	−1.20
View9902	0.02	0.03	0.90	−3.08	0.91	−2.66
View9903	−0.69	0.04	0.97	−0.61	0.97	−0.62
View9904	−0.32	0.03	0.98	−0.69	0.98	−0.57
View9905	−0.47	0.03	0.93	−2.15	0.93	−2.00
View9906	0.40	0.03	0.76	−7.20	0.74	−7.09
View9907	−0.73	0.04	0.99	−0.20	1.02	0.42
View9908	0.99	0.04	0.98	−0.30	1.01	0.22
View9909	0.53	0.03	0.97	−0.67	1.00	0.08
View9910	0.59	0.04	0.97	−0.67	0.97	−0.66
View9911	0.54	0.04	1.02	0.40	1.01	0.23
View9912	−0.03	0.04	1.19	4.87	1.21	5.34
View9913	0.11	0.03	1.16	4.34	1.20	5.34
View9914	−0.06	0.03	0.76	−7.92	0.76	−7.70
View9915	0.47	0.03	1.12	3.48	1.13	3.47
View9916	0.50	0.03	0.92	−2.30	0.91	−2.25
View9917	−0.55	0.04	1.03	0.82	1.03	0.96
View9918	−0.67	0.04	1.20	5.00	1.23	5.68

Comparing the two tables, item difficulties are roughly similar, and the standard errors of the difficulty estimates are nearly the same. However, one difference is quite noticeable. Looking at the standardized unweighted mean square fit statistics, four items show significant misfit to the PCM, while five items show misfit to the RSM. One possible reason for the misfit is that these items do not discriminate as well as the others. Another possible reason why the RSM has more misfitting items is that forcing all items to have the same threshold parameters may not be tenable.

TABLE 9.8 ● Item Difficulties for the Rating Scale Model						
Item	Difficulty	Std. Error	WMS	Std. WMS	UMS	Std. UMS
View9901	−0.58	0.03	0.59	−13.57	0.59	−12.97
View9902	0.07	0.03	1.18	5.05	1.18	4.94
View9903	−0.87	0.04	1.02	0.44	1.00	0.12
View9904	−0.30	0.03	0.93	−2.00	0.94	−1.70
View9905	−0.50	0.03	1.03	0.78	1.03	0.89
View9906	0.46	0.04	0.92	−2.06	0.91	−2.52
View9907	−0.85	0.04	0.96	−0.98	0.98	−0.43
View9908	1.38	0.05	1.27	4.76	1.25	4.10
View9909	0.63	0.04	1.14	3.33	1.14	3.32
View9910	0.39	0.04	0.70	−9.26	0.71	−8.72
View9911	0.36	0.04	0.79	−6.14	0.79	−6.10
View9912	−0.09	0.03	1.07	1.91	1.10	2.72
View9913	0.09	0.03	1.17	4.59	1.20	5.45
View9914	−0.05	0.03	0.91	−2.76	0.91	−2.75
View9915	0.35	0.03	1.14	3.82	1.14	3.73
View9916	0.56	0.04	1.19	4.77	1.18	4.32
View9917	−0.48	0.03	0.97	−0.96	0.98	−0.67
View9918	−0.58	0.03	0.99	−0.22	1.05	1.40

One way to view the tenability of the equal threshold assumption of the RSM is to graph the threshold parameters from the PCM. Figure 9.17 connects the three thresholds across the 18 items. This graph was created by exporting the item statistics table from jMetrik into EXCEL. If the RSM is viable, then we would expect to see three distinct and roughly parallel lines, one above the other. Instead, the lines cross each other. In particular, there are six items in which a lower threshold exceeds a higher one. For example, the thresholds for item View9902 are −0.36, 0.57, and −0.21. The graph for this item, produced by jMetrik, is shown in Figure 9.18. When the thresholds are out of order, the response curve for one of the response choices is

FIGURE 9.17 ⬡ Thresholds for Partial Credit Model

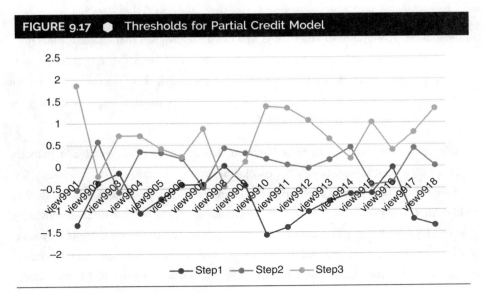

FIGURE 9.18 ⬡ Response Curves for View9902

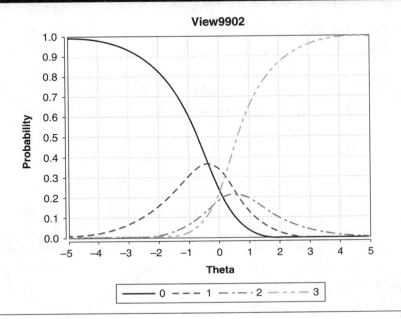

submerged below all others. In this case, the response curve for a score of 2 is never the most likely answer choice. You may as well not even have had that choice for this item. To sum up, there are problems with both models. For the RSM, the assumption of equal item thresholds clearly does not hold. For the PCM, six of the thresholds are out of order. This means that the test developer's assumption that response choices are ordered the same way does not hold for all items.

Another way to compare the fit of Rasch models to data is to use relative fit statistics. Two widely used fit statistics are the Akaike information criterion (AIC) (Akaike, 1974) and Bayesian information criterion (BIC) (Schwarz, 1978). Both use a value of the log-likelihood function. Most applications for Rasch models show this value. For jMetrik, it can be found in the Log file under View log. This file displays the log-likelihood at each iteration of item and ability estimation. The AIC and BIC use the last value in the table. For the PCM, this value is $-22,038.383$, and for the RSM, the value is $-22,564.450$. The fit indices are calculated using the following formulas:

$$AIC = -2\ln L + 2 \times (\text{number of parameters}) \qquad (9.11)$$

$$BIC = -2\ln L + \ln(N) \times (\text{number of parameters}) \qquad (9.12)$$

When this is calculated for both models, the model with the smallest AIC or BIC is the better fitting model. For the PCM:

$$AIC = -2(-22,038.383) + 2 \times (54) = 44,184.765$$
$$BIC = -2(-22,038.383) + \ln(1,047) \times (54) = 44,452.264$$

For the RSM:

$$AIC = -2(-22,564.450) + 2 \times (20) = 45,168.900$$
$$BIC = -2(-22,564.450) + \ln(1,047) \times (20) = 45,267.973$$

For both fit statistics, the PCM has the lower value and therefore provides better fit to the data than the RSM. So, if we have to choose between these two models, it would be the PCM at this point.

Although the PCM seems to fit the political viewpoint data better than the RSM, it does have a serious problem with the thresholds being out of order on one-third of the items. This leads to one of the response choices never being the most probable one. That in turn challenges the substantive/response process validity evidence for the test. We intend for each answer choice to represent an increasingly conservative viewpoint, but the data do not confirm this. Furthermore, all of the answer choices that were submerged by disordered thresholds were either Disagree or Agree. One possible fix to this problem is to collapse categories. In this case, Strongly Disagree and Disagree could be combined into one category, and Agree and Strongly Agree could be combined into a second category, essentially converting each item into a dichotomously scored Disagree or Agree item. This strategy is called *optimization* of the response choices. For this model, the fit statistics are as follows:

$$\text{AIC} = -2(-10{,}445.643) + 2 \times (18) = 20{,}927.285$$

$$\text{BIC} = -2(-22{,}564.450) + \ln(1{,}047) \times (18) = 21{,}016.452$$

This optimized model fits much better than either of the original two models. However, before plunging ahead and using this model for these data, it is important to realize that this was not the test to which persons responded. If Disagree or Agree were given as the only possible answer choices, the respondents might have answered in a totally different way.

9.9 ASSUMPTIONS, INFORMATION, AND LID

Beyond the differences between binary and polytomous Rasch models themselves, all of the other theoretical ideas discussed for the binary Rasch model apply equally to polytomous items. The three assumptions—unidimensionality, model fit, and local item independence—also must hold for polytomous models. Model fit was addressed above. Q_3 statistics can be calculated from the residuals of either polytomous model. There was some evidence of LID between pairs of items. For the PCM, of the possible 153 possible correlations between item residuals, 13 were outside the range of 0.0 ± 0.2. For the RSM, 19 correlations were outside this range. One possible explanation is that some of the items measure a different construct to some extent, in other words, the test is multidimensional. The dimensionality of the political viewpoint data will be explored in Chapter 11.

There are information functions for both the PCM and RSM. For the political viewpoint test, Figure 9.19 shows the test information function for the PCM. The test information function for the RSM looks very similar. In addition, the property that all persons who receive the same raw score have the same ability estimate is also true for polytomous models as it was for dichotomous models.

Finally, I should point out that there are a number of other Rasch models. These are generally developed to be applied to particular item formats, for example, if multiple raters score a constructed response item or if an item is designed to measure more than one construct. The models differ in how they are parameterized, but they all have the same properties of the ones discussed here, including item and test information, determining model fit and the presence of LID.

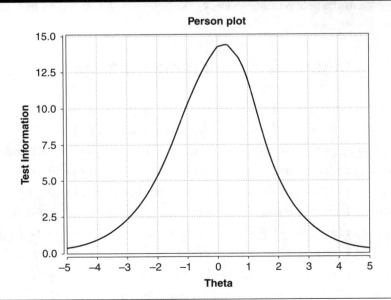

9.10 COMPARING RASCH ABILITY ESTIMATES WITH CTT RAW AND NORMALIZED z-SCORES

As discussed in Chapter 3, raw scores are ordinal data at best. Figure 9.20 shows a scatterplot of raw scores against Rasch ability estimates for the TIMSS Booklet 1 data, using jMetrik. This plot is typical of most raw score and ability estimate comparisons. Their relationship is clearly nonlinear. As raw scores approach 0 and a perfect score, the increments to ability estimates become greater. But what about the normalized z-scores, which were presented as a classical way to obtain a more equal-interval score? A scatterplot of normalized z-scores versus ability estimates is shown in Figure 9.21. This relationship is more linear but still nonlinear to some degree at the extreme scores. The greater curvilinearity at the lower end may be due in part of the failure of the Rasch model to account for guessing in multiple-choice items. Still, the two scores do not necessarily produce the same results. How does one choose? This depends on the test theory on which the test was developed, CTT or Rasch. That is,

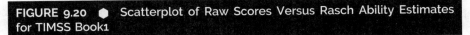

FIGURE 9.20 ● Scatterplot of Raw Scores Versus Rasch Ability Estimates for TIMSS Book1

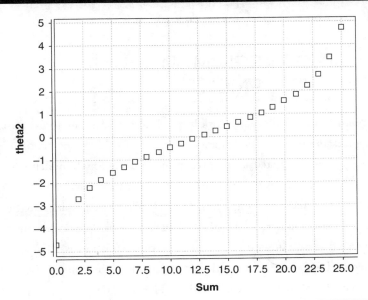

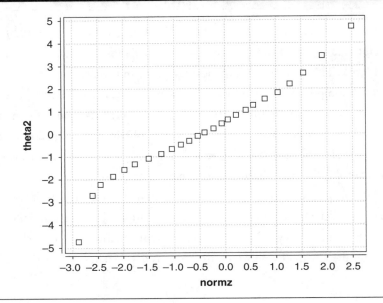

FIGURE 9.21 ● Scatterplot of Normalized Z-scores Scores Versus Rasch Ability Estimates for TIMSS Book1

use Rasch ability estimates if the test was developed using Rasch Theory and the normalized z-score if the test was developed from CTT.

9.11 USING RASCH MODELS IN TEST DEVELOPMENT

At this point, a logical question to ask is: when is it appropriate to use Rasch models to scale and score tests? A general answer is: after a field test of the final version of the instrument is completed. I don't recommend using Rasch models with pilot test data. First, Rasch models will not make poor items into better items. Poor items will tend to look like misfitting items. Second, pilot test samples may be too small for accurate item parameter estimation. A number of sample size recommendations have appeared in the literature. A general recommendation is about 300 or more respondents. That number depends somewhat on high item quality, test length, and the choice of model itself. With field test data, you can estimate item parameters and person abilities and examine model fit, dimensionality, and local item independence.

Quite often, items will appear to misfit the Rasch model. It's possible that these are high quality items from a CTT point of view based on an item analysis of pilot test data. Unequal item discrimination and guessing (on multiple-choice items) could be the cause. What should be done? If feasible, you could select only items that fit the model for further test scaling. If misfitting items are needed, there are several options. First, you can keep the items in the test and still apply the Rasch model. If there are a small number of such items, say one or two, the scaling might not be affected. A second option is to use other probability models, called item response theory (IRT) models, that include discrimination and guessing item parameters in the model. A third option is to use CTT and transformed normalized z-scores.

9.12 CHAPTER SUMMARY

This chapter introduced Rasch Measurement Theory. Rasch models specify the probability that a person will obtain a specific item score, given the characteristics, or parameters, of the item and the "ability" (the term is used generically here) of the person. They were developed to address several notable shortcomings of CTT. The models themselves are tied to specific item formats. They can be roughly divided into the binary Rasch model for dichotomously scored items and models for polytomously scored items. This chapter presented two such models, the partial credit and rating scale models.

All three Rasch models, however, adhere to a set of assumptions and properties. They assume that the test is measuring only one construct, that the data fit the model, and that item responses are locally independent of each other. Several ways of investigating model fit and local item independence were discussed. The dimensionality assumption will be discussed in Chapter 11. One advantage of using Rasch models is that score precision can vary among persons with different abilities. Another advantage is that test development can be guided by a target test information function so that the score precision is greatest where it needs to be on the ability scale. A number of large-scale testing programs use Rasch models for scaling and scoring, including state-level educational achievement assessments and licensure/certification exams.

9.13 EXERCISES AND ACTIVITIES

Estimate item parameters and ability estimates from TIMSS Booklet 1. The results should Agree with the tables shown in this chapter.

1. Then, answer the following:

   a. Which are the easiest and most difficult items?

   b. Are there any items with poorly estimated difficulties?

   c. Are there any items that do not fit the Rasch model?

2. Insert a plot of the characteristic curve and information function for the first item. Then, indicate the location of the item's difficulty.

3. Insert an item map. Does the difficulty of the items seem to match well to the abilities of the persons?

4. Insert a plot of the test characteristic curve and test information function. Where does this instrument provide the most and least measurement precision?

5. Is there evidence of LID?

Estimate item parameters and ability estimates for the political viewpoint data using the PCM. The results should Agree with the tables shown in this chapter.

1. Then, answer the following:

   a. Which are the easiest and most difficult items?

   b. Are there any items with poorly estimated difficulties or category thresholds?

   c. Are there any items that do not fit the Rasch model?

2. Insert a plot of the characteristic curve and information function for the first item. Then, indicate the location of the item's difficulty and category thresholds.

3. Insert an item map. Does the difficulty of the items seem to match well to the abilities of the persons?

FURTHER READING

For Rasch Measurement Theory, the Seminal Reference is

Rasch, G. (1960). *Probabilistic models for some intelligence and attainment tests*. Copenhagen: Danmarks Paedagogiske Institut.

For more Accessible (i.e., Less Mathematical) Presentations of Rasch Measurement Theory, I Recommend the Following

Bond, T. G., & Fox, C. M. (2007). *Applying the Rasch model: Fundamental measurement in the human sciences* (3rd ed.). New York, NY: Routledge.

Wilson, M. (2004). *Constructing measures: An item response modeling approach*. New York, NY: Routledge.

REFERENCES

Akaike, H. (1974). A new look at the statistical identification model. *IEEE Transaction Automatic Control*, 19, 716–723.

Andrich, D. (1978). Rating formulation for ordered response categories. *Psychometrika*, 43(4), 561–573.

Chalmers, P., Pritikin, J., Robitzsch, A., Zoltak, M., KwonHyun, K., Falk, C. F., … King, D. (2017). *Multidimensional item response theory (MIRT)*.

Linacre, J. M. (2021). *Winsteps® Rasch measurement computer program* [Computer software] Beaverton, OR: Winsteps.com.

Masters, G. N. (1982). A Rasch model for partial credit scoring. *Psychometrika*, 47(2), 149–174.

Meyer, J. P. (2014). *Applied measurement with jMetrik*. New York, NY: Routledge.

Schwarz, G. (1978). Estimating the dimension of a model. *Annals of Statistics*, 6, 461–464.

Vector Psychometric Group. (2020). *IRTPRO5* [Computer software]. Chapel Hill, NC: Vector Psychometric Group.

Yen, W. M. (1984). Effects of local item dependence on the fit and equating performance of the three-parameter logistic model. *Applied Psychological Measurement*, 8, 125–145.

VALIDATION

10

FAIRNESS, DIF, AND ITEM BIAS

10.1 FAIRNESS IN TEST DEVELOPMENT AND USE

Chapter 7 introduced the concept of fairness in the context of writing test items that are fair to all respondents and subgroups of respondents. The emphasis on fairness in test development and in use in the 2014 *Standards* is revealed not only with its own chapter but that chapter being located immediately after chapters on validity and reliability. The *Standards* view fairness as a validity question: Is the intended score interpretation valid for all respondents and subgroups of respondents from the target population? A fair test is essentially one in which the answer to this question is Yes. A No answer means that some aspect of the test itself, its administration, or usage undermines score validity.

It is important to note that fairness as an issue arose during the civil rights movement of the 1960s. The first two editions of *Educational Measurement*, in 1951 and 1971, make no mention of fairness, equity, or test or item bias. In the 1989 third edition, a separate chapter, "Bias in Test Use," by Nancy Cole and Pamela Moss (1989), discussed the concept of measurement bias, a subject of increasing research from the 1970s to the present day. The fourth and most recent edition features a chapter by Gregory Camilli titled "Test Fairness." Additional resources can be found in the *Code of Fair Testing Practices in Education* (1988) and *ITC Guidelines for the Large-Scale Assessment of Linguistically and Culturally Diverse Populations* (2018).

The *Standards* address two major aspects of fairness: measurement bias and accessibility. Measurement bias means that scores are misleadingly higher or lower for particular population subgroups. During the 1960s, large-scale standardized tests, such as the SAT, came under attack for being culturally biased, alleging that scores of some groups, such as racial/ethnic minorities were lower because the items on the test reflected the culture of the dominant subgroup, namely white and middle class students. To investigate these claims, the psychometric profession developed a set of methodologies, called *differential item functioning*, or DIF, to detect potentially biased items. These methods have evolved into a common practice for test development and are the focus of this chapter. A second aspect of fairness, accessibility, has been addressed more recently. Even if a test's items are not biased, unfairness may still be present because some respondents or subgroups of respondents may not have access to the skills or processes needed to achieve desired scores. A common example is online assessment, now used by many testing programs. Some individuals do not have sufficient internet access. A better example is the prevalence of test preparation programs in wide use for many high-stakes tests. These cost money, a barrier for low-income respondents. What results is a validity question: if two respondents achieve the same score, but one has had the benefit of an intensive test preparation program, do the two scores really mean the same thing? Another aspect of accessibility has to do with accommodations for respondents with disabilities or limited proficiency in the primary language of the test. Common accommodations include extended time, private room, a dictionary for nonnative language speakers, braille versions, and versions in alternative languages. These accommodations are intended to "level the playing field." For many test development projects, such as those for research purposes, accommodations may not be an issue. The researchers could simply exclude these respondents. However, for high-stakes tests, where everyone must have access to the test, accommodations may be necessary. In my own university (and I suspect in most institutions), there is a disabilities office that determines what accommodations will be required for each individual who requests them. As an instructor, the office informs me what accommodations must be provided to a student without informing me what the student's actual disability is.

10.2 DIFFERENTIAL ITEM FUNCTIONING AND ITEM BIAS

Cole and Moss (1989) present a definition of test and item bias that is widely accepted within the psychometric community:

> *Bias is differential validity of a given interpretation of a test score for any definite, relevant subgroup of test takers. (p. 205)*

In other words, overall group differences by themselves do not constitute bias. To illustrate this point, let us look at the mean raw scores of male and female eighth grade students on the 20 mathematics items from Booklet 1 of the 2003 TIMSS. These are shown in Table 10.1. There is a small difference, 0.294 on a 0–20 raw score scale, between male and female students. According to Cole and Moss's definition of bias, we would expect no bias to look like a 0.294 difference on the *p*-value of every item. If, for example, we found that female students scored significantly higher than male students on an item, then this item would show DIF in favor of the female students. This does not mean that the item is necessarily biased. DIF in an item warrants further investigation. Typically, subject matter experts examine DIF items for possible bias. Most of the time, experts are not able to explain why an item

TABLE 10.1 ● Descriptive Statistics of Male and Female Students on TIMSS Booklet 1

	Mean	*N*	Std. Dev.
Female	12.289	402	4.1693
Male	12.583	355	4.5771
Total	12.427	757	4.3648

shows DIF. In that case, the test developer must decide what action to take: keep the item, discard it, or keep it but continue to monitor it.

10.3 METHODS FOR DETECTING DIFFERENTIAL ITEM FUNCTIONING

Since the 1980s, dozens of DIF detection methods have been developed and researched. Most of them are based on comparing two groups. The *focal* group is one that test developers are concerned about because that group may be disadvantaged, disabled, or at risk. The *reference* group tends to be advantaged and not at risk. The groups may be defined according to variables, such as sex, race/ethnicity, age, or type of community. The analysis is intended to support the notion that the test's items are not biased against a particular population subgroup. For example, for DIF analysis based on race/ethnicity, the reference group is usually white respondents, and the focal group is one of the minority groups.

As mentioned above, DIF is based on comparing item performance by group to overall performance by group. Figure 10.1 shows frequency polygons of female and male students on the 20 mathematics TIMSS items. In conducting a DIF analysis, it is critical to *match* students in some fashion, to eliminate the effect of the overall difference. The most common way to do this is to match on raw score. In other words, respondents who achieved the same raw score, regardless of group, can be considered equal on the construct being measured, in this case, grade 8 mathematics skills. A practical issue that often arises in matching is that the sample size may be too small to match on every possible raw score. If so, then matching could be done on raw score intervals, a technique called thick matching. In Figure 10.1, the frequencies

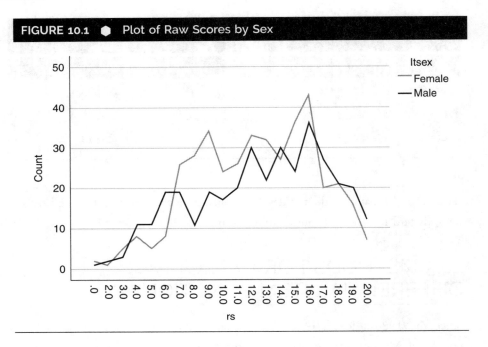

FIGURE 10.1 ● Plot of Raw Scores by Sex

below a raw score of 4 are small (note that chance level raw scores are about 4 or 5). Thus, one may decide to collapse scores of 4 or 5 or less into a single score interval for the DIF analysis.

There are two types of DIF. Uniform DIF occurs when the direction of differential item performance favors one group throughout the score scale. This is illustrated in Figure 10.2 for a hypothetical dichotomously scored item. The x-axis is the raw score on the test. The y-axis is the probability, or proportion, of respondents at each score level for each group. In this graph, at every score level, a higher proportion of reference group members answered the item correctly than focal group members. This item therefore shows *uniform* DIF favoring the reference group.

The other type of DIF is called nonuniform DIF and is illustrated in Figure 10.3. Above a score of 10, the DIF favors the focal group, while scores below 10 favor the reference group. What is actually occurring here is that the item discriminates differently in the two groups. In this case, the item has a higher discrimination for the focal group. Finally, it is quite common for uniform and nonuniform DIF to both be present for an item, as shown in Figure 10.4. Here, there is uniform DIF favoring the reference group for a large part of the score range, but the curves cross at a score of 13.

FIGURE 10.2 ● Plot of Uniform DIF

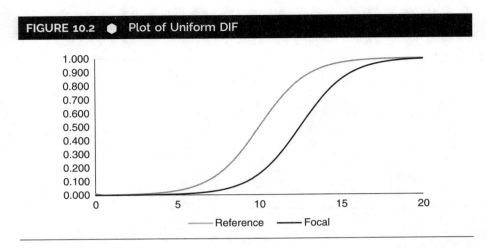

FIGURE 10.3 ● Plot of Nonuniform DIF

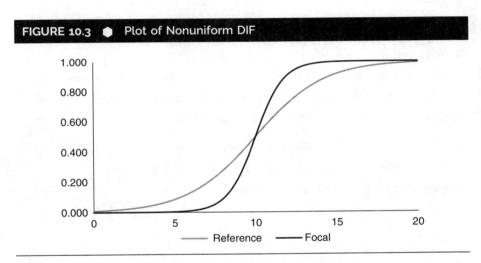

Above that score, DIF slightly favors the focal group. Below that score, DIF favors the reference group. In the following sections, several DIF detection methods will be introduced, and results will be compared for the TIMSS and political viewpoint data.

10.4 DIF METHODS FOR DICHOTOMOUSLY SCORED ITEMS

10.4.1 Mantel–Haenszel Methods

By far, the most popular DIF methods are based on the Mantel–Haenszel chi-square statistic. Holland and Thayer (1988) adapted this statistic for detecting DIF for

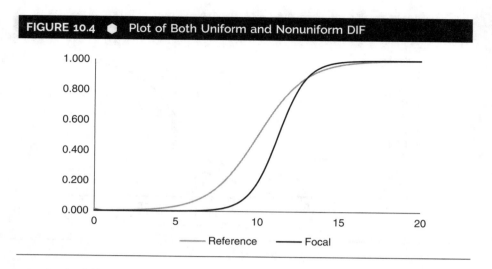

FIGURE 10.4 ● Plot of Both Uniform and Nonuniform DIF

dichotomously scored items. Consider the graph in Figure 10.1. If one takes one of the raw score points or intervals, then a 2 × 2 contingency table can be constructed for frequencies of respondents who belong to the reference or focal group and who score 0 or 1 on item j, as shown in Table 10.2.

DIF is present if there is a significant relationship between group membership and item score within this score interval. The Mantel–Haenszel statistic for item j is formed by summing across all score intervals.

$$M - H_{\chi^2 \text{M-H}} = \frac{\left(\left|\sum_j A_j - \sum_j E\left(A_j\right)\right| - 0.5\right)^2}{\sum_j \text{var}\left(A_j\right)} \qquad (10.1)$$

TABLE 10.2 ● Contingency Table at a Single Raw Score. Score on Item j

Group	1	0	Total
Reference	A_j	B_j	N_{Rj}
Focal	C_j	D_j	N_{Fj}
Total	M_{1j}	M_{0j}	T_j

$$E(A_j) = \frac{N_{Rj}M_{1j}}{T_j} \tag{10.2}$$

$$\text{var}(A_j) = \frac{N_{Rj}N_{Fj}M_{1j}M_{0j}}{T^2(T_j - 1)} \tag{10.3}$$

This statistic is a chi-square with one degree of freedom, meaning that DIF is present at the 0.05 level of significance if the $M–H$ chi-square value exceeds 3.84. However, significance tests depend to a large extent on sample size. As a complement to this significance test, it is important to consider the practical effect size. For dichotomously scored items, the effect size is the odds ratio:

$$\alpha_{M-H} = \frac{\sum_j A_j D_j / T_j}{\sum_j B_j C_j / T_j} \tag{10.4}$$

α_{M-H} can range from 0 to infinity. A value of 1 indicates no DIF is present. Holland and Thayer (1988) suggested the following transformation:

$$\Delta_{M-H} = -2.35 \ln(\alpha_{M-H}) \tag{10.5}$$

A Δ_{M-H} value of 0 means no DIF. A positive value indicates DIF favoring the focal group while a negative value indicates DIF favoring the reference group. Educational Testing Service (ETS) uses the following classification system for negligible, moderate, and large levels of DIF, as shown in Table 10.3.

A great deal of research has been conducted on the Mantel–Haenszel method. According to Clauser and Mazor (1998) and Meyer (2014), its advantages include computational efficiency (you would not want to calculate this by hand, but

TABLE 10.3 ● ETS DIF Levels for Mantel–Haenszel

ETS DIF	$M–H\ \chi^2$	Δ_{M-H}	DIF Level
A	$p > .05$	$|\Delta| < 1$	Negligible
B	$p < .05$	$1 \leq |\Delta| < 1.5$	Moderate
C	$p < .05$	$|\Delta| \geq 1.5$	Large

psychometric software can do it very quickly), acceptable Type I error rates on tests of at least 20 items, effectiveness with samples as small as 200 per group, and enough power to detect uniform DIF. On the other hand, the method does not detect nonuniform DIF very well and has an inflated Type I error rate for short tests, for tests with a wide variation in item difficulty and discrimination, and where the two groups are considerably different in overall score.

10.4.2 Mantel–Haenszel Analysis of TIMSS Items

Two software applications for running the Mantel–Haenszel method are jMetrik and the difR R package. Since jMetrik was used for item analysis of the TIMSS items in Chapter 8, the DIF analysis can be carried out in just a few additional mouse clicks. The first step is to create a test score on which the matching will take place. I suggest creating a raw score (called sum score in jMetrik) from the Transform/Test Scaling menu. To run the DIF analysis, click Analyze/DIF: Mantel–Haenszel. In the dialog box, enter the variables as shown in the screen shot below in Figure 10.5. Note that we are examining DIF with respect to sex, where females are coded 1, and males are coded 2. We'll also arbitrarily label females as the focal group. The results are shown in Table 10.4.

These initial results show one item with a C, or large level, DIF and five items with a B or moderate level of DIF. However, each item was analyzed by matching on the overall raw score which means that the items showing DIF were used to match the groups. As a result, some of the DIF could be a statistical artifact of matching with items that show DIF. To counteract this effect, we can *purify* the matching score to include only items that showed no DIF. In jMetrik, purification can be carried out by creating a new raw score that includes only those 14 items that showed negligible, A Class, DIF and then rerunning the analysis by matching on the purified raw score. When this is done, the new results are shown in Table 10.5. The difference from the initial results is that item M022251 no longer shows DIF but that item M012015 now does at a moderate level.

Let's take a closer look at the single C-level item, M012004, identified by jMetrik. Since the ETS Δ is negative, the DIF for this item favors the reference group, male students. Figure 10.6 shows the text of this item. Additionally, jMetrik can provide a graph of what the DIF looks like. This graph can be produced by clicking

FIGURE 10.5 ● *jMetrik* Mantel–Haenszel Dialog Box

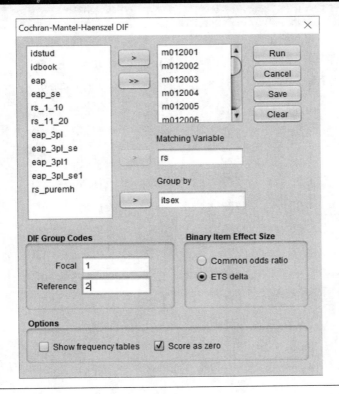

Graph/Nonparametric Curves and setting up the dialog box as shown in Figure 10.7. Figure 10.8 shows the resulting graph. Nonparametric curves are based on the data at each score point. The curves show that the reference group, male students, has a uniform advantage, except at the lower end of the score scale. Since all items are multiple-choice (with 4 or 5 options), this lower end represents chance level scoring and can therefore be ignored. At this point, the logical question for subject matter experts is: what is it about this item that gives US male 8th graders a differential advantage over female 8th graders? For this item, a logical explanation for the DIF is hard to come by, a common result. The decision for the test developer is what action to take. For ETS and many other large-scale testing organizations, the decision would be to retain the item but reanalyze later. My own advice to test developers is to remove the item if a high-quality replacement item is available, or to keep the item and further investigate if a replacement is not available.

TABLE 10.4 ⬡ Mantel–Haenszel Results for TIMSS Booklet 1 by Gender						
Item	Chi-square	p-Value	Valid N	E.S.	(95% C.I.)	Class
M012001	11.99	0.00	654	−1.61	(−0.69, −2.54)	B−
M012002	2.80	0.09	735	−0.73	(0.12, −1.59)	A
M012003	0.05	0.83	699	−0.09	(0.77, −0.96)	A
M012004	31.14	0.00	732	−2.42	(−1.55, −3.29)	C−
M012005	1.21	0.27	732	0.42	(1.17, −0.33)	A
M012006	5.69	0.02	696	0.99	(1.80, 0.17)	A
M012037	1.27	0.26	727	0.46	(1.26, −0.34)	A
M012038	0.01	0.93	732	0.04	(0.92, −0.84)	A
M012039	3.71	0.05	735	−0.73	(0.02, −1.49)	A
M012040	0.54	0.46	654	−0.39	(0.64, −1.42)	A
M012041	6.97	0.01	724	1.23	(2.15, 0.30)	B+
M012042	9.84	0.00	696	1.49	(2.43, 0.55)	B+
M032570	3.18	0.07	654	−0.78	(0.08, −1.65)	A
M032643	0.19	0.66	705	0.18	(1.00, −0.64)	A
M012013	0.32	0.57	724	−0.22	(0.55, −0.99)	A
M012014	2.70	0.10	649	−0.92	(0.18, −2.03)	A
M012015	17.13	0.00	735	1.85	(2.74, 0.97)	B+
M012016	2.85	0.09	699	−0.65	(0.11, −1.41)	A
M012017	2.96	0.09	724	0.70	(1.50, −0.10)	A
M022251	5.78	0.02	716	1.05	(1.90, 0.19)	B+

10.4.3 SIBTEST

The Mantel–Haenszel method has two main limitations. First, as noted above, it is not effective in detecting nonuniform DIF. Second, the DIF analysis is limited to investigating each individual item. It is quite possible for groups of items that share some characteristic, such as content or skill level, to show DIF as a group, which is referred to as differential *bundle* functioning (DBF). Specifically, each individual item in a group could show negligible DIF, but the group of items together could show

Item	Chi-square	p-Value	Valid N	E.S.	(95% C.I.)	Class
M012001	12.44	0	754	−1.52	(−0.67, −2.36)	B−
M012002	2.07	0.15	703	−0.63	(0.22, −1.48)	A
M012003	0.06	0.81	703	0.11	(0.97, −0.75)	A
M012004	24.26	0.00	754	−1.94	(−1.16, −2.72)	C−
M012005	1.82	0.18	703	0.52	(1.27, −0.23)	A
M012006	7.03	0.01	703	1.12	(1.94, 0.29)	B+
M012037	1.49	0.22	703	0.50	(1.30, −0.30)	A
M012038	0.06	0.81	707	0.11	(0.98, −0.77)	A
M012039	3.22	0.07	696	−0.71	(0.07, −1.49)	A
M012040	0.06	0.81	654	−0.13	(0.90, −1.16)	A
M012041	7.89	0.00	750	1.21	(2.07, 0.35)	B+
M012042	7.97	0.00	754	1.21	(2.06, 0.37)	B+
M032570	2.60	0.11	658	−0.71	(0.15, −1.57)	A
M032643	0.39	0.53	680	0.26	(1.08, −0.56)	A
M012013	0.22	0.64	703	−0.19	(0.59, −0.97)	A
M012014	1.94	0.16	654	−0.78	(0.32, −1.87)	A
M012015	15.86	0.00	754	1.64	(2.45, 0.82)	B+
M012016	3.08	0.08	703	−0.69	(0.08, −1.45)	A
M012017	3.97	0.05	684	0.79	(1.57, −0.00)	A
M022251	4.02	0.04	743	0.83	(1.63, 0.02)	A

TABLE 10.5 ◆ Purified Mantel–Haenszel Results of TIMSS Items

large DIF, a phenomenon called DIF *amplification*. A second DIF method called SIBTEST (Shealy & Stout, 1993) addresses these limitations. SIBTEST is a flexible approach to DIF by conceptualizing two subtests, a matching or valid subtest which consists of items believed to show no DIF, and a suspect or studied subtest of one or more items suspected of having some degree of DIF.

To run a SIBTEST analysis of TIMSS item M012001, make M012001 the suspect subtest and the remaining 19 items the matching subtest. Figure 10.9, which is a

---

FIGURE 10.6 ⬢ TIMSS Item M012004

> Alice can run 4 laps around a track in the same time that Carol can run 3 laps. When Carol has run 12 laps, how many laps has Alice run?
>
> Ⓐ   9
>
> Ⓑ   11
>
> Ⓒ   13
>
> Ⓓ   16

FIGURE 10.7 ⬢ Screenshot of Setup for Nonparametric Curves

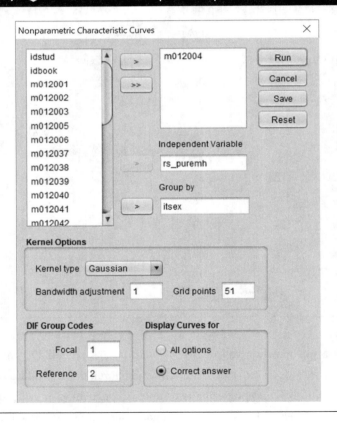

cumulative frequency version of the matching subtest. At each score point on the matching subtest, the difference in proportion correct on the suspect subtest between the reference and focal groups can be calculated, then summed, weighted by the

FIGURE 10.8 ● Nonparametric Curves of Item M012004

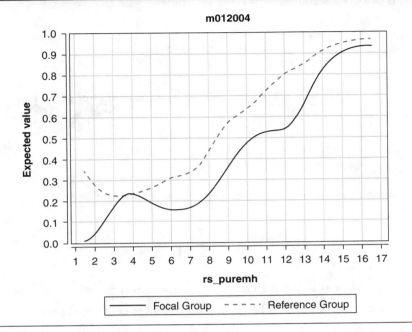

FIGURE 10.9 ● Cumulative Frequencies of Raw Scores by Sex

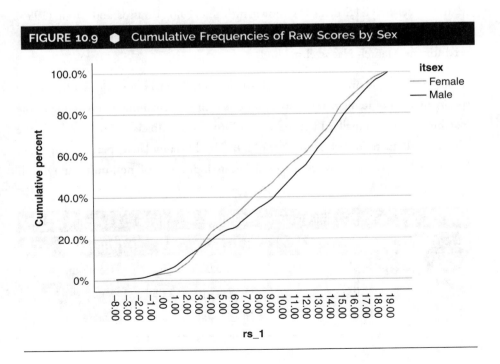

overall proportion of respondents at each matching subtest score. This forms the SIBTEST Beta statistic for item j:

$$\beta_j = \sum_j p_j \left(\bar{Y}_{Rj} - \bar{Y}_{Fj} \right) \tag{10.6}$$

If there is no DIF, Beta is expected to be 0. The standard error of Beta is:

$$\text{SE}_{\beta_j} = \sqrt{\sum_j p_j^2 \left[\frac{s^2(Y|R,j)}{n_{Rj}} + \frac{s^2(Y|F,j)}{n_{Fj}} \right]} \tag{10.7}$$

A significance test is created by dividing Beta by its standard error:

$$Z_{\text{SIB}} = \frac{\beta_j}{\text{SE}_{\beta_j}} \tag{10.8}$$

This Z_{SIB} statistic is asymptotically normal, meaning that ± 1.96 can serve as critical values. It is important to note here that positive beta values favor the reference group while negative beta values favor the focal group, which is the opposite of the Mantel–Haenszel ETS delta. As shown in Table 10.6, Roussos and Stout (1996) proposed effect sizes to parallel the ETS negligible, moderate, and large levels of DIF used for the Mantel–Haenszel method.

In addition to studying each item individually, DBF can be investigated by simply specifying a set of items as the suspect subtest with the remaining items acting as the matching subtest. Finally, Li and Stout (1996) and Chalmers (2018) modified the SIBTEST Beta to detect nonuniform DIF. If the cumulative percent curves in Figure 10.9 were to cross, that would be an indication of non-uniform DIF. If

TABLE 10.6 ● ETS DIF Levels for SIBTEST			
ETS DIF	**M–H χ^2**	**β**	**DIF Level**
A	$p > .05$	$|\beta| < 0.059$	Negligible
B	$p < .05$	$0.059 \leq |\beta| < 0.088$	Moderate
C	$p < .05$	$|\beta| \geq 0.088$	Large

SIBTEST Beta were calculated for that scenario, positive and negative differences would cancel out each other. For the modification, called Crossing SIBTEST, the absolute value of all differences would be summed to calculate Beta.

At the time of this writing, Shealy and Stout's original software is no longer available, but SIBTEST can be run in two R packages, difR and mirt. Both packages calculate Crossing SIBTEST, but the difR package only calculates individual item analyses and only for dichotomously scored items. To obtain DBF results and results for polytomously scored items, the mirt package is needed. As a result, the mirt package will be used to illustrate SIBTEST with the TIMSS data. The R code to run the following SIBTEST analyses from the mirt package can be found in Appendix B. Using the Roussos and Stout guidelines, Table 10.7 shows the partial output from the analysis. For effect size, four items (in bold) show C-level DIF, and four items show B-level DIF.

However, there is still the issue of purification of the matching subtest. In mirt, purification is done by specifying which items constitute the matching subtest, which are the remaining twelve items that show negligible DIF. As shown in Table 10.8, after purification, item M022251 no longer shows DIF. Six other items show C-level DIF, and one item shows B-level DIF. Six of these seven items were also flagged by the Mantel–Haenszel method. This is a common finding, that at the individual item level, Mantel–Haenszel and SIBTEST tend to identify the same items, even though the DIF levels may not match. Crossing SIBTEST identified the same items. Items with large SIBTEST beta values will also have crossing SIBTEST beta values at least as large (Chalmers, 2018). However, it could be that items showing negligible uniform DIF do show significant nonuniform DIF. This will occur if the crossing point is within the score range of the test. The fact that the Crossing SIBTEST and SIBTEST beta values are so similar is an indication that a crossing point does not occur within the raw score range of the test.

As mentioned above, SIBTEST can also be used to detect DBF, or DIF in a group of items. To illustrate DBF with the TIMSS data, a suspect test was formed for the four items in the Algebra content domain: M012002, M012040, M012017, and M022251. The results are shown in Figure 10.10.

While there was no uniform DIF, there was significant nonuniform DIF. No further diagnostics are available from the SIBTEST function in the mirt package. However,

TABLE 10.7 ● SIBTEST Results for TIMSS Items			
Item	Beta	SE	p
M012001	**0.131**	**0.035**	**0**
M012002	0.048	0.035	0.172
M012003	−0.019	0.035	0.575
M012004	**0.169**	**0.036**	**0**
M012005	−0.041	0.037	0.265
M012006	−0.079	0.033	0.018
M012037	−0.050	0.035	0.151
M012038	−0.005	0.033	0.890
M012039	0.055	0.038	0.146
M012040	0.015	0.034	0.653
M012041	−0.085	0.032	0.008
M012042	**−0.090**	**0.033**	**0.007**
M032570	0.047	0.036	0.199
M032643	−0.003	0.035	0.936
M012013	0.027	0.037	0.464
M012014	0.037	0.035	0.293
M012015	**−0.125**	**0.031**	**0**
M012016	0.056	0.036	0.122
M012017	−0.071	0.036	0.048
M022251	−0.075	0.033	0.022

as shown in Figure 10.11, a line chart (created in Excel) of the groups by Algebra domain raw score shows what the crossing DIF looks like. Female students appear to be advantaged in the middle of the score range while male students are advantaged at the upper and lower ends. I'll leave it to the middle grade mathematics specialists to try to interpret what this means.

TABLE 10.8 ● Purified SIBTEST and Crossing SIBTEST Results for TIMSS Items

Item	SIBTEST			Crossing SIBTEST	
	Beta	SE	p	Beta	p
M012001	0.090	0.035	0.009	0.098	0.015
M012004	0.134	0.036	0	0.134	0
M012006	−0.087	0.035	0.013	0.087	0.013
M012041	−0.114	0.033	0	0.114	0
M012042	−0.112	0.033	0.001	0.102	0.003
M012015	−0.153	0.035	0	0.136	0
M012017	−0.095	0.037	0.011	0.095	0.011
M022251	−0.059	0.034	0.081	0.06	0.167

10.5 MANTEL–HAENSZEL AND SIBTEST METHODS FOR POLYTOMOUSLY SCORED ITEMS

For polytomously scored items, a more general form of the Mantel–Haenszel chi-square statistic can be used (Cochran, 1954; Mantel, 1963). In this form, instead of a 2×2 contingency table at each score interval, there is a $2 \times$ (number of item score points) contingency table at each interval. For effect size, jMetrik uses sP-DIF, an effect size indicator proposed by Dorans, Schmitt, and Bleistein (1992). Its values can range from 0 to 1. Dorans et al. recommend items at the negligible "AA" level have an sP-DIF value of less than 0.05, and items with large DIF, at the "CC" level, have an sP-DIF value of 0.10 or larger. "BB" items, indicating moderate DIF, have values of 0.05 or greater but less than 0.10. For SIBTEST, no modification of the method is necessary since it operates on the scores of the matching and suspect subtests, whether the items are scored dichotomously or polytomously.

FIGURE 10.10 ● DBF Results for TIMSS Booklet 1 Content Domain

```
          focal_group n_matched_set n_suspect_set    beta    SE     X2  df       p
SIBTEST            1           16              4  -0.039  0.068  0.324   1   0.569
CSIBTEST           1           16              4   0.168    NA   6.604   2   0.037
```

FIGURE 10.11 ● Crossing SIBTEST DBF of Algebra Domain

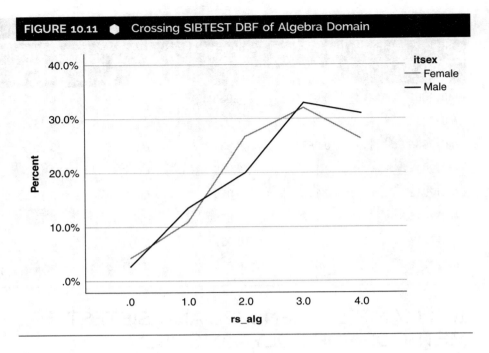

A DIF analysis of the political viewpoint data was carried out using the Mantel method with jMetrik and the SIBTEST function from the mirt package. After purification of the matching raw score, the following results were obtained with the Mantel method, shown in Table 10.9. Twelve of the 18 items showed some degree of DIF. These results are following purification, but the results are largely the same without purification. When using SIBTEST, all but six of the items, View9906, View9910, View9911, View9912, View9914, and View9918 showed some level of uniform DIF. Three of these items, View9906, View9911, and View9914, exhibited significant nonuniform DIF. While the two sets of results appear to differ, the correlation between the Mantel effect size and SIBTEST beta was 0.62, which would be 0.88 if one outlier (View9908) were removed. What is clear is that SIBTEST in this context was the more powerful method, that is, it tended to produce higher levels of significance.

Table 10.10 shows the text of the items showing moderate or large levels of DIF from the Mantel method. A plus sign indicates DIF favoring the focal group, in this case female incoming freshmen (in 1999). A negative sign favors the reference group, male incoming freshmen. As was the case with the TIMSS mathematics items, logical

Item	Chi-square	p-Value	Valid N	E.S.	(95% C.I.)	Class
View9901	0.00	0.98	1,043	0.01	(−0.07, 0.09)	AA
View9902	4.76	0.03	1,043	−0.16	(−0.30, −0.01)	BB−
View9903	8.77	0.00	1,041	−0.15	(−0.25, −0.05)	BB−
View9904	23.64	0.00	1,043	0.29	(0.17, 0.41)	BB+
View9905	5.53	0.02	1,043	0.17	(0.04, 0.29)	BB+
View9906	79.07	0.00	1,043	−0.55	(−0.67, −0.42)	CC−
View9907	4.34	0.04	1,041	0.11	(−0.00, 0.22)	AA
View9908	85.57	0.00	1,018	−0.45	(−0.54, −0.35)	CC−
View9909	94.51	0.00	1,043	−0.58	(−0.70, −0.46)	CC−
View9910	0.20	0.66	1,041	−0.01	(−0.10, 0.07)	AA
View9911	2.18	0.14	1,043	−0.07	(−0.16, 0.01)	AA
View9912	7.45	0.01	1,041	0.14	(0.04, 0.25)	AA
View9913	16.95	0.00	1,041	−0.26	(−0.39, −0.14)	BB−
View9914	61.63	0.00	1,043	−0.51	(−0.64, −0.37)	CC−
View9915	83.97	0.00	1,043	0.56	(0.44, 0.68)	CC+
View9916	55.88	0.00	1,043	−0.47	(−0.59, −0.34)	CC−
View9917	26.30	0.00	1,043	−0.30	(−0.42, −0.18)	BB−
View9918	2.96	0.09	1,041	0.09	(−0.01, 0.19)	AA

TABLE 10.9 ● Mantel Purified Results for Political Viewpoint Data

reasons for the DIF are not clear. However, there are some trends. Four of the six CC-level items relate to social issues. Five of the six BB-level items either reflect legal or racial issues. In the next chapter, an analysis of the political viewpoint data will suggest some degree of multidimensionality that divides along social, legal, and racial issues. It's possible that political viewpoint had different meaning among female and male students. This possibility appears even more strongly in the SIBTEST results. If most items show DIF, then the matching subtest is not really functioning as intended, and it is likely that those items are measuring something different than the items showing DIF.

TABLE 10.10 ⬡ Political Viewpoint Items Showing DIF From Mantel Method		
Level	**Item ID**	
CC−	View9906	It is important to have laws prohibiting homosexual relationships.
CC−	View9908	Just because a man thinks that a woman has "led him on" does not entitle him to have sex with her.
CC−	View9909	The federal government should do more to control the sale of handguns.
CC−	View9914	Same sex couples should have the right to legal marital status.
CC+	View9915	Material on the internet should be regulated by the government.
CC−	View9916	The activities of married women are best confined to the home and family.
BB−	View9902	Abortion should be legal.
BB−	View9903	The death penalty should be abolished.
BB+	View9904	If two people really like each other, it's all right for them to have sex even if they've known each other for only a very short time.
BB+	View9905	Marijuana should be legalized.
BB−	View9913	Colleges should prohibit racist/sexist speech on campus.
BB−	View9917	Affirmative action in college admissions should be abolished.

10.6 OTHER DIF DETECTION METHODS

As mentioned above, many DIF methods besides the Mantel–Haenszel and SIBT-EST have been developed and implemented. I'll describe several of the more popular ones.

Logistic Regression. This approach to DIF (Swaminathan & Rogers, 1990) involves regressing a dichotomous item score on test score, group membership, and a score-by-group interaction variable in successive models. If the group membership variable is significant, it means that there are group differences on the item score while controlling for overall test score. This amounts to a test of uniform DIF. If the interaction variable is significant, the relationship between test score and item score is different between the two groups. The interaction variable is then a test of nonuniform DIF. A primary appeal of logistic regression is that uniform and non-uniform DIF (along with a combined DIF) can be studied within a single model. The method can be implemented in most statistical software packages, but it is more efficiently run as part of the difR R package.

Raju's DFIT. DFIT (Raju, van der Linden, & Fleer, 1995) is based on latent variable models, such as Rasch models, in which item parameters are estimated separately for focal and reference groups. A significant difference in item difficulty indicates uniform DIF while a significant difference in discrimination indicates non-uniform DIF. DFIT's appeal is its flexibility in that it can be used for both dichotomously and polytomously scored items, and it can examine DBF and differential test functioning (DTF). Because it is based on latent variable models, DFIT does require relatively large sample sizes. At present, DFIT is most extensively available in the *DFIT* R package. A more limited version is available in the difR package.

Standardization. The standardization method (Dorans & Kullick, 1986; Dorans, Schmitt, & Bleistein, 1992) was one of the first uniform DIF methods, but it is still in use primarily because of its intuitive appeal, ease of calculation, and lack of assumptions. The method calculates the average difference in proportion correct between the two groups across matched score intervals, weighted by the frequency of the focal group in each interval. Standardization is currently available in the difR package.

10.7 USING DIF ANALYSIS AS VALIDITY EVIDENCE

DIF, DBF, and DTF analyses on data from developing tests are important pieces of validity evidence. Optimally, these analyses are conducted before a test is used operationally to allow for the opportunity to replace items that suggest some degree of bias. This most likely would occur using field test data rather than pilot test data. The 2014 *Standards* list DIF as a type of internal structure evidence. This is because the presence of DIF, DBF, or DTF indicates a type of multidimensionality that is typically not desired by test developers. In Kane's validity framework, DIF comes under the extrapolation inference as a construct-irrelevant source of invalidity that undermines score interpretation.

If a test appears to be free of DIF/DBF/DTF, does that mean that the test is free from bias, or in other words fair? Not necessarily. A test with no DIF would seem to be free from one type of bias: something about the items that gives one subgroup an unfair advantage. A test can still be biased in other ways. As mentioned at the beginning of this chapter, the 2014 *Standards* discuss accessibility as a fairness issue. Consider the above DIF analysis of the TIMSS items. At least one item (depending on which DIF statistic was calculated) showed a large level of DIF and several others showed moderate levels of DIF. It is difficult to explain why these items show DIF. What is it about being a female or male 8th grader that gives that subgroup an advantage? On the other hand, it could be that female and male 8th graders do experience differences in instruction in terms of which mathematics classes they have taken prior to responding to the TIMSS survey. If that is the case, then unfairness could exist in the form of accessibility.

A different kind of validity issue surfaced with the DIF analysis of the political viewpoint items, namely, that most of the items showed some degree of DIF. Since DIF is by definition *differential* item performance, the fact that most items show DIF is indicative of issues of underlying internal structure. The potential multidimensionality of the political viewpoint construct could lead to revisiting the construct map and internal model. This is an example of the iterative nature of Wilson's construct map framework to test development that was presented in Chapter 5.

Both the TIMSS and political viewpoint DIF analyses show the judgment that is necessary after running the DIF analyses. When items show DIF, the test developer must make a judgment on whether or not to retain the item. DIF is usually analyzed for groups based on sex, race/ethnicity, and special populations, such as limited English proficiency (LEP). Examples of DIF analyses for tests measuring noncognitive constructs, particularly small-scale projects, are difficult to find. Some examples for the MBTI can be found (e.g., van Zyl & Taylor, 2012), but DIF does not appear to be widely practiced.

My recommendation is that DIF/DBF/DTF analyses be a part of any test's validation plan. While groupings based on sex, race/ethnicity, or LEP/disability are important, it may be more informative to include groupings based on relevant background variables, such as instructional differences for achievement constructs, that may underlie group differences.

10.8 CHAPTER SUMMARY

This chapter introduced the concept of fairness as a validity issue in terms of both measurement bias and accessibility. The focus then turned to analyzing test data for potential item bias, as illustrated in methods for detecting DIF, or the case when target population subgroups under- or overperform relative to overall group differences. The chapter focused on two popular DIF methods, the Mantel–Haenszel and SIBTEST, methods that are used by many large-scale testing programs. While running the DIF analyses in jMetrik and the mirt R package is relatively straightforward, interpreting the results is often difficult. For the TIMSS items, it was difficult to explain why some items showed DIF for groups based on sex. For the political viewpoint items, the majority of items showed DIF, which could lead to possible respecification of the construct as being multidimensional rather than unidimensional.

DIF for the political viewpoint data will resurface in the next chapter on dimensionality. DIF as an important piece of validity evidence will reappear in the last chapter, on validation plans.

10.9 EXERCISES AND ACTIVITIES

1. Use jMetrik to calculate the Mantel–Haenszel DIF method for the TIMSS Booklet 1 data and the Mantel method for the political viewpoint data. Use the mirt R package to calculate the SIBTEST method for both data sets, for individual items. For all analyses, purify the matching score. The results should agree with those presented in this chapter.

2. For the TIMSS data:

   a. Compare the nonparametric curves for items exhibiting A, B, and C levels of DIF.

   b. Examine the items showing B levels of DIF. Can you think of any logical explanation for the observed gender DIF?

   c. Run a DBF SIBTEST analysis of the set of items that measure mathematics at the "Reasoning" level. Is there evidence of gender DBF?

3. For the political viewpoint data, run a DBF SIBTEST analysis of the subset of items that concern regulation of behavior (View9907, View9913, View9915, and View9917). Is there evidence of gender DBF? If so, can you think of a logical explanation?

Test Development Project

In addition to gender and race/ethnicity, what other subgroups of your target population would benefit from a DIF/DBF analysis?

FURTHER READING

Camilli, G. (2006). Test fairness. In R. L. Brennan (Ed.), *Educational measurement* (4th ed., pp. 221–256). Westport, CT: Prager Publishers.

Clauser, B. E., & Mazor, K. M. (Spring 1998). Using statistical procedures to identify differentially functioning test items. *Educational Measurement: Issues and Practice*, 17(1), 31–44. NCME ITEM http://ncme.org/publications/items/

International Test Commission. (2018). ITC guidelines for the large-scale assessment of linguistically and culturally diverse populations. Retrieved from www.InTestCom.org

Joint Committee on Testing Practices. (1988). *Code of fair testing practices in education.* Washington, DC: Author.

REFERENCES

Chalmers, R. P. (2018). Improving the crossing SIBTEST statistic for detecting non-uniform DIF. *Psychometrika*, 83(2), 376–386.

Cochran, W. G. (1954). Some methods for strengthening the common χ^2 tests. *Biometrics*, 10, 417–451.

Cole, N. S., & Moss, P. A. (1989). Bias in test use. In R. L. Linn (Ed.), *Educational measurement* (pp. 201–219). New York, NY: Macmillan Publishing; American Council on Education.

Dorans, N. J., & Kullick, E. (1986). Demonstrating the utility of the standardization approach to assessing unexpected differential item performance on the Scholastic Aptitude Test. *Journal of Educational Measurement*, 23, 355–368.

Dorans, N. J., Schmitt, A. P., & Bleistein, C. A. (1992). The standardization approach to assessing comprehensive differential item functioning. *Journal of Educational Measurement*, 29(4), 309–319.

Holland, P. W., & Thayer, D. T. (1988). Differential item performance and the Mantel-Haenszel procedure. In H. Wainer, & H. I Braun (Eds.), *Test validity* (pp. 129–145). Hillsdale, NJ: Lawrence Erlbaum.

Li, H.-H., & Stout, W. (1996). A new procedure for detection of crossing DIF. *Psychometrika*, 61, 647–677.

Mantel, N. (1963). Chi-square tests with one degree of freedom; extensions of the Mantel-Haenszel procedure. *Journal of the American Statistical Association*, 58, 690–700.

Meyer, J. P. (2014). *Applied measurement with jMetrik*. New York, NY: Routledge.

Raju, N. S., van der Linden, W. J., & Fleer, P. F. (1995). An IRT-based internal measure of test bias with applications for differential item functioning. *Applied Psychological Measurement*, 19, 353–368.

Roussos, L. A., & Stout, W. F. (1996). Simulation studies of the effects of small sample size and studied item parameters on SIBTEST and Mantel-Haenszel Type I error performance. *Journal of Educational Measurement*, 33(2), 215–230.

Shealy, R. T., & Stout, W. F. (1993). A model-based standardization approach that separates true bias/DIF from group ability differences and detects test bias/DTF as well as item bias/DIF. *Psychometrika*, 58, 159–194.

Swaminathan, H., & Rogers, H. J. (1990). Detecting differential item functioning using the logistic regression procedures. *Journal of Educational Measurement*, 27, 361–370.

Van Zyll, C. J. J., & Taylor, N. (2012). Evaluating the MBTI Form M in South African context. *South African Journal of Industrial Psychology*, 38(1), 11–26.

11

DIMENSIONALITY

11.1 DIMENSIONALITY, INTERNAL MODELS, AND CONSTRUCT MAPS

In Chapter 6, I recommended that test developers create a construct map and internal model prior to writing items. The purpose of the construct map is to conceptualize the construct measured by the test as a single continuum between two extremes. Both respondents and items can be placed on this continuum. The construct map serves to define how respondents with higher test scores will differ from respondents with lower scores. The internal model further explicates the intended structure of the test by describing how the construct can be composed of parts based on content, skills, or cognitive processes.

After data have been collected on the test by respondents, either through a field test or operationally, an important piece of validity evidence is to show that item response data actually support the proposed internal structure of the test. This is typically done through analyses designed to investigate the dimensionality of the test. Dimensions, sometimes called factors or components, are the parts of the test as described in the construct map and internal model. Those two development activities could conceptualize a single dimension, multiple but strongly correlated dimensions, or uncorrelated dimensions. Such a structure points to a single test score, an overall score with subscores, or two or more test scores. Additionally, using one of the Rasch models introduced in Chapter 9 requires support for the assumption that a single dimension underlies test performance, a condition we referred to as unidimensionality.

This chapter introduces the two most popular statistical methods for investigating dimensionality: exploratory and confirmatory factor analysis. Dimensionality is a highly technical topic. This chapter is intended to provide an overview of several popular methods for assessing dimensionality with some worked examples from the political viewpoint and TIMSS datasets. For a more technical treatment, the reader is referred to the references at the end of this chapter. To become proficient in these methods, I recommend additional coursework or workshops.

11.2 METHODS FOR ASSESSING DIMENSIONALITY

A number of methods for assessing dimensionality have been developed. These include the following:

> *Exploratory Factor Analysis (EFA):* EFA determines the extent to which the
> correlations between a large number of variables (i.e., items or parts of a test)
> can be explained by a small number of factors (or dimensions or
> components).

Confirmatory Factor Analysis (CFA): CFA tests whether a hypothesized or intended internal structure (proposed by the test developer) fits the data.

Principal Components Analysis (PCA) of Residuals: This method is intended for Rasch models. It determines if there are meaningful additional dimensions after a unidimensional model is fit to the data.

Essential Dimensionality: This method tests whether a single dimension is so strong that any other smaller dimensions do not affect person ability estimates.

Likelihood Ratio Test: This test can be used to test whether a Rasch or IRT model with more dimensions fits the data better than a model with fewer dimensions.

The last three methods are intended for use with Rasch models or other latent variable models. The two factor analytic models, EFA and CFA, can be used with both latent variable and classical test theory models. They are also the two most popular models. As a result, this chapter will take up EFA and CFA and illustrate the methods with the TIMSS and political viewpoint data.

11.3 EXPLORATORY FACTOR ANALYSIS

Over one hundred years ago, the psychologist and statistician Charles Spearman (1904) investigated theories of intelligence using data from Binet's intelligence test. He noticed that all parts of Binet's scale correlated positively with each other, as shown graphically in Figure 11.1. The arrows represent the parts of the test. They all point in the same general direction. Spearman interpreted this to mean that the parts did not measure independent mental abilities, as Binet thought. He considered two possibilities: (1) the correlations between the parts reduce to a small number of independent traits, or (2) the correlations reduce to a single underlying general factor, plus a specific factor for each part. Spearman decided to go with the second explanation, and thus was born his *g* theory of intelligence. In this case, F1 is the single general intelligence factor correlated with all of the parts. F2 is uncorrelated with F1 and is therefore represented as a right angle. You could have a third factor that is uncorrelated with the first two factors, and so on up to as many factors as there are parts of the test.

FIGURE 11.1 ● Intercorrelated Parts of Binet's Intelligence Scale

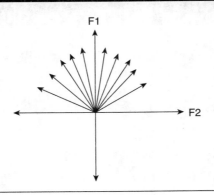

To support the *g* theory of intelligence, Spearman invented the first method of EFA. Without computers or calculators, this analysis was laborious and often carried out by students who sometimes took several weeks to work out the solution. The method operated on the correlation matrix between the scored parts of a test. Consider the correlation matrix between seven items claiming to measure job satisfaction, as shown in Table 11.1. If an EFA were conducted on this correlation matrix, the result would likely show two factors. Items 1–4 are strongly correlated with each other, while items 5–7 are strongly correlated, but the two sets of items are relatively uncorrelated with each other. It could turn out that items 1–4 measure one aspect of job satisfaction, say working conditions, while items 5–7 measure a different aspect, such as personal fulfillment. When Spearman conducted factor analyses of the Binet scale, the results showed one dominant factor that all parts were related to, and a series of minor factors that seemed to be specific to just one part or a small group of parts. Spearman interpreted these results as support for his *g* theory of intelligence.

In the late 1930s, the psychologist L. L. Thurstone came to quite a different view of intelligence than Spearman's *g*. He noticed that with Spearman's factor analysis method, there was a tendency for all items or test parts to be related, or load on, the first factor and also on one or more of the secondary factors. This situation made it difficult to interpret the meaning of the factors. He thought that the goal of factor analysis should be *simple structure*, where each item or part loads primarily on just one factor and that each factor loads primarily on a distinct subset of the items or parts. To accomplish this, Thurstone (1938) developed the idea of a geometrical rotation of

| TABLE 11.1 ⬤ Hypothetical Seven Item Correlation Matrix | | | | | | |
	1	2	3	4	5	6	7
1	1						
2	0.75	1					
3	0.83	0.82	1				
4	0.68	0.92	0.88	1			
5	0.03	0.01	0.05	0.01	1		
6	0.05	0.02	0.04	0.07	0.89	1	
7	0.02	0.06	0.03	0.03	0.91	0.76	1

factors. This is illustrated in Figure 11.2. The original two factors (from Figure 11.1) are shown as dotted arrows. By rotating these two factors, the new factors, F1 and F2, now align with separate groups of items or parts. It could be that the items aligned with the new F1 are associated with verbal comprehension, while the items aligned with the new F2 are associated with number facility. By rotating the initial factor analysis of intelligence test data, Thurstone (1935) theorized that there were a small number (seven) types of intelligence, which he called primary mental abilities, instead of a dominant *g*.

In the decades since Spearman's and Thurstone's work on developing factor analysis, EFA has evolved into a three-stage process. In the first stage, similar to Spearman's

FIGURE 11.2 ⬤ Rotation of Initial Factors

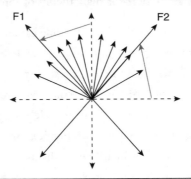

work, an initial extraction of factors is carried out on the correlation matrix between test items or parts. Second, a determination is made about the number of significant factors. In the third stage, as in Thurstone's method, the initial extraction is rotated to attempt to produce a simple structure that can help identify and interpret the factors. In the following sections, some of the most popular extraction and rotation methods are described, followed by their applications to the political viewpoint and TIMSS data.

11.3.1 Extraction Methods

Principal Components Analysis (PCA). PCA is considered to be an alternative analytic method to EFA (Osborne, 2014). It is designed to produce weighted linear combinations, or components of items and/or parts of a test, similar to a weighted raw score. The weights, or loadings, are intended to produce combinations with the greatest variance. The items or parts are considered to be measured without error, meaning that all of the data are used. The major difference of PCA with EFA is that EFA is intended for the factors to be interpretable as latent variables, or constructs, while no such claim is made about PCA.

That said, PCA is the default option for some statistical software packages, including SPSS. PCA works with the correlation matrix between test items or parts. The items or parts have first been converted to z-scores. The first factor, or component, is extracted to have the maximum possible variance. The variance of a factor is called its *eigenvalue*. This factor is a linear combination of item scores, each weighted by a factor loading to indicate its importance for the factor. The second factor is extracted to have maximum variance and be uncorrelated with the first factor. PCA extraction continues until there are as many factors as there are items. All factors will be uncorrelated and will have decreasing variance. The sum of the eigenvalues, or the total variance of all of the factors, will equal the number of items or parts.

Principal Axes Factoring (PAF). PAF works similarly to PCA, except that the 1.0s that appear in the diagonal of a correlation matrix are replaced by communality estimates. Communalities are the estimated proportions of variance that items or parts share with all of the significant factors. This method effectively extracts the factors only on the shared variance between items or parts and the factors, thus acknowledging that items or parts contain measurement error (as estimated in 1 minus the communality estimate).

Maximum Likelihood (ML). ML is an iterative process in which factors and factor loadings are estimated to best reproduce the correlation matrix between items and parts. This method assumes that all items or parts are normally distributed and together they are multivariate normal. If these assumptions are not met, then PAF is a better alternative.

Unweighted Least Squares (ULS) and Generalized Least Squares (GLS). These methods are iterative like ML, but ULS is more robust to violating the multivariate assumption of ML. GLS weights items or parts according to their correlations with other items or parts.

Minimum Residual (minres). Minres is similar to ULS but seeks to minimize the squared differences (or squared residuals) between observed and predicted correlations. Because minres operates only on the off-diagonal entries of the correlation matrix, commonality estimates are not needed.

Whatever method is used for extraction, a linear model is the result:

$$F_{ik} = b_{k1}X_{i1} + b_{k2}X_{21} + b_{k3}X_{31} + \cdots + b_{kj}X_{ij} \qquad (11.1)$$

where F_{ik} is the score on Factor k by person i, and the $b_{kj}X_{ij}$ terms are the item or part scores (X_{ij}) weighted by their factor loadings (b_{kj}). Alternatively, the linear model can be written as follows:

$$X_{ij} = b_{j1}F_{i1} + b_{j2}F_{i2} + b_{j3}F_{i3} + \cdots + b_{jk}F + U_{ij} \qquad (11.2)$$

where U_{ij} is the item residual after the factors have been fit, or one minus the communality. If you were to square and sum the factor loadings for a factor, you would obtain the factor's eigenvalue (i.e., its variance). If you were to square and sum the factor loadings for a single item or part, you would obtain the communality of that item or part.

Is there a preferred extraction method? Osborne (2014) echoes many practitioners by recommending ML when multivariate normality holds and PAF when it doesn't. On the other hand, minres has received increasing use and is the default option for the psych R package.

11.3.2 The Number of Factors

After the extraction phase of EFA, a critical decision to be made is the number of factors to be extracted. It's important to note that EFA is primarily exploratory. The goal is to find a solution that enables identification of the factors. Several methods for determining this number have been proposed. These are guidelines that provide advice. They are not rules to be obeyed.

One of the most popular and oldest methods is the Kaiser (1960) criterion, in which the number of factors is simply the number of eigenvalues greater than 1.0. Because the items or parts have been converted to z-scores, they all have a variance of 1.0. Any eigenvalue less than 1.0 means that factor has less variance than a single item or part. A second criterion for the number of factors is Cattell's (1966) scree test. The scree plot is a graph of eigenvalues. An example of a scree plot of the political viewpoint data is shown in Figure 11.3. The decline in eigenvalues is steep for the initial factors, then proceeds more slowly. The scree test looks for a point where the plot "bends" from steeper to flatter. Here, this occurs after the third factor or after the fifth factor. The bend point is ultimately a judgment call. A third popular criterion is to look at the proportion of total variance accounted for by each factor. Cutoff values are likewise judgment decisions, but many practitioners use 10 percent of total variance for a single factor or 80 percent for all factors combined.

FIGURE 11.3 ● Scree Plot of Political Viewpoint Data

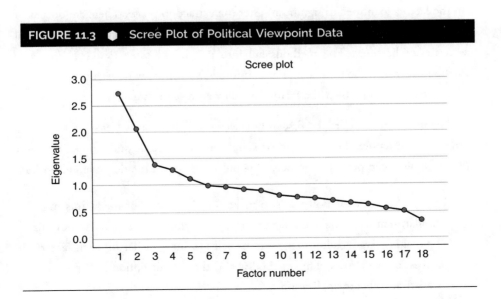

Parallel analysis (Horn, 1965), a variation on the scree test, has been a popular approach in recent years. First, a scree plot of factor eigenvalues is plotted. Then, an extraction is carried out on a random dataset with the same test length, sample size, and item scoring as the test being investigated. The random eigenvalues are plotted with the actual eigenvalues. The number of factors from actual data that have larger eigenvalues than the random data are estimated to be the optimal number of factors. Parallel analysis is implemented in the psych R package.

Finally, one could use as a starting point the number of factors theoretically hypothesized for the construct being measured. Alternatively, in addition to specifying an intended number of factors, the test developer could analyze the data with a range of numbers of factors and look for the most meaningful solution. This strategy would be most appropriate for constructs that have no clearly articulated theory behind them. Again, EFA is exploratory in nature. The goal is to discover the factor solution that is the most interpretable for the construct being measured. It may turn out that this solution differs from the proposed internal structure for the test. This outcome, however, may suggest a revision to the internal model.

11.3.3 Rotation Methods

The third phase of EFA is rotation. Its goal is to provide a simple structure that enhances interpretation of the meaning of the factors. The rotation is carried out only on the factors identified as significant after the extraction phase. There are dozens of rotational methods, and there is great variation in the methods offered by statistical software applications. The methods fall into two broad categories: (1) *orthogonal* methods, in which the factors are not permitted to correlate with each other, and (2) *oblique* methods, in which the factors are allowed to correlate.

Orthogonal methods were the first to be developed. Thurstone's (1938) rotation was orthogonal in nature. They tend to be simpler mathematically and worked well at a time of limited computer power. Several popular orthogonal rotation methods include

> *Varimax.* Varimax rotation tends to make the eigenvalues of the factors more similar, that is, to make the factors have more similar variances. It does this by making large loadings larger and small loadings smaller for each factor across items or parts. This method is also the default option in some statistical software applications.

Quartimax. Quartimax minimizes the number of factors needed to explain each item or part. It does this by making large loadings larger and small loadings smaller for each item or part across the factors. As a result, this method tends to produce a first factor on which most items or parts load.

Equimax. Equimax is a compromise between varimax and quartimax rotations.

Oblique methods have been developed more recently as computer capabilities have increased. Two popular oblique rotation methods are *Promax* and *Direct Oblimin*. The technical details of these methods are beyond the scope of this book. The reader is referred to Gorsuch (1983) for a review of these methods. In both methods, the researcher can control the limit on how strongly factors can be correlated. Comparing the two methods, Promax is often faster, especially for large datasets, but this advantage has become minimized with recent increases in computing power.

If an orthogonal rotation is used, a rotated factor matrix of loadings is produced. The entries of this matrix consist of the correlations between the factors and items or parts. If an oblique rotation is used, two matrices are produced. The structure matrix consists of the correlations between factors and items or parts. The pattern matrix consists of regression coefficients for each item or part in predicting each factor. In general, the interpretation of these two matrices will be nearly identical in terms of identifying which items or parts load on each factor. Additionally, an oblique rotation will estimate a matrix of the correlations between the factors.

Which rotation method is to be recommended? In measuring constructs in social science and educational research, we usually think of factors being correlated, so oblique methods are used most often. Also, if the factors do turn out to be uncorrelated, then orthogonal and oblique rotations will produce nearly the same results. In the end, this decision should be guided by the theory of the construct, construct map, and internal model to determine whether or not the component parts of the internal model are theorized to be correlated. Correlated component parts point to an oblique rotation. Uncorrelated parts suggest an orthogonal rotation.

11.3.4 EFA Example Using the Political Viewpoint Data

For an example of EFA, I will use data from the 18 political viewpoint items. It is important to recall that this set of items appears as a group of opinion Likert items.

The original survey reported these as 18 independent variables. The question at hand is whether these 18 items can be used as a test measuring a construct called political viewpoint. As we saw in Chapter 5, the construct map shows a single dimension for political viewpoint that ranges from liberal to conservative. The purpose of this EFA is therefore to investigate viability of this possible test.

First, a note about software. Most statistical software packages, such as SPSS and SAS, offer EFA. However, for this example, I will use the psych R package for several reasons. First, you have already seen this package in operation in Chapters 4 and 8. Second, this package produces very similar results as the commercial packages. And most importantly, the psych package contains more up-to-date methods. The R code to run the EFA on the TIMSS and political viewpoint data can be found in Appendix B. You will notice that the opening lines of code are identical to those presented in Chapters 4 and 8. These lines simply open the political viewpoint dataset and reverse score some of the items.

First, a parallel analysis was carried out to get some idea of the number of factors suggested by the data. The results are shown in Figure 11.4. Since we are conducting

FIGURE 11.4 ● Results of Parallel Analysis

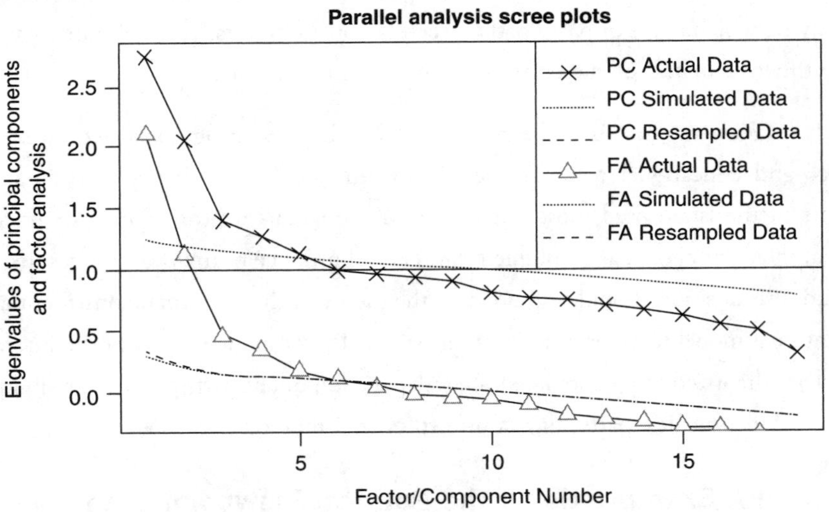

Parallel analysis scree plots

```
> fa.parallel(poliscored,fm="minres")
Parallel analysis suggests that the number of factors = 5 and the
number of components = 5
```

a factor analysis, we look at the graphs for the lines denoted FA. These results suggest five factors. Keeping with this recommendation, an EFA was run with rotating five factors.

The first output from the EFA is shown in Table 11.2. This consists of the factor loadings, commonalities (h2), uniquenesses (u2), and complexities (com). For interpretative purposes, factor loadings greater than the absolute value of 0.30 are in bold. The first thing to notice is the commonalities column. This shows the proportion of variance that each item shares with the five factors. For two items, View9912 and View9918, this proportion is less than 0.10. That results in these

TABLE 11.2 ⬡ Factor Loadings for Five-Factor Solution								
	MR1	**MR2**	**MR4**	**MR3**	**MR5**	**h2**	**u2**	**com**
View9901	0.22	−0.02	−0.09	**0.40**	0.01	0.22	0.78	1.7
View9902	**0.40**	**0.33**	0.12	−0.20	−0.06	0.40	0.60	2.7
View9903	0.00	0.05	0.11	**0.63**	−0.03	0.41	0.59	1.1
View9904	0.04	**0.64**	0.03	−0.05	−0.08	0.43	0.57	1.1
View9905	0.08	**0.54**	−0.13	0.16	0.09	0.40	0.60	1.4
View9906	**0.83**	−0.04	−0.04	0.02	0.03	0.67	0.33	1.0
View9907	−0.10	**0.43**	−0.06	0.13	0.18	0.23	0.77	1.7
View9908	0.26	**−0.34**	0.08	0.08	0.00	0.17	0.83	2.1
View9909	0.04	0.00	0.71	0.05	0.05	0.53	0.47	1.0
View9910	0.06	0.02	0.10	−0.10	**0.50**	0.26	0.74	1.2
View9911	0.20	−0.23	−0.10	0.05	0.20	0.13	0.87	3.4
View9912	−0.05	−0.06	−0.19	−0.04	0.11	0.06	0.94	2.1
View9913	−0.09	−0.06	**0.35**	0.01	−0.13	0.15	0.85	1.5
View9914	**0.75**	0.06	0.07	0.02	−0.01	0.63	0.37	1.0
View9915	0.06	0.23	**−0.36**	−0.02	−0.03	0.20	0.80	1.8
View9916	**0.39**	−0.04	0.02	−0.01	0.05	0.16	0.84	1.1
View9917	−0.02	0.00	0.18	0.07	**0.27**	0.12	0.88	1.9
View9918	−0.09	−0.15	−0.11	0.04	−0.07	0.06	0.94	3.3

items not loading on any factor, meaning they seem to be measuring something other than political viewpoint. A third item, View9911, has a relatively small commonality of 0.13. As a result, this item loads weakly on two factors but has no loading greater than |0.30|. Of the remaining items, one item, View9902 loads on two factors, a situation that makes it difficult to interpret the factors.

The remaining items primarily load onto one factor each. Table 11.3 shows the text of those items with each factor. Like many, if not most, EFAs conducted on survey data, the results are not totally clear. Factors 1 and 2 deal mostly with social issues. Factor 1 may be concerned with societal mores, while Factor 2 may relate to personal behavior, although there are exceptions to these generalizations. View9902 (Abortion should be legal.) loads on both of these factors. Factor 3 is about legal issues. Factor 4 is not clear, but two of the three items are related to government regulation. Finally, Factor 5 is concerned about racial issues. You will note that there are only two items

TABLE 11.3 ● Political Viewpoint Items Loading on Each Factor		
Factor	**Item**	**Text of Item**
1	View9906	It is important to have laws prohibiting homosexual relationships.
	View9914	Same sex couples should have the right to legal marital status.
	View9916	The activities of married women are best confined to the home and family.
2	View9904	If two people really like each other, it's all right for them to have sex even if they've known each other for only a very short time.
	View9905	Marijuana should be legalized.
	View9907	Employers should be allowed to require drug testing of employees or job applicants.
	View9908	Just because a man thinks that a woman has "led him on" does not entitle him to have sex with her.
3	View9901	There is too much concern in the courts for the rights of criminals.
	View9903	The death penalty should be abolished.
4	View9909	Realistically, an individual can do little to bring about changes in our society.
	View9913	Colleges should prohibit racist/sexist speech on campus.
	View9915	Material on the Internet should be regulated by the government.
5	View9910	Racial discrimination is no longer a major problem in America.
	View9917	Affirmative action in college admissions should be abolished.

TABLE 11.4 ⬡ Correlations Between Factors					
	MR1	MR2	MR4	MR3	MR5
MR1	1.00	0.29	0.28	0.11	0.20
MR2	0.29	1.00	−0.12	0.00	−0.02
MR4	0.28	−0.12	1.00	0.08	0.01
MR3	0.11	0.00	0.08	1.00	0.24
MR5	0.20	−0.02	0.01	0.24	1.00

for Factors 3 and 5, making their interpretation more difficult. Table 11.4 shows the estimated correlations between factors. These range from −0.12 to 0.29. The strongest correlation is 0.29, between Factors 1 and 2, raising the question if this is really two factors, or just one.

Table 11.5 shows the size of the eigenvalues (SS loadings) and their proportion of the variance explained. Even with rotation, the eigenvalues decrease in magnitude. Factors 3 and 5 show variances smaller than 1.0. This is due to there being only two items loading on these factors. Finally, the psych package shows some fit indices indicating how well the data fit the five-factor model. Among these are the RMSR, RMSEA, and TLI. Using criteria from Hu and Bentler (1999), these indicate relatively good fit (<0.05 for RMSR and RMSEA, and >0.90 for TLI).

So, what can be determined from this EFA? First, the data clearly do not justify a single political viewpoint liberal-to-conservative score. There are multiple dimensions

TABLE 11.5 ⬡ Eigenvalues and Proportion of Variance Explained					
	MR1	MR2	MR4	MR3	MR5
SS loadings	1.81	1.29	0.95	0.69	0.47
Proportion Var	0.10	0.07	0.05	0.04	0.03
Cumulative Var	0.10	0.17	0.23	0.26	0.29
Proportion Explained	0.35	0.25	0.18	0.13	0.09
Cumulative Proportion	0.35	0.60	0.78	0.91	1.00

to political viewpoint, including possibly, separate dimensions for social, legal, and racial issues. These dimensions also seem to be weakly correlated, so someone could appear liberal on some dimensions but conservative on others. Could these items then be used to produce multiple political viewpoint scores? This also is problematic because two of the factors consist of only two items, two other factors consist of only three items. These small numbers make it difficult to clearly define these factors. Finally, three items do not appear to load onto any single factor. At best, these items suggest a way to develop a new test with multiple scores corresponding to different aspects of political viewpoint. At this point in using Wilson's construct map approach to test development, it would seem advisable to revisit and revise the political viewpoint construct map itself.

11.3.5 EFA of Dichotomously Scored Data

To conduct an EFA of the TIMSS data, we run into a technical problem. The correlation matrix between dichotomously scored items is actually a correlation matrix of phi coefficients. As shown in the computational formula for phi coefficients in Chapter 1, phi is totally dependent on the p-value, or proportion correct, of the item. As a result, EFA often produces factors based on item difficulty (e.g., difficult items loading on one factor). There are several alternatives to using phi coefficients for EFA. One solution, implemented in the *IRTPRO* or *HOHARM* (Fraser & McDonald, 2012) software packages, is to use a nonlinear model. More specifically, these packages use logistic models such as Rasch or other IRT models. Another alternative, implemented in the psych package, is to have the initial extraction performed on tetrachoric correlations in the case of dichotomously scored items. These correlations assume an underlying normal distribution of the item scores.

The TIMSS Booklet 1 test is organized around five broad content domains. For the TIMSS data, the key structural question is whether a single score is justified, essentially combining item scores across domains, or whether separate scores are more valid measures of mathematical skill. A third possibility is a single score with subscores for each domain. With this in mind, two rotations will be conducted. Quartimax rotation will look at the viability of a fewer number of factors, while oblimin will look at whether factors break down according to content or skill domains and how strongly related they are. The R code for running the EFA can be found in Appendix B. The argument cor="tet" correlations indicate tetrachoric correlations are to be analyzed. The argument fm="ml" tells the psych package to use the maximum likelihood method of extraction. This was used because both the ml method and tetrachoric correlations assume normality, but very similar results can be obtained by using principal axis factoring.

The results of the parallel analysis are shown in Figure 11.5. Eight factors are suggested, but the graph shows that the first factor dominates the others. Table 11.6 shows the eight factors using a quartimax rotation. As expected, all items except one load on the first factor. The remaining factors, except for Factor 6, show only one item loading on that factor. For only four items are the loadings greater than the loadings for Factor 1. Together, these results suggest support for a single test score. Table 11.7 shows the results from an oblimin rotation. Here, the first two factors are the only ones with loadings from more than a single item. The items loading on Factor 1 are all from the Number domain, but the items loading on Factor 2 come from all five domains. So, Factor 1 might plausibly represent the Number domain, but there is no clear pattern for the remaining domains on the remaining factors. The major content domains therefore do not appear to be distinct factors. Overall, the fit

---

FIGURE 11.5 ● Results of Parallel Analysis

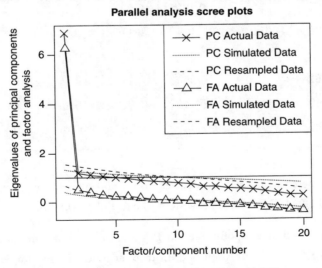

Parallel analysis scree plots

```
> fa.parallel(bk1scored,cor="tet",fm="ml")
Parallel analysis suggests that the number of
factors =  8 and the number of components =  1
```

TABLE 11.6 ● Quartimax Rotation of TIMSS Data								
	F1	**F2**	**F3**	**F4**	**F5**	**F6**	**F7**	**F8**
M012001	**0.80**	0.02	0.12	0.09	−0.09	**−0.31**	−0.01	−0.05
M012002	**0.34**	0.05	0.93	0.05	0.05	0.00	0.00	0.00
M012003	**0.62**	0.11	0.03	0.04	0.05	0.09	−0.01	−0.02
M012004	**0.67**	0.04	0.01	0.03	0.00	**−0.34**	0.11	0.10
M012005	**0.33**	0.12	−0.04	0.19	−0.08	0.07	0.13	**0.30**
M012006	**0.38**	0.09	0.05	0.04	0.00	0.17	−0.12	0.09
M012037	0.29	**0.95**	0.04	0.07	0.01	0.00	0.00	0.00
M012038	**0.49**	0.03	0.11	0.10	**0.73**	0.01	0.00	−0.01
M012039	**0.34**	0.22	0.11	−0.03	0.21	−0.08	0.17	0.03
M012040	**0.57**	0.06	0.03	0.09	0.12	0.04	0.06	0.25
M012041	**0.65**	0.07	0.20	−0.05	−0.01	0.26	−0.04	−0.03
M012042	**0.69**	0.13	0.05	0.28	0.12	0.20	−0.21	0.12
M032570	**0.59**	0.03	−0.02	0.06	0.08	−0.10	−0.25	−0.16
M032643	**0.50**	0.10	0.06	**0.85**	0.06	−0.02	0.02	0.00
M012013	**0.49**	−0.02	0.03	0.10	0.02	−0.04	**0.45**	−0.01
M012014	**0.64**	0.12	0.10	0.12	0.11	0.13	0.18	**−0.31**
M012015	**0.61**	0.12	0.11	−0.08	0.07	0.32	0.08	0.03
M012016	**0.40**	−0.02	0.10	0.09	0.11	−0.24	0.01	0.25
M012017	**0.51**	0.20	0.16	−0.04	−0.02	0.03	0.02	0.02
M022251	**0.31**	0.00	0.00	0.06	0.15	0.11	0.11	0.06

statistics to these two models show mixed results and suggest borderline good fit (for both models: RMSEA = 0.67, RMSR = 0.02, TLI = 0.868).

For both the political viewpoint test and TIMSS Booklet 1, it is important to keep in mind that EFA is exploratory. In both of these analyses, a pure simple structure did not emerge. At this point, the test developer can try additional analyses with different numbers of factors, different extraction methods, and different types of rotation in the hope that an optimal solution will emerge.

TABLE 11.7 ⬡ Oblimin Rotation of TIMSS Data								
	F1	**F2**	**F3**	**F4**	**F5**	**F6**	**F7**	**F8**
M012001	**0.79**	0.04	0.08	0.01	0.09	−0.05	0.01	−0.07
M012002	0.00	0.00	0.01	0.00	**0.99**	0.01	−0.01	0.01
M012003	0.22	**0.36**	0.04	0.07	−0.02	0.08	0.03	−0.07
M012004	**0.72**	−0.02	−0.02	0.04	−0.03	0.06	0.12	0.10
M012005	0.03	**0.30**	0.21	0.08	−0.05	−0.11	0.15	0.27
M012006	0.03	**0.41**	0.03	0.05	0.03	−0.01	−0.09	0.05
M012037	−0.01	−0.01	0.00	**1.01**	0.00	−0.01	−0.01	0.00
M012038	−0.02	0.00	0.01	0.00	0.02	**0.89**	0.00	0.00
M012039	0.14	−0.04	−0.09	0.23	0.08	0.27	0.17	0.03
M012040	0.19	**0.35**	0.06	0.02	−0.01	0.16	0.08	0.21
M012041	0.09	**0.58**	−0.04	0.01	0.17	−0.01	0.02	−0.11
M012042	0.09	**0.52**	0.29	0.05	0.00	0.13	−0.17	0.06
M032570	**0.48**	0.14	0.03	0.01	−0.07	0.14	−0.23	−0.19
M032643	0.00	−0.02	**0.99**	0.01	0.02	0.01	0.01	−0.01
M012013	0.20	0.09	0.14	−0.05	−0.01	0.05	**0.49**	−0.04
M012014	0.11	0.20	0.17	0.08	0.04	0.15	0.23	**−0.37**
M012015	−0.04	**0.62**	−0.07	0.06	0.06	0.08	0.15	−0.06
M012016	**0.40**	−0.02	0.03	−0.03	0.09	0.15	0.00	0.27
M012017	0.23	0.25	−0.07	0.19	0.14	−0.01	0.05	−0.02
M022251	−0.03	0.22	0.07	−0.04	−0.04	0.18	0.14	0.03

11.4 CONFIRMATORY FACTOR ANALYSIS

For the TIMSS dataset, there exists a specific internal structure to investigate. Because the TIMSS test's content is organized around five content domains, Numbers, Measurement, Geometry, Data, and Algebra, we can investigate the viability of three internal structures based on a single mathematics score, five distinct but correlated domain scores, or a single overall score with five domain subscores. To see how well item response data fit a specific internal structure, CFA is used. CFA is offered in several commercial software packages, such as *MPlus*, *LISREL*, and *EQS*. It is also offered by the *lavaan* R package (Rosseel, 2012), which I will use for this example. The lavaan package is an extensive latent variable modeling application, of which CFA is just one available analysis. It also carries out structural equation modeling (SEM), growth curve modeling, and multilevel SEM. The code for running a CFA with lavaan can be found in Appendix B. The website (https://lavaan.ugent.be/index.html) contains extensive tutorials and resources for using lavaan.

There are two internal models to be tested with CFA. The first is one with five scores with each one representing one of the domains. They are hypothesized to correlate with each other, as shown in the graphical representation in Figure 11.6. The arrows to the left of each domain show the items associated with that domain. The two-way arrows between domains indicate that they are correlated. The second model is for a single overall score. This path diagram looks like the previous figure except that there is just one circular figure for an overall score with arrows pointing to each item.

Table 11.8 shows the parameter estimates for the five-score model.[1] With the exception of the first item, each item has a hypothesis test of its significance. Note that the first item in each domain contains an estimate of 1.00. This is done by default to set the scale for the factors, so it does not have a significance test. The important result from this table is that all items are significant predictors of the domain score. In factor analytic language, all items significantly load on their assigned factors.

Table 11.9 shows the correlations between the five domains. These are not the actual correlations between observed scores on each domain but rather the correlations estimated from the model (which is why some exceed 1.00). These correlations are essentially near 1.00, challenging the idea that the domains are distinct. The results for the single-score model also show every item loading significantly on the single score. And the model shows excellent fit. Is there then a preferred model?

---

[1]It is important to point out here that I am referring to domains, items, and internal model as they have been in this book so far. I do note that the standard CFA/SEM language would refer to domain scores as factors or latent variables, items as observed variables, and Figure 11.6 as a five-factor model.

FIGURE 11.6 ● Graphical Representation of Five Correlated Scores From TIMSS

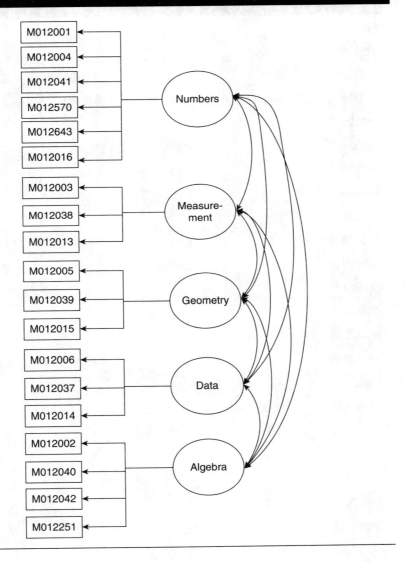

Table 11.10 shows a comparison between the two models on various fit indices. Both models fit the data very well. On all indices, the single-score model shows a very slightly better fit. In summary, either model could be used, but the five-score model is essentially five scores of nearly the same thing.

TABLE 11.8 ● Parameter Estimates for the Five-Score Model				
	Estimate	Std. Err	z-Value	P (> |z|)
Number	=~			
M012001	1.00			
M012004	0.84	0.07	11.90	0.00
M012041	0.68	0.06	11.11	0.00
M032570	0.65	0.06	10.41	0.00
M032643	0.81	0.07	11.53	0.00
M012016	0.55	0.07	8.29	0.00
Measurement	=~			
M012003	1.00			
M012038	0.87	0.09	9.21	0.00
M012013	0.85	0.10	8.41	0.00
Geometry	=~			
M012005	1.00			
M012039	1.19	0.21	5.56	0.00
M012015	1.66	0.26	6.41	0.00
Data	=~			
M012006	1.00			
M012037	1.15	0.19	6.00	0.00
M012014	1.32	0.19	6.95	0.00
Algebra	=~			
M012002	1.00			
M012040	1.02	0.14	7.33	0.00
M012042	1.79	0.21	8.38	0.00
M022251	0.63	0.13	4.99	0.00

TABLE 11.9 ⬡ Estimated Correlation Between Domain Scores

	Number	Measurement	Geometry	Data	Algebra
Number	1.00				
Measurement	0.98	1.00			
Geometry	0.86	1.10	1.00		
Data	0.87	1.00	1.08	1.00	
Algebra	1.01	1.08	1.04	0.98	1.00

TABLE 11.10 ⬡ Comparison of Fit Indices for Five- and Single-Score Models

	RMSEA	TLI	CFI	AIC	BIC
fit5d	0.031	0.933	0.945	16,885.77	17,107.98
fit1d	0.031	0.932	0.939	16,885.47	17,061.38

11.5 BIFACTOR MODEL: AN EFA THAT LOOKS LIKE A CFA

For the TIMSS data, there is one other internal model worth testing out. This is called the bifactor model, in which each item loads onto a dominant first factor and onto one other more specific factor. This model reflects a single overall score with subscores. In some software applications, such as *IRTPRO*, the bifactor model is run as a CFA with there being specific factors predicted to load on specific items. In the psych R package, the bifactor model is run as an EFA where the data drive which secondary factor is associated with each item. The setup is as shown above, except the fa function that runs the EFA is as follows:

$$\text{fa}(r = bk1scored, nfactors = 6, fm = \text{“ml”},\ cor = \text{“tet”}, rotate = \text{“bifactor”})$$

There are six factors in this analysis because of one overall factor and five subfactors that we hope will correspond to the five domains. The factor loadings are shown in Table 11.11. These results overall are similar to the quartimax rotation shown above.

Thirteen of the 20 items do not have a large loading on any factor other than the first. The seven items that do load on a second factor do not exhibit any domain-related pattern. For example, Numbers items appear in both Factors 3 and 4. The fit statistics are mixed but generally indicate borderline good fit of the data to the model (RMSEA = 0.70, RMSR = 0.03, TLI = 0.856) but slightly worse fit than the EFAs shown above. However, the secondary factors do not correspond to the content domains.

TABLE 11.11 ◗ EFA Loadings for Bifactor Model						
	ML1	ML2	ML3	ML4	ML5	ML6
M012001	**0.74**	−0.08	0	**0.46**	−0.01	−0.09
M012002	**0.47**	0.06	−0.05	0.01	0.02	−0.13
M012003	**0.63**	0.00	−0.08	0.00	−0.05	−0.03
M012004	**0.61**	−0.01	−0.04	**0.43**	0.10	0.11
M012005	**0.38**	−0.12	0.10	−0.05	0.07	**0.31**
M012006	**0.41**	−0.04	−0.06	−0.10	−0.18	0.08
M012037	**0.44**	−0.07	0.01	−0.13	−0.02	0.04
M012038	**0.56**	**0.83**	0.01	−0.01	0.00	−0.01
M012039	**0.40**	0.14	−0.10	0.03	0.16	0.06
M012040	**0.59**	0.07	−0.02	0.04	0.00	0.22
M012041	**0.66**	−0.05	−0.19	−0.10	−0.09	−0.12
M012042	**0.76**	0.05	0.12	−0.09	**−0.31**	0.08
M032570	**0.54**	0.06	−0.01	0.21	−0.23	−0.16
M032643	**0.66**	0.01	**0.75**	−0.01	−0.01	0.01
M012013	**0.51**	−0.02	0.01	0.09	**0.37**	0.01
M012014	**0.68**	0.05	−0.01	−0.06	0.16	−0.29
M012015	**0.65**	0.00	−0.23	−0.20	−0.01	−0.02
M012016	**0.39**	0.08	0.04	0.27	0.01	0.23
M012017	**0.54**	−0.06	−0.15	0.02	0.00	−0.02
M022251	**0.33**	0.11	−0.01	−0.06	0.07	0.06

11.6 USING FACTOR ANALYSIS RESULTS AS VALIDITY EVIDENCE

The goal of these analyses is to provide validity evidence in support of the proposed construct map and corresponding internal model. In Messick's validity framework, as represented in the 2014 *Standards*, this evidence falls under the heading of structural fidelity or internal structure. In Kane's framework, factor analyses fall as evidence within the extrapolation inference, that is, that test scores do in fact measure the construct as it is defined. If the structural evidence is consistent with the test developer's intended structure, then there is support for the intended meaning and use of test scores.

So, what do the above analyses have to say about the political viewpoint and TIMSS tests? First, if the 18 political viewpoint items were intended to measure respondents on a single liberal-to-conservative continuum, these results definitely do not support that meaning. Instead, political viewpoint seems to be multidimensional, with separate dimensions possibly for legal, social, and racial issues. Unfortunately, there are not enough items in each dimension to provide reliable scores. These analyses suggest the development of a new political viewpoint test with a multidimensional construct map and internal model.

Additionally, if you reexamine the DIF results presented in Chapter 10, you will notice that all of the items in Table 10.9 that showed some level of DIF also appeared above in Table 11.2 as being associated with a particular factor. All of the Factor 1 items showed a CC DIF level favoring the reference group. Of the six items showing little or no DIF, three were not clearly associated with any factor. The relationship between the DIF and EFA analyses is not completely clear, but there is some indication that at least some DIF is caused by multidimensionality, that is, respondents are matched on a different dimension than the one measured by the studied item. This situation would be like matching respondents on social studies scores to examine DIF on mathematics items.

For TIMSS, the structural validity issue is quite different. In its development, grade eight mathematics is subdivided into five content domains. The intent is to report a single overall score, but domain subscores are a possibility. Because of this specific proposed structure, CFA as well as EFA become important analytic tools. The EFA results with a quartimax rotation suggested a single dominant factor and a number of smaller factors. However, the smaller factors had no apparent relationship to the five domains. The oblimin rotation did not produce an interpretable set of factor loadings, but the factors were moderately correlated. The CFA and bifactor model results both indicated a strong factor related to most, if not all, items. No secondary factors related to domains emerged. Furthermore, the CFA results for the five-score model indicated that the domains correlated near perfectly. This means that, if domain subscores were provided, most students would achieve the same relative result on all five, for example, high in all five or low in all five domains. Profiles of strengths and weaknesses would not appear for most students. In sum, a single overall score is supported by these analyses. Domain scores, as distinct sets of skills, is not supported.

11.7 CHAPTER SUMMARY

This chapter presented an overview of EFA and CFA, a set of widely used tools to investigate the internal structure of tests. I have intended this chapter to be as nontechnical as possible. Issues such as sample size, pros and cons of various extraction and rotation methods, and other dimensionality methods were not addressed deeply in this chapter. Readers who want to know more about these issues are referred to the readings below.

For test development, the purpose of factor analysis is to provide validity evidence pertaining to the intended definition of the construct as evidenced in the construct map and to the intended structure of the test as evidenced in the internal model. If the results of the factor analyses do not support the intended structure, then it may be necessary to revisit how the construct is defined.

11.8 EXERCISES AND ACTIVITIES

1. Using the political viewpoint data, run the five-factor EFA from this chapter. You should obtain the same results as shown. Still using the political viewpoint data, run new EFAs with six factors and four factors. Highlight factor loadings with an absolute value greater than 0.30. Compared to the five-factor solution, do either of these solutions provide greater simple structure?

2. Using the TIMSS data, run the eight-factor EFA from this chapter. You should obtain the same results as shown. Still using the TIMSS data, run a new EFA with two factors and an oblimin rotation. Highlight factor loadings with an absolute value greater than 0.30. Compared to the eight-factor solution, does this solution provide greater simple structure or support for single dominant factor?

3. Using the TIMSS data, use the lavaan R package to run the five- and one-factor CFA from this chapter. You should obtain the same results as shown. For the same data, run a CFA for two factors. Assume that the intended structure of the test is two factors as follows:

   a. Factor 1 (Numbers and Measurement)

   b. Factor 2 (Geometry, Data, and Algebra)

   Does this model fit the data better than the five- or one-factor models?

4. Using the psych R package, run the six-factor bifactor model as shown in this chapter. You should obtain the same results as shown. For the same data, run a bifactor model for three factors, with the second and third factors being the ones used above for the CFA. Do the loadings suggest that Factors 2 and 3 correspond to the factors used in the above CFA?

FURTHER READING

Gorsuch, R. L. (1983). *Factor analysis* (2nd ed.). Hillsdale, NJ: Lawrence Erlbaum Associates.

Osborne, J. W. (2014). *Best practices in exploratory factor analysis*. Seattle, WA: Amazon.com.

Rosseel, Y. (2012). lavaan: An R package for structural equation modeling. *Journal of Statistical Software*, 48(2), 1–36. Retrieved from http://www.jstatsoft.org/v48/i02/

REFERENCES

Cattell, R. B. (1966). The scree test for the number of factors. *Multivariate Behavioral Research*, 1(2), 245–276.

Fraser, C., & McDonald, R. P. (2012). *NOHARM 4: A Windows program for fitting both unidimensional and multidimensional normal ogive models of latent trait theory*. [Computer software]. Retrieved from http://www.noharm.software.informer.com

Horn, J. L. (1965). A rationale and test for the number of factors in factor analysis. *Psychometrika*, 30(2), 179–185.

Hu, L.-t., & Bentler, P. M. (1999). Cutoff criteria for fit indexes in covariance structure analysis: Conventional criteria versus new alternatives. *Structural Equation Modeling: A Multidisciplinary Journal*, 6(1), 1–55.

Kaiser, H. F. (1960). The application of electronic computers to factor analysis. *Educational and Psychological Measurement*, 20(1), 141–151.

Spearman, C. (1904). "General intelligence," objectively determined and measured. *The American Journal of Psychology*, 15(2), 201–292.

Thurstone, L. L. (1935). *The vectors of mind: Multiple-factor analysis for the isolation of primary traits*. Chicago, IL: University of Chicago Press.

Thurstone, L. L. (1938). *Primary mental abilities* (Psychometric Monographs 1). Chicago, IL: University of Chicago Press.

12

STANDARD SETTING

Many tests are intended to provide a criterion-referenced score interpretation. Instead of, or in addition to, information about how a respondent compares to others, the primary test score shows how respondents perform relative to a specific performance standard, such as pass/fail, basic/proficient/advanced, selected/not selected, or respondent needs/does not need a therapeutic intervention. These categorizations imply that there is a *cut score* that divides respondents into performance levels. If that is the case, then some form of *standard setting* is needed so that cut scores are set in a way that supports score validity. This chapter presents several rigorous and widely accepted methods for setting performance standards.

One commonly accepted definition of standard setting is:

The task of deriving levels of performance on educational or professional assessments, by which decisions or classifications of persons (and corresponding inferences) will be made.

(Cizek, 2001, p. 3)

A less formal version of this definition is:

Standard setting refers to the process of establishing one or more cut scores on a test.

(Cizek & Bunch, 2007, p. 13)

The goal of standard setting is to align the performance standard with the cut score. As with every test development activity, the goal is to provide evidence of test score validity. In the case of standard setting, implementing a rigorous method supports claims about a decision inference in Kane's validity framework or substantive evidence or response processes in the Messick/*Standards* framework. In other words, the cut score represents the consensus border between adjacent performance levels, as judged by subject matter experts and stakeholders. Furthermore, implicit in the implementation of standard setting is the idea that the outcome is "fundamentally fair" (Cizek & Bunch, 2007, p. 15).

An example of criterion-referenced score reporting based on the results of a standard setting process is shown in Figure 12.1 for the 2010 NAEP Geography.

FIGURE 12.1 ◆ Score Reporting for a Criterion-Referenced Test

Students At or Above *Proficient* Level

Twenty-seven percent of students performed at or above the *Proficient* level in 2014

27%

Race/ethnicity

Asian/Pacific Islander	44%
White	39%
Hispanic	11%
Black	7%

Gender

Male	30%
Female	24%

A performance level called Proficient is defined by the National Assessment Governing Board (NAGB), the sponsoring organization, as *solid academic performance and competency over challenging subject matter* (NCES, https://nces.ed.gov/nationsreportcard/NDEHelp/WebHelp/achievement_levels.htm). What this means specifically for each grade level in geography is provided in the assessment framework for geography (NAGB, 2010). Determination of what score on the test resulted in a category called Proficient came from implementing a standard setting method, discussed below, called the *modified Angoff method*.

It is important to note that standard setting methods have been developed in the context of high-stakes testing in which important decisions about the respondent are based on a test score, notably in educational achievement and credentialing tests. And the applications of such methods reside almost exclusively in these areas. However, developers of noncognitive tests may also wish to use standard setting for decision-making about respondents, for example, as a screening device for a clinical intervention or as a way to place participants into groups for a research study.

12.1 BACKGROUND

Before 1950, setting cut scores was commonly applied to pass/fail decisions for credentialing tests. For these decisions, the most common method of standard setting was what I call the "arbitrary method:" picking a number, most often between 60 and 80 percent of the items correct, that seems to reflect the required level of rigor to reach a performance standard. Even today, some testing programs use this method. For example, one organization decided that 80 percent of the items correct would be the passing score for certification. That number seemed to be an acceptable level of mastery of the knowledge and skills deemed necessary for certification. The problem is that 80 percent mastery of the relevant knowledge and skills and 80 percent correct do not necessarily mean the same thing. The items may be relatively easy, and so 80 percent correct could actually be below the performance standard. The reverse could be true for a test consisting of relatively difficult items. Consideration must be made of the properties of the items as well as the needs of stakeholders and users of the test.

The first systematic standard setting method that considered the difficulty of individual items was proposed by Nedelsky (1954) for a test consisting of multiple-choice items. For this method, a panel of subject matter experts is convened to set a standard. For each multiple-choice test item, their task is to identify the number of options that the typical borderline examinee could reject as incorrect. The reciprocal of the remaining number of options is the probability of a correct response by borderline candidates. In other words, this is the probability of guessing correctly among the answer choices that the borderline respondent cannot reject as being incorrect. Add these up across all items for the cut score. For example, for a four-item test, with five options for each item, if a panelist could identify 1, 3, 3, and 4 options, respectively, that a borderline candidate could reject, then that panelist's cut score would be $\frac{1}{4} + \frac{1}{2} + \frac{1}{2} + \frac{1}{1} = 2\frac{1}{4}$.

Nedelsky's method was a forerunner of many modern standard setting methods in several respects. First was the idea of convening panels of subject matter experts and stakeholders to recommend a cut score, rather than members of the sponsoring organization. Second, instead of recommending a cut score directly, the cut score was determined instead by making judgments on individual items and aggregating those judgments across the items. In this way, individual item difficulty was considered in arriving at the final cut score. Third, the idea of a borderline respondent was introduced. The borderline respondent is one that scores right at the boundary between adjacent levels with an equal probability of being categorized into either performance level. Fourth, since no data were needed to implement this method, a cut score could be set before any respondent actually responded to the test. The Nedelsky method is still used operationally, most notably in medical contexts, where defining borderline candidacy is relatively straightforward, i.e., a competent practitioner should be able to reject those options that would cause harm to patients.

However, some limitations to the method exist. First, it's restricted to multiple-choice items. Many current large-scale tests employ alternative item formats. Second, research on the method suggests that panelists tend not to assign probabilities of 1.0 (meaning that the borderline examinee could eliminate all distractors), resulting in lower cut scores than intended. Third, the method is difficult to implement for multiple performance levels and cut scores.

During the 1960s and 1970s, measuring educational achievement began to transition from primarily norm-referenced score reporting to criterion-referenced scoring. This change was driven by perceptions that American public education was not meeting the needs of society. Evidence for this perception was rising youth unemployment, declining scores on the SAT and NAEP, much-publicized stories of senior class valedictorians who could not effectively read or write (Resnick, 1980), and an analysis by John Cannell (1989) that suggested that all states were erroneously above average, the Lake Woebegone effect, a nod to Garrison Keillor's news from Lake Woebegone (where "all the women are strong, the men are good looking, and the children are all above average"). In response, many states, beginning with Florida in 1976, began to implement Minimum Competency Testing. The idea was to require at least a minimal level of academic skills as a high school graduation requirement. This requirement led to the need to establishing a passing score. Most states at the time used norm-referenced achievement tests, and the passing score was determined by an examination of state-level performance on these exams, sometimes by making an arbitrary decision (Resnick, 1980, p. 10).

Limitations of the Nedelsky method and the need to determine a cut score on minimum competency tests led to the development of other standard setting methods during the 1970s and early 1980s. In 1982, Samuel Livingston and Michael Zieky published *Passing Scores* (Livingston & Zieky, 1982), a resource that outlined procedures for aspects of the methods, such as selecting judges, choosing a method, and dealing with political and social issues. As these new methods became more widely used for credentialing and educational achievement tests, they also came under withering criticism from several measurement scholars, mostly for the judgmental nature of standard setting methods, which they saw as arbitrary. For example,

> *Setting performance standards on tests and exercises by known methods is a waste of time or worse. (Glass, 1978)*

As a result, efforts were made in the 1980s and 1990s to bring rigor into standard setting methods. In 1983, the National Commission on Excellence in Education reported in *A Nation at Risk* that the low quality of American public schools put the nation at future risk. After this report was published, a growing consensus of educators began to coalesce around the idea that minimal competency tests produced just that—minimal competency. What was needed were rigorous academic standards. In 1988, Congress passed a law that created the National Assessment Governing Board (NAGB), a board charged with setting achievement goals. NAGB decided in

1990 to report NAEP results according to four achievement levels: below basic, basic, proficient, and advanced. Until this point, NAEP had been a low-profile survey program in which the same test was administered over a long period of time to track achievement longitudinally.

NAEP used the relatively new modified Angoff method to determine the cut scores for each subject and grade level. The new NAEP standards ultimately led to individual states developing their own assessments and standards for educational achievement as well as comparisons between states on NAEP. Because many states adopted achievement levels as a graduation requirement, the setting of the levels became high-stakes, resulting in a brighter spotlight being shone on standard setting methods. Greater scrutiny of the methods resulted in an increase in research on standard setting methods and the development of new methods.

This wider scrutiny has also led to much controversy as well. Probably the most famous criticism of NAEP's standard setting methodology was issued by the National Research Council's (1999) evaluation of NAEP, calling the methodology "fundamentally flawed" (NRC, 1999, p. 7). Much of the controversy existed because standard setting sits at a crossroads between psychometrics, policy, and politics, and it is often unclear into which of these three areas standard setting should be seen. Nevertheless, the primary goal in many test development projects is to make decisions about respondents. In those cases, some form of standard setting is required. Validation necessitates setting cut scores in a way that is defensible and contributes to validity evidence. What follows in this chapter is a discussion of several standard setting methods that have been widely used and researched.

12.2 *STANDARDS* FOR STANDARD SETTING

The 2014 *Standards* make a number of references to standard setting. In Chapter 1, on validity, Standard 1.9 states:

> *When a validation rests in part on the opinions or decisions of expert judges, observers, or raters, procedures for selecting such experts and for eliciting judgments or ratings should be fully described. The qualifications and experience of the judges should be presented. The description of procedures should include any training and instructions provided, should indicate whether participants reached their decisions*

independently, and should report the level of agreement reached. If participants interacted with one another or exchanged information, the procedures through which they may have influenced one another should be set forth. (p. 25)

Although this standard does not explicitly refer to standard setting, such methods rely on expert judgment. This standard therefore is aimed at demonstrating that participants are representative and well-qualified, and their judgments are sound and well-documented.

In Chapter 2, on reliability, Standard 2.16 states:

When a test or combination of measures is used to make classification decisions, estimates should be provided of the percentage of test takers who would be classified in the same way on two replications of the procedure. (p. 46)

That is, some measure of judgment precision, such as a standard error of measurement at the cut score, should be reported.

Chapter 5 discusses scoring, scaling, norming, linking, and cut scores. Three standards address cut scores in particular. Standard 5.21 states: "When proposed score interpretations involve one or more cut scores, the rationale and procedures used for establishing cut scores should be documented clearly" (p. 107). In other words, transparency in the standard setting process is required. Standard 5.22 states: "When cut scores defining pass-fail or proficiency levels are based on direct judgments about the adequacy of item or test performances, the judgmental process should be designed so that the participants providing the judgments can bring their knowledge and experience to bear in a reasonable way" (p. 108). This means that the judgment tasks asked of participants result in defensible cut scores. Finally, Standard 5.23 states: "When feasible and appropriate, cut score defining categories with distinct substantive interpretations should be informed by sound empirical data concerning the relation of test performance to the relevant criteria" (p. 108). Wherever possible, data should be collected that demonstrate the relationship between test scores and a criterion measure, that is, the appropriateness of the cut score. I mention these standards in detail because the test developer often has to make some modifications to a standard setting method to accommodate particular constraints. The *Standards* offer general guidance when any type of standard setting is undertaken. Together, these standards address the validity of the cut score and standard setting process.

12.3 THE PROCESS OF STANDARD SETTING

The implementation of a defensible standard setting method typically depends on several important steps: (1) selection of an appropriate standard setting method, (2) selection of participants, (3) development of performance level descriptors (PLDs), (4) implementation of the chosen method in a panel meeting, resulting in a cut score recommendation, and (5) collection of validity evidence to support the cut score recommendation(s).

Selection of a Standard Setting Method. There are at present dozens of standard setting methods. Several popular standard setting methods are described below. The choice of methods depends on the format of the test, the purpose of the cut score, the data that are available, single versus multiple cut scores, and the resources of the sponsoring organization.

Selection of Participants. Most standard setting methods require a panel meeting during which the participants work through a group decision-making process to arrive at one or more recommended cut scores. Since the credibility of the recommendations will be determined by these participants, their selection deserves careful consideration. The panelists are usually subject matter experts and/or stakeholders. Selecting individuals to be panelists is sometimes considered an art form, much like selecting a jury for a trial. To ensure the legitimacy of the proposed cut score, it is important that all relevant viewpoints be represented and heard during the meeting. Raymond and Reid (2001) list a number of criteria to be used in selecting participants. These include:

1. Panelists must have expertise in the subject matter of the test.

2. Panelists must be familiar with the target population.

3. Panelists must have knowledge of the instructional environment of respondents. For example, if the test measures knowledge in a subject area, panelists need to know what instruction respondents will have received.

4. Panelists must generally support and appreciate the consequences of the performance standard, that is, if the decision is pass/fail, referral/nonreferral, accept/reject, etc.

5. Panelists must represent the community of stakeholders or groups of individuals or organizations that will be impacted by the cut score determination.

6. Panelists should be representative demographically.

Finally, some knowledge of the viewpoints of potential panelists is valuable. For example, it may be that the most experienced and prominent professionals in a field may recommend relatively high standards. Or, the reverse could be true! Similarly, panel meeting facilitators have often lamented on the difficulty of managing one or more panelists who have extreme views of the performance standard and try to dominate the conversation.

How many panelists should be selected? There is no definitive answer to this question. Examples in the literature report panels ranging from 5 to 30 participants (Hambleton, Pitoniak, & Copella, 2012; Livingston & Zieky, 1982; Loomis, 2012; Raymond & Reid, 2001). Panel size is a compromise between having a panel large enough to be representative and provide stable results and having a panel small enough to be manageable. Raymond and Reid, using generalizability theory, calculated that 10–15 panelists would produce a sufficient degree of precision in many contexts. In the panel meeting itself, in order to facilitate discussion, it is often advantageous to seat panelists in small tables of 5–6.

Here are some examples of panel membership.

- *Virginia Standards of Learning (SOL).* In a recent standard setting for high school mathematics tests, approximately 12 teachers were selected for each panel (VDOE, 2018). The selection was based on regional representation, expertise in the mathematics content area, knowledge of the relevant SOLs, and experience with students with disabilities or limited English proficiency.

- *NAEP.* NAGB policy on NAEP standard setting panels does not dictate a panel size but does prescribe that 55 percent of the panel consists of classroom teachers, 15 percent of other educators (e.g., administrators, curriculum specialists), and 30 percent of noneducators (e.g., parents, employers, professionals). NAGB policy also dictates representation demographically by geographic region, type of community (i.e., rural, urban, suburban), race/ethnicity, and gender. Most NAEP panels have ranged from 20 to 30 in size.

- *GED ESL Test (1999).* For a GED Test that measures English language literacy for candidates taking the GED Test battery in a language other than English, a panel of 15 subject matter experts and stakeholders from constituencies impacted by the GED Tests—community colleges, prisons, adult basic education, state departments of education, business leaders—was formed to recommend a cut score.

Performance Level Descriptors (PLDs). For a cut score recommendation to have any validity, the sponsoring organization or research team must be able to articulate what the performance levels mean. This articulation is called a PLD. PLDs can range in specificity from a single sentence general statement to a lengthy and detailed essay. In whatever form, PLDs indicate what exceeding and not reaching the cut score mean. In credentialing exams, exceeding the cut score usually means pass. For any specific discipline, the sponsoring organization specifies what it means to be "certified" or "licensed."

In most instances, the sponsoring organization develops the PLDs rather than the standard setting panelists. What the panelists may do is develop greater specificity of a PLD that is more of a policy statement. For example, the performance level *Proficient* is used by NAEP and many state educational achievement assessment programs. The meaning of that label varies slightly across the states and NAEP but in general means "solid academic performance and competency over challenging subject matter." What panelists for NAEP do is apply that policy PLD to a specific grade and content area. Figure 12.2 shows the PLD for Proficient in 8th grade Civics.

However, the use of PLDs is not restricted to educational achievement or credentialing tests. For example, a hospital recently developed a test to quickly identify the level of mental health risk among referred teens. The hospital identified five levels of risk. One of them, for which a standard setting was applied, was labeled *Extreme*, which meant that the teen "needed immediate psychiatric intervention." A team of

FIGURE 12.2 ● PLD for NAEP 8th Grade Civics

Eighth-grade students performing at the *Proficient* level should understand and be able to explain purposes that government should serve. These students should have a good understanding of differences between government and civil society and of the importance of the rule of law. They should recognize discrepancies between American ideals and reality and be able to describe continuing efforts to address them. They should understand the separation and sharing of powers among branches of government and between federal and state governments, and they should be able to explain how citizens influence government. They should be able to describe events within the United States and other countries that have international consequences.

https://nces.ed.gov/nationsreportcard/civics/achieve.aspx

clinicians developed a more detailed PLD, in which specific risk behaviors were identified that met the criterion.

A detailed set of PLDs was developed by the Smarter Balanced Assessment Consortium (SBAC, 2013) for its assessment programs in English language arts/literacy and mathematics. These tests were based on the Common Core State Standards. Although there are four performance levels (labeled 1 through 4 at each grade level), the primary goal is a performance level called *College Content Readiness*, which corresponds to Level 3 in 11th grade. Smarter Balanced defines College Content-Readiness as shown in Figure 12.3.

In addition to this general policy PLD, four different types of PLDs, proposed by Egan, Schneider, and Ferrara (2012), were created to serve different purposes for different audiences:

- *Policy.* Policy PLDs represent the sponsoring organization's vision of the meaning of a performance level. In the case of Smarter Balanced, to supplement the overall policy PLD shown in Figure 12.3, additional policy PLDs were written for each performance level at each grade level and broad content domain.

- *Range.* Range PLDs are intended for item writers. They specify in detail the knowledge, skills, and processes (KSPs) to be covered and at what level of understanding.

- *Threshold.* Threshold PLDs are intended for panelists in standard setting meetings. They describe the KSPs of borderline respondents.

FIGURE 12.3 ● Policy PLD for SBAC College Readiness Performance Level (SBAC, 2013)

English Language Arts/Literacy[3]	Students who perform at the College Content-Ready level in English language arts/literacy demonstrate reading, writing, listening, and research skills necessary for introductory courses in a variety of disciplines. They also demonstrate subject-area knowledge and skills associated with readiness for entry-level, transferable, credit-bearing English and composition courses.
Mathematics	Students who perform at the College Content-Ready level in mathematics demonstrate foundational mathematical knowledge and quantitative reasoning skills necessary for introductory courses in a variety of disciplines. They also demonstrate subject-area knowledge and skills associated with readiness for entry-level, transferable, credit-bearing mathematics and statistics courses.

- *Reporting.* Reporting PLDs are intended to provide test score interpretations to users and respondents. They describe the KSPs demonstrated by respondents.

Table 12.1 shows examples of the first PLDs for Level 3 (College Content Ready) for 11th grade Mathematics. There are Range PLDs for each assessment target and Threshold PLDs for each content category. The table shows one example of each of these for Concepts and Procedures/Target O: Define trigonometric ratios and solve problems involving right triangles. All of these PLDs were developed by Smarter Balanced or by expert panels convened by Smarter Balanced, and not by the standard setting panels. While most test development efforts do not require this level of detail, the PLD framework proposed by Egan et al. (2012) illustrates the types of information needed to validate the decision process for criterion-referenced score interpretations.

Implementation of the Chosen Method in a Panel Meeting. As mentioned above, most standard setting methods require a panel meeting during which subject matter experts and stakeholders work through a standard setting method to arrive at a cut score recommendation. Although the procedures for the meeting vary widely depending on the standard setting method, the number of performance levels, and the formats of the items, most methods share a number of activities. Here is a basic outline of a standard setting panel meeting:

1. *Introduction.* A meeting facilitator, typically someone experienced in managing panel meetings and not from the sponsoring organization, will

TABLE 12.1 ● PLDs for 11th Grade Mathematics (SBAC, 2013)

Type of PLD	PLD
Policy	The Level 3 student can adequately explain and adequately apply mathematical concepts. The Level 3 student interprets and carries out mathematical procedures with adequate precision and fluency.
Range	Concepts and Procedures/Target O: Level 3 students should be able to use the Pythagorean Theorem, trigonometric ratios, and the sine and cosine of complementary angles to solve unfamiliar problems with minimal scaffolding involving right triangles, finding the missing side or missing angle of a right triangle.
Threshold	Concepts and Procedures/Target O: The student who just enters Level 3 should be able to Use trigonometric ratios and the sine and cosine of complementary angles to find missing angles or sides of a given right triangle with minimal scaffolding.
Reporting	The student has met the achievement standard and demonstrates progress toward mastery of the knowledge and skills in mathematics needed for likely success in entry-level credit-bearing college coursework after completing high school coursework.

lead in introducing panel members, state the purpose of the meeting, and go over any logistical details.

2. *Training.* Whatever standard setting method is used, panelists must be trained in the activities they are expected to complete. Typically, three types of training are offered:

   a. Panelists take the test as if they were the respondents. They then discuss general impressions of the items and what they measure.

   b. Panelists discuss the PLDs. As mentioned above, these are usually provided by the sponsoring organization, although the panelists could be asked to refine them. There is then a discussion of how the KSPs described by the PLDs align with the KSPs measured by the items in the test.

   c. Panelists practice the judgment task. The standard setting methods differ on the type of judgments panelists are asked to make. Panelists need to practice these, often on a small scale, and then discuss and possibly modify the process they used to make the judgments.

3. *Round 1*. Panelists independently make the judgment tasks required by the standard setting method.

4. *Round 2*. The facilitator leads a discussion of the results of Round 1 and may supply additional feedback, such as item statistics and impact data. Then, panelists again make the judgment tasks required by the standard setting method. There may also be a Round 3, in which impact data (i.e., estimates of the percentages of respondents that will be at each performance level as a result of implementing a particular cut score) are provided to panelists, followed by panelists making the judgment tasks.

Panel meetings can last from 1 to 5 days depending on resources. NAEP panel meetings tend to last four to five days, due to multiple performance levels and item formats. For two performance levels, e.g., pass/fail, refer/don't refer, and a single item format, e.g., multiple-choice or Likert, a single day or a day and a half may suffice.

12.4 STANDARD SETTING METHODS

There are dozens of standard setting methods. I will briefly describe the most frequently used methods according to the judgment task required by panelists, the item format, how the cut score is calculated, and some pros and cons for each method. It should be pointed out that these methods are more properly thought of as frameworks rather than a specific set of procedures. Their actual use usually requires modifications in particular situations. If the reader plans to implement one of these methods, I suggest accessing the references listed in the "Further Reading" section at the end of this chapter, or the primary sources for each method, for details.

12.4.1 Borderline Group and Contrasting Group Methods

Two well-regarded standard setting methods are the borderline group (Zieky & Liviningston, 1977) and contrasting group methods (Berk, 1976). Both methods rely on a judgment of the *true* performance level of actual respondents. In most applications of these methods, this judgment task is done by the panelists who have some knowledge of the individual respondents. The panelists judge whether each respondent has met the performance standard, has not met the standard, or are borderline. Once this task is completed, the cut score is calculated from the scores of the respondents on the test.

Borderline Group Method. In this method, a frequency distribution is formed using the test scores of the group of respondents categorized as borderline. A hypothetical distribution is shown in Figure 12.4. For a symmetrical distribution like this one, the mean is the most appropriate statistic for a cut score. For a skewed distribution, the median is preferable. However, there are some practical issues to consider. I shall illustrate these with the political viewpoint test. Suppose that what is desired is a test score that is meant to identify students as either liberal or conservative. It is insufficient to simply choose the middle score because the items themselves could lean liberal or conservative.

Instead of panelists identifying liberal, conservative, and borderline students, the students themselves self-identified their overall political viewpoint from the following item that appeared on the CIRP questionnaire: "How would you characterize your political views?" The answer choices were (1) Far Left, (2) Liberal, (3) Middle-of-the-road, (4) Conservative, and (5) Far Right. If we considered those who answered Middle-of-the-road to be the borderline students, then we could calculate a frequency distribution of their political viewpoint scores on the 18-item test. Using that frequency distribution, a line chart shown in Figure 12.5 was constructed. As you can see, this distribution is very "jagged" or "toothy." The mean, median, and mode are 43.4, 43.0, and 43.0, respectively. However, scores of 41–45 all have similar frequencies, so it is not entirely clear that 43 should be the

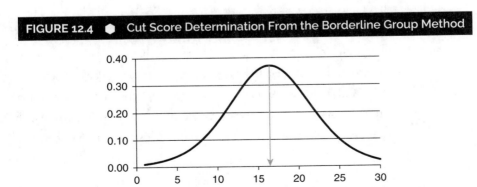

FIGURE 12.4 ● Cut Score Determination From the Borderline Group Method

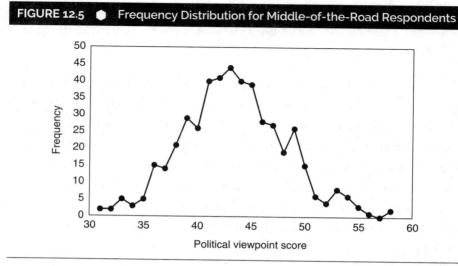

FIGURE 12.5 ● **Frequency Distribution for Middle-of-the-Road Respondents**

cut score. To clarify, we could "smooth" the frequency distribution to give it a more distinctive shape. There are a wide variety of smoothing methods. In this example, a simple rolling weighted average was used. Each smoothed frequency is calculated by averaging the frequency in question and the two frequencies above and below it. The smoothed distribution is shown in Figure 12.6. Here, there is a definite peak at a score of 43, which is the median. The mean of the smoothed distribution is 43.4. The sponsoring organization would then need to decide which recommended cut score to use, and if it is the mean, whether to round it down.[1] The smoothed distribution is intended to approach the true population distribution. As a result, the smaller the sample size of respondents, the greater weight should be given to the smoothed distribution.

Contrasting Groups Method. In this method, test score distributions are calculated separately for two groups of respondents, those that have been judged to meet the performance standard and those that have not met the standard. The cut score, as shown in Figure 12.7, is the test score that best distinguishes between the two groups. As you can see from the graph, there is overlap between the two distributions, which is almost always the case. No matter what cut score is chosen, there will be some

---

[1] If 43.4 is the cut score, then a respondent with a score of 43 has not reached the cut score.

FIGURE 12.6 ● Smoothed Frequency Distribution for Middle-of-the-Road Respondents

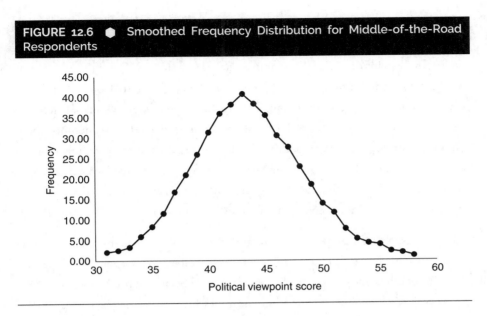

FIGURE 12.7 ● Cut Score Determination From the Contrasting Groups Method

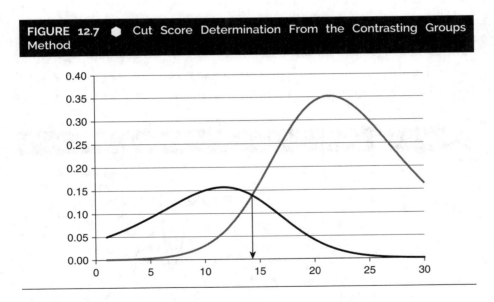

respondents who are misclassified. The goal is to find the cut score that minimizes classification errors. This will be the point of intersection between the two distributions, or the point at which the probability of belonging to each group is equal and equal to 0.50.

However, as was the case for the borderline group method, there is the issue of smoothing the frequency distributions. This can again be demonstrated using the political viewpoint data. For this example, the answer choices "Far left" and "Liberal" were combined into a single Liberal group, and "Far right" and "Conservative" were combined into a Conservative group. The students responding "Middle-of-the-road" were excluded. Figures 12.8 and 12.9 show the unsmoothed and smoothed distributions, respectively. The smoothing method here was the same rolling weighted average used above for the borderline group. As you can see, the two cut scores are close but not the same. Determining the cut score visually means that choice of smoothing method can exert an influence on the cut score.

For this reason, it is common to use an analytical method to determine the cut score. One simple method is to find the midpoint between the two group means or medians. The unsmoothed means for the conservative and liberal groups are 46.7 and 39.8, respectively. A midpoint cut score would be 43.3 which would then be truncated to 43 or rounded up to 44, depending on the sponsoring organization's policy. The group medians were 46.0 and 40.0, respectively, resulting in a midpoint cut score of 43.0.

The most common and defensible method of cut score determination involves the use of logistic regression. In this analysis, the test score is used to predict group membership, where the groups are coded 0 and 1. The cut score is the score for

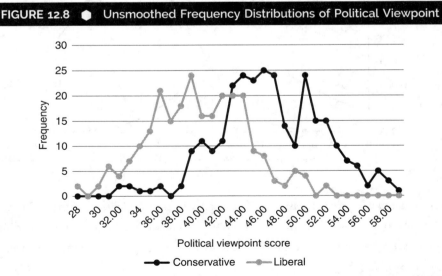

FIGURE 12.8 ● Unsmoothed Frequency Distributions of Political Viewpoint

Political viewpoint score

—●— Conservative   —●— Liberal

FIGURE 12.9 ⬡ Smoothed Frequency Distributions of Political Viewpoint

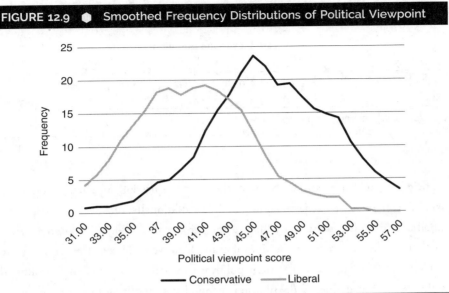

which there is an equal probability of 0.50 of belonging in either group. The SPSS Binary Logistic Regression program produced the results shown in Figure 12.10.

The logistic regression equation for predicting group membership is

$$\text{Probability(liberal)} = 12.838 - 0.300*\text{polivw} \qquad (12.1)$$

Polivw is the raw, or observed, score on the 18-item test. What is being predicted is the probability of a respondent with a raw score of polivw being in the group coded 1. Setting the probability equal to 0.50 produces a political viewpoint score of 41.1. The SPSS analysis also indicates that approximately 77 percent of the students would be correctly classified by using this cut score.

These two methods are generally well regarded by measurement experts. They are data-driven and are easily understood by the test's stakeholders, who are usually not measurement experts. In practice, however, the methods are often difficult to implement. The main difficulty is obtaining the data needed for either method. To make the classification judgment, panelists need to know the respondents well enough to classify them. Ten to twenty panelists each need to judge the classification of enough respondents to be able to carry out the analyses. It is uncertain that, even if

FIGURE 12.10 ● Logistic Regression Results for Political Viewpoint Data

Variables in the Equation

		B	S.E.	Wald	df	Sig.	Exp(B)
Step 1[a]	Poliview	−.300	.027	121.892	1	.000	.741
	Constant	12.838	1.175	119.418	1	.000	376387.861

a. Variable(s) entered on step 1: poliview.

sufficient sample size can be obtained, there is the question of whether this sample will be representative of the target population. Additionally, one of the groups may be small in size. This is particularly likely if the performance standard is located near the extreme of the construct dimension, for example, if we had been attempting to select students with a Far left or Far right political viewpoint. For very small groups, the estimate of their frequency distributions is unreliable, resulting in a cut score that is itself unstable.

12.4.2 Angoff Methods

Modified Angoff Method. The Modified Angoff Method (Angoff, 1971, p. 514, Footnote 4) requires panelists to make a very different kind of judgment than the preceding two methods. This method is applicable only to dichotomously scored items. Here, after extensive training to identify the KSPs of borderline respondents, panelists are asked to estimate the *p*-values of each item for a group of borderline respondents. For example, suppose a panel is attempting to recommend a cut score on a middle school mathematics test that would indicate that a student is ready to take Algebra I as their next course. Directions to panelists look like the following:

1. Imagine an entire classroom made up completely of students who are barely ready to take Algebra I.

2. Look at the first item in the algebra readiness test: Based on what you yourself believe a barely ready student to be, what percentage of these students do you think would answer this test item correctly? Record your answer on the participant rating form.

3. Repeat Step 2 for each of the remaining items in the algebra readiness test.

As an example, suppose that ten multiple-choice items from the TIMSS Booklet 1 were used as the algebra readiness test. Each panelist is tasked with estimating the proportion, or percent, correct for each item, for borderline students (referred to in this case as barely ready for Algebra I). Table 12.2 shows the *p*-value judgments for ten TIMSS items by nine panelists (These estimates actually came from my class of doctoral students studying test development.). Since the estimates were made independently, we consider these to be Round 1 judgments. For example, Panelist 1 estimated that 70 percent of the barely ready students would answer item M012001 correctly. The far right column shows the mean percent correct for each panelist across the ten items. For this first item, estimates ranged from 50 to 90 percent correct, with a mean of 70.56 percent correct and a standard deviation of 14.24. The standard deviations for the other items ranged from 12.88 to 27.40. This is a considerable amount of variability, more than most operational standard settings, because the panelists have been minimally trained (due to the constraints of class time) and because they were not middle school mathematics experts.

The cut score for each panelist is the mean (or median) percent correct across all items. For Panelist 1, this is 47.5 percent correct, or 4.7 correct out of 10 items. Likewise, cut scores for the other panelists range from 50.0 to 76.7, again a wider than expected range for the reasons noted above. Overall, the mean cut score is 59.2 percent correct (bolded in table), which would be the recommended cut score from these panelists.

After Round 1, the meeting facilitator would likely begin a conversation about how the panelists made their judgments. The judgments from each panelist would generally not be revealed to the rest of the group. However, the facilitator would point to the item with the most variability, in this case item M012013, and ask the panel to discuss how they arrived at their judgments. Following this, the facilitator would work through the remaining items in descending order of standard deviation, until no new comments were forthcoming. The facilitator might also provide the panel with empirical *p*-values (these are found in the last row of the Table 12.2), those calculated from the entire respondent sample, not just barely-ready students, as a "reality check." Then, the panelists would make Round 2 judgments, with the direction that, based on the discussion after Round 1, they could keep the same estimates or change them. As mentioned above, there could be an additional

TABLE 12.2 ⬡ Round 1 Judgments for the Modified Angoff Method

Panelist	M012001	M012002	M012003	M012039	M012040	M012041	M012042	M012013	M012016	M022151	Ave. Pct.
1	70	30	40	30	30	80	50	30	75	40	47.50
2	50	50	75	50	25	75	75	25	25	50	50.00
3	75	97	95	70	45	80	75	85	95	50	76.70
4	80	75	70	50	70	45	30	60	75	40	59.50
5	60	35	40	75	73	40	70	85	20	33	53.10
6	80	80	70	80	80	80	60	70	70	30	70.00
7	80	50	60	90	50	50	70	70	50	50	62.00
8	50	40	80	70	70	50	40	40	80	70	59.00
9	90	70	70	80	40	60	70	10	30	30	55.00
Mean	70.56	58.56	68.89	66.11	53.67	62.22	60.00	52.78	57.78	43.67	**59.20**
SD	14.24	22.91	15.16	19.00	20.18	16.60	16.39	27.40	27.28	12.88	9.40
Empirical p	58.92	72.26	67.11	45.44	82.17	74.37	64.99	53.76	57.33	25.36	60.171

discussion, followed by a Round 3. One additional piece of information that is sometimes provided between Rounds 2 and 3 is impact data, or the estimated percentage of respondents who will meet the standard if the cut score recommended in Round 2 is adopted.

Yes/No Method. At this point, you may be wondering if there is an *Unmodified* Angoff Method. Yes, there is, and it's called the Yes/No Method (Impara & Plake, 1997). Angoff (1971, pp. 514–515) suggested that panelists could estimate whether a borderline respondent could correctly answer each item. As Impara and Plake developed this idea, panelists would first be asked to consider a single, typical borderline respondent that they know. Then, for this respondent, the judgment task would be simply to judge, yes or no, would this respondent likely answer each item correctly. The rationale is that this yes/no task for a respondent the panelist knows is less complex, and hence more reliable, than asking for a p-value judgment. The recommended cut score for each panelist is simply the number of Yes judgments.

Extended Angoff Method. Another variation, the Extended Angoff Method (Hambleton & Plake, 1995), is intended for use with polytomously scored items, including constructed response and Likert items. The judgment task for panelists is to estimate either the expected score point for a typical borderline respondent or the average score for a group of borderline respondents. Using the above example, suppose a panel is convened to set a cut score that distinguishes liberal from conservative viewpoint. The same panel of students that was used above for the TIMSS items (there are only eight panelists here because one student was absent that day) completed this method for the political viewpoint test. Table 12.3 shows the judgments of each panelist on each political viewpoint item, that is, the expected item scores for a typical borderline liberal respondent. Again note the wide variation in judgments, due to the panelists being a class of doctoral students who are not experts on political viewpoint. And yet, the mean cut score across the panelists was 45.50. This compares to 43.40 from the Borderline Group Method and 41.10 from the Contrasting Groups Method. These results do not mean that the Extended Angoff Method necessarily results in higher cut scores than the other two methods. It means simply that different methods tend to produce different results.

Advantages and Limitations of Angoff Methods. The Modified Angoff Method has been widely used on many prominent tests, including NAEP and state educational

TABLE 12.3 ⬡ Round 1 Judgments for the Extended Angoff Method										
Item	1	2	3	4	5	6	7	8	Mean	SD
View9901	2	2	2	3	3	2	2	3	2.38	0.52
View9902	2	2	2	2	1	3	3	3	2.25	0.71
View9903	4	3	4	3	4	4	3	4	3.63	0.52
View9904	3	3	2	3	3	4	4	3	3.13	0.64
View9905	3	4	4	4	4	3	3	3	3.50	0.53
View9906	3	2	2	2	3	2	1	1	2.00	0.76
View9907	4	4	3	3	4	4	3	4	3.63	0.52
View9908	1	1	2	3	4	1	2	1	1.88	1.13
View9909	1	2	2	2	1	3	2	2	1.88	0.64
View9910	1	2	2	2	2	2	1	1	1.63	0.52
View9911	1	2	2	3	2	2	1	1	1.75	0.71
View9912	2	3	3	3	3	2	2	3	2.63	0.52
View9913	3	3	2	2	2	2	3	2	2.38	0.52
View9914	2	3	2	2	3	4	2	2	2.50	0.76
View9915	1	2	2	1	2	2	1	1	1.50	0.53
View9916	2	2	2	2	1	2	1	3	1.88	0.64
View9917	3	4	3	4	3	3	3	4	3.38	0.52
View9918	3	4	4	4	4	3	4	3	3.63	0.52
Sum	41.00	48.00	45.00	48.00	49.00	48.00	41.00	44.00	45.50	3.25
SD	1.02	0.91	0.79	0.84	1.07	0.91	1.02	1.10	0.76	

achievement programs. Tests with mixed item formats can be used by treating sets of items with a common format as a single test and then combining cut scores on each set. For example, the Modified Angoff could be used for multiple-choice items, while the Extended Angoff could be used for constructed response items. The Angoff methods can also be used for tests that require multiple cut scores.

On the other hand, Angoff methods have been criticized because there is evidence that the judgment tasks themselves are conceptually difficult for panelists. For example, in the above table for the algebra readiness example, the correlation between actual and panelists' *p*-values is 0.38. With better trained panelists who are subject matter experts, Impara and Plake (1998) reported only moderate correlations, around 0.50, between actual and estimated *p*-values. Furthermore, panelists often experience the Angoff methods as making arbitrary judgments (Dawber, Lewis, & Rogers, 2002; McGinty, 2005). Additionally, there is evidence to suggest that, in some applications, panelists have resorted to heuristics, or simplifications, to make their judgments (Hein & Skaggs, 2009, 2010).

12.4.3 Bookmark Standard Setting Methods

Bookmark Method. The Bookmark Method (Mitzel, Lewis, Patz, & Green, 2001) is based on a Rasch (or IRT) measurement model. This means that, instead of the panelists recommending a raw score, the recommended cut score is actually a location on the logit scale, as discussed in Chapter 9. Panelists are presented with an *ordered item booklet* (OIB), in which items are arranged in order of difficulty, from least to most difficult. The judgment task for the panelist is to decide the item in the OIB that separates adjacent performance levels. That is, they are asked to find the item such that they think a borderline respondent will respond correctly to the items preceding it but not that item or later ones. For the Algebra readiness test example, directions to panelists look like the following:

1. Imagine an entire classroom made up completely of students who are barely ready to take Algebra I.

2. Look at the first item in the OIB: Do you think that 2/3 of the students who are barely ready to take Algebra I will answer this item correctly?

3. Go through the booklet and ask yourself the same question about each item.

4. Then, place your bookmark at the item where you think that 2/3 of the barely proficient students would likely answer the previous items correctly but not this item and later items.

Each panelist will bookmark a specific page in the OIB. Each bookmark will correspond to a specific cut score in logit units. The recommended cut score for the panel is the mean (or median) cut score across the panelists. Bookmarking would seem to be a relatively straightforward task for panelists, but there are several complexities. The first one you'll note is the 2/3 direction. This is called the response probability (RP) criterion. When asking panelists whether or not a borderline respondent will answer an item correctly, it is necessary to specify some degree of certainty. One hundred percent certainty will elicit a different judgment than, say, "more likely than not" to answer correctly. An extensive amount of research has been devoted to determining an optimal RP value. Huynh (2000) recommended 0.67, or 2/3, a value that has been used frequently in operational standard settings.

As an example, suppose we look at the same ten items from the TIMSS Booklet 1 that were used in the above Angoff example. The panelists are the same nine doctoral students. The initial step was to estimate item difficulties for the Rasch model, in this case, using jMetrik as done in Chapter 9. A graph of the ten items, in order of difficulty, is shown in Figure 12.11. The curves are all parallel because we are using the Rasch model, and they are not equally spaced because the item difficulties themselves are not equally spaced. Also shown on this graph is a horizontal line indicating the RP of 0.67.

FIGURE 12.11 ● Response Curves for Ten TIMSS Items

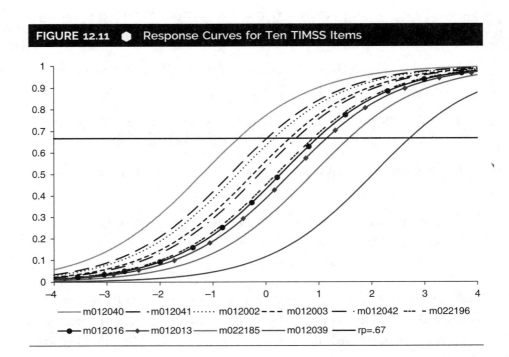

Next, an OIB is created showing the ten items in order of difficulty with one item per page. The OIB is organized as shown in Table 12.4. The first two rows show which items appear on each page. The third row shows the Rasch difficulty estimate for each item. The fourth row shows the logit value of each item when the probability of a correct answer is 0.67. These values are always higher than the item difficulty, which corresponds to a probability of 0.50. The last row shows the cut score for each page bookmarked by a panelist. For example, if a panelist selects page 4 (item M012003), then the cut score is half the logit distance between that item and the preceding one (item M012002), at the RP value of 0.67. The cut score for this panelist is therefore $(0.47-0.17)/2 + 0.17 = 0.32$.

These cut scores, as mentioned above, are on the Rasch logit scale. For a test developed from the Rasch model, the logit value can be converted to a raw score using the test characteristic curve (see Chapter 9). For these panelists, their bookmarks, logit cut scores, and raw score cut scores are shown in Table 12.5. The panelists bookmarks ranged from page 4 to page 8. The cut score in logits ranged from 0.32 to 1.11, with a mean of 0.88. When converted to raw scores, panelists cut scores ranged from 5.52 to 7.08 out of 10, with a mean of 6.64. This compares to a cut score of 5.82 when the same panelists used the modified Angoff method. Like other standard setting methods, it is no surprise that different methods produce different cut scores. If this had been an operational standard setting meeting, there would likely be a discussion of bookmarks after Round 1, focusing on how panelists made their bookmark decisions. This discussion could likewise be followed by Round 2, or even Round 3.

Single Passage Bookmark Method. One of the major benefits of the Bookmark Method is that it is not restricted to dichotomously scored items. The method works well for a test composed of mixed item formats. For polytomously scored items, a separate page is created in the OIB for each score point. For example, if a test consists of multiple-choice items and a constructed response or essay item, then a score of 1 on this item would appear as a separate page, followed later on in the OIB with another page for a score of 2, and so forth.

However, there is a practical limit to this. For example, if a test consists entirely of polytomously scored items, then the OIB is likely to be unworkable. A panelist may have to understand and decide between different scores from different items. Does a score of 3 on one item represent a higher degree of difficulty than a score of 2 on another item? As an alternative, Skaggs, Hein, and Awuor (2007) proposed a Single

TABLE 12.4 ◆ Arrangement of OIB and Cut Scores

Page No.	Page1	Page2	Page3	Page4	Page5	Page6	Page7	Page8	Page9	Page10
Item ID	M012040	M012041	M012002	M012003	M012042	M012001	M012016	M012013	M012039	M022251
b	−1.210	−0.670	−0.540	−0.240	−0.120	0.200	0.280	0.460	0.880	2.030
b at 0.67	−0.50	0.04	0.17	0.47	0.60	0.93	1.04	1.18	1.59	2.74
Cut	−0.50	−0.23	0.10	0.32	0.54	0.76	0.99	1.11	1.38	2.16

TABLE 12.5 ⬤ Bookmarked Page Logit and Raw Score Cut Scores

Panelist	Bookmark Page	Logit Cut Score	Raw Score Cut
1	8	1.11	7.08
2	6	0.76	6.43
3	6	0.76	6.43
4	8	1.11	7.08
5	6	0.76	6.43
6	4	0.32	5.52
7	7	0.99	6.86
8	7	0.99	6.86
9	8	1.11	7.08
Mean		0.88	6.64
SD		0.26	0.51

Passage version of the Bookmark Method. Here, separate OIBs are created for each set of items with a common stimulus, such as a reading passage or graphic.

Mapmark Method. One distinguishing feature of the Bookmark Method is that extensive training with the OIB is required. That is, much time is spent discussing how and why each succeeding item is more difficult than the one before it. Even so, many panelists will still perceive the items to be out of order, that a later item is actually less difficult than an earlier one. As a result, some variations of the Bookmark Method focus on the information presented to panelists to assist their judgment task. One of these, the Mapmark Method (Schulz & Mitzel, 2005) provides detailed information in the form of spatial item maps that show visually what items measure and why they are located where they are on the logit scale.

Advantages and Disadvantages of the Bookmark Methods. The Bookmark Method has been widely used in educational achievement and credentialing tests. Since it is Rasch/IRT-based, it makes sense to use it only when the test itself has been developed according to one of these models. As a result, the assumptions of Rasch (and IRT) measurement theory—dimensionality, model fit, and local item independence—must also hold when using the Bookmark Method. The method is appealing for two reasons:

(1) the judgment task for panelists appears straightforward, and (2) the method is easily adaptable for mixed format tests.

Still, the judgment task is a complex one cognitively for panelists. They do not need to know the basics of Rasch measurement theory or IRT, but they still need to balance the concept of the RP criterion, borderline performance, the performance standard, and the properties of each item. And so, while panelists can usually narrow the OIB down to a smaller set of possible items to bookmark, they often feel that within this smaller set, they are making an arbitrary judgment, particularly if they perceive some of the items to be out of order. This perceived disordinality is a particular problem if some of the items are close together in difficulty. And yet, as was the case of the Angoff method, while individual panelists' judgments can vary widely, a reasonable group cut score is usually produced.

12.4.4 Other Standard Setting Methods

The above methods described in some detail are the ones most widely used. There are a number of other methods that require different kinds of judgments from panelists. Here, I will briefly describe several of these and point to situations in which they might be considered.

Body of Work. The Body of Work Method (Kingston, Kahl, Sweeney, & Bay, 2001) was developed for state educational achievement assessments, but it can be used for a wide range of tests, particularly those with mixed item formats, including portfolios. Panelists examine "work samples" from actual respondents and holistically judge the performance level of each work sample. An initial "rangefinding" round provides a general idea of where cut scores could be, followed by a "pinpointing" round that fine tunes cut score ranges. Then, logistic regression is used to finalize the cut score that most effectively distinguishes work samples in adjacent performance levels. The Body of Work method seems especially suited to content areas, such as language arts or a psychological evaluation, where a test score is a holistic judgment coming from different types of evidence.

Hofstee and Beuk Methods. These two methods are simple to implement and are designed to offer a compromise between a purely criterion-referenced cut score and a cut score that considers norm-referenced information. For example, panelists may have in mind a minimum or maximum that should not be exceeded (e.g., less than 50 percent correct is too low for being proficient, or 95 percent correct or greater should be required for passing or being certified), even if a standard setting method recommends as such. Both methods were developed for tests with a pass/fail outcome.

Hofstee's (1983) Method asks panelists to respond to the following four questions:

1. What is the highest cut score that would be acceptable, even if every respondent attains that score?

2. What is the lowest cut score that would be acceptable, even if every respondent attains that score?

3. What is the maximum acceptable failure rate?

4. What is the minimum acceptable failure rate?

The answers to these four questions permit plotting a straight line between two points on a Percent failing by Percent correct coordinate plane. On this same graph, the cumulative score distribution is plotted. The cut score is the point of intersection between these two lines.

The Beuk Method (1984) asks panelists just two questions:

1. What should be the minimum raw score required to pass this test?

2. What passing rate should be expected on this examination?

The panelists' mean of the answers to these questions also creates a point on the passing rate by raw score coordinate plane. Additionally, for each possible raw score, the percentage of respondents that would pass is plotted on the same coordinate plane. Then, a straight line is drawn from the means point to the percent passing with a slope equal to the ratio of the standard deviations from the answers to the two questions. The point of intersection is the cut score.

Because these two methods take so little time, they are often used in conjunction with other standard setting methods as additional estimates of cut scores. For example, the questions posed by both methods could be asked of panelists after a panel meeting that implemented another method, such as an Angoff or Bookmark Method.

Item-Descriptor Matching Method. The Item-Descriptor Matching Method (Ferrara, Perie, & Johnson, 2002) requires each panelist to carefully review the PLDs for each performance level and examine the KSPs measured by each test item. Items are presented to panelists in an OIB, from least to most difficult. Then, panelists use the PLDs to match each item to a performance level. From this task, "threshold regions" are identified in which there is variation in judgments about a group of items. Cut scores are then calculated by averaging the highest and lowest difficulties of the items in the threshold region. As in the Bookmark Method, item difficulties are in the form of Rasch (or IRT) difficulty estimates. Unlike the Bookmark Method, panelists do not have to address item sequencing.

12.5 VALIDATING STANDARD SETTING

The defensibility of implementing a standard setting method and its resulting cut score(s) is an issue of validity. Validity here is not a property of the test or the standard setting method. It is a property of the interpretation or meaning associated with a performance standard.

That is, if someone takes a test and achieves "proficient" or "licensed," what exactly does that mean and what evidence can be brought to bear to support that claim?

Kane (1994, 2001) has written extensively on this topic by developing a framework for validating performance standards. In this framework, Kane first draws a distinction between the *passing*, or *cut score*, which is a test score point, and the *performance standard*, which he defines as "the minimally adequate level of performance for some purpose" (Kane, 1994, p. 425). The passing or cut score is about the standard setting method. The performance standard is about a policy decision. According to Kane (1994):

> *Validation then consists of a demonstration that the proposed passing score can be interpreted as representing an appropriate performance standard. (pp. 425–426)*

With this in mind, validation can proceed along two distinct lines:

1. Does the cut score validly represent the performance standard?

2. Is the performance standard itself a valid operationalization of the desired level of competence?

Kane proposes three types of validity evidence to answer these two questions. This evidence fits into the decision inference in his more general validity framework introduced in Chapter 2.

Procedural Evidence. Procedural evidence centers on the appropriateness of the standard setting method and the quality of its implementation. Evidence of this sort includes:

- Justification for the selection of the standard setting method

- Justification for the selection of panelists

- Adequacy of the training of panelists

- Appropriateness and clarity of the performance standard

- Proper collection and handling of data

- Clarity of directions to panelists

- Clear management of the meeting by the facilitator

It is quite common for the meeting facilitator to administer brief evaluation questionnaires at various points in the panel meeting. For example, a questionnaire asking about the clarity of various aspects of the training, including discussion of the PLD and practice with the judgment task, can be administered after the last training activity and before Round 1. The facilitator reads the responses on the spot. That way, if panelists raise an issue, the facilitator can make immediate corrections. Another questionnaire can be administered after the discussion in Round 1. This one asks about how clear the directions were to the panelists, how confident they were in their judgments, and how well the facilitator ensures that all panelists' views were respected. Again, the facilitator can intervene if a problem occurs. A final questionnaire at the end of the meeting addresses overall experiences of the panelists, their confidence level in Round 2, and what information influenced their judgments. In addition, informal procedural evidence can also be documented. Facilitators and observers will generally know when things are going well or badly. For example, one thing that can happen in a panel meeting is that one panelist dominates the discussion. As a result, the cut score may be biased toward that judge's position rather than a consensus.

There is a debate on how important procedural evidence is. For the first question, about the cut score, this type of evidence does not directly support the use of the cut score, but it could invalidate any cut score interpretation if the evidence is not favorable, much the same way that poor items can invalidate the validity of a test score. For the second question, about the performance standard, procedural validity evidence is important. If a policy decision has been made according to procedural rules applied correctly, it gains some legitimacy.

Internal Consistency Evidence. This type of evidence focuses on the judgments of the panelists and the degree to which they are consistent, between and within panelists. The results of a standard setting panel meeting are hopefully replicable, that a different set of judges would likely come to a similar cut score recommendation. Figure 12.12, using data from an operational bookmark standard setting meeting, shows the book-mark cut scores, in logit units, across three rounds. Notice that in each round the panelists' cut scores become closer together, that is, the standard deviation of their cut scores decreases across rounds. This would be considered internal evidence that a greater consensus was achieved in each round. There is no requirement from any standard setting method that there be unanimity, so it is not surprising that there was not complete agreement after the last round. Unanimity is rarely achieved, but there is hope that greater consensus is achieved across rounds. On the other hand, the graph reveals that four panelists changed their judgments dramatically between rounds. Two panelists seemed to waffle back and forth. These panelists showed some degree of internal inconsistency. For these two panelists, a perception that several items in the OIB to be out of order led to the inconsistency. The remaining panelists were highly consistent from round to round. Another type of internal consistency evidence can be examined if the test has multiple item formats and/or multiple content areas. Do the same cut scores get recommended for different formats and content areas?

Internal evidence provides a check on the correspondence between the cut score and the performance standard. There is also indirect support for the policy question about the performance standard in the sense that there seems to be a consensus, but this evidence cannot directly infer that this is the intended or correct consensus.

External Evidence. External evidence concerns validation of the cut score through comparisons with external sources of information. This is arguably the most important type of evidence, and yet it tends to be the least frequently collected. It is difficult to collect, and it is often not available for a long time after the test and cut score have been used. Does it look as though those who pass or achieve the standard really deserve it? In licensure/certification testing, it will eventually be noticed how individuals who meet the standard, that is, are certified or licensed, perform in their profession. In educational achievement testing, this question is harder to answer.

FIGURE 12.12 ● Three Rounds of Bookmarking (Skaggs, 2007)

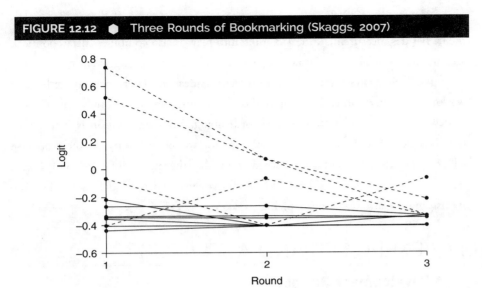

Outcomes, such as basic, proficient, and advanced, can be compared with grades, teacher judgments, and other test scores, but all of these contain some degree of measurement error. However, if the cut score is perceived to be too high or too low, controversy eventually ensues. An example of this occurred in my home state of Virginia. When cut scores on the state assessment were first determined, a very low, and to many educators too low, percentage of students achieved the level of Proficient. As a result, standard setting was revisited, and the cut scores were modified. Similarly, NAEP consistently reports a low percentage of students at the Proficient level. Some educators and policymakers have attacked the standard setting methods as being "fundamentally flawed" (see NRC (1999) and the beginning of this chapter). External evidence is mostly directed at the policy question. It gets at the heart of the appropriateness of the performance standard.

12.6 CHAPTER SUMMARY

This chapter presents an historical overview of standard setting, typical aspects of modern standard setting, and a look at several methods that have been used with some success. In order to conduct a standard setting procedure for your test, I recommend accessing the general resources listed below as well as the primary publications for a specific method.

Standard setting is less like psychometrics than any other topic in mental measurement. Besides measurement ideas coming into play, it also combines social, political, and artistic considerations. Some people think of standard setting as entirely a policy setting exercise rather than a measurement endeavor. There are strengths and weaknesses to any standard setting method, and critics often stress the weaknesses as evidence that standard setting is not worth doing. My own position is that any of methods described in this chapter are superior to the Arbitrary Method because whatever cut score is eventually adopted at least has the support of a group of subject matter experts and stakeholders. This is ultimately much more defensible than the sponsoring organization simply picking a score.

12.7 EXERCISES AND ACTIVITIES

Test Development Project

For tests with a criterion-focused score interpretation:

1. Write a brief PLD for the target performance level.

2. Select an appropriate standard setting method.

3. Determine the composition and size of the standard setting panel.

4. Develop a panel meeting agenda that includes the types of training, number of rounds, and what information will be provided between rounds.

For a classroom or small group meeting, carry out a mock standard setting meeting on a small scale (i.e., much reduced length of time). This mock meeting should include:

1. PLD provided by the instructor or facilitator. If a test and item response data are not available, the TIMSS and political viewpoint tests and data for this book could be used along with the provided PLD.

2. Brief training exercises: (a) taking the test as a respondent, followed by a discussion of what KSPs the items measure, and (b) discussion of the borderline respondent (given the group size, it may be advantageous to divide the group into small groups of five or six panelists for discussion and then report the results to the full group).

3. Carry out at least two standard setting methods, for example, the modified Angoff method followed by the bookmark method (and if time, followed by the Hofstee and Beuk methods).

4. Discuss the results of the methods. How different are they? How did panelists experience the standard setting process?

5. For this mock panel meeting, describe how you would collect the three types of validity evidence proposed by Kane.

FURTHER READING

General Sources for Standard Setting Methodology

Cizek, G. J. (Ed.). (2001). *Setting performance standards: Concepts, methods, and perspectives.* Mahwah, NJ: Erlbaum.

Cizek, G. J., & Bunch, M. B. (2007). *Standard setting: A guide to establishing and evaluating performance standards on tests.* Thousand Oaks, CA: SAGE.

Cizek, G. J. (Ed.). (2012). *Setting performance standards: Foundations, methods, and innovations.* New York, NY: Routledge.

Hambleton, R. K., & Pitoniak, M. J. (2006). Setting performance standards. In R. L. Brennan (Ed.), *Educational measurement* (4th ed., pp. 433–470). Westport, CT: Praeger.

REFERENCES

Angoff, W. H. (1971). Scales, norms, and equivalent scores. In R. L. Thorndike (Ed.), *Educational measurement* (pp. 508–600). Washington, DC: American Council on Education.

Berk, R. A. (1976). Determination of optimal cutting scores in criterion-referenced measurement. *Journal of Experimental Education, 45,* 4–9.

Beuk, C. H. (1984). A method for reaching a compromise between absolute and relative standards in examinations. *Journal of Educational Measurement, 21,* 147–152.

Cannell, J. J. (1989). *How public educators cheat on standardized achievement tests.* Albuquerque, NM: Friends for Education.

Dawber, T., Lewis, D. M., & Rogers, W. T. (April 2002). The cognitive experience of bookmark standard setting participants. Paper presented at the Annual Meeting of the American Educational Research Association, New Orleans, LA.

Egan, L. E., Schneider, M. C., & Ferrara, S. (2012). Performance level descriptors. In G. J. Cizek (Ed.), *Setting performance standards: Foundations, methods, and innovations* (pp. 79–106). New York, NY: Routledge.

Ferrara, S., Perie, M., & Johnson, E. (December 2002). *Matching the judgmental task with standard setting panelist expertise: The item-descriptor (ID) matching procedure.* Washington, DC: American Institutes for Research.

Glass, G. V. (1978). Standards and criteria. *Journal of Educational Measurement, 15,* 237–261.

Hambleton, R. K., Pitoniak, M. J., & Copella, J. M. (2012). Essential steps in setting performance standards. In G. J. Cizek (Ed.), *Setting performance standards: Foundations, methods, and innovations* (pp. 47–76). New York, NY: Routledge.

Hambleton, R. K., & Plake, B. S. (1995). Using an extended Angoff procedure to set standards on complex performance assessments. *Applied Measurement in Education, 8,* 41–56.

Hein, S. F., & Skaggs, G. (2009). A qualitative investigation of panelists' experiences of standard setting using two variations of the bookmark method. *Applied Measurement in Education, 22*(3), 207–228.

Hein, S. F., & Skaggs, G. (2010). Conceptualizing the classroom of target students: A qualitative investigation of panelists' experiences during standard setting. *Educational Measurement: Issues and Practice, 29*(2), 36–44.

Hofstee, W. K. B. (1983). The case for compromise in educational selection and grading. In S. B. Anderson, & J. S. Helmick (Eds.), *On educational testing* (pp. 109–127). San Francisco, CA: Jossey-Bass.

Huynh, H. (April 2000). On item mappings and statistical rules for selecting binary items for criterion-referenced interpretation and bookmark standard setting. Paper presented at the Annual Meeting of the National Council on Measurement in Education, New Orleans, LA.

Impara, J. C., & Plake, B. S. (1997). Standard setting: An alternative approach. *Journal of Educational Measurement, 34,* 353–366.

Impara, J. C., & Plake, B. S. (1998). Teachers' ability to estimate item difficulty: A test of the assumptions of the Angoff standard setting method. *Journal of Educational Measurement, 35,* 69–81.

Kane, M. (1994). Validating the performance standards associated with passing scores. *Review of Educational Research, 64*(3), 425–461.

Kane, M. (2001). So much remains the same: Conception and status of validation in standard setting. In C. J. Cizek (Ed.), *Setting performance standards: Concepts, methods, and perspectives* (pp. 53–88). Mahwah, NJ: Lawrence Erlbaum Associates.

Kingston, N. M., Kahl, S. R., Sweeney, K., & Bay, L. (2001). Setting performance standards using the body of work method. In C. J. Cizek (Ed.), *Setting performance standards: Concepts, methods, and perspectives* (pp. 219–248). Mahwah, NJ: Lawrence Erlbaum Associates.

Livingston, S., & Zieky, M. (1982). *Passing scores: A manual for setting standards of performance on educational and occupational tests.* Princeton, NJ: Educational Testing Service.

Loomis, S. C. (2012). Selecting and training standard setting participants: State of the art policies and procedures. In G. J. Cizek (Ed.), *Setting performance standards: Foundations, methods, and innovations* (pp. 107–134). New York, NY: Routledge.

McGinty, D. (2005). Illuminating the "black box" of standard setting: An exploratory qualitative study. *Applied Measurement in Education*, 18, 269–287.

Mitzel, H. C., Lewis, D. M., Patz, R. J., & Green, D. R. (2001). The bookmark procedure: Psychological perspectives. In C. J. Cizek (Ed.), *Setting performance standards: Concepts, methods, and perspectives* (pp. 249–281). Mahwah, NJ: Lawrence Erlbaum Associates.

National Assessment Governing Board. (2010). *Geography framework for the 2010 National Assessment of Educational Progress*. Author.

National Commission on Excellence in Education. (1983). *A nation at risk: The imperative for educational reform*. Washington, DC: U. S. Government Printing Office.

National Research Council. (1999). *Grading the nation's report card*. Washington, DC: National Academy Press.

Nedelsky, L. (1954). Absolute grading standards for objective tests. *Educational and Psychological Measurement*, 14, 1–19.

Raymond, M. R., & Reid, J. B. (2001). Who made thee a judge? Selecting and training participants for standard setting. In G. J. Cizek (Ed.), *Setting performance standards: Concepts, methods, and perspectives* (pp. 119–157). Mahwah, NJ: Erlbaum.

Resnick, D. P. (1980). Minimum competency testing historically considered. *Review of Research in Education*, 8, 3–29.

Schulz, E. M., & Mitzel, H. C. (April 2005). The Mapmark standard setting method. Paper presented at the Annual Meeting of the National Council on Measurement in Education, Montreal, Quebec, Canada.

Skaggs, G. (2007). Bookmark locations and item response model selection in the presence of local item dependence. *Journal of Applied Measurement*, 8(1), 65–83.

Skaggs, G., Hein, S., & Awuor, R. (2007). Setting passing scores on passage-based tests: A comparison of traditional and single-passage bookmark methods. *Applied Measurement in Education*, 20(4), 405–426.

Smarter Balanced Assessment Consortium (SBAC). (April 2013). *Initial achievement level descriptors and college content-readiness policy*. Olympia, WA: Author.

Virginia Department of Education. (2018). *Superintendent's Memo #229-18*. Richmond, VA: Author. Retrieved from www.doe.virginia.gov/administrators/superintendents.../229-18.docx.

Zieky, M. J., & Livingston, S. A. (1977). *Manual for setting standards on the basic skills assessment tests*. Princeton, NJ: Educational Testing Service.

13

VALIDITY EVIDENCE AND VALIDATION PLANS

13.1 CURRENT VALIDITY FRAMEWORKS

In most cases, tests are intended to be used in a context broader than the initial data collections (pilot and field tests) used to develop them. A test could be used for research or to make decisions about respondents. And quite often, individuals or groups other than the developers will administer and score the test. As a result, it is important for the developers to have evidence to support the intended uses of the test and the intended meanings of the test scores. In other words, what validity evidence is available? Chapter 2 presented two major validity frameworks for organizing validity evidence: Messick/*Standards* and Kane frameworks. Both frameworks indicate what evidence should be collected, but as pointed out in Chapter 2, validity is an ongoing process. There is never a point in which proof of validity is obtained. Essentially, every data collection with a test can be viewed as a validity study. One central question therefore is: what evidence and how much of it is sufficient before a test can be used operationally? A second question is: what validity evidence should be collected in the future? These questions are addressed in this chapter.

13.2 VALIDATION USING MESSICK/ *STANDARDS* FRAMEWORK

Messick proposed six types of validity evidence. The 2014 *Standards* relabels these types and combines generalizability and external evidence into "relations with other variables." If you have followed the procedures described in the preceding chapters in developing a test, you have already collected a body of evidence. In the next sections, I describe what has been collected so far and what future validation projects might seek to determine.

Content evidence refers to content relevance, representativeness, and item technical quality. In developing a test, there is likely to be considerable evidence of this type. In particular, many validity questions can be answered using the following evidence:

1. Documentation of purpose and intended uses of the test:

   - Is there a clearly defined purpose?

   - Is there a rationale for each intended use for the test for which validity evidence will be investigated?

2. Development of test specifications:

   - Do the specifications follow from the purpose and intended uses?

   - Does the test adequately represent the universe of all possible tasks?

   - Do the item types, time limits, scoring criteria, etc., lead to a reasonable representation of the construct?

3. Documentation of the test development process:

   - Was the test developed on a sound scientific basis?

4. Documentation of the use of expertise in reviewing items:

   - What were the qualifications and training of reviewers?

   - Does expert review support the content quality and representativeness of the test in measuring the construct?

5. Item technical quality:

   - Do the items demonstrate sufficient statistical quality (e.g., item difficulty and discrimination)?

   - Do the items fit the proposed measurement model?

For content evidence, this is a fairly complete set of documentation. For the future, these various documents may need to be revised or updated. If there are major changes to the test, e.g., change from paper/pencil administration to computer-based administration, additional content evidence supporting these changes will be needed.

Substantive/Response processes evidence refers to empirical evidence that the intended thought processes are actually engaged in by respondents. Some work has been done during test development:

1. Construct map:

   - Is the development of the construct supported by theory or research?

2. Theoretical framework of the construct:

   - Does the internal model follow from the construct map, theory, and research?

   - Do theory and research support the external model?

3. Operational definition:

   - Is the operational definition of the construct consistent with the construct map, theory, and research?

4. Rationale for item format (multiple-choice, rating scale, and/or constructed response)

   - Do the selected item formats support the operational definition of the construct?

This information is admittedly indirect in nature. It is important to know what the intended thought processes actually are in order to support the claim that they are taking place, but more direct evidence should be collected:

1. Think-alouds or cognitive labs:

   - Are respondents thinking processes consistent with the conceptual basis of the construct?

2. Distractor/rating scale functioning:

   - Do the responses to the distractors support the intended cognitive processes for which the distractors were developed?

   - Do the responses to the rating scale (e.g., Likert scale) correspond to the intentions of the test developers?

3. Item hierarchy:

   - Do the actual item difficulties agree with those expected when the test was developed?

Historically, such substantive evidence has not been collected by many test programs. However, in recent years, think-alouds and cognitive labs have been used increasingly as a prepilot test of item quality because they can reveal item flaws prior to investing in more extensive and expensive data collection.

Structural/Internal structure evidence refers to the degree to which relationships between items or parts of a test conform to the theoretical view of the construct. Unlike substantive evidence, structural evidence seems to be commonly collected. During test development, the following can be documented:

1. Development of the internal model:

   - Does the internal model define a structure for the test? What are the component parts of the construct and how are they related?

2. Rationale for adoption of the measurement model:

- Does the internal model meet the assumptions of the measurement model? For example, if a unidimensional Rasch model is adopted, is there evidence that the test is unidimensional?

Given the resources of the project, the following may or may not have been completed during development:

1. Correlational analyses:

- Are the correlations between component parts consistent with the internal model of the construct?

2. Dimensionality:

- Is the dimensional structure suggested by the data consistent with the internal model (using exploratory and/or confirmatory factor analysis)?

3. Differential item functioning:

- Do items have the same characteristics across different subgroups of respondents?

Data for these analyses require reasonably large sample sizes, such as would be collected during a field test or operationally. As mentioned above, reporting results of factor analyses is fairly common. Many test users may want to see this type of structural evidence before using it operationally.

Generalizability evidence refers to the degree to which test score properties and interpretations generalize to and across population groups, settings, and tasks including validity generalization of test criterion relationships. Evidence likely collected during development includes the following:

1. Specification of the target population:

- Is the test appropriate for the target population?

2. Reliability:

- Do test scores have sufficient reliability and precision?

- If raters are used, do they sufficiently agree in their judgments of human performances?

3. Selection of norming sample:

- Does the norming sample represent the target population?

Generalizability evidence uses data collected from a field test, but this is one type of evidence that can be collected indefinitely. This could include the following:

1. Validity generalization:

- Do the relationships between the test and other variables generalize to other settings and groups of respondents?

External evidence refers to how the construct is expected to relate to other constructs and variables. Generally, external evidence is collected after the initial test development, as the test is used operationally, but it is sometimes collected as part of the development process (see the Grit Scale example below). Many types of external evidence are possible, including the following:

1. Group and within-individual comparisons:

- Experimentation: Are the outcomes of a randomized experiment consistent with theory of the construct?

- Comparison of Groups: Are differences between subgroups of respondents consistent with theory of the construct?

- Changes Over Time: Do individuals change as expected over time?

2. Convergent and discriminant validity:

- Does the construct correlate with other variables with which it is expected to correlate?

- Does the construct correlate less well with variables with which it is not expected to correlate?

3. Multiple regression/Structural equation modeling:

- Do data fit the external model? These methodologies are attempts to investigate the entire external model rather than individual pairs of variables.

As was the case with generalizability, external evidence can and should be collected over time. As mentioned above, every operational use of a test can be thought of as a validity study. Many test developers create a system for tracking applications of their test and use those results to update support for the validity of test scores.

Consequential/Consequences of testing evidence refers to the value implications of score interpretation as well as the actual and potential consequences of test use, especially regarding bias, fairness, and distributive justice. During development, attempts are made to produce items that are fair to all respondents:

1. Bias/fairness review of items:

- Do items show bias toward any population of respondents?

- Do items show any offensive or stereotypic language?

However, the critical consequential evidence is collected after the test has been used operationally:

1. Positive or negative impact on individuals:

- Is this impact a result of a source of invalidity? (e.g., lack of access, cultural bias)

- Does test use result in stigmatization of some respondents?

2. Positive or negative impact on systems:

- Are the intended outcomes of test use realized?

- Do unintended negative outcomes arise after instituting a new testing program or changing an existing testing program?

A common consequential evidence threat comes from tests in which respondents provide self-reports, such as many tests measuring personality, attitude, and psychological constructs. On these, if respondents are unsure how their scores will be used, they may not answer honestly. For example, for a test measuring self-efficacy administered by an employer, respondents may be concerned about the potential negative impact of a low score.

13.3 VALIDATION PLAN FOR GRIT SCALE—MESSICK/*STANDARDS* VERSION

Creating a validation plan involves examining the validity evidence that is available as a test is launched for operational use, and then proposing additional data collection to fill in the types of evidence which is lacking. As an example, I will examine the original 12-item Grit Scale, developed by Angela Duckworth and her colleagues (Duckworth, Peterson, Matthews, & Kelly, 2007). The Grit Scale was discussed in Chapter 6 in the context of test specifications. Here, we look at the validity evidence presented in the 2007 publication and a follow-up set of validity studies (Duckworth & Quinn, 2009) on a shortened eight-item version. Although a considerable amount of research on the construct of grit has been undertaken since those articles were published, we'll look at what is offered in just those two articles because they were the seminal publications that launched the Grit Scale into operation. And so, based on Messick's (and the 2014 *Standards*) framework, what evidence has been collected so far and what would a validation plan for the future look like?

Content Evidence

- Clearly defined purpose: to test research hypotheses about grit (Duckworth et al., 2007, p. 1089).

- Definition of grit: "perseverance and passion for long-term goals" (2007, p. 1087). Construct of grit hypothesized to consist of two components—Consistency of Interests and Perseverance of Effort.

- Clear target population: adults 25 years or older (2007, p. 1090).

- Frame of reference: Norm-referenced for research purposes. Respondents to the Grit Scale are given a percentile rank.

- Test specifications: Item format: five-point Likert items rated on 1 = not at all like me to 5 = very much like me (2007, p. 1090).

- Test development:

  - Item ideas "generated from interviews with lawyers, businesspeople, academics, and other professionals" (2007, p. 1090).

  - 27 draft items that "tapped the ability to sustain effort in the face of adversity" (2007, p. 1090).

- Item Quality: Draft items piloted on a website inviting respondents to participate. Sample size was large (over 1,500), but it was self-selecting, so it is not clear how representative it was of the target population. Item analysis resulted in selecting 17 items for further study that met statistical criteria, e.g., positive discrimination (2007, p. 1090).

Substantive Evidence

- Construct map: A construct map was not explicitly presented but could be constructed from the theoretical description of grit (2007, p. 1090).

- Operational definition: "the attitudes and behaviors characteristic of high-achieving individuals" (2007, p. 1090). These were collected during interviews with high-achieving individuals.

- Rationale for the Likert item format was not explicitly stated, but the selected items do correlate positively with test scores, suggesting that the preferences of the answer choices performed as expected (2007, p. 1090).

Structural Evidence

- Internal model: two components equally weighted and hypothesized to be moderately to strongly correlated, supported by an oblique rotation from an EFA (2007, p. 1090).

- Measurement model: Classical sum score calculated for each component and for the total score (2007, p. 1090).

- Dimensionality: An EFA with an oblique rotation indicated a two-factor solution was the closest model to simple structure. The two factors corresponded to the test developers intended two components of grit, and the items loaded on the factor that was intended by the developers. Further item selection trimmed the test to 12 items, six for each component. A CFA was also carried out on the 12-item two-factor test. Model fit was moderately good (2007, p. 1090). The CFA analyses were replicated on the eight-item test on all samples. Fit was improved.

Generalizability Evidence

- Reliability: Both the 12-item and eight-item tests demonstrated adequate reliability (coefficient alpha) for both components separately and combined (2007, p. 1091; 2009, p. 167). For a sample of secondary magnet school students, test–retest reliability was adequate (2009, p. 170).

- Application to different populations: Original field test sample consisted of adults 25 and over. The test was also administered to samples from other populations: Ivy League undergraduates, West Point cadets in two different classes, and National Spelling Bee finalists. The results showed adequate reliability and model fit for all samples (2007, p. 1092; 2009, pp. 167–169).

External Evidence

- Much evidence of verification of hypothesized relationships:

  - Grit correlated positively with educational attainment and age, with and without controlling for the Big Five Traits.

  - Grit correlated positively with GPA, negatively or not at all with SAT.

  - Grit was a better predictor of completing summer training among freshman West Point cadets than the Candidate score, with and without controlling for the Big Five Traits.

  - Grit predicted who would advance to later rounds in a spelling bee competition.

Consequential Evidence

- Since these two articles detailed the launch of the Grit Scales along with several validity studies, no consequential evidence was offered at that time. However, because the tests are self-reported and susceptible to social desirability bias, the authors caution against using the Grit Scale for high-stakes decisions.

Given the validity evidence presented in these articles, what additional evidence could be recommended in a validation plan? I will approach this question in the context of the stated purpose of the test—to conduct research on grit and its relationship to other constructs. If the purpose were to change, say for example, to be used as a personnel selection test, then all types of evidence need to be rethought.

Content Evidence. As mentioned above, the preponderance of this type of evidence is produced during test development. As a test with a history of implementation in research studies, there is likely little need to revisit the underpinnings of the test. Further content evidence would be needed if there were a need to create additional forms or if the specifications needed to be updated.

Substantive Evidence. Like most tests measuring noncognitive constructs, less attention was paid to this type of evidence. As noted above, the items were derived from asking high-achieving individuals what attitudes and behaviors led to their success, e.g. "I finish what I begin." On the other hand, the attitudes and behaviors of "low achievers" might not necessarily be the opposite of those of high achievers. These could be explored with think-alouds or cognitive labs with respondents that score at different levels on the Grit Scale.

Structural Evidence. The evidence presented in these articles for EFA and CFA is quite strong. A validation plan could include replication analyses with different subgroups of the target population. There was no indication of DIF analyses in these two articles. It would be worthwhile to conduct DIF analyses with important subgroups of the population. In particular, does the Grit Scale function the same way in these subgroups?

Generalizability Evidence. The developers have used the Grit Scale to conduct research with numerous population subgroups. So far, the reliability of the test remains strong across the subgroups. This could continue as the authors' research program expands to new settings.

External Evidence. Like the preceding two sections, every administration of the Grit Scale for a research study is also a validity study. Such research has continued since 2009. Additionally, a validation plan could include an expansion of the research methodology. In these two articles, correlational and regression analyses were the prime vehicles for examining predictive validity. More advanced methods, such as HLM and SEM, could provide more nuanced interpretations of the relationships between high achievement, grit, and other variables while controlling for measurement error. As a result, if predictive hypotheses are true, both the theory of grit and the Grit Scale itself are supported.

Consequential Evidence. No consequential evidence is reported in either article. Because the intended use of the Grit Scale is to conduct research, and because the developers took great care to protect the identities of the participants, no adverse impacts or unintended consequences were anticipated. Still, the validation plan should include some attention to this type of evidence. The 2014 *Standards* generally point to the test developers as being responsible for consequences pertaining to the intended uses of the test, but for other uses, the test user is responsible for investigating consequences. This would include any consequences or adverse impact resulting from participating in a research study or from responding to the test on Dr. Duckworth's website. I mentioned in Chapter 6 the possibility of "purpose creep," or using a test for additional purposes beyond its original intent. For grit, there have been articles debating using the Grit Scale for high-stakes testing in K-12 schools (e.g., https://www.nytimes.com/2016/03/01/us/testing-for-joy-and-grit-schools-nationwide-push-to-measure-students-emotional-skills.html). If this were to come to pass, then additional validity evidence would be needed to support this use (I note here that Dr. Duckworth does not support using the Grit Scale in this way.)

13.4 VALIDATION USING KANE'S FRAMEWORK

Kane's framework is based on a series of inferences, each of which makes a relevant claim backed by validity evidence. Because the inferences are sequential, failure to make a validity case in an earlier inference undermines any subsequent inferences.

However, the actual evidence itself is much the same as in the Messick/*Standards* framework. Below, I will outline what evidence can be used for each of the six inferences listed in Chapter 2. The first three inferences largely deal with test development while the last three inferences pertain to test use. As a result, the first three inferences will tend to be strongly supported by evidence from the test development process. For the last three inferences, evidence will often overlap. For example, evidence pertaining to consequences is an issue for any use of a test.

Scoring Inference. The scoring inference claims that items are of high quality and that they are scored correctly and reliably. The evidence to support this claim could include the following:

- Documentation of purpose and uses of the test:

  - Is there a clearly defined purpose?

  - Is there a rationale for each intended use?

- Documentation of the test development process:

  - Is the development process consistent with best practice, e.g., consistent with the 2014 *Standards*?

- Documentation of use of expertise in reviewing items:

  - Are the items judged to be appropriate by subject matter experts?

- Item technical quality:

  - Difficulty and discrimination: Is item difficulty targeted appropriately? Do the items discriminate sufficiently?

  - Is there a rationale for the item format (multiple-choice, rating scale, and/or constructed response)?

  - Distractor/rating scale functioning: Are the answer choices appropriate?

  - Do the items fit the proposed measurement model?

- Expert judgment of scoring, interrater reliability, quality control for raters:

  - If human scorers are needed, do they show sufficient interrater reliability?

Generalization Inference. The generalization inference claims that the items selected for the test are a representative sample of all possible items (i.e., universe of generalization) and that this sample is large enough to control for sampling error. Evidence could include the following:

- Construct map:

    - Is the development of the construct supported by theory or research?

- Operational definition:

    - Is the operational definition of the construct consistent with the construct map, theory, and research?

- Development of test specifications:

    - Do the specifications follow from the purpose and intended uses?

    - Does the test adequately represent the universe of all possible tasks?

    - Do the item types, time limits, scoring criteria, etc. lead to a reasonable representation of the construct?

- Reliability:

    - Does the test show sufficient reliability for all scores?

Extrapolation Inference. This inference claims the test score (universe score) actually does represent the measurement of the construct (target score). This claim can be supported by the following:

- Development of internal model:

    - Does the internal model represent the construct?

- Rationale for adoption of reference framework (criterion versus normative)

- Verifying of use of the proposed processes by respondents:

    - Do think-aloud/cognitive lab methods indicate that respondents are thinking about their responses in the way developers intend?

    - Do debriefing interviews likewise indicate that respondents are thinking about their responses in the way developers intend?

- Dimensionality:

  - Is the internal structure of the test consistent with the internal model?

- Differential item functioning:

  - Do the items function the same way for relevant population subgroups?

Implication Inference. This inference claims validity for the proposed interpretation of test scores. This claim can be supported by the following:

- Predicted relations with other variables:

  - Do test scores relate to other variables as predicted by the external model?

- Expected group differences:

  - Do subgroups differ on test scores as predicted?

- Consequences for respondents:

  - Is there evidence that any intended consequences do occur?

  - Is there any evidence of unintended consequences or adverse impacts from the use of the test?

Theory-based Inference. This inference claims that the theory behind the construct accounts for variation in test scores and that scores can be used in theory-based interpretations. Some evidence in support for this claim could be:

- Predicted relations with other variables:

  - Do test scores relate to other variables as predicted by the external model?

- Theoretical framework of the construct:

  - Does the internal model follow from the construct map, operational definition, theory, and research?

  - Does theory and research support the external model?

- Consequences for groups of respondents or systems:

  - Is there evidence that intended consequences do occur?

  - Is there evidence of unintended consequences or adverse impacts from the use of the test?

Decision Inference. If the test is intended to be used to make decisions about respondents, e.g., as a selection test, this inference claims that the decision rule is appropriate. Evidence in support of that claim could include the following:

- Standard setting:

  - Is the standard setting appropriate for the test?

  - Is there evidence to support the validity of the standard setting process (using Kane's validity framework for standard setting)?

- Positive or negative impact on individuals:

  - Is this impact a source of invalidity (e.g., lack of access, cultural bias)?

  - Does test use result in stigmatization of some respondents?

- Positive or negative impact on systems:

  - Are the intended outcomes of test use realized?

  - Do unintended negative outcomes arise after instituting a new testing program or changing an existing testing program?

13.5 VALIDATION PLAN FOR GRIT SCALE—KANE VERSION

So, how does the development of the Grit Scale fit within Kane's framework?

Scoring. As mentioned above, there is a clearly defined purpose for the Grit Scale. Since all items are objectively scored, there is no need for any evidence of interrater reliability. The statistical quality of the items is documented in the 2007 article. A rationale for using a five-point Likert format is not explicit in the article, but that format, as pointed out in Chapter 7, is quite common for measuring noncognitive constructs. All in all, the evidence for the scoring inference seems quite strong.

Generalization. As mentioned above, a construct map was not explicit in the articles, but a theory of grit and an operational definition are clearly articulated. The test's specifications are not laid out in much detail, but I suspect that many specification decisions made during development were not included in the articles. DIF analyses were not mentioned in either article and should be a part of future validation work. Whether the items are representative sample of all possible items is difficult to determine. This could be a task for future investigation. Finally, there is extensive evidence that both versions of the Grit Scale are sufficiently reliable.

Extrapolation. The developers proposed a two-factor internal structure. Numerous EFA and CFA results support this model. As mentioned above, one possible future validation study would be to see if the attitudes and behaviors articulated in the items apply to low achievers as well as high achievers. Think-alouds, cognitive labs, and/or debriefing interviews could be used in this study.

Among the next three inferences, I would argue that the theory-based inference is of primary importance to the developers. The main purpose of the Grit Scale is a tool for investigating how grit plays a role in achievement. Because respondents receive a normative score report online, the implication inference is also important.

Implication. Anyone is welcome to complete the Grit Scale on Dr. Duckworth's website. All respondents receive a score and a percentile rank. The articles do not provide much information about the norming sample, so it's difficult to determine what population the percentile rank comes from.

Theory-based. The two articles together present a number of studies in which the predicted relationships between grit and other variables were confirmed, thus supporting the theory of grit. For the future, this research program should continue. Additionally, a validation plan could include research on the consequences of using the Grit Scale and on the consequences of grit itself in individuals' quality of life.

Decision. Because the developers did not intend, and do not recommend, that the Grit Scale be used in a high-stakes fashion, there is no evidence available for a decision-making inference.

At present, formal validation plans are commonly developed for large-scale testing programs. A good example can be found from the Smarter Balanced Assessment Consortium, in a chapter from their *2017–2018 Technical Report* (SBAC, 2019b). This chapter explains what validity evidence has been collected to date and what validity questions it answers. Future work is outlined in their *Strategic Plan 2017–2022* (SBAC, 2019a). Formal plans are much rarer for smaller-scale efforts, but I strongly recommend the practice of creating one for your test. Such a plan would likely be a part of a technical report that potential test users will want to see.

13.6 CHAPTER SUMMARY

This chapter introduced validation plans, which are plans to collect and present evidence to support score interpretations and the intended uses of the test. Two prominent validity frameworks, first introduced in Chapter 2, are the Messick/ *Standards* and Kane frameworks. These are offered as vehicles for organizing the types of evidence that is most useful to collect. Done this way, validation is seen as an ongoing project. Much evidence is collected during test development, enough to justify using the test operationally. However, every application of a test is also a validity study, and it is beneficial to have some direction to these studies at the outset of implementation.

13.7 BOOK SUMMARY

This book has attempted to root the test development process in the concept of validity. The target audience here includes students, faculty, professionals, researchers, and small organizations who are planning to develop a test measuring a construct. Large-scale testing organizations have the resources to assign parts of the process to specialists, but you may be faced with having to carry out all of the parts yourself. Each of the recommended procedures in this book is intended to produce a specific type of validity evidence. The sum total of the process is the generation of a compelling justification for the score interpretations and the test's intended uses. At the same time, if you are a researcher or practitioner in search of a test for a particular purpose, the validity frameworks give you a way of evaluating the validity evidence of possible tests. What types of evidence are provided? Which inferences have the most support? What evidence is lacking?

13.8 EXERCISES AND ACTIVITIES

Test Development Project

For the test you developed for your ID project, create a validation plan that will support the claim you will make about scores from the test (this is the purpose of the test). Use either the Messick/*Joint Standards* or Kane validity framework to organize your plan.

1. If using the Messick framework, list the six (according to Messick) or five (according to the *Standards*) types of validity evidence. Briefly describe under each type the validity evidence you have already collected through the ID project and what it says to support test score validity. Then, for each type of evidence, list and describe the evidence you would like to collect (if you had unlimited resources) and what you hope each type of evidence shows.

2. If using the Kane framework, integrate the proposed validity evidence into a coherent argument, as described by Kane. This means that, whatever purpose your test has, you will have three inferences: scoring, generalization, and extrapolation. For each of these inferences, briefly describe (or list) the validity evidence you have collected from the test development project and how it supports each inference. Then, list and describe the evidence you would like to collect and what you hope each type of evidence shows. Additionally, you should have a fourth inference based on the primary purpose: implication, theory-based interpretation, or decision. For each inference, list and describe the evidence you would like to collect (if you had unlimited resources) and what you hope each type of evidence shows.

REFERENCES

Duckworth, A. L., Peterson, C., Matthews, M. D., & Kelly, D. R. (2007). Grit: Perseverance and passion for long-term goals. *Journal of Personality and Social Psychology*, 92(6), 1087–1101.

Duckworth, A. L., & Quinn, P. D. (2009). Development and validation of the Short Grit Scale (Grit-S). *Journal of Personality Assessment*, 91(2), 166–174.

Smarter Balanced Assessment Consortium. (2019). *Smarter Balanced Strategic Plan 2017–2022*. Los Angeles, CA: Author.

Smarter Balanced Assessment Consortium. (2019). *2017–2018 Summative technical report*. Los Angeles, CA: Author.

APPENDIX A

GUIDE TO SAMPLE DATA SETS

TIMSS 2003 8th Grade Mathematics, Booklet 1, US Sample

The data can be found in the excel file: TIMMS 2003 Math data—booklet 1.xlsx

The text and information for the items can be found at: https://timssandpirls.bc.edu/PDF/T03_RELEASED_M8.pdf

CIRP Political Viewpoint Data

The data can be found in the excel file: political viewpoint data.xlsx

The survey itself can be found at: https://www.heri.ucla.edu/researchers/instruments/CIRP/1999SIF.pdf

The excel file contains data from items 1, 28, and 31. The data come from a random sample of incoming freshmen at a higher education institution.

APPENDIX B

R CODE FOR ANALYSES

This appendix contains the R code for running the analyses presented in the book. I strongly recommend running these analyses in R Studio. In R Studio, it is particularly useful to create an R project in a convenient folder. Data and R codes should be copied to this folder. This makes it easier to keep track of files and their location.

Chapter 8

Item analysis for TIMSS Booklet 1:

```
## load packages
library(psych)
library(readxl)
## TIMSS 2003 Math Book 1 (US data, dichotomous example)
## Response Data
bk1 <- read_excel("TIMMS 2003 Math data.xlsx",sheet = "book 1")
names(bk1)
str(bk1)

## Extract Test Items
resp_bk1 <- bk1[-1:-3]
dim(resp_bk1)

##use score.multiple.choice function from psych package
bk1key <- c(1,3,4,4,2,3,2,3,3,2,4,5,1,3,1,4,1,2,2,3)
bk1scored <- score.multiple.choice(bk1key,resp_bk1,score=FALSE)

#sink function directs output to a text file.
sink("book1 item analysis.txt", append=TRUE)

## descriptive statistics (using psych package)
describe(bk1scored)
```

```
## item analysis & reliability analysis (using psych package)
psych::alpha(bk1scored)

sink() # return output to console
```

Item analysis of political viewpoint data:

```
## load packages
library(psych)
library(readxl)
## CIRP poliview data 1999
## Response Data
poliview <- read_excel(path = "political viewpoint data.xlsx", sheet = "poliview")
poliview <- as.data.frame(poliview)

## Extract Test Items
resp_pol <- poliview[,2:19]
dim(resp_pol)

##use reverse.code function from psych package
polikey <- c(1,-1,-1,-1,-1,1,1,-1,-1,1,1,1,-1,-1,1,1,1,-1)
poliscored <- reverse.code(polikey,resp_pol,mini=rep(1,18),maxi=rep(4,18))
str(poliscored)
head(poliscored)

#sink function directs output to a text file.
sink("poliview item analysis.txt", append=TRUE)

## descriptive statistics (using psych package)
describe(poliscored)
## item analysis & reliability analysis (using psych package)
psych::alpha(poliscored)
sink() # return output to console
```

Chapter 10

DIF/SIBTEST analysis for TIMSS Booklet 1:

```
## load packages
library(psych)
library(readxl)
library(mirt)
bk1 <- read_excel("TIMMS 2003 Math data.xlsx",sheet = "book 1")
names(bk1)
str(bk1)
```

```
## Extract Test Items
resp_bk1 <- bk1[-1:-3]
dim(resp_bk1)

##use score.multiple.choice function from psych package
bk1key <- c(1,3,4,4,2,3,2,3,3,2,4,5,1,3,1,4,1,2,2,3)
bk1scored <- score.multiple.choice(bk1key,resp_bk1,score=FALSE)

## combine sex and scored item responses
bk1combo <- data.frame(bk1$ITSEX,bk1scored)
dim(bk1combo)

## descriptive statistics (using psych package)
describe(bk1combo)

#sink function directs output to a text file.
sink("dif of timss booklet 1 w difr & mirt.txt", append=TRUE)

## Mantel-Haenszel
results_bk1_MH <- difMH(bk1combo[,2:21],group=bk1$ITSEX,focal.name=1)
results_bk1_MH

## MH with purification
results_bk1_MH_pure <- difMH(bk1combo[,2:21],group=bk1$ITSEX,focal.name=1,
purify=TRUE)
results_bk1_MH_pure

## running SIBTEST from mirt package

#DIF (all other items as anchors)
SIBTEST(bk1scored, bk1$ITSEX, suspect_set = 1, focal_name='1')
SIBTEST(bk1scored, bk1$ITSEX, focal_name='1',2)
SIBTEST(bk1scored, bk1$ITSEX, focal_name='1',3)
SIBTEST(bk1scored, bk1$ITSEX, focal_name='1',4)
SIBTEST(bk1scored, bk1$ITSEX, focal_name='1',5)
SIBTEST(bk1scored, bk1$ITSEX, focal_name='1',6)
SIBTEST(bk1scored, bk1$ITSEX, focal_name='1',7)
SIBTEST(bk1scored, bk1$ITSEX, focal_name='1',8)
SIBTEST(bk1scored, bk1$ITSEX, focal_name='1',9)
SIBTEST(bk1scored, bk1$ITSEX, focal_name='1',10)
SIBTEST(bk1scored, bk1$ITSEX, focal_name='1',11)
SIBTEST(bk1scored, bk1$ITSEX, focal_name='1',12)
SIBTEST(bk1scored, bk1$ITSEX, focal_name='1',13)
SIBTEST(bk1scored, bk1$ITSEX, focal_name='1',14)
```

```
SIBTEST(bk1scored, bk1$ITSEX, focal_name='1',15)
SIBTEST(bk1scored, bk1$ITSEX, focal_name='1',16)
SIBTEST(bk1scored, bk1$ITSEX, focal_name='1',17)
SIBTEST(bk1scored, bk1$ITSEX, focal_name='1',18)
SIBTEST(bk1scored, bk1$ITSEX, focal_name='1',19)
SIBTEST(bk1scored, bk1$ITSEX, focal_name='1',20)

##purified
#DIF purification: matched is a vector of non-DIF items
matched <- c(2,3,5,7:10,13:16,18)

SIBTEST(bk1scored, bk1$ITSEX, match_set = matched, focal_name='1',1)
SIBTEST(bk1scored, bk1$ITSEX, match_set = matched, focal_name='1',4)
SIBTEST(bk1scored, bk1$ITSEX, match_set = matched, focal_name='1',6)
SIBTEST(bk1scored, bk1$ITSEX, match_set = matched, focal_name='1',11)
SIBTEST(bk1scored, bk1$ITSEX, match_set = matched, focal_name='1',12)
SIBTEST(bk1scored, bk1$ITSEX, match_set = matched, focal_name='1',17)
SIBTEST(bk1scored, bk1$ITSEX, match_set = matched, focal_name='1',19)
SIBTEST(bk1scored, bk1$ITSEX, match_set = matched, focal_name='1',20)

#DBF: differential bundle functioning: example for algebra
suspect_alg <- c(2, 10, 19, 20)

SIBTEST(bk1scored, bk1$ITSEX, suspect_set=suspect_alg, focal_name='1')

#example for reasoning
suspect_reas <- c(7, 17, 19)

SIBTEST(bk1scored, bk1$ITSEX, suspect_set=suspect_reas, focal_name='1')

#purify dbf
matched_alg <- c(3,5,8:9,13:16,18)

SIBTEST(bk1scored, bk1$ITSEX, match_set = matched_alg, suspect_set=suspect_
alg, focal_name='1')

#example for reasoning
matched_reas <- c(2,3,5,8:10,13:16,18)

SIBTEST(bk1scored, bk1$ITSEX, match_set = matched_reas, suspect_set=suspect_
reas, focal_name='1',)

#DIF purification of crossing SIBTEST: matched is a vector of non-DIF items
crossmatch <- c(2,3,5,7:10,13:16,18)

SIBTEST(bk1scored, bk1$ITSEX, match_set = matched, focal_name='1',1)
SIBTEST(bk1scored, bk1$ITSEX, match_set = matched, focal_name='1',4)
```

```
SIBTEST(bk1scored, bk1$ITSEX, match_set = matched, focal_name='1',6)
SIBTEST(bk1scored, bk1$ITSEX, match_set = matched, focal_name='1',11)
SIBTEST(bk1scored, bk1$ITSEX, match_set = matched, focal_name='1',12)
SIBTEST(bk1scored, bk1$ITSEX, match_set = matched, focal_name='1',17)
SIBTEST(bk1scored, bk1$ITSEX, match_set = matched, focal_name='1',19)
SIBTEST(bk1scored, bk1$ITSEX, match_set = matched, focal_name='1',20)

sink() # return output to console
```

DIF/SIBTEST analysis for political viewpoint data:

```
## load packages
library(psych)
library(readxl)
library(mirt)

## CIRP poliview data 1999
poliview <- read_excel(path = "political viewpoint data.xlsx", sheet = "poliview")
poliview <- as.data.frame(poliview)

## listwise deletion of missing data needed for sibtest
poliviewr <- na.omit(poliview)
dim(poliviewr)

## Extract Test Items
resp_pol <- poliviewr[,2:19]
dim(resp_pol)

##use reverse.code function from psych package
polikey <- c(1,-1,-1,-1,-1,1,1,-1,-1,1,1,1,-1,-1,1,1,1,-1)
poliscored <- reverse.code(polikey,resp_pol,mini=rep(1,18),maxi=rep(4,18))
str(poliscored)
head(poliscored)

## descriptive statistics (using psych package)
describe(poliscored)

## combine sex and scored item responses
polivwcombo <- data.frame(poliviewr$sex,poliscored)
dim(polivwcombo)

## descriptive statistics (using psych package)
describe(polivwcombo)
```

```
#sink function directs output to a text file.
sink("sibtest of poliview w mirt.txt", append=TRUE)
## running SIBTEST from mirt package

#DIF (all other items as anchors)
SIBTEST(poliscored, poliviewr$sex, suspect_set = 1, focal_name='2')
SIBTEST(poliscored, poliviewr$sex, suspect_set = 2, focal_name='2')
SIBTEST(poliscored, poliviewr$sex, suspect_set = 3, focal_name='2')
SIBTEST(poliscored, poliviewr$sex, suspect_set = 4, focal_name='2')
SIBTEST(poliscored, poliviewr$sex, suspect_set = 5, focal_name='2')
SIBTEST(poliscored, poliviewr$sex, suspect_set = 6, focal_name='2')
SIBTEST(poliscored, poliviewr$sex, suspect_set = 7, focal_name='2')
SIBTEST(poliscored, poliviewr$sex, suspect_set = 8, focal_name='2')
SIBTEST(poliscored, poliviewr$sex, suspect_set = 9, focal_name='2')
SIBTEST(poliscored, poliviewr$sex, suspect_set = 10, focal_name='2')
SIBTEST(poliscored, poliviewr$sex, suspect_set = 11, focal_name='2')
SIBTEST(poliscored, poliviewr$sex, suspect_set = 12, focal_name='2')
SIBTEST(poliscored, poliviewr$sex, suspect_set = 13, focal_name='2')
SIBTEST(poliscored, poliviewr$sex, suspect_set = 14, focal_name='2')
SIBTEST(poliscored, poliviewr$sex, suspect_set = 15, focal_name='2')
SIBTEST(poliscored, poliviewr$sex, suspect_set = 16, focal_name='2')
SIBTEST(poliscored, poliviewr$sex, suspect_set = 17, focal_name='2')
SIBTEST(poliscored, poliviewr$sex, suspect_set = 18, focal_name='2')

#DBF: differential bundle functioning: example for regulation
suspect_reg <- c(7, 13, 15, 17)

SIBTEST(poliscored, poliviewr$sex, suspect_set=suspect_reg, focal_name='2')
sink() # return output to console
```

Chapter 11

EFA of political viewpoint data:

```
## load packages
library(psych)
library(readxl)

## CIRP poliview data 1999
poliview <- read_excel(path = "political viewpoint data.xlsx", sheet = "poliview")
poliview <- as.data.frame(poliview)
```

```
## listwise deletion of missing data needed for sibtest
poliviewr <- na.omit(poliview)
dim(poliviewr)

## Extract Test Items
resp_pol <- poliviewr[,2:19]
dim(resp_pol)

##use reverse.code function from psych package
polikey <- c(1,-1,-1,-1,-1,1,1,-1,-1,1,1,1,-1,-1,1,1,1,-1)
poliscored <- reverse.code(polikey,resp_pol,mini=rep(1,18),maxi=rep(4,18))
str(poliscored)
head(poliscored)

sink("poliview efa 5 factors.txt", append=TRUE)

##parallel analysis to estimate number of factors
fa.parallel(poliscored,fm="minres")

## EFA on poliview data
fa(r=poliscored,nfactors=5,rotate= "oblimin")

sink() # return output to console
```

EFA of TIMSS Booklet 1:

```
## load packages
library(psych)
library(readxl)

bk1 <- read_excel("TIMMS 2003 Math data.xlsx",sheet = "book 1")
names(bk1)
str(bk1)

## Extract Test Items
resp_bk1 <- bk1[-1:-3]
dim(resp_bk1)

##use score.multiple.choice function from psych package
bk1key <- c(1,3,4,4,2,3,2,3,3,2,4,5,1,3,1,4,1,2,2,3)
bk1scored <- score.multiple.choice(bk1key,resp_bk1,score=FALSE)

sink("efa timss booklet 1.txt", append=TRUE)

##parallel analysis to estimate number of factors
fa.parallel(bk1scored, cor="tet",fm="ml")
```

```
## EFA on timss data
fa(r=bk1scored,nfactors=8,fm="ml", cor="tet",rotate= "quartimax")
fa(r=bk1scored,nfactors=8,fm="ml", cor="tet",rotate= "oblimin")
fa(r=bk1scored,nfactors=6,fm="ml", cor="tet",rotate= "bifactor")

sink() # return output to console
```

CFA of TIMSS Booklet 1:

```
## load packages
library(lavaan)
library(psych)
library(readxl)

bk1 <- read_excel("TIMMS 2003 Math data.xlsx",sheet = "book 1")
names(bk1)
str(bk1)

## Extract Test Items
resp_bk1 <- bk1[-1:-3]
dim(resp_bk1)

##use score.multiple.choice function from psych package
bk1key <- c(1,3,4,4,2,3,2,3,3,2,4,5,1,3,1,4,1,2,2,3)
bk1scored <- score.multiple.choice(bk1key,resp_bk1,score=FALSE)

#sink function directs output to a text file.
sink("cfa of timss book1 w lavaan.txt", append=TRUE)


## lavaan code starts here. First, the model is specified.
timss.mod5 <- 'number =~ M012001 + M012004 + M012041 + M032570 + M032643 + M012016
            measurement =~ M012003 + M012038 + M012013
            geometry =~ M012005 + M012039 + M012015
            data =~ M012006 + M012037 + M012014
            algebra =~ M012002 + M012040 + M012042 + M022251
            '
## Then, lavaan runs the CFA.
fit5 <- cfa(timss.mod5, data=bk1scored)

##The next three lines extracts various outputs.
##Inspect lets the user verify that the model is setup correctly.
```

```
##Summary provides the basic results.
##lavInspect provides the correlation matrix between the five domains.

inspect (fit5)
summary(fit5, standardized=TRUE, fit.measures=TRUE)
lavInspect(fit5, "cor.lv")

timss.mod1 <- 'math =~ M012001 + M012004 + M012041 + M032570 + M032643 + M012016
               + M012003 + M012038 + M012013
               + M012005 + M012039 + M012015
               + M012006 + M012037 + M012014
               + M012002 + M012040 + M012042 + M022251
               '
fit1 <- cfa(timss.mod1, data=bk1scored)
inspect (fit1)
summary(fit1, standardized=TRUE, fit.measures=TRUE)

##This code provides a comparison of fit indices between the 5- and 1-score models.
fit5d <- fitmeasures(fit5,fit.measures = c("rmsea","tli","cfi",'rmsr',"AIC","BIC"))
fit1d <- fitmeasures(fit1,fit.measures = c("rmsea","tli","cfi",'rmsr',"AIC","BIC"))
rbind(fit5d,fit1d)

sink() # return output to console
```

INDEX

Correction for attenuation, 101
Credentialing, test development, 10–11
Criterion model of validity, 32–33, 37
Criterion-referenced score interpretation, 19–20, 66, 186, 203, 309
  frame of reference, 130
  polytomously scored items, 210
  scaling, 72–73
Criterion-related evidence, 35
Cronbach, L. J., 34–35, 37, 39
CTT. *See* Classical Test Theory (CTT)
Cureton, E. E., 32, 33
Cut scores, 52

D

Data sets, 369
DBF. *See* Differential bundle functioning (DBF)
Decision inference, 52, 363
  Grit Scale—Kane version, 364
Descriptive statistics
  census, 21
  central tendency, 22–23
  correlation coefficient, 24
  dispersion, 23
  parameters, 21
  Pearson correlation, 24, 26
  phi coefficient, 26
  point biserial correlation coefficient, 26
  quantitative variables, 23–24
  summation operator, 21–22
Dichotomously scored items
  binary Rasch model, 231, 232 (table), 251
  biserial conversion factors, 196, 196 (table)
  differential item functioning (DIF), 261–273
  distractor analysis, 196–197, 197 (table)
  exploratory factor analysis (EFA), 296–298, 297 (figure), 298 (table), 299 (table)
  item difficulty, 193–194
  item discrimination, 194–195
  item-total correlation, 195, 195 (table)
  Mantel–Haenszel methods, 261–265
  multiple-choice items, 202–204
  SIBTEST, 266–272
  TIMSS Booklet 1, 198–201 (figure), 198–202
Differential bundle functioning (DBF), 266, 277
  TIMSS Booklet 1, 273 (figure)
Differential item functioning (DIF), 257
  amplification, 266–267
  detection methods, 259, 261

dichotomously scored items, 261–273
  focal group, 259
  item bias, 258–259, 259 (table)
  logistic regression, 276–277
  Mantel method, 273
  Mantel-Haenszel method, 261–266
  Raju's DFIT, 277
  raw scores, by sex, 259–260, 260 (figure)
  reference group, 259
  SIBTEST, 266–273
  standardization, 277
  types, 260
  validity evidence, 277–278
Differential test functioning (DTF), 277
Dimensionality, 282–283
  assessing, 283–284
  confirmatory factor analysis (CFA), 284. *See* Confirmatory factor analysis (CFA)
  essential dimensionality, 284
  exploratory factor analysis (EFA), 283. *See also* Exploratory factor analysis (EFA)
  likelihood ratio test, 284
  principal components analysis (PCA) of residuals, 284
Direct Oblimin oblique rotation method, 291
Disattenuated correlation, 101–102
Distractor analysis, 196–197, 197 (table)
Dorans, N. J., 190, 273
Downing, S. M., 157
Duckworth, A. L., 127, 355

E

ECD. *See* Evidence-centered design (ECD)
Educational achievement, 16–17
Educational Measurement (Cureton), 16, 32, 38, 49, 257
Educational needs, 12
Educational Testing Service (ETS)
  Mantel–Haenszel methods, 263, 263 (table)
  SIBTEST, 270, 270 (table)
Education Longitudinal Survey, 187, 189 (figure)
EFA. *See* Exploratory factor analysis (EFA)
Egan, L. E., 320
Eigenvalues, 287
  exploratory factor analysis (EFA), 289, 290, 295, 295 (table)
Elements (Euclid), 5
Elman, B. A., 10
Emotional and Social Competence Inventory (ESCI), 137, 139
  external relationship model, 139–140

Łódź Ghetto Album

Łódź Ghetto Album

Photographs by Henryk Ross
Selected by Martin Parr & Timothy Prus
Foreword by Robert Jan van Pelt
Text by Thomas Weber

Boot

**ARCHIVE
OF MODERN
CONFLICT**

Contents

Foreword

Robert Jan van Pelt

Leafing through a binder with photos taken by Henryk Ross in the Lodz ghetto, I could not escape the anger and compassion that always rises when I confront the abomination of the Nazi ghettos in Poland. The rage and the pity are not difficult to explain. Even after working as a Holocaust historian for two decades, I have not become used to the pictures of the rag-clad urchins scavenging scraps of food, the dejected grown-ups trading their last meagre possession which no-one needs, and the harrowed people pulling the excrement wagons. The stolen images of the public hangings, the corpses awaiting burial and the anguish of the deportations to the death camps still nauseate me. These are the photos I know well: images that have been published in general histories of the Holocaust, or more focused accounts of the Lodz ghetto.

But as I turned the pages of the binder, there were other photos that I had never seen before; pictures that caused a feeling of apprehension and even an unexpected annoyance. There were photos showing well-dressed children enjoying a party, of grown-ups acting up for the camera, and of the pleasures of a wedding reception. For me, and not only for me, these pictures testify to the uncomfortable fact that, amongst the pauperized and starving mass of ghetto inmates, in the wrenching situation imposed by the Germans, a small minority fared relatively well. These included those who occupied positions in the Jewish Council or its administration, or people who had been able to save some of their wealth, or opportunists who adapted to whatever opportunities existed in the bewildering ordeal of segregation, starvation, disease and slave labour.

I had read about these people, and the way they had been able to carve out small enclaves of relative privilege amidst a hell of cruelty and suffering. Both survivors, and others who had never suffered the world of the Nazi ghettos, reproached the favoured after the war for their lack of solidarity with those who had died just steps away. And they condemned those who had bought an exemption from deportation – one person's exemption being at the expense of someone else having to go. Many felt a shame that so many had grasped the opportunity to endure the ordeal with a degree of comfort – or with an illusion of control over a very uncertain future. How much more edifying was the self-sacrifice of a Janusz Korczak, who had protected his orphans while he could, and who then chose to share their death rather than seek his own safety. And thus these photos showing privilege amidst general destitution – some cheer amidst despair – did not find a place in the histories we published, to remain hidden in forbidden drawers and closed files.

Two generations after the Germans liquidated the Lodz ghetto, we are ready for the whole picture, and therefore need every single photograph. As I consider all of the images that Henryk Ross took and saved, the differences between the seemingly privileged and the obviously destitute fade in the knowledge that almost all of the people caught by his camera were murdered shortly thereafter. The pathos of this halts my all-too-easy reflections on the meaning and memory of social and economic distinctions in the anteroom of Auschwitz. It makes me shudder that, very likely, each of the pictures in this album is the last record of each of these people's unique lives. In the face of this forlorn fact, there remains nothing but to cease conversation and return to observation.

Robert Jan van Pelt, Toronto, March 2004

Introduction

Thomas Weber

When it became clear to Nazi leaders in the summer of 1944 that their dream of establishing a 1,000-year Germanic Reich in Central and Eastern Europe was about to be crushed by the Red Army, they decided to liquidate their last remaining Jewish ghetto: Lodz. As the news reached the ghetto, a Jewish photographer rushed to hide his most precious possession. Henryk Ross, who had taken thousands of pictures of life under German occupation, buried his prints, negatives and other documents in the ground of the ghetto, either to be dug up so that they could bear witness to the persecution of European Jewry, or to vanish forever.

Ross's photographs were not lost. He and his wife Stefania were lucky to be among the few ghetto inmates (approximately five per cent) who survived the ghetto. After liberation, he salvaged the photos and began to make those depicting the atrocities of the ghetto available to the public. Together with the work of Mendel Grossman, the other Jewish photographer employed in the ghetto, Ross's photos provided a visual image for the horrors that were detailed in the written documents of Nazi perpetrators and described by survivors. His powerful accounts of the ghetto – dark pictures of faces of hunger and despair, of children searching the ground for something to eat, of deportations and hangings – became icons of the horrors of the Holocaust.

Yet for the next six decades, the majority of Ross's photos remained as unavailable as they had been when they lay buried in the ghetto's frozen ground. Only a small proportion were released during his lifetime, and it was not until 1997 – six years after his death – that they became accessible to independent scrutiny, when Ross's son made his collection available to the Archive of Modern Conflict in London. It consists of more than 6,000 items, including some 3,000 negatives, original copies of ghetto newspapers, 41 ghetto announcements, ghetto money, and personal effects such as Ross's identification card. In terms of its scope, all other photographic records of ghetto life pale in comparison.

'He did not seek beauty, for there was no beauty in the ghetto.' So wrote ghetto survivor Arieh Ben-Menahem about Mendel Grossman, in his afterword to Grossman's book of photographs *With a Camera in the Ghetto*. But Ross did see beauty – in mothers with their babies, lovers posing for the camera, the joy of children at a birthday party. And he saw it in the milieu of the ghetto's relatively privileged minority. These previously unpublished photographs are unexpected and challenging, and contrast vividly with the selection of images he made available for publication during his lifetime. What we begin to realize is that his prior selection served to illustrate a particular interpretation of ghetto life – one that was wholly in keeping with the collective memory of survivors. The new photographs, meanwhile, begin to change our iconography of ghetto life.

This book represents only the first inspection of the unseen photographs in Ross's collection, and the beginning of a process of their exploration. Most of the negatives are yet to be printed as individual photographs, and there is still much to learn from them. Ultimately, the collection has the potential to revolutionize the way in which we understand ghetto life during the Holocaust. The new photos encourage alternative readings of ghetto society and its leadership, class system and solidarity in the face of violence. They suggest that the ghetto population at large had to face many of the same dilemmas as the Jewish councillors, and lead us to revisit the question of collaboration and resistance across all social strata within the ghetto.

As soon as Nazi Germany occupied Poland in 1939, Poland's Jews were rounded up – forced to live in the newly established ghettos before ultimately being sent to the gas vans and chambers of death camps such as Auschwitz and Chelmno. The two most notorious ghettos were established in Warsaw and Lodz, the European towns with the largest Jewish

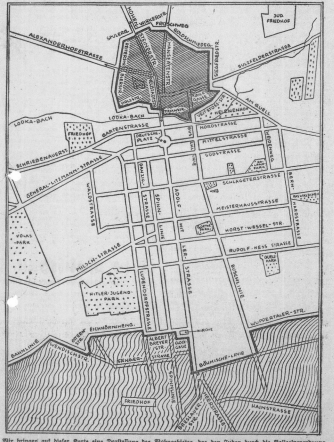

Die Wohngebiete der Juden und Polen

Wir bringen auf dieser Karte eine Darstellung des Wohngebietes, das den Juden durch die Polizeiverordnung vom 8. Februar als ausschließlicher Aufenthaltsraum zugewiesen wurde (schräg schraffiert), sowie der beiden Durchfahrtsstraßen durch dieses Gebiet (durch durchgehende Pfeile gekennzeichnet). Durch Wellenlinien ist das Gebiet bezeichnet, das als neuer Wohnraum der Polen bestimmt wurde. Die Abgrenzung dieses Viertels nach Osten, Süden und Westen zu bildet von der Verlängerung der Nordgrenze an die Stadtgrenze.

Map of Lodz published in the German newspaper *Der Lodscher Tag* on 11/12 February 1940, at the time of the first German order for Jews to move to the ghetto. The area of the ghetto was later enlarged, before it was fenced in.

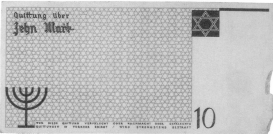

'The above photograph shows the excavation of the box containing documents and photographs of life in the Lodz ghetto from 1940 to 1944. The excavation was attended by my wife Stefania Ross, Zenon Goldreich with his wife, and Jacob Urbach, all of whom were in the Lodz ghetto. We buried the box with documents and my photographs in the ghetto (12 Jagielonska Street) during the final liquidation' – Ross in *The Last Journey*.

A ten-Mark note of ghetto currency. The German authorities confiscated the money of all Jews in the ghetto, replacing it with ghetto currency by way of a 'receipt'. The only legal tender inside the ghetto, it had no value outside.

populations. Lodz alone had a pre-war Jewish population of 223,000, which made up 34 per cent of the local population.

Initially, the ghettos were established as a provisional measure pending a decision on the fate of European Jewry. Soon, Polish Jews were joined by Jews deported from 'Greater Germany' and other occupied territories. Having little in common with the traditional Jewish quarters that had existed in European cities prior to Jewish emancipation, the ghettos fenced Jews into confined areas. Often referred to as the 'antechambers of hell', they were in fact an integral part of the hell the Nazis constructed for European Jewry; Joseph Goebbels, the German propaganda minister, simply called them 'death boxes'. It is estimated that approximately 500,000 Jews, or one in twelve Holocaust victims, died in a ghetto.

Following the German occupation of Poland, the country was partitioned according to a secret agreement between Hitler and Stalin. The western part came under German control, and this territory was itself divided, so that the western portion was incorporated into the German Reich as the so-called Warthegau. Lodz, the second-largest city in Poland, lay at the heart of this area. The Germans confined Jews from all over the Warthegau at Lodz – or Litzmannstadt as they renamed it in 1940, after Karl Litzmann, the German general who had conquered the city in World War I.

In May 1940, Lodz became the first ghetto to be hermetically sealed off by fences and barbed wire. Ross and approximately 164,000 other Jews (as well as people who were considered to be Jews under Nazi-German law) were squeezed into an area of roughly 1.5 square miles. Anybody trying to approach the fence from the inside with the suspected intention of crossing over to the 'Aryan' side was shot.

The Germans ran the ghetto through the principle of 'indirect rule', establishing a Jewish Council, or self-administration, under Chaim Rumkowski, who was more willing to comply with German orders than most other Jewish leaders and was to become one of the most controversial Jewish figures of the Holocaust. After the start of the full-scale implementation of the 'Final Solution' in late 1941 and 1942 (calling for the annihilation of all the Jews in Europe), tens of thousands were transported from the ghetto directly to the extermination camp of Chelmno, where they were killed in gas vans. Yet for the Germans, the ghetto was not just a place in which to concentrate the Jews before sending them to their deaths; it provided a huge source of cheap labour. It has been estimated that the ghetto administration made a profit of 350 million Reichsmark by exploiting it.

In the final phase of the war, as the Red Army was advancing towards the region, the German authorities liquidated the ghetto, sending most of its remaining 70,000 inhabitants to Auschwitz and subsequently to other camps. Allied forces arrived before their work was complete; 5,000 to 7,000 Jews were saved, the largest number of survivors in any Jewish ghetto in the East.

We know relatively little about Henryk Ross's life. Born on 1 May 1910 in Warsaw, he worked in Lodz for a Warsaw newspaper before the war, accredited as a sports photographer. Shortly before the Germans invaded Poland, Ross was called to arms. He fought with the Polish army against the invading forces, returning to Lodz after Germany's victory in October 1939. In January 1940, he was forced to move to the part of the city that was designated as the ghetto, and soon found himself confined there. He became one of two official Jewish ghetto photographers at Lodz, employed from late 1940 by the Jewish administration's Department of Statistics. Along with his colleague Mendel Grossman, Ross's job was to take official propaganda pictures and to produce the thousands of identification photographs of ghetto inhabitants required by the Germans.

Both Ross's and Grossman's work gave them permanent access to cameras, film and darkroom equipment, which they used to document the horrors of the ghetto, risking their lives in the process. 'The conditions for taking photographs were extremely difficult', Ross recalled. 'The photographic materials were smuggled to me in exchange for bread, of which I had far too little.' Recounting the circumstances behind a photograph of deportations that he took at the ghetto's railway station in 1944 (see page 87), Ross explains how railway workers smuggled him into the station:

I was locked in a store from where I was able, through a hole in the wood, to photograph this deportation. After being locked in for fourteen hours, the workers who conspired with me

let me out. It was extremely dangerous for me. When the remaining residents of the ghetto were deported to Auschwitz in August 1944, Ross was one of about 800 men and women who stayed behind as members of a clean-up commando. The German authorities had planned to liquidate the members of this team and, as survivors later recorded, a mass grave had already been dug for them, but a German had tipped them off, allowing them the opportunity to go into hiding. They escaped detection and in January 1945, Soviet troops liberated Lodz.

After the war, Henryk and Stefania Ross stayed in Lodz. There, they had two sons, and Ross continued to work as a photographer. In 1950, like many other Polish Jews who had survived the Holocaust, they decided to emigrate to the newly founded Israel, where Ross worked as a photographer and zincographer. In Israel, he embarked on the difficult task of getting his ghetto photos out of Poland. He later described how some were destroyed in Poland, with those saved sent to Israel through the Israeli consulate; how 'for some reason' negatives were lost in Israel, but 'thanks to the intervention of David Ben-Gurion and Consul Satat, some of the negatives were found.'

Grossman, unlike Ross, did not survive the Holocaust, but his photos were rescued after liberation and were taken to Palestine, where the vast majority disappeared during the Israeli War of Independence. The surviving pictures of both photographers soon became keystones in the visual representation of German-inflicted horrors of ghetto life by Holocaust museums and books on the Shoah. They were also used as evidence in the trial of the main administrator of the Holocaust, Adolf Eichmann, in Jerusalem in 1961. Ross himself appeared in the witness box and also gave evidence in 1974 in a German trial against a member of the Gestapo. In the catalogue of his photos compiled in 1987, four years before his death, he expressed what had driven him in the ghetto. 'I wanted to leave a record of our martyrdom', he wrote, stressing the mortal dangers to which he had exposed himself.

This account of Ross's life is the story of a man who met the challenge of German terror with bravery. War and genocide transformed him into a hero, and his life represented the moral victory of the forces of good against evil. But is this the full story? Does the unpublished part of his collection support such a reading? And why did he not make more of his pictures public during his lifetime?

One straightforward explanation for Ross's decision not to release many of his photographs during his lifetime could be that he simply considered them private – being domestic scenes, many featuring his wife, recorded for personal reasons or for the albums of the people depicted. It would hardly be surprising if he considered these historically less interesting or important than photos of executions and deportations. Furthermore, there's the question of how public taste and historical interest has shifted over time. Photographs of quieter, less dramatic moments may now be considered more powerful than was the case after the war. We have become familiar with scenes of Holocaust atrocities, as well as with violent news imagery in general, while arguably more receptive to intimate domestic pictures. An illustration of this is provided by a scene in Roman Polanski's film about the Warsaw ghetto, *The Pianist* (2003). The father of a family rounded up for deportation spends his last few coins buying a piece of chocolate, dividing

Ghetto identity card of
Henryk Ross.

Henryk Ross taking ID photos
in the ghetto. Producing
several ID photos in a single
frame allowed him to save film
for other purposes.

The wooden bridge crossing Zigerska, the 'Aryan' street, connecting the two main parts of the ghetto, as published by Ross in *The Last Journey*. See also page 29.

Two pages from Ross's book *The Last Journey*.

it into six parts with his penknife to become the final shared meal of the family before they are separated, en route to the death camp. It proves to be far more devastating than the film's more sensational or violent scenes.

But these explanations do not wholly account for why Ross did not make more of his photographs available during his lifetime. Comparing those he released with those he withheld, it seems clear that his post-war decisions were specifically intended to serve a particular interpretation of ghetto history. Indeed, the published photographic record of the ghetto generally should be treated with the same degree of caution that one should apply to any historical account based on memory, including Holocaust survivors' written and oral accounts. True, authentic images of the ghetto provide contemporary documentary evidence, free from the mediating influence of memory, trauma and post-Holocaust identity. Yet once survivors become involved in the process of choosing which photos to include or exclude, inevitably they will be offering a version of life in the ghetto based on post-war experiences. Hence they cease to be either unmediated accounts of experiences, or pure snapshots of history.

The issue is not whether this is right or wrong. It is simply to underline the problems that arise when one treats photographs as unbiased documents that 'speak for themselves'. Only recently, in the wake of the controversial exhibition *War of Annihilation: Crimes of the Wehrmacht* (opened in Hamburg in 1995 and then presented throughout Germany) did a broad discussion begin about the danger of using photographs as illustrations for a particular historical interpretation – rather than as historical sources in their own right.

Examples of the selective use of Lodz photographs to present a particular interpretation of ghetto life are the two photographic books of Ross and Grossman's work – Ross's *The Last Journey of the Jews of Lodz*, published in an undated edition in Israel during the 1960s, and *With a Camera in the Ghetto*, Grossman's posthumously edited photographs published in Tel Aviv by the Ghetto Fighters' House in 1970. Ross himself chose the photographs for the first book, while Aleksander Klugman, another survivor of the ghetto, was the book's editor. While *With a Camera* was not edited by survivors of the ghetto, the selection of photos was clearly influenced by survivors; the editors acknowledge the help of Grossman's sister, and of another two survivors, Nachman Zonabend and Arieh Ben-Menahem, in bringing the book together.

The photos in both books depict scenes of hunger, despair and death. Typical examples would be the picture of an emaciated boy lying in the street, or the image of the distressed woman on a cart during a deportation (see pages 44 and 74). There is no doubt these are true testimonies of the horrors of the ghetto, and yet they are not presented as documents in their own right. Rather they are used as powerful illustrations of a particular understanding of ghetto life – as shaped by the emerging collective memory of survivors.

Ross even modified at least one photo in his book so that it would support this view more effectively. One can see this by comparing the image reproduced, without retouching, from a damaged negative (see page 29) with the repaired image that appeared in Ross's book (opposite). The photograph depicts the 'Aryan street' running through the ghetto, and it is clear that Ross added liberal quantities of barbed wire to the fences on either side, thus dramatizing his source material to support his memory of the ghetto.

Another photograph of a heap of decapitated corpses (see page 48) appears in Ross's book with the caption: 'The corpses "supplied" the fat, the fat became soap …'. Opposite it he placed a photograph of a bar of soap bearing the letters 'RIF', explaining this as 'RIF – soap – made out of Jewish fat'. Ross was contributing to a story that had at some

Bekanntmachung Nr 391.

Betr.:

Allgemeine Gehsperre im Getto.

Ab Sonnabend,
den **5.** September **1942** **um 17 Uhr,**
ist im Getto bis auf Widerruf eine

ALLGEMEINE GEHSPERRE.

Ausgenommen hiervon sind:

Feuerwehrleute, die Transportabteilung, Fäkalien- und Müllarbeiter, Warenannahme am Baluter Ring und Radegast, Aerzte und Apothekerpersonal.

Die Passierscheine müssen beim Ordnungsdienstvorstand — Hamburgerstrasse 1 — beantragt werden.

Alle Hauswächter

sind verpflichtet darauf zu achten, dass keine fremden Personen in die für sie zuständigen Häuser gelangen, sondern sich nur die Einwohner des Hauses dortselbst aufhalten.

Diejenigen, die ohne Passierscheine auf der Strasse angetroffen werden, werden evakuiert.

Die Hausverwalter

müssen in ihrem Häuserblock mit den Hausbüchern zur Verfügung stehen.

Jeder Hauseinwohner hat seine Arbeitskarte bei sich zu halten.

ARCHIWUM I.ROSS

CH. RUMKOWSKI
Der Aelteste der Juden in Litzmannstadt.

Litzmannstadt-Getto, 5. September 1942.

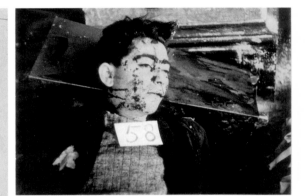

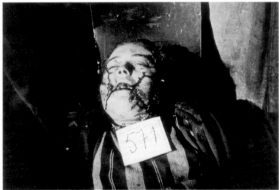

Ghetto announcement No. 391 from 5 September 1942, announcing the 'Gehsperre' (literally, 'curfew') during which some 20,000 children, sick, and elderly of the ghetto were deported to Chelmno.

The bodies of two Jews, killed during the Gehsperre of September 1942, lying in the eulogy hall of the ghetto's cemetery, awaiting burial. It is not clear whether these photographs were made as part of the photographer's official duties, or secretly as a way of allowing relatives to link the gravediggers' number to a particular person, and hence to a particular burial site.

point entered the collective memory of a section of the Holocaust survivor community, but research has shown that it is almost certainly a myth. 'RIF' did not stand for 'Reines Jüdisches Fett' (Pure Jewish Fat), as popularly believed, but for 'Reichstelle für Industrielle Fettversorgung' (Reich Agency for Supply of Fats). Soap bearing these initials had been in circulation before the Holocaust started, and chemical examinations of 'RIF' soap have uncovered no traces of human fat. That being so, Ross could not have witnessed what he suggests. Thus we need to treat his book less as a collection of documentary evidence, and more as an expression of mediated experience.

There are also some apparent contradictions between Ross's statements about how he gathered photographs and evidence within the pictures themselves. He repeatedly stressed the danger involved in taking the photographs of deportees being loaded on to trains destined for the death camps, telling us that he was able to do this only by being smuggled by railway workers out of the ghetto to the train station. Yet if that was true, how could he have taken photographs of deportations underway, outside the ghetto perimeter and under the eyes of the ghetto police (see pages 84 and 85)? Without doubt, Ross would have been shot had he been caught recording the German guards at work, herding Jews on to train carriages. But was he exaggerating the danger posed by the Jewish police? Perhaps in an attempt to portray himself as part of the underground? Or to distance himself from their milieu and in turn from their relationship to the Jewish Council?

Ross is by no means alone in his selective and sometimes rhetorical use of Holocaust images. This can be seen in the iconography surrounding Rumkowski. His vanity and obsession with power soon earned him the name 'King of the Ghetto', 'Chaim I' or 'Dictator', and he has often been seen as the archetypal traitor for the extent of his co-operation with the Germans. He is accused of ruthlessly handing over tens of thousands of Jews to the Germans, whilst excusing himself with the claim that he had to 'act decisively, like a surgeon who cuts a limb so the heart won't stop beating'. He is also accused by some survivors of sexually abusing children. According to a widely believed myth, Rumkowski was thrown alive into the furnace at Auschwitz by former ghetto inmates for his crimes against the community. It is little surprise, then, that photos of the Council leader in publications on ghetto life and in the world's Holocaust museums have tended to select photos that depict him as an aggressive, autocratic and brutal ruler, often using an unflattering low-angle shot of him taken whilst making a speech.

Likewise, the condemnation of ghetto policemen, accused after the war of willingly becoming the Germans' henchmen, has been translated into an iconography that supports this reading. It is no surprise that it is the photo of ghetto policemen arresting Jews trying to escape from the hospital (during the mass deportations of the Gehsperre in September 1942, see page 70) that has become one of the best-known representations of their work.

The underlying message conveyed by these traditional representations is that Jews in the ghetto were at the mercy not only of the barbarism of the Germans but also of the ghetto administration itself. In recent years, however, an increasing number of historians and observers have been more favourable in their portrayal of Rumkowski, pointing out that his collaboration with the Germans was a potentially viable survival strategy. Realizing that the only value the Jews had for the Germans was in terms of their labour, he concluded that the best chance of survival for as many Jews as possible was to employ a 'Rescue through Work' strategy. Thus he turned the ghetto into a thriving workshop, specializing in the production of clothing and military uniforms. And for a while, it seemed effective: the Lodz ghetto both survived longer than any other ghetto in Poland and had the highest survival rate. It should also be stressed that Jewish leaders had no way of knowing what the future would bring. Had the Russian advance moved faster in 1944, tens of thousands of Jews may have been liberated before the liquidation of the ghetto began. And had Hitler died on 20 July 1944, when he narrowly escaped an attempt on his life by German officers, 70,000 Jews would almost certainly have survived in the ghetto.

Unlike the traditional representation of Rumkowski, photographs in Ross's collection render him a more benign figure, more like a good-natured grandfather than a traitor to his people (see page 50). More significantly, many of Ross's pictures defy the canonical representation of ghetto policemen, depicting them as friendly community figures who cared for others as lovers, husbands and fathers. Again, this supports the view that the negative visual representation of Rumkowski and the Jewish police has been the result of a tendency to find and publish photos that reflected a particular point of view about ghetto life.

There may be other reasons contributing to Ross only making available those photos that supported the conventional reading of ghetto life. It may stem from an increasing marginalization from the section of the survivor community that was most closely involved with the institutions dedicated to Holocaust remembrance. Generations of writers and publishers on the Lodz ghetto have largely ignored him. Institutions such as YIVO, the Institute of Jewish Research in New York, which held many Lodz ghetto photographs, had little contact with him. What seems to have occurred is a falling out within the survivor community.

To understand what happened it is necessary to go back to the immediate post-war period and look at the interaction of those who were to become some of the key players in the visual remembrance of the ghetto. After the war, the Lodz survivor Aleksander Klugman accused another survivor, Nachman Zonabend, of having been a Gestapo agent. Zonabend recalled the incident in 1991:

In the summer of 1948 the Warsaw paper Dos Naye Leben published an article by a certain Aleksander Klugman, an aspiring Party hack from Lodz, keen to make a quick career. The article – entitled 'How a Gestapo man, Nachman Zonabend, became a martyr in the New York "Yedijes fun Yivo"' – presented me as a Gestapo agent stained with the blood of Jewish victims.

Zonabend had been a Lodz postman, subsequently employed by the Department of Construction at the ghetto railway station and at the meat packing centre. He later stated that he was friends with Grossman and Ross in the ghetto.

Like Ross, Zonabend survived the ghetto and after liberation retrieved documents and photographs hidden there, donating them to institutions in Israel, and to YIVO in New York, where they are held in a collection bearing his name. In 1955, Zonabend sent at least two letters from Sweden, where he then lived, to Ross in Israel, attempting to persuade him to collaborate on a book of photos, along with Mendel Grossman's, to commemorate the tenth anniversary of the liberation of the ghetto. As drafts of a design for the book indicate (opposite), Ross started work on the project but the book was never published. It would seem that Ross and Zonabend had some kind of disagreement since Ross chose instead to bring out his own book, with Zonabend's nemesis Aleksander Klugman as its editor.

A few years after Ross's book appeared, Mendel Grossman's *With a Camera in the Ghetto* was published, with the help of Zonabend. Curiously, it contained a number of photos that had already appeared in Ross's book. Since then, many publications and archives have attributed photos to Grossman for which negatives exist in the Ross collection. At least seven of the photos published in this book, for example, have been attributed to Grossman elsewhere.

Even the catalogue of *Unser Weg ist Arbeit* (*Our Way is Work*), the large photographic exhibition on the history of Lodz held in 1990 at the Jewish

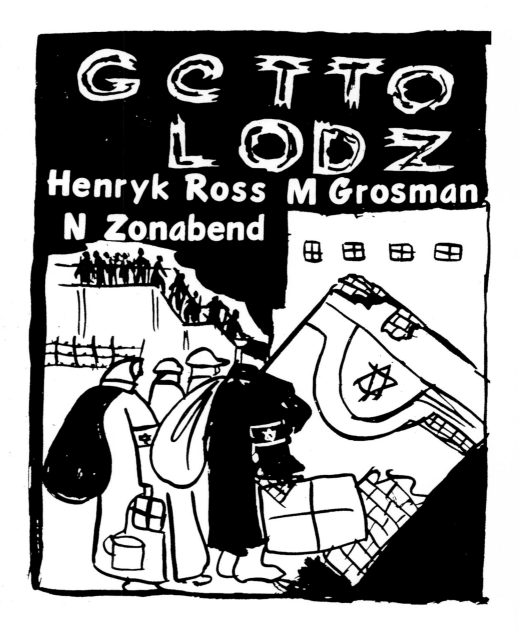

GCTTO LODZ
Henryk Ross M Grosman
N Zonabend

Design for a book of
ghetto photographs that
Henryk Ross and Nachman
Zonabend, another survivor
of the ghetto, started work on
during the 1950s. The book
never was published and
Ross and Zonabend seem
to have fallen out.

Members of the postal service of the ghetto – an official photograph of the kind Ross was required to produce. Prints of some of Ross's official photographs survive in the archive, without negatives.

Montage, showing Ross and two of his ghetto co-workers at the Department of Statistics. The poster in the background advertises an exhibition about the economic success of the ghetto, referring to 1,048,290 uniforms and other items of workers' clothing produced in the ghetto at the time. It was part of Ross's work to produce propaganda posters such as this. The superimposed ghetto postage stamp shows the head of Chaim Rumkowski,

the Chairman of the Jewish Council, as well as Ross's photograph of the ghetto's defining landmark – the wooden bridge across Zigerska Street.

Museum of Frankfurt while Ross was still alive, did not dignify his post-war history beyond a buried reference in a caption to page 178: 'Henryk Ross survived the liquidation of the ghetto in hiding and now lives in Tel Aviv'. The omission is all the more surprising given that the catalogue, published for the general book market, included many articles about the ghetto and its photographic history, as well as pieces written by survivors. Similarly, the 1990 *Encyclopedia of the Holocaust* included an entry on Grossman, written by Arieh Ben-Menahem, yet none on Ross. When, four years later, the English edition of the memoirs of the Lodz survivor Riva Chirurg were published, the editor informed readers that 'apart from Grossman both Rumkowski and the Germans photographed the life of the Jews in Lodz', without even mentioning Ross.

The photos published here for the first time raise the question of whether Ross might have been more involved with the ghetto elite than he was willing to admit. His pictures of ghetto 'dignitaries' often depict their private and domestic lives, rather than showing them at official occasions. They have the intimate character of family photographs. How could Ross have gained access to their gardens and houses if he was not privy to this life himself? The dignitaries, policemen and their families depicted do not seem to be responding to a stranger, or even to an official photographer, but appear to be at ease in his presence. This suggests the possibility that Ross had been shunned by part of the survivor community because they knew, or assumed, that he had intermingled with the privileged of the ghetto; that he had been able to live a relatively easy life whilst others around him were dying.

Tempting though this explanation might be, it is ultimately unsatisfactory since it follows the tendency among survivors, historians and other observers to discuss collaboration and resistance as a problem only faced by the Jewish councils, ghetto policemen and the very small group of people around them. According to this view, ghetto life beyond the Council and its policemen was characterized by humane solidarity. As the historian Yehuda Bauer recently remarked, 'The Poor helped those that were poorer'.

Reality was less lofty. In the face of violence, human bonds disintegrated as often as they were strengthened. Yet this aspect of the ghetto experience has often been edited out of the story. Even beyond the question of the degree to which Ross intermingled with the ghetto 'elite', in both his case and in Grossman's, resistance and collaboration were not mutually exclusive concepts. No doubt, both photographers exposed themselves to mortal dangers when taking documentary pictures of executions or deportations. This work was certainly an act of resistance. Had they been caught, these acts of bravery would have meant their instant death. In an article on Grossman, Arieh Ben-Menahem has stressed that the Department of Statistics of the Jewish Council, for whom both Grossman and Ross worked, collected 'all the true information concerning the ghetto', thus allocating it a heroic role. At the same time, however, it was the very institution that drew up the list of deportees. And since they agreed to be employed by it, Ross and Grossman could be called collaborators. The Germans were dependent on the department's work in order to carry out the Holocaust, and rejection of its terms of employment would have meant they, rather than others, ended up on the deportation lists.

In September 1942, during the Gehsperre, the German authorities decreed that all children, as well as the sick and elderly in the ghetto, were to be deported, since they had no 'labour value'. However, it was not only the German SD (Sicherheitsdienst) – as Ross incorrectly claimed when he gave his graphic testimony in the witness box in the Eichmann trial – who rounded up the children for deportation. The German authorities maliciously delegated a major part of the job to Rumkowski, allowing him a certain number of exemptions. He used his power to exclude the children of policemen, fire fighters and anyone who would volunteer to participate in the rounding-up of the ghetto's children. Contrary to the orthodox view, therefore, all inmates who wished to save their offspring from deportation had to face the same kinds of dilemma as those confronting the Council and the police force.

For ghetto inhabitants to have survived until 1944, and thus to have maintained even a slim chance of survival, tended to require more than good luck. The Germans had delegated the power to distribute food rations to the Council, and all those who were fit and willing to work received higher rations. This meant that the ability and, equally importantly, the willingness to work, as well as compliance with Rumkowski's orders, ensured better food rations at a time when death rates from starvation (or from tuberculosis, often triggered by malnutrition) were staggering.

But specific choices enabling survival often went further than that. The German authorities gave Rumkowski and his Council the choice either to draw up lists for deportation to the extermination camp at Chelmno, or to face the liquidation of the entire ghetto. The Council first entered the names of all those who had ever spoken up against it, as well as 'criminals', along with their entire families. Often the only crime that many of these had committed was to steal potato peelings in order to save their families from starvation. When the Germans demanded yet more Jews for deportation, the Jewish administration earmarked for death everybody unfit or unwilling to work (and thus unable to contribute to and collaborate with the German war effort). In other words, it was not only the policemen who had to face the dilemma of whether or not to increase their families' chances of survival by effectively doing the Germans' work. 'Ordinary' ghetto inmates were given the choice of whether to collaborate with the Germans by working in the ghetto's factories, or to receive food rations that were so low they made survival well nigh impossible – or to face deportation.

Ultimately, the vast majority of ghetto inhabitants (at least 95 per cent), irrespective of their position in the ghetto and of the decisions they had taken there, perished in the Holocaust. A third of the prisoners died of starvation or disease within the ghetto. After liquidations recommenced in 1944 with the Red Army advancing, almost the entire ghetto population, including Rumkowski himself, died in Auschwitz or on death marches. As he later stated, Ross had become so emaciated that by the time of liberation he weighed a mere 38 kg.

The picture that emerges is that generally only those inhabitants who chose to accept certain positions within the ghetto and to comply with Rumkowski's Council and thus with the Germans maintained any chance of survival. Ghetto residents were therefore, to a small degree at least, not just the objects of the Council and the Germans but, within narrow confines, also subjects of their own life and death decisions. Yet, if Jews actively took these decisions, can we still maintain that collaboration was only a phenomenon affecting a tiny minority of people around Rumkowski?

The conventional understanding of 'collaboration' is that it results from a positive decision, driven by personal and/or ideological gain, while 'co-operation' or 'involuntary collaboration' is forced upon victims without bringing them personal benefit. This distinguishes the behaviour of the Vichy collaborator (or the Quislings in Norway) and the Jews. However the Jewish administrators of Lodz do not fit neatly into this model, a problem that Primo Levi addressed in his essay 'The Grey Zone'. He argued that the moral behaviour of people like Rumkowski was not black or white, good or bad, but grey and ambiguous. Still, Levi's argument depends on the idea that 'good' and 'bad' behaviour in the ghetto was possible – with the moral conduct of some Jewish councillors, policemen or Kapos falling somewhere in the middle.

Yet, as we have seen, human behaviour in the Holocaust generally involved collaboration and resistance *at the same time*. Jews who clearly did

A montage depicting the clandestine photographic activity of members of the ghetto's Department of Statistics. In the background is the reproduction of a decree that no members of the Department could leave their workplace without prior permission.

not agree with Nazi ideology often decided to co-operate with the Nazis, and thus to contribute to the machinery of the Holocaust, in the hope that they would receive the most precious personal gain imaginable – survival – if only temporarily.

Even though the impossible dilemmas that the Nazis imposed on ghetto inmates made them collaborators of a kind, for the vast majority of survivors this was a long way away from the immoral collaboration of profiteers. For some, maybe for most, collaboration went hand in hand with resistance, the two intimately and necessarily related. Often, collaboration was the prerequisite to launch effective resistance. Rather than following the trend to categorize almost any Jewish behaviour during the Holocaust as either resistance or collaboration, a more nuanced discussion is required, distinguishing between the conscious and unconscious, voluntary and involuntary, informed and uninformed, ideological and opportunistic, collusive and combative. As Bernard Wasserstein has argued:

> Collaboration … is best understood … as a palimpsest in which old loyalties are erased, new ones are written, those are rubbed out, and yet others are written, all to reflect a rapidly changing external environment. Modern war tries to reduce all loyalties to one. But in real life there are many and war does not get rid of them: loyalties to family, nation, class, ideology, army unit, generation, institutions, community all continue and indeed are often accentuated under pressure of war. The reality that war often brings to the fore is that these are frequently cross-cutting and sometimes competing loyalties.

Thus the picture of the Lodz ghetto that evolves from a critical exploration of the Ross Collection differs significantly from that offered by the traditional iconography and by an uncritical use of survivor accounts. However, it is not the intention here to criticize the decisions made by survivors in the ghetto in order to save their families. Nor is it to overlook the concerns of survivors that, as time passes, they will lose control over their memory of the Holocaust, or see Holocaust photos scrutinised in ways that detract from their function as sites for mourning. Nor does this account provide succour to Holocaust deniers, who threaten to rear up every time historians point to the dissonance between historic evidence and survivors' memories, ready to spin and misconstrue the evidence. On the contrary. The unfamiliar picture of life in the ghetto that Ross's previously unreleased photographs present only adds to our understanding of the diabolical crimes of Nazi Germany.

The decisions that Henryk Ross made during the Holocaust – as a Jew, a husband and a photographer – are marked by the navigation of competing loyalties and an almost-inevitable combination of heroism and compromise, collaboration and resistance. This does not make him exceptional. The scrutiny he is placed under here may be precisely what he sought to avoid during his lifetime by the selective release of his photographs. But he did not seek to avoid scrutiny indefinitely; he kept and preserved his archive and, before he died, prepared and catalogued it for future generations to make sense of. This decision may seem minor by comparison with his actions during the war, but it is brave all the same. What is exceptional is the archive that he leaves us. It deserves proper appreciation and attention by those of us seeking deeper knowledge and understanding of the Holocaust, and by students of the photograph exploring the moments where art and history collide.

Ross's photograph of the post-war trial of Hans Biebow (seated), Nazi administrator of the ghetto 1940-1944. Biebow was arrested in Germany after the war, tried in the Law Courts in Lodz, and executed in 1947.

Henryk Ross in the witness box at the trial of Adolf Eichmann, the administrative brain behind the Holocaust. Jerusalem, 2 May 1961.

The Photographs

Selected by Martin Parr & Timothy Prus

An explanation of the catalogue and a description of the photographs illegally taken by me in the Lodz ghetto (1940-1945).

In the above mentioned period, I took approximately 6,000 photographs of life in the Lodz ghetto.

I was engaged by the Department of Statistics for the Jewish community in the Lodz ghetto. My task was to take photographs for the above department which gave me the authority to have a camera. All the photographs I took for the Department of Statistics were buried by them and totally lost.

Having an official camera, I was secretly able to photograph the life of the Jews in the ghetto. Just before the closure of the ghetto (1944) I buried my negatives in the ground in order that there should be some record of our tragedy, namely the total elimination of the Jews from Lodz by the Nazi executioners. I was anticipating the total destruction of Polish Jewry. I wanted to leave a historical record of our martyrdom.

Having an official camera, I was able to capture all the tragic period in the Lodz ghetto. I did it knowing that if I were caught my family and I would be tortured and killed. The conditions for taking photographs were extremely difficult. The photographic materials were smuggled to me in exchange for bread, of which I had far too little. Unfortunately, some of the negatives were destroyed (in Poland). I sent the negatives which were saved to Israel through the Israeli consulate in Poland. For some reason, negatives were lost in that country [Israel]. Only thanks to the intervention of David Ben-Gurion and Consul Satat, some of the negatives were found (about 3,000).

I also brought from Poland about 2,000 photographs and original documents from the Lodz ghetto.

The negatives I made I have put in order, catalogued and provided explanations. These descriptions I was able to make with the help of my wife Stefania. During the whole of the time in the ghetto, she helped and sheltered me during the dangerous task of photographing.

It is forty-two years since the Lodz Ghetto was liquidated so there may be some small inaccuracies in the chronology.
Henryk Ross, Jaffa, 1987

A note on the photographs and captions
The photographs were selected in 2003 from the Henryk Ross Collection, acquired by the Archive of Modern Conflict in 1997. They were chosen from new contact sheets made from the surviving 3,000 negatives. Many bear the scars of damage that we assume results from their burial in the ghetto, and no attempt has been made to enhance or repair the photographs for publication.

The 'public' section features photographs that Ross released during his lifetime, along with previously unpublished photographs that are similar to or from the same sequences as those released by Ross. As far as we are aware, none of the 'private' photographs (or others similar to them) have been previously published.

Wherever possible, the photographs are captioned from Ross's 1987 catalogue, translated from the original Polish. Where a particular photograph is not referred to in the catalogue, its caption is sourced from his 1960s book *The Last Journey of the Jews of Lodz*. Some photographs are not captioned in either source. Additional captions and caption notes, shown in italics, are by Thomas Weber.
Martin Parr & Timothy Prus London, 2004

Public

The 'Aryan' street – Zigerska – cuts the ghetto in two.

*Remains of the synagogue
in Wolborska Street, which
was blown up by the German
authorities in 1940.*

Photograph of a Jew who
saved the Torah from
the rubble of the Synagogue
in Wolborska Street.

31

Street trading.

People 'borrowed' pieces of coal from time to time even if it was guarded. *This photograph appears to have been taken outside the ghetto perimeter.*

Window display of a shop
selling sweets and spices.

35

Winter street scene in the ghetto.

Street trading in winter.

Children washing items recovered from the ground of the ghetto.

Searching for food on
the ground.

Distribution of soup
in front of the kitchen.

The spoon scrapes the
bottom in vain.

43   Lunch break – soup for lunch.

Falling in the street
from hunger.

A corpse is taken away.

The gallows is in operation.

The corpses 'supplied' the fat, the fat became soap… *However, it was almost certainly a myth that human bodies were used to make soap at Lodz. This leaves no satisfactory explanation as to what exactly was being done with the human bodies in the scene depicted.*

Probably a ghetto hearse.

*Chaim Rumkowski,
the Chairman of the Jewish
Council.*

'Let them work till the
bitter end.'

Men carrying sewing-machine tables.

Tailoring Department.

One of the ghetto's garment
factories, with feathers being
attached to hats.

Removal of faeces.
An assignment as a 'fecal worker' was usually a death sentence, as workers soon contracted typhus.

At work.
Mendel Grossman is shown photographing the excavation of a central cesspit, dug at the end Francizkanska Street in 1941, supervised by ghetto policemen.

In the tannery.

The place for sorting.

We received a ration of potatoes, all of them frozen and not suitable for consumption.
Several ghetto records confirm that rations of potatoes frequently arrived frozen, and inedible, although this particular photograph appears not to have been taken during winter.

Veterinary hospital.

Cleaners.

Management of the
hospital kitchen.

Workers of the
hospital kitchen.

Ghetto police.

Great distress, deportation
from hospital. Attempted
escapes from being deported
from hospital in Lagiewnickiej.
*Photographed during the
Gehsperre, September 1942.*

Temporary asylum for children of ghetto 'dignitaries'. *During the Gehsperre, all children under 10 were deported from the ghetto apart from those of officials, and of volunteers willing to assist in the deportations.*

1941. Deportation –
registration and pinning
on numbers. 'There must
be order'.

Before deportation –
sale of belongings.
*Elsewhere, this is attributed
to Mendel Grossman and is
captioned 'Deportees from
towns in the area arrive at
the Lodz ghetto carrying their
possessions'.*

Transport of the sick and aged by horse-drawn carts. *This photograph is attributed to Mendel Grossman in* With a Camera, *where it is captioned 'Jews from Germany, Czechoslovakia, Austria and Luxembourg who were brought to the Lodz ghetto, are now being sent to the Chelmno death camp. 1942'.*

Farewells at the gate of the prison in Czarnecki Street. *Deportees were incarcerated at the ghetto prison before being deported.*

Scenes with other families.

What to do? How to save
or help them?
*At the prison in Czarnecki
Street.*

At the prison in Czarnecki Street.

At the prison in Czarnecki Street.

Transportation by tram
to the railway station at
Radogoszcz, thence to
the extermination camp.

More deportations.

Deportations.

Deportations.
An iconic image, sometimes attributed to Grossman, it has been previously published with different captions including 'Deportees from Vienna, October 1941' and 'Jews being deported to the Chelmno death camp, huddled on the ground at an assembly point, c. 1942.'

Radogszcz Station, from which the Lodz ghetto Jews were transported to concentration camps, was situated outside the boundaries of the Lodz ghetto. The right of entry was only for workers at the station. In order to immortalize the removal of the people from the ghetto, I stole into the station with a group of railway workers. I was locked in a store from where I was able, through a hole in the wood, to photograph this deportation (1944).

The scarecrow too has to
carry the yellow star.
*The photo was taken in the
garden of the ghetto hospital
at 36 Lagiewnicka Street.*

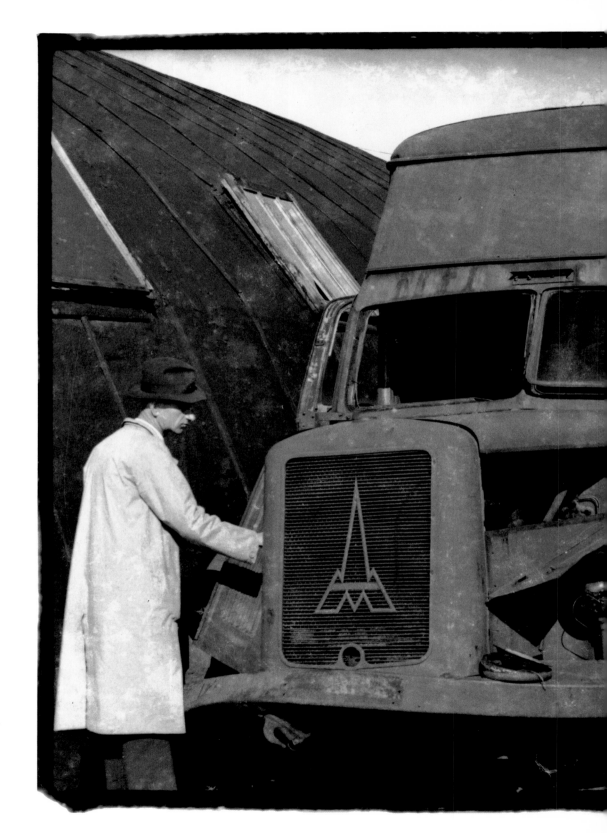

The death truck (picture taken after the Polish army entered Chelmno). *In Chelmno, unlike in other extermination camps, Jews were gassed in mobile gas vans, using a technique that had been developed for the T4 programme, the systematic killing of approximately 70,000 mentally-impaired people.*

Chelmno, the remains of
the crematorium.

Private

Life in the ghetto.
With happiness sometimes.

Ghetto residents.

Ghetto residents.

Ghetto residents.

Ghetto residents.
The above photograph shows
Ross's wife Stefania.

Ghetto residents.

Ghetto life.

Private photographs
of the Ghetto police.

Ghetto residents.
Another photo in the same sequence, unpublished here, shows the ghetto policeman (in the background above) as part of the group, suggesting the series depicts the social milieu of the police.

One of a series captioned by Ross as 'Personal guard of Ch. M. Rumkowski. Guard Ajzenman with his wife and children'.

113

A party involving members of the ghetto police.

This wooden bridge at Koscielny Square (Church Square) crossing Zigerska, the 'Aryan' street that cut through the ghetto – identified as likely to have been photographed from the building of the Statistics Department of the Jewish Council, Ross's employers.

Residents of the
Lodz ghetto.
*Ross photographs this boy
and his family at least 41
times although the only detail
he provides about them in
his catalogue is that they are
people 'with more money'.*

Children of the ghetto.
Playing as ghetto policemen.
*According to the information
provided by the Ghetto
Fighters' House, the photos
were taken on 22 October
1943 – more than a year after
the majority of ghetto children
were deported.*

Children of the ghetto.
Playing as ghetto policemen.

Ghetto children at a
reception given by those
with more money.

Ghetto children at a reception given by those with more money. *According to the Ghetto Fighters' House, this and the preceding photograph were taken in September 1943, one year after the deportation of the majority of the ghetto's children during the Gehsperre.*

Pictures from the hospital.
The photo depicts Dr. Kagan,
the administrative director
of the ghetto hospital at
36 Lagiewnicka Street.

Children of the ghetto. 1940.

Children in the ghetto.

128

Ghetto life.

In the bakery.

N. Kleinman.
At present in Israel.

Telephone exchange
workers in the ghetto.

Jubilee of the Holz-Wolle
factory. Manager A. Rosen.
1942.

B.P.
RÓŻA KLEINMAN
URODZ. REISFELD
LAT 36
ZMARŁA 17 XI 1942
ה כסלו תש״ג

137

The ghetto photographer's wife, Stefania.

Wedding of Stefania and Henryk Ross in the ghetto in 1941.

A wedding reception.

Probably taken during a religious holiday in the ghetto.

Ghetto residents.

Extermination camp in
Jakub Street. Remaining
prisoners celebrating
liberation.
January 1945.

Chronology of the Lodz Ghetto

Thomas Weber

1809 24 Jewish families live in Lodz.

1840 Lodz is recorded as being the smallest Jewish community of Congress Poland.

1939 Rapidly industrialized from the mid-19th century onward, Lodz is now a booming textile town, with a population of 700,000 including 233,000 Jews and 60,000 ethnic Germans. More than half of Lodz's large and mid-sized businesses and larger artisan shops are owned by Jews.

1 September 1939 Germany invades Poland, beginning the Second World War. On 8 September German troops reach and occupy Lodz.

13 October 1939 Chaim Rumkowski is appointed 'Eldest of the Jews of Lodz' and a newly established Jewish Council replaces the Kehillah, the Jewish communal leadership.

11 November 1939 The Germans burn down the synagogues of Lodz. Over the following days, the Jewish Council is dissolved and most of its members killed. Rumkowski is forced to set up a new Jewish Council.

14 November 1939 A German decree forces Jews to wear yellow armbands.

11 December 1939 A new decree is issued forcing Jews to wear a yellow Star of David on the chest and back, instead of yellow armbands.

8 February 1940 A German decree establishes the ghetto in the northern suburbs of Lodz. Jews who do not live in this area of Lodz are instructed to move there. 62,000 Jews already live in the area, and are soon joined by another 100,000.

1 March 1940 A decree forbids Jews living in the ghetto to leave its confines.

6–7 March 1940 During the forced move of Jews from other parts of Lodz into the ghetto, the Germans shoot 200 Jews in their apartments or in the street. By the end of April, all non-Jews residing in the area of the ghetto are forced to move out of the ghetto.

15 March 1940 A postal service is set up within the ghetto.

11 April 1940 Hitler decrees the renaming of Lodz to Litzmannstadt, after the German general Karl Litzmann who captured Lodz during the First World War.

30 April–1 May 1940 The ghetto is hermetically sealed off with barbed wire. The outer boundary is guarded by regular German police who have orders to shoot any Jew approaching it.

1 May 1940 Rumkowski sets up the Jewish police force, which by 1943 numbered approximately 1,200 men.

8 July 1940 The German Reichsmark ceases to be legal tender within the ghetto, with ghetto residents forced to change Reichsmarks for Lodz ghetto currency – which has no value outside the ghetto.

7 June 1941 The chief of the SS and German Police, Heinrich Himmler, visits the ghetto.

22 June 1941 Germany invades the Soviet Union. Most historians assume that the decision to physically exterminate the Jews of Europe was taken sometime between this date and the Wannsee Conference of 20 January 1942.

July 1941 Approximately 140,000 Jews live in the ghetto, of whom 7,316 work for the ghetto administration.

October–November 1941   The ghetto population increases by approximately 20,000 Jews, deportees from various German towns as well as from Vienna, Prague and Luxembourg.

November 1941   A camp for approximately 5,000 Austrian Roma is set up inside the ghetto, internally sealed-off from the Jewish section.

December 1941   The first experimental gassing to death of humans takes places in gas vans in Chelmno, the first SS extermination camp, using technology developed for the systematic killing of the mentally impaired – the T4 programme.

2–19 January 1942   Approximately 4,500 Roma (the entire Roma population of the ghetto) and 10,009 Jews are deported to Chelmno and gassed.

February 1942   7,000 Jews are deported to Chelmno.

March 1942   24,700 Jews are deported to Chelmno.

April 1942   2,350 Jews are deported to Chelmno.

May 1942   Approximately 10,900 Jews are deported to Chelmno.

May–August 1942   Tens of thousands of Jews from communities in the Warthegau are forced into the Lodz ghetto.

September 1942   The 'Gehsperre' (curfew) is announced by the Germans, during which approximately 15,700 Jews (primarily children, the sick, and the elderly) are deported to Chelmno.

Late 1943   Adolf Eichmann visits Lodz. His immediate plans to transform the ghetto into a concentration camp are later shelved.

June 1944   Himmler decrees that the Lodz ghetto is to be liquidated. The Chelmno extermination camp is reactivated and approximately 7,200 Jews are deported there between 23 June and 14 July.

20 July 1944   Hitler narrowly escapes attempt on his life. 68,000 Jews are still alive in the Lodz ghetto.

2 August 1944   The final liquidation of the ghetto is ordered. More than 60,000 Jews are deported from Lodz to Auschwitz from August onwards.

19 January 1945   The Red Army liberates Lodz. Approximately 880 Jews, members of the clean-up commando, survive inside the ghetto.

8 May 1945   VE Day.

April 1947   The German Administrator of the ghetto, Hans Biebow, is tried in Lodz and sentenced to death.

1961–1962   Adolf Eichmann, the Nazi mastermind of the Holocaust, is tried in Jerusalem and sentenced to death.

'Give me your children!'

Chaim Rumkowski speech. Lodz, 4 September 1942

A grievous blow has struck the ghetto. They are asking us to give up the best we possess – the children and the elderly. I was unworthy of having a child of my own, so I gave the best years of my life to children. I've lived and breathed with children. I never imagined I would be forced to deliver this sacrifice to the altar with my own hands. In my old age I must stretch out my hands and beg: Brothers and sisters, hand them over to me! Fathers and mothers, give me your children!

[Transcriber's note – Horrible, terrifying wailing among the assembled crowd.]

I had a suspicion something was about to befall us. I anticipated 'something' and was always like a watchman on guard to prevent it. But I was unsuccessful because I did not know what was threatening us. I did not know the nature of the danger. The taking of the sick from the hospitals caught me completely by surprise. And I give you the best proof there is of this: I had my own nearest and dearest among them, and I could do nothing for them.

I thought that that would be the end of it, that after that they'd leave us in peace, the peace for which I long so much, for which I've always worked, which has been my goal. But something else, it turned out, was destined for us. Such is the fate of the Jews: always more suffering and always worse suffering, especially in times of war.

Yesterday afternoon, they gave me the order to send more than 20,000 Jews out of the ghetto, and if not – 'We will do it!' So, the question became: 'Should we take it upon ourselves, do it ourselves, or leave it for others to do?' Well, we – that is, I and my closest associates – thought first not about 'How many will perish?' but 'How many is it possible to save?' And we reached the conclusion that, however hard it would be for us, we should take the implementation of this order into our own hands.

I must perform this difficult and bloody operation – I must cut off limbs in order to save the body itself! I must take children because, if not, others may be taken as well, God forbid.

[Horrible wailing.]

I have no thought of consoling you today. Nor do I wish to calm you. I must lay bare your full anguish and pain. I come to you like a bandit, to take from you what you treasure most in your hearts! I have tried, using every possible means, to get the order revoked. I tried – when that proved to be impossible – to soften the order. Just yesterday I ordered a list of children aged nine – I wanted, at least, to save this one age group, the nine- to ten-year-olds. But I was not granted this concession. On only one point did I succeed, in saving the ten-year-olds and up. Let this be a consolation in our profound grief.

There are, in the ghetto, many patients who can expect to live only a few days more, maybe a few weeks. I don't know if the idea is diabolical or not, but I must say it: 'Give me the sick. In their place, we can save the healthy.' I know how dear the sick are to any family, and particularly to Jews. However, when cruel demands are made, one has to weigh and measure: who shall, can and may be saved? And common sense dictates that the saved must be those who can be saved and those who have a chance of being rescued, not those who cannot be saved in any case.

We live in the ghetto, mind you. We live with so much restriction that we do not have enough even for the healthy, let alone for the sick. Each of us feeds the sick at the expense of our own health: we give our bread to the sick. We give them our meagre ration of sugar, our little piece of meat. And what's the result? Not enough to cure the sick, and we ourselves become ill. Of course, such sacrifices are the most beautiful and noble. But there are times when one has to choose: sacrifice the sick, who haven't the slightest chance

148

of recovery and who also may make others ill, or rescue the healthy.

I could not deliberate over this problem for long; I had to resolve it in favour of the healthy. In this spirit, I gave the appropriate instructions to the doctors, and they will be expected to deliver all incurable patients, so that the healthy, who want and are able to live, will be saved in their place.

[Horrible weeping.]

I understand you, mothers; I see your tears, all right. I also feel what you feel in your hearts, you fathers who will have to go to work the morning after your children have been taken from you, when just yesterday you were playing with your dear little ones. All this I know and feel. Since four o'clock yesterday, when I first found out about the order, I have been utterly broken. I share your pain. I suffer because of your anguish, and I don't know how I'll survive this – where I'll find the strength to do so.

I must tell you a secret: they requested 24,000 victims, 3,000 a day for eight days. I succeeded in reducing the number to 20,000, but only on the condition that these would be children below the age of ten. Children ten and older are safe. Since the children and the aged together equal only some 13,000 souls, the gap will have to be filled with the sick.

I can barely speak. I am exhausted; I only want to tell you what I am asking of you: Help me carry out this action! I am trembling. I am afraid that others, God forbid, will do it themselves.

A broken Jew stands before you. Do not envy me. This is the most difficult of all the orders I've ever had to carry out at any time. I reach out to you with my broken, trembling hands and I beg: Give into my hands the victims, so that we can avoid having further victims, and a population of a hundred thousand Jews can be preserved. So they promised me: if we deliver our victims by ourselves, there will be peace.

[Shouts: 'We all will go!' 'Mr. Chairman, an only child should not be taken; children should be taken from families with several children!']

These are empty phrases! I don't have the strength to argue with you! If the authorities were to arrive, none of you would shout.

I understand what it means to tear off a part of the body. Yesterday I begged on my knees, but it didn't work. From small villages with Jewish populations of seven to eight thousand, barely a thousand arrived here. So which is better? What do you want: that eighty to ninety thousand Jews remain, or, God forbid, that the whole population be annihilated?

You may judge as you please; my duty is to preserve the Jews who remain. I do not speak to hotheads. I speak to your reason and conscience. I have done and will continue doing everything possible to keep arms from appearing in the streets and blood from being shed. The order could not be undone; it could only be reduced.

One needs the heart of a bandit to ask from you what I am asking. But put yourself in my place, think logically, and you'll reach the conclusion that I cannot proceed any other way. The part that can be saved is much larger than the part that must be given away.

Eichmann Trial

Henryk Ross's Testimony, May 1961

Session No. 23
6 Iyar 5721 (2 May 1961)

Attorney General: I call now our next witness, Mr. Henryk Ross. Mr. Ross will have to testify in Polish, and Advocate Riftin will be able to assist us in translating from Polish to Hebrew and vice versa. I would be grateful to the Court, if it will swear in Advocate Riftin as a interpreter. [Advocate Riftin is sworn as interpreter.]

Presiding Judge: What is your full name?

A: Avraham Riftin.

Q: Are you an advocate? An Israeli?

A: An Israeli advocate, previously a Polish advocate until 1939.
[Witness Ross is sworn.]

Presiding Judge: What is your full name?

Witness: Henryk Ross.

Attorney General: Do you live in Jaffa, Rehov 402/6?

Witness Ross: Yes.

Q: Do you work at Orit Zincography in Tel Aviv?

A: Yes.

Q: You were born in the year 1910?

A: Yes. On 1 May 1910.

Q: When the Second World War broke out, you were in the Polish army. In November 1939 you moved to Lodz where you resided?

A: Yes.

Q: The ghetto at Lodz was established in 1940, is that correct?

A: Yes. That is correct. The ghetto was established in 1940. Notices about the ghetto appeared beforehand, but the ghetto was closed off on 1 May.

Q: Were food ration cards distributed to the population?

A: Yes.

Q: Was it possible to exist on the food rations that were given?

A: It was impossible.

Q: What food was given to the Jews of Lodz?

A: It was precisely this: We received a loaf of bread for eight days. Apart from this there were food rations in small quantities, which were sometimes rotten. Everyone rejoiced at the prospect of potatoes, but finally it became clear that they were all rotten and unfit to eat.

Q: What did the people eat?

A: Those who worked received an extra ration of soup. The soup consisted of 800 grams of water, 60 grams of potatoes, 3 grams of some cereal and 50 to 60 grams of what was called in German *Kiloriben*. Here in Israel there is no such thing. I haven't seen it. When there were no potatoes, they added this to the soup.

Presiding Judge: Aren't you referring to *Kuhlrüben* or beet?

A: Yes, *Kuhlrüben*.

Attorney General: By the way, it exists in Israel. You worked before the war as a journalist and photographer, and at the time of the occupation you worked in the statistical department of the ghetto management?

A: Yes, before the year 1939 – that is to say before the outbreak of the war – I was employed as a photographer for more than ten Polish newspapers in Poland. When the war broke out and I returned from the war, when the ghetto was established, I was given the post of photographer in the statistical department. I worked there from the year 1940, approximately until August 1944.

Q: We shall soon come to your photographs, Mr. Ross. But meanwhile tell us something about the statistics. How many Jews were there in Lodz at the time the Ghetto was set up?

Presiding Judge: When, Mr. Hausner?

Attorney General: He told us, in May 1940.

Witness Ross: In May 1940, when the ghetto was officially sealed, 203,000 Jews were registered, according to what I saw in our department.

Presiding Judge: When the ghetto was established?

Witness Ross: Yes, when the ghetto was sealed and closed off.

Attorney General: After this were Jews from other places added to the ghetto?

Witness Ross: Afterwards more Jews arrived who had been transferred from small townlets such as Zdunska Wola, Pabianice, and other townlets. In 1942, Jews who had been expelled from Germany, Czechoslovakia, Luxembourg and Austria were brought into the ghetto. They numbered 21,000. Most of them consisted of the intelligentsia. Amongst them were also rich people as well as non-Jews, whose forefathers of the third preceding generation only were Jewish.

Q: Perhaps you would tell us something about these offspring of mixed marriages who reached the Litzmannstadt Ghetto?

A: There were women who, according to the German racial law, were pure Aryans, but they came to the ghetto together with their Jewish husbands. According to the German racial law, the fourth generation was already exempted from being in the ghetto – they were pure Germans. There were cases where people did not even know where they were travelling to. And they even had with them children who, already of the fourth generation, were not Jews, so to say cleansed of Jewish blood.

Q: Were there also members of the 'Hitler Jugend' [Hitler Youth] amongst them?

A: Yes. There were instances where the children arrived together with their parents and walked around for the first days in the uniform of the Hitler Jugend.

Q: What was the attitude of these children to the Jews of the ghetto?

A: In the first two or three days they went around in the streets singing 'Hei-li, hei-la' in German, and naturally beating up the Jews. This thing continued for two or three days. Afterwards they understood, their parents explained to them that things were not good for them. They did not have anything to eat.

Q: You said that at the beginning there were in the ghetto 203,000 Jews. 21,000 persons were added from the villages and from abroad. What happened to this quarter of a million Jews, approximately, during the years 1940-1944?

A: Throughout this time, during the five years of the ghetto, they died from starvation and they worked very hard. The food rations were not adequate. People either swelled up from hunger or became emaciated. There were cases of people collapsing in the street; there were cases where they collapsed at work and at home because of the difficult conditions. We were six to eight persons to one room, depending on the size of the room. People froze from the cold. There was no heating. The hunger and the frost caused much distress.

I saw instances while at work where men collapsed, and help that could have come, arrived too late. Matters reached such a state that during a single day they used to bring 120 people to the cemetery. There was a Burial Society with its vehicles. To begin with they were taking for burial two or three victims of starvation. But afterwards, when the number reached 120, it became necessary to construct special carts to transport the bodies. I saw entire families, skeletons of people, who during the night were dying with their children.

When the neighbours entered in the morning, they saw that all of them had died from frost and starvation. Surrounding the ghetto was a fence guarded by Germans. In the beginning they were Volksdeutsche police in blue uniforms. Afterwards there were other guards on behalf of the German ruling power – amongst them men of the NSDAP.

Q: Mr. Ross, you dealt with statistics?

A: I worked in the statistical department.

Q: Do you know how many people, roughly, died from starvation in Lodz?

A: More than 120,000 people, approximately, died of starvation.

Q: What happened to the remaining 100,000?

A: Meanwhile, from 1940 to 1944, there were deportations. Already in 1940 there were deportations of 1,000 – 500 persons in each operation.

Q: Mr. Ross, at the beginning were the deportations

voluntary? Were the people invited to register for deportation?

A: Yes. After the year 1940, the Germans wrote to the Judenrat, the Jewish Council, asking them to register for departure, saying that it would be good for them and that they would receive work and good food.

Q: Did you in the ghetto know at that time where the transports were going to?

A: In the year 1940, it was still not known, but in 1941, at the time of the further deportations, the Jews began to make enquiries and it became known to them that they were going into the 'frying pan'.

Q: What was the 'frying pan'?

A: This was a routine expression of the people in the ghetto. They knew they were going to be burned, they used to call this 'going to the frying pan'. The largest deportation was in 1942. Then many Germans of the SD came in, they conducted an Aktion [operation]. They took people from blocks of houses, surrounded them, removed from the apartments children and aged people through a process of selection, loaded them on to carts; they even loaded them on to tramcars, sometimes making them run on foot.

During this time of deportation in 1942, they expelled from the ghetto more than 20,000 Jews, snatched children from the arms of their mothers; I do not have to say that this was not voluntary, and I do not see the necessity for talking here about the shouts and the blows. I saw an instance where they collected children in a particular hospital in Drewnowska Street. Drewnowska Street was partly in the ghetto and partly in the city. There was a fence on the pavement. The hospital was in the ghetto and the street was in the city. I once saw vehicles come up with two trailers, large vehicles with eight wheels. These were open trucks, they called them 'Roll Kommando', I do not know if this was only a nickname used by the people of the ghetto or whether this was the official name – I had no knowledge of this.

In these vehicles there were sick people, women and men. The Germans concluded that too few people were riding in the vehicles. They said they had to load more. The trucks came to the front of the hospital where the children were assembled. The Germans threw the children from the second floor and from the balconies. The children were of various ages, from one year to approximately ten years. The Germans threw them from the balconies on to these open trucks, on top of the sick people. A few children wept, but most of them were already not crying . The children scratched the walls with their fingernails. The children did not cry any more, they knew what awaited them, they had heard about it. They could not cry.

The Germans were running around in these rooms, they beat them and threw them from the windows and the balconies into these trucks. I was not there for a long time, for it was dangerous even for me to be there. But seeing that I had the instinct of a reporter, of a photographer, I went in there and took the risk. But I quickly fled from there for the sight was not a pleasant one.

Q: Mr. Ross, you were a photographer in the ghetto?

Presiding Judge: Mr. Hausner, what is the position? Will this witness be able to complete his testimony in a short while?

Attorney General: I am not sure, Your Honour. The witness was a photographer and I want to submit a number of the illegal photographs he took. The legal pictures are not in our possession. I would like him to identify them and explain them. This can take about half an hour.

Presiding Judge: We shall continue with this evidence in the afternoon, and thereafter we shall hear the application of Dr. Servatius for hearing witnesses from abroad.

Session No. 24
16 Iyar, 5721 (2 May 1961)

Presiding Judge: I declare the twenty-fourth Session of the trial open. We continue hearing the evidence of the witness Henryk Ross. Will the interpreter please tell him that he continues to testify under oath. [The interpreter tells the witness accordingly.]

Attorney General: Mr. Ross, you told us that you worked as a photographer in the Lodz Ghetto. Whom were you working for as a photographer?

Witness Ross: I was an official in the Department of Statistics and I worked there in the photographic section. This section operated legally, having been set up in accordance with an order of the Germans.

Q: What did you have to photograph?

A: Whatever the Jewish Council instructed us to do according to orders they received from the Germans. For example, everyone in the ghetto had to be photographed for identity cards signed by Amtsleiter Biebow. Every person who worked had to carry such an identity card and it had to have a photograph. Apart from this, we used to photograph people who died on the streets and on whom no documents were found, and under an order of the German authorities we had to mark them as 'unidentified', without names. In addition to this, we photographed samples of products manufactured in the factories for the army, such as uniforms and shoes. When an order came from the Germans to destroy a particular building or neighbourhood, we had to photograph the building from all angles and to forward the photographs, as required by the Germans, to the headquarters in the market which was called Baluty market, where the German headquarters were situated.

Q: Did you say to destroy a building or a neighbourhood?

A: They used to destroy both buildings and neighbourhoods.

Q: Apart from the photographs you prepared for the Ghetto Council, did you also take other photographs?

A: When I had more free time, I also used to take photographs which it was forbidden to take.

Q: When? Towards the end?

A: In July 1944, when I heard and saw that the ghetto was about to be liquidated, that they were going to expel all of us, I hid the negatives in barrels and concealed them in the ground. I only took them out after I had been liberated.

Q: Did you succeed in saving some of the negatives and bringing them with you to Israel?

A: Yes. Some were destroyed owing to water seeping in, but the greater part was saved. I hid them in the ground in the presence of several of my friends, so that if we died and one of us survived, the photographs would remain for the sake of history. Fortunately I remained alive and I dug them up.

Q: How much did you weigh when you were liberated after the war?

A: I did not weigh myself after the war, I was ill, but towards the end, when I was weighed for the last time in the ghetto, my weight was 38 kilograms. I even have photographs showing how I looked then.

Attorney General: [To Presiding Judge] May I approach the witness?

Presiding Judge: Certainly.

Attorney General: Thank you.
[Approaches witness-box.]
[To witness] What was this picture, Mr. Ross? [Shows the picture to the witness.]

Witness Ross: This is a child who was deported in the year 1941.

Q: Please submit it. I now submit some of your photographs. You gave us these – is that correct?

A: Yes.

Presiding Judge: This photograph will be T/223. Was this at the time of deportation? What does this picture show?

Witness Ross: At moments when no German was seen in the vicinity, when they had gone elsewhere to beat up people, I took advantage of that moment to take photographs.

Presiding Judge: This boy was about to be deported? This is what I understand.

Witness Ross: The deportation was on the same day, possibly a minute later, and on that same day the Germans entered the place and beat up and chased children and old people alike. The moment the Germans approached, I fled out of fear.

Attorney General: What is this picture, Mr. Ross? [Shows a picture to the witness.]

Witness Ross: I still want to explain what I said previously. A number of people have approached me who did not understand what I said previously regarding potatoes.

Presiding Judge: Let us come back to the potatoes after the photographs have been submitted.

Attorney General: Explain to us what this picture is.

Presiding Judge: If this correction relates to the picture, please proceed.

Witness Ross: I said previously that the potatoes were not fit to be eaten. I was wrong. They used to arrive in very good condition, but they were frozen, like stones. When they reached the kitchen and thawed, it was seen that they were not fit to eat. They then distributed the potatoes to the people, but they were not able to eat them; but despite everything, seeing that they were very hungry, they used to dig them up, since the ghetto authorities used to bury them in the ground in chlorine, as they were not suitable for use. The children knew where they were to be found and dug them up.

Attorney General: What does this picture show, Mr. Ross?

Witness Ross: This picture shows how the children were digging up the rotten potatoes from the earth – they were so hungry that it didn't matter to them what they ate.

Q: I see that even little children were wearing the Jewish badge. Were they also obliged to do so?

A: Even babies in their cradles were obliged to wear the badge on their right arm and on their back.

Attorney General: I submit the picture.

Presiding Judge: Has Dr. Servatius received copies of these pictures?

Attorney General: No. Dr. Servatius has received a list of the pictures and what they portray.

Presiding Judge: Very well. This will be T/224 – the children taking the potatoes out of the ground.

Attorney General: What is this? [He shows a photograph to the witness.]

Witness Ross: This is a picture of a woman who fell asleep, simply from hunger. The next morning she was no longer alive. She died in her sleep.

Q: Did you see her there, in her room? You photographed this?

A: I saw her and I took the photograph. I developed the picture myself.

Presiding Judge: This will be T/225.

Attorney General: What is this? [Shows the witness a photograph.]

Witness Ross: This is one of my many photographs showing how a person looks who has died of hunger. People like this used to die or become swollen from starvation or emaciated like skeletons as I said previously.

Presiding Judge: This will be T/226.

Attorney General: What is this? [Shows the witness a photograph.]

Witness Ross: This is a group being taken for deportation.

Presiding Judge: This will be T/227.

Attorney General: And what is this picture? This is also a picture of people on their way to deportation. Is that correct? [Shows the witness the photograph.]

Witness Ross: Yes, the same thing.

Q: And at the side, the Jewish police also with the same yellow badge. Is that correct?

A: The men in uniform are the Jewish police.

Presiding Judge: This will be T/228.

Attorney General: What is this? [Shows the witness a photograph.]

Witness Ross: This shows Jews who were brought into the ghetto. There was an order:

All the Jews to the ghetto! The Jews in the town were robbed. They carried the remains of their possessions into the ghetto.

Presiding Judge: This will be T/229.

Attorney General: What is this, Mr. Ross? [Shows the witness a photograph.]

Witness Ross: This is a line of 200 or 300 people or more, for deportation.

Presiding Judge: This will be T/230.

Attorney General: And what is this picture? [Shows the witness a photograph.]

Witness Ross: This is also a deportation group. This picture shows the same scene as the previous picture. Thousands of people went.

Presiding Judge: This will be T/231.

Attorney General: What is this scene near the place on which it says *Zentralgefän* [Central Prison]? [Shows the witness a photograph.]

Witness Ross: The Germans gave orders to build a prison in that ghetto. Criminals and smugglers were supposed to be there. In the picture, there are no smugglers or criminals. In this picture we see people who were expelled from their homes or who were taken from factories or from the street. When the people ended their work at five o'clock, they used to hurry home to their families, to their children and their wives to bid farewell to them or to take them along if they decided to go together with them.

Q: Does this show such leave-taking of members of a family?

A: Yes.

Presiding Judge: This will be T/232.

Attorney General: What is this? [Shows the witness a photograph.]

Witness Ross: This is a mother who was deported. I didn't ask at the time whether it was from a factory or from the street. The mother is standing on the other side of the fence.

Q: And on the inside of the fence?

A: A child or two – I don't know exactly. The mother is no criminal. She is crying – she was carried off during the raid on the streets. The children are standing there, not knowing what to do.

Presiding Judge: This will be T/233.

Attorney General: What is this? [Shows the witness a photograph.]

Witness Ross: This is a family on the way to deportation, a father and mother and two children. Deportation in fact meant death.

Q: Deportation – where to?

A: This was deportation to Chelmno.

Presiding Judge: This will be T/234.

Attorney General: Did you manage to take a picture of the loading on to railway waggons? Actually two such pictures?

Witness Ross: There are more.

Q: But I have two here. How did you succeed in photographing this? [Shows the witness a photograph.]

A: On one occasion, when people with whom I was acquainted worked at the railway station of Radegast, which was outside the ghetto but linked to it, and where trains destined for Auschwitz were standing – on one occasion I managed to get into the railway station in the guise of a cleaner. My friends shut me into a cement storeroom. I was there from six in the morning until seven in the evening, until the Germans went away and the transport departed. I watched as the transport left. I heard shouts. I saw the beatings. I saw how they were shooting at them, how they were murdering them, those who refused. Through a hole in a board of the wall of the storeroom I took several pictures.

Q: Is that one of the pictures that you are holding in your hand?

A: Yes, this is one of those pictures.

Presiding Judge: This will be T/235.

Attorney General: And what is this photograph? [Shows the witness a photograph.]

Witness Ross: This, too, was taken on the same day – I was there only once – some time later.

Presiding Judge: This will be T/236.

Attorney General: What is this picture?

[Shows the witness a photograph.]

Witness Ross: This place marks where the ghetto ended, and where the road leading to the Radegast railway station began. It was along this road that the Germans conveyed the transports to Auschwitz.

Presiding Judge: This will be T/237 – people marching on the way to deportation.

Attorney General: Is this a photocopy of the decree of the mayor of Lodz ordering the evacuation of the ghetto?

[Shows the witness a photograph.]

Witness Ross: Yes.

Q: And what is this?

A: The same thing. This is the order and the notice.

Q: Did you photograph it?

A: Yes. If the original notice will be required, it is in my possession.

Presiding Judge: This will be T/238.

Attorney General: This is the order of the Elder of the Ghetto, giving an instruction to greet anyone wearing a German uniform. Is that correct?

[Shows the witness a photograph.]

Witness Ross: Yes. All these notices were sent by the Germans from the market at Baluty to the Council of the Jewish Elders. The Jewish Council was obliged to print them, to send them to the German censorship, and only after that was it permitted to paste them on the walls.

Q: I have here two more such orders. Were these also photographed by you?

[Shows the witness two photographs.]

A: Yes. I also have the original notices.

Q: Was this the Allgemeine Gehsperre [General Curfew]?

A: Yes.

Q: And is this an order to hand in and collect all rings – all articles of silver and gold?

A: Yes, to turn over all rings, all articles of silver and gold.

Presiding Judge: Do you have additional copies of this?

Attorney General: No. He brought these to us at the last moment.

Presiding Judge: These photographs have been marked T/239, T/240 and T/241.

Attorney General: [Receives the album from Mr. Bodenheimer.] Mr. Ross, you are acquainted with picture 34 on page 13. What is it?

Witness Ross: This is not my photograph, but I know what it is. The ghetto was in the old quarter of the town. Tramcars, motor vehicles and carts used to pass through the ghetto. In order to prevent contact with the Jews, fences were erected on both sides of the road. We were obliged to pass over the road via a bridge built for this purpose, from one part of the ghetto to the other. This was an opportunity for the Germans to amuse themselves, to beat us in order to compel us to walk faster.

Q: This is the last picture we intend to show to you. This is a photograph of places of work in the Lodz Ghetto which you took. Is that right?

[Shows the witness a photograph.]

A: This is an official list of all the places of work.

Presiding Judge: This picture will be marked T/242.

Attorney General: [To Presiding Judge] That is all, Your Honour.

Presiding Judge: Dr. Servatius [Defence Attorney for Adolf Eichmann], do you have any questions to the witness?

Dr. Servatius: I have no questions.

Presiding Judge: Thank you, Mr. Ross, you have completed your evidence.

Bibliography

Thomas Weber

The Ghetto System in its Historical Context

Bartov, Omer (ed.), *The Holocaust: Origins, Implementation, Aftermath* (London, 2000)

Bennett, Rab, *Under the Shadow of the Swastika: The Moral Dilemma of Resistance and Collaboration in Hitler's Europe* (Basingstoke, 1999)

Corni, Gustavo, *Hitler's Ghettos: Voices from a Beleaguered Society, 1939-1944* (London, 2002)

Dwork, Deborah; van Pelt, Robert Jan, *Holocaust: A History* (London, 2002)

Gutman, Israel and Half, Cynthia (eds.), *Patterns of Jewish Leadership in Nazi Europe 1933-1945: Proceedings of the Third Yad Vashem International Historical Conference* (Jerusalem, 1977)

Hilberg, Raul, *The Destruction of the European Jewry* (abridged edition) (New York, 1985)

Jones, David H., *Moral Responsibility in the Holocaust: A Study in the Ethics of Character* (Lanham, 1999)

Trunk, Isaiah, *Judenrat: The Jewish Councils in Eastern Europe under Nazi Occupation* (New York, 1972)

The Lodz Ghetto

Adelson, Alan and Lapides, Robert (eds.), *Lodz Ghetto – Inside a Community under Siege* (New York, 1989)

Baranowski, Julian, *The Lodz Ghetto, 1940-1944* (Lodz, 1999)

Dobroszycki, Lucjan (ed.), *The Chronicle of the Lodz Ghetto, 1941-1944* (New Haven, 1984)

Eilenberg-Eibeshitz, Anna (ed.), *Preserved Evidence – Ghetto Lodz* (2 vols) (Haifa, 2000)

Huppert, S., 'King of the Ghetto: Mordechai Haim Rumkowski, the Elder of the Lodz Ghetto', *Yad Vashem Studies, xv* (1983)

Krakowski, Shmuel, 'Lodz', in Gutman, Israel (ed.), *Encyclopedia of the Holocaust, iii* (New York, 1990)

Lodz Ghetto Photography

Adelson, Alan, 'The Photographs and Photographers', in Adelson, Alan (ed.), *Diary of D. Sierakowiak: Five Notebooks From the Lodz Ghetto* (London, 1996)

Ben-Menahem, Arieh, 'Grossman, Mendel', in Gutman, Israel (ed.), *Encyclopedia of the Holocaust, ii* (New York, 1990)

Grossman, Mendel and Smith, Frank Dabba, *My Secret Camera: Life in the Lodz Ghetto* (London, 2000)

Loewy, Hanno and Schoenberger, Gerhard (eds.), *'Unser einziger Weg ist Arbeit': Das Ghetto in Lodz 1940 – 1944,* (Exhibition catalogue of the Jüdisches Museums Frankfurt/Main) (Vienna, 1990)

Klugman, Aleksander (ed.), *The Last Journey of the Jews of Lodz, photographed by Henryk Ross* (Tel Aviv, undated)

Unger, Michal (ed.), *The Last Ghetto: Life in the Lodz Ghetto, 1940-1944* (Jerusalem, c. 1995)

Szner, Zvi and Sened, Alexander (eds.), *Mendel Grossman – With a Camera in the Ghetto* (Tel Aviv, 1970)

Holocaust and War Photography

Brothers, Caroline, *War and Photography: A Cultural History* (London, 1997)

Hamburg Institute for Social Research, *The German Army and Genocide: Crimes against War Prisoners, Jews, and Other Civilians in the East, 1939-1944* (New York, 1999)

Liss, Andrea, *Trespassing through Shadows: Memory, Photography, and the Holocaust* (Minneapolis, 1998)

Sontag, Susan, *Regarding the Pain of Others* (New York, 2003)

Struk, Janina, *Photographing the Holocaust: Interpretations of the Evidence* (London, 2003)

Map of the Lodz ghetto as it appeared in *The Last Journey*.

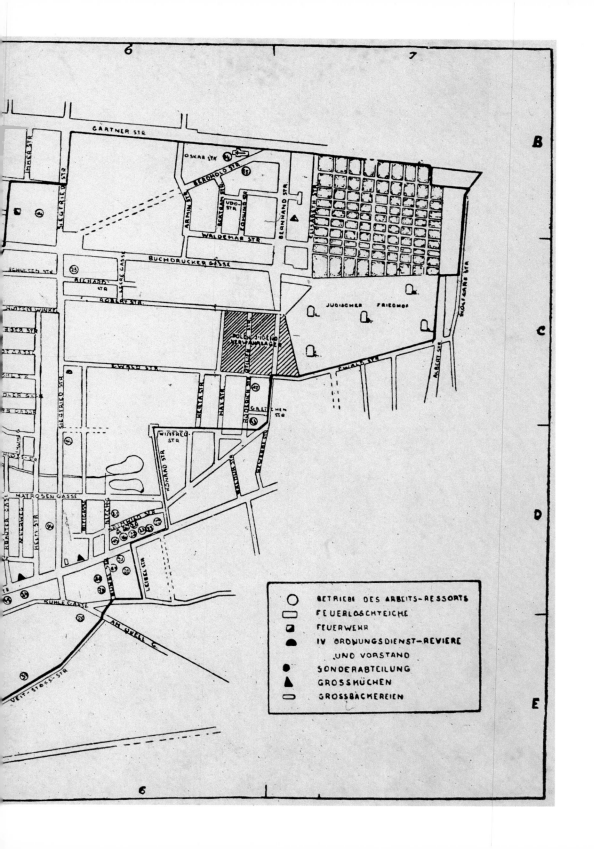

Author's Note

This book could not have been written without the generous help, advice and encouragement of Barbara Adams, Dr. Frank Bialystok, Sandra Bialystok, Dr. Ruth Bettina Birn, Katie Boot, Anina Comber, Sarah Y. Cooper, Bonnie Einav, Prof. Niall Ferguson, Carsten Firscher, Krysia Fisher, Gregor Gehrke, Dr. Elwira Grossman, Irene Kohn, Melissa Larner, Felix and Sheila Prus, Henia Reinhartz, Prof. Simon Newman, Prof. Roger Simon and Prof. Bernard Wasserstein; participants of conferences and seminars at Yale, the Imperial War Museum, Flossenbürg and Wolverhampton; the staff at YIVO in New York, the Zentralstelle der Jandesjustizverwaltungen zur Verfolgung Nationalsozialistischer Gewaltverbrechen in Ludwigsburg, and the university libraries at Glasgow, Oxford, and Freiburg/Breisgau. Needless to say, the mistakes remain my own.
Thomas Weber, Glasgow, 2004

Lodz Ghetto Album
© Archive of Modern Conflict, 2004
© Chris Boot Ltd, 2004

First published 2004
by Chris Boot
79 Arbuthnot Road
London SE14 5NP
www.chrisboot.com

Photographs © Archive of Modern Conflict
Text © Thomas Weber
Foreword © Robert Jan van Pelt
Photographic prints by Glen Brent
Project management by Bree Seeley
Design by Untitled

Extract records of the Eichmann Trial transcripts reproduced from the recordsof the Israeli Ministry of Justice. Chaim Rumkowski speech reproduced from *Lodz Ghetto – Inside a Community Under Siege* by Alan Adelson and Robert Lapides, © the Jewish Heritage Project, New York. Used with kind permission.

A CIP catalogue record for this book is available from the British Library.

ISBN 0-9542813-7-3

Printed by EBS, Italy